FEMINIST ETHNOGRAPHY

THINKING THROUGH METHODOLOGIES, CHALLENGES, AND POSSIBILITIES

DÁNA-AIN DAVIS & CHRISTA CRAVEN

ROWMAN & LITTLEFIELD
Lanham • Boulder • New York • London

Senior Editor: Leanne Silverman
Assistant Editor: Karie Simpson
College Marketing Manager: Karin Cholak
Senior Marketing Manager: Deborah Hudson
Cover Designer: Meredith Nelson
Cover Art: Thinkstock

Credits and acknowledgments of sources for material or information used with permission appear on the appropriate page within the text.

Published by Rowman & Littlefield
A wholly owned subsidiary of The Rowman & Littlefield Publishing Group, Inc.
4501 Forbes Boulevard, Suite 200, Lanham, Maryland 20706
www.rowman.com

Unit A, Whitacre Mews, 26-34 Stannary Street, London SE11 4AB, United Kingdom

British Library Cataloguing in Publication Information Available

Library of Congress Cataloging-in-Publication Data
Names: Davis, Dána-Ain, 1958– author. | Craven, Christa, 1975– author.
Title: Feminist ethnography : thinking through methodologies, challenges, and possibilities / by Dána-Ain Davis and Christa Craven.
Description: Lanham, MD : Rowman & Littlefield, 2016. | Includes bibliographical references and index.
Identifiers: LCCN 2015045939 (print) | LCCN 2016008411 (ebook) | ISBN 9780759122444 (cloth : alk. paper) | ISBN 9780759122451 (pbk. : alk. paper) | ISBN 9780759122468 (Electronic)
Subjects: LCSH: Feminist theory. | Feminism—Research. | Women's studies—Methodology. | Social sciences—Research—Methodology. | Feminists—Biography.
Classification: LCC HQ1190 .D385 2016 (print) | LCC HQ1190 (ebook) | DDC 305.4201—dc23
LC record available at http://lccn.loc.gov/2015045939

∞™ The paper used in this publication meets the minimum requirements of American National Standard for Information Sciences—Permanence of Paper for Printed Library Materials, ANSI/NISO Z39.48-1992.

Printed in the United States of America

Brief Contents

Contents

Acknowledgments

Many people have contributed to this book, so here is where we want to express our gratitude. Feminist anthropologist, activist, and friend Sandi Morgen inspires the acknowledgements for this project. We had several conversations with her as we pursued work on this book that got us thinking deeply about the debts we owe to academic friendships. She recalled finding herself explaining to baffled family and friends how the academic friendships that she has built over the years—connecting for 20 minutes at conferences year after year, collaborating on panels, generating scholarship and activism—are essential to her well-being, as a scholar, but also as a person. Likewise, the scholarly connections that have inspired and nurtured our scholarly, activist, and personal journeys are many, and deeply valued.

Throughout our work on this book, collectively—as coauthors, coeditors, and friends—and individually—as feminist ethnographers and activist-scholars—we have been the recipients of tremendous support. During the production of this book, we received ideas, critiques, and feedback from Ujju Aggarwal, Florence Babb, Elizabeth Chin, LeeRay Costa, Nancy Grace, Faye Harrison, Dorothy Hodgson, Katie Holt, Antoinette Jackson, Shannon King, Ellen Lewin, Laura Mauldin, Jennifer Nelson, and David Valentine. We thank Wendi Schnaufer for starting us on the road to writing this textbook. We are grateful to Leanne Silverman, Karie Simpson, and Jehanne Schweitzer at Rowman and Littlefield, Anita Singh at Deanta Global, and Sherri Barnes at Moonlight Indexing for helping us to bring it to fruition. We also thank Tine Davids and Karin Willemse, who published a special issue in *Women's Studies International Forum (2014)* "Embodied Engagements: Feminist Ethnography at the Crossing Knowledge of Production and Representation," and conference attendees at the Queer Kinship and Relationships Conference, held by the Institute of Psychology, Polish Academy of Sciences, Zalesie Mazury, Poland, especially Aspa Chalkidou, Ulrika Dahl, Ruth Preser, Damien Riggs, Antu Sorainen, Agata Staniszińska, and Gracia Trujillo, for drawing our attention to a range of exciting feminist ethnographic work outside of North America. We are grateful for the enthusiasm we have received from so many supportive colleagues. We thank Rowman & Littlefield's reviewers for their insightful comments and helpful references: Ujju Aggarwal, Center for Place, Culture and Politics, The Graduate Center, City University of New York (CUNY); Michelle Fine, The Graduate Center, CUNY; Holly Hassel, University of Wisconsin-Marathon County; Martin F. Manalansan IV, University of Illinois, Urbana-Champaign; and two anonymous reviewers.

The College of Wooster and Queen's College, CUNY, our home institutions, both granted us timely research leaves, during which we wrote the bulk of this text. The Henry Luce III Fund for Distinguished Scholarship enabled us to travel and work together to bring this manuscript to completion. During Fall 2014, both Dána-Ain and Christa taught courses, Feminist Ethnographies and Ethnographic Research, respectively, and in Spring 2015, Christa introduced portions of the textbook to David McConnell's "Contemporary Anthropological Theory." Students in those classes contributed immeasurably to both the content and the structure of this text. Some gave constructive comments on early drafts of chapters, and Dána-Ain's graduate students conducted some of the interviews spotlighted in the text.

For their assistance with research and transcription, we would like to thank Jacob Danko, Evangeline Smith, and Sara Tebeau from the College of Wooster. We also appreciate the efforts of two research assistants, Brenna McCaffrey a doctoral student in the anthropology program at the CUNY Graduate Center and Regina McCullough, at the College of Wooster, who helped us with revisions, the timeline, and the glossary. And we thank Jackson Siegel, graduate of College of Wooster, for designing artwork to demarcate elements, such as Essentials and Spotlights, throughout the text.

We have also received tremendous support from our families, who have sustained us—emotionally, physically, and intellectually—during this project. Dána-Ain is blessed to have an amazing family of choice and birth: Toni, Ricci, LaFredia (aka Fefa), India-Rose, Deirdre, Dan, Liz, Alex, and Ethan. And Christa is grateful for the support of Donna, Stephen, and David Craven, B Murphy for understanding the bizarre madness that is writing, and her 5-year-old twins Rosalie and Braxton Murphy-Craven for especially fun writing breaks. On the day that we turned in the first draft of the manuscript, Braxton poignantly asked, "When are you going to be done with your chapterbook?" Braxton, we are done, now!

It has been a journey and we thank each other. It is an amazing experience to collaborate with someone who knows how to motivate you. When one of us was distracted or bound by other obligations, the other held things together and moved this project forward. All academics should be so fortunate to have someone to collaborate with who makes the work such a joy. Cheers to enduring friendship, critical conversations, and more collaborative scholarship long into our futures.

Preface

A Note for Instructors

What happens when you want a text that can help teach your students about the thinking and the doing of feminist ethnography—and you can't find one? This was a dilemma we both faced and ultimately, we decided to create the textbook we wished to use.

We wrote *Feminist Ethnography: Thinking through Methodologies, Challenges and Possibilities* to share with students how to integrate activism, theory, and research into crafting ethnography from a feminist perspective. This is accomplished by using examples that address gender in conversation with race, disability, sexuality, class, and nation. To facilitate students' ability to learn about feminist ethnography we use a problem-based approach. Problem-based learning, which is based on inquiry, is an opportunity to consider how to respond to questions asked, as well as employing assignments or tasks to enhance the integration of the ideas presented. We draw on the concept of "*un choque*," or "cultural collisions," discussed by Gloria Anzaldúa.[1] which describes the "cultural collision." In her work, the collision of cultures forces *la mestiza* to engage in self-making, that is the creation of her own identity. We apply the concept of "*un choque*" in the text through examples that contribute to the making of feminist ethnography.

For instance, you will find a departure from previous work in the field in that men are included in this conversation, because they too can do feminist ethnography. Although it is clear that gender binaries and inequities exist within the field, we also work toward deconstructing these dichotomies. We have also been attentive to the historical marginalization of women of color in academia; thus, half of the textboxes in the book feature their voices. We also want to impress upon readers the importance of exploring the possibilities that can exist within feminist ethnography, which may serve as one response to what is a troubling predicament: the global shredding of, limitations to, and stratification of rights and access to resources. Examples of how struggles and movements have been undermined include how race is used to stratify pregnant women in public health institutions, how research on LGBTQI+ people has been based on perceived deficits, or when young people of color are the targets of military recruitment because they have too few employment options.

Although we offer a concise overview of feminist ethnography in subsequent chapters, here we highlight the contemporary texts that have influenced feminist ethnographic research and production, and may be useful to your students as they engage further with feminist ethnographic projects. Some of the texts contributing to contemporary feminist ethnography include sociologist Shulamith Reinhartz's *Feminist Methods in Social Research* in 1992, which situated feminist ethnography as a grounded multimethod approach that plays "a special role in upholding a non-positivist perspective."[2] Indigenous education scholar Linda Tuhiwai Smith's *Decolonizing Methodologies: Research and Indigenous Peoples* in 1999 explored the intersections of imperialism and research, arguing that the decolonization of research methods will help to reclaim control over indigenous ways of knowing and being.[3] In 2000, Chicana studies scholar Chela Sandoval's *Methodology of the Oppressed* developed her idea of an oppositional consciousness, based on the resistance of binary identity categories in favor of a fluidity that moves between them,[4] and sociologist Patricia Hill Collins's *Black Feminist Thought: Knowledge, Consciousness, and the Politics of Empowerment* in 2000 highlighted the complexity of gendered, raced, and classed oppression and possibilities for empowerment through knowledge.[5] Anthropologist Irma McClaurin's important volume in 2001, *Black Feminist Anthropology: Theory, Politics, Praxis and Poetics* demonstrated key theoretical and methodological contributions of Black women ethnographers.[6] Sociologist Nancy A. Naples's *Feminism and Method: Ethnography, Discourse Analysis and Activist Research* in 2003 utilized different research topics as the lens through which dilemmas of feminist research are explored.[7] In 2005, sociologist Joey Sprague's *Feminist Methodologies for Critical Researchers* foregrounded institutional ethnography,[8] the approach adopted by Marxist feminist sociologist Dorothy E. Smith in *Institutional Ethnography: A Sociology for People*, which articulated the importance of feminist standpoint theory.[9] In 2010, Kath Browne and Catherine J. Nash published the edited collection *Queer Methods and Methodologies: Intersecting Queer Theories and Social Science Research,*[10] which underscored various approaches to feminist and queer ethnography from researchers in the United Kingdom, the United States, Canada, Sweden, New Zealand, and Australia in a variety of disciplines, including sociology, anthropology, women's/gender studies, communication studies, and geography. And in 2014, Sharlene Nagy Hesse-Biber edited the second edition of *Feminist Research Practice: A Primer,* which offers a useful overview of both epistemological approaches and specific research methods as applied by feminist researchers.[11]

What we want to do for students is untangle some of the threads of feminist ethnography—its multiple histories, meanings, hopes, dilemmas, praxis, and necessity—by foregrounding the importance of feminist ethnography to the development of ethnographic methods. Some have claimed feminist ethnography is an impossibility, others have attempted to neutralize its often political intent, and even those who count themselves among this field sometimes find feminist ethnography difficult to fully and unequivocally define. This textbook is devoted to the task of drawing out its important interdisciplinary lineages and charting a path for feminist ethnography into the future.

The interdisciplinarity of the field is not to be taken for granted. While we trace some of the history of feminist ethnography through anthropology, where we both received much of our academic training, we aimed throughout the text to include examples and discussions that span a range of disciplines. Feminist anthropologists have frequently "reclaimed" female ethnographers from the late nineteenth and early twentieth centuries, they produced theoretical explorations of women's roles in the 1970s (in edited volumes such as *Woman, Culture, and Society and Toward an Anthropology of Women),*[12] they experimented with feminist writing in the 1980s and 1990s (exemplified in *Women Writing Culture),*[13] and they helped to establish an anthropology of gender (and sexuality) into the twenty-first century (for example, *Gender at the Crossroads of Knowledge, Situated Lives: Gender and Culture in Everyday Life,* and *Black Genders and Sexualities).*[14] We demonstrate how those influences, insights, and applications have invigorated the field of feminist ethnography, although our discussion is partial because much of the work we present on feminist thinking and ethnography centers on English-language publications. Our hope is that this textbook serves as inspiration for future work on the global production of feminist ethnography.

Origins of Our Collaboration

Nearly 15 years after we first sat next to each other, quite by accident, at an American Anthropological Association (AAA) conference, this book has come to fruition. Our scholarly collaboration began by building on our connections with other scholars through two sessions we organized on feminist ethnography: the first at the AAA in 2005 and then at the National Women's Studies Association in 2006. Subsequently, in 2011 we published "Revisiting Feminist Ethnography: Methods and Activism at the Intersection of Neoliberal Policy" in the journal *Feminist Formations*, exploring the links between neoliberalism and U.S.-based feminist ethnography and activism.[15] Following the publication of that article we edited a volume incorporating the work of other feminist ethnographers, *Feminist Activist Ethnography: Counterpoints to Neoliberalism in North America*.[16] It was this last project that inspired us to write this textbook, a more historical, cross-cultural, and interdisciplinary discussion of feminist ethnography.

We worked collaboratively on this textbook over the course of several years, via innumerable phone calls, texts, emails, and back-and-forth chapter drafts. The bulk of the textbook was written during one semester, when we were able to work together in person for a week in Wooster, Ohio, and a week in New York, our respective homes. Even our "downtime" during these visits reinforced the importance of writing this text. During Dána-Ain's visit to Wooster, we had the pleasure of meeting philosopher and activist Angela Y. Davis during the College of Wooster's Colloquium on Global and Postcolonial Ethics, when she spoke with faculty about teaching in the context of liberation and transnational solidarity. Davis is well known for her political activism around prison reform, her leadership in the Communist party, and her scholarship. On the day we saw Davis, what was profound about her talk on teaching was her reminder about the impact one can make in classrooms—by professors, but also by students engaging deeply with texts and materials that promote social change. Indeed, we aim for this text to prompt discussions, including how feminist ethnography can contribute to a more transformative politics. Likewise, during Christa's visit to New York, we took a break from writing to attend a Kehinde Wiley exhibit at the Brooklyn Museum—described in more detail in the introduction. After the exhibit we talked about what it means to bring historically marginalized people's lives into the foreground as subjects, as artists, and as authors. It is important to be aware of the issue of representation, who is represented, and how they are represented—be it in museums, ethnographies, or other spaces. That is central to what we are trying to accomplish in the textbook and have tried to model this throughout.

Organization of the Text

The material presented is supplemented by information organized into three categories: *Spotlights, Essentials, and Thinking Through . . .* elements. These features introduce students to important texts, people, and ideas, and offer them creative opportunities to further engage with the field. *Spotlights* are aimed at familiarizing students with a variety of contemporary feminist ethnographic projects and approaches. We draw attention to a range of scholars and activists—from seasoned feminist ethnographers who have participated in the growth of the field since the 1970s, those who witnessed the debates that emerged during the 1980s and 1990s, and newer scholars and activists inspired to incorporate feminist ethnography in their work, including several students. *Essentials* are excerpts or reprints of material—many that we would consider "classics" or canonical texts that have deeply influenced the field—and will give students a deeper sense of the history and practice of feminist ethnography. By paying homage to important figures in feminist ethnography we aim to both catalogue and contribute to crafting the continued history of feminist ethnography. We recognize that this project could never be complete, nor include every voice we would like. On the other hand we are thrilled that there is so much important scholarship on feminist ethnography for students to explore!

Each chapter also includes activities that encourage students to engage in further *Thinking Through . . .* the concepts that we have presented. These may be used as direct assignments in class, or as an opportunity to continue to expand students' knowledge. Our goal in the *Thinking Through . . .* exercises is to encourage students to move beyond a merely textual engagement with this book. After reading about a variety of feminist ethnographic approaches and strategies—including methodology, production, and circulation—students will be well positioned to think through possibilities for their own projects and critically engage with a range of scholarship. The *Thinking Through . . .* assignments are also compiled as an online resource available on the text's catalog page at www.rowman.com. An additional feature of the book is that there is a *Timeline* of events in feminism and feminist ethnography. Also, at the close of each chapter, we provide a list of additional *Suggested Resources* for students who wish to pursue the topics we present in more depth. These are largely materials we have not explored in depth within the chapter. Finally, throughout the text, we present words and phrases in **bold**, which we define on first mention, as well as in a *Glossary* of definitions.

In the spirit of collaborative feminist practice, we welcome comments, critiques, and suggestions from teachers, students, and activists who engage with the book. Please feel free to contact us.

Notes

[1] Gloria Anzaldúa, "Towards a New Consciousness," in *The Post-Colonial Reader, Bill Ashcroft, Gareth Griffiths*, Helen Tiffin, eds., 2006, 208.

[2] Shulamith Reinharz, *Feminist Methods in Social Research*, 1992, 46.

[3] Linda Tuhiwai Smith, *Decolonizing Methodologies*, 2012 *[orig 1999]*.

[4] Chela Sandoval, *Methodology of the Oppressed*, 2000.

[5] Patricia Hill Collins, *Black Feminist Thought*, 2009 *[orig 1990]*.

[6] Irma McClaurin, *Black Feminist Anthropology*, 2001.

[7] Nancy A. Naples, *Feminism and Method*, 2003.

[8] Joey Sprague, *Feminist Methodologies for Critical Researchers*, 2005.

[9] Dorothy E. Smith, *Institutional Ethnography*, 2005.

[10] Kath Browne and Catherine J. Nash, *Queer Methods and Methodologies: Intersecting Queer Theories and Social Science Research*, 2010.

[11] Sharlene Nagy Hesse-Biber, *Feminist Research Practice*, 2014.

[12] Michelle Zimbalist Rosaldo and Louise Lamphere, eds., *Woman, Culture, and Society*, 1974; Rayna Reiter, *Toward an Anthropology of Women*, 1975.

[13] Ruth Behar and Deborah A. Gordon, *Women Writing Culture*, 1996.

[14] Micaela di Leonardo, ed., *Gender at the Crossroads of Knowledge*, 1991; Louise Lamphere, Helena Ragoné, and Patricia Zavella, eds., *Situated Lives*, 1997; Shaka McGlotten and Dána-Ain Davis, eds., *Black Genders and Sexualities*, 2012.

[15] Dána-Ain Davis and Christa Craven. "Revisiting Feminist Ethnography: Methods and Activism at the Intersection of Neoliberal Policy in the U.S.," *Feminist Formations*, 2011.

[16] Christa Craven and Dána-Ain Davis, eds. *Feminist Activist Ethnography: Counterpoints to Neoliberalism in North America*, 2013.

Timeline

Some people set the origins of feminism to coincide with specific revolutionary women in early history—for example, Sappho in Greece (5 BCE)—while others point to waves of activism around particular issues—such as women's suffrage. For the sake of highlighting the long, rich, and geographically diverse history of feminism(s) in a manageable overview, the following Timeline presents key dates in feminist ethnography against the backdrop of representative issues raised in this text, including events and dates from varied strands of feminism and intersecting social movements. When we mention specific individuals featured in the Spotlights or Essentials boxes, we also include chapter numbers.

To explore the history of feminism and related movements through alternative lenses, see the following timelines and resources:

- Riki Anne Wilchins's "Selected Chronology of the Transexual Menace and Gender PAC," in *Read My Lips: Sexual Subversion and the End of Gender.* Riverdale, NY: Mangus Books, 209–35, 2013 [orig 1997].
- Nan D. Hunter's "Contextualizing the Sexuality Debates," in *Sex Wars: Sexual Dissent and Political Culture*, by Lisa Duggan and Nan D. Hunter, 15–28. New York: Routledge, 2006.
- The website "Women's Suffrage and Beyond" has regional timelines for women's suffrage in Africa, Asia, Central and South America, Europe, the Middle East, North America, and Oceania, available at: http://womensuffrage.org/.
- United Nations Foundation, "Key Dates in International Women's History," available at: http://www.unfoundation.org/assets/pdf/key-dates-in-international-womens-history.pdf.
- "A Brief History of African Feminism," *Ms. Afropolitan*, July 2, 2013, available at: http://www.msafropolitan.com/2013/07/a-brief-history-of-african-feminism.html.
- The Women's Struggle Timeline, 1905–2006 (South Africa), available at: http://www.sahistory.org.za/topic/womens-struggle-timeline-1905-2006.
- Cross-national timeline of the women's movement in Asia in *Women's Movements in Asia: Feminisms and Transnational Activism*, edited by Mina Roces and Louise Edwards, 224–42. London: Routledge, 2010.
- Australian Women's History Forum, "Timeline," available at: https://womenshistory.net.au/timeline/.
- British Women's History Timeline, available at: http://www.historyofwomen.org/timeline.html.
- Donna Goodman's "The Struggle for Women's Equality in Latin America," in *Dissident Voice*, March 13, 2009, available at: http://dissidentvoice.org/2009/03/the-struggle-for-womens-equality-in-latin-america/.
- "Timeline of Canadian Women's History: From Moira Armour and Pat Stanton," in *Canadian Women in History: A Chronology*, 2nd ed. Toronto: Green Dragon Press, 1992. Available at: http://people.stfx.ca/nforeste/308website/women'shistorytimeline.html.
- Denize Oliver Velez's "Women's History: Native Americans," March 2, 2014, available at: http://www.dailykos.com/story/2014/3/2/1280488/-Women-s-History-Native-Americans.
- National Women's History Project's "Detailed History of Women in the United States" (2013), available at http://www.nwhp.org/resources/womens-rights-movement/detailed-timeline/.

TIMELINE

Key Dates in Feminist Ethnography

1837 British writer Harriet Martineau, often cited as the first female sociologist, published *Society in America* based on her long trip to the U.S. in the mid-1830s, which criticized the state of women's education

1885 Matilda Coxe Stevenson became the first president of the Women's Anthropological Society of America

1911 Alice Fletcher and Omaha collaborator Francis LaFlesche (see Ch. 2) published *The Omaha Tribe*

Margaret Mead published *Coming of Age in Samoa* on adolescence **1928**

Ruth Benedict published *Patterns of Culture*, a cross-cultural analysis of culture and personality **1934**

Zora Neale Hurston (see Ch. 2) published *Mules and Men*, a novel on Black American folk tales **1935**

The Waves of Feminism and Other Social Movements

"1st Wave" of Feminism

Labor Movement

Abolitionist Movement

Birth Control Movement

Temperance Movement

Key Dates in Feminisms and Social Movements

1691 Mexican nun Sor Juana Inés de la Cruz wrote a letter, *Respuesta a Sor Filotea (Reply to Sister Philotea)*, in which she defended women's right to education

1792 British writer Mary Wollstonecraft published *The Vindication of the Rights of Women*, where she argued for women's education

1832 African American journalist Maria W. Stewart became the first American woman to speak to a mixed audience of men and women, whites and Blacks, addressing women's rights and the abolition of slavery

1836 Jarena Lee published *The Life and Religious Experience of Jarena Lee, A Coloured Lady*, cited as the first autobiography to be published in the U.S. by an African American woman

1840 French journalist Flora Tristan published *Promenades dans Londre* criticizing working conditions in London, including the exploitation of prostitutes

1848 *Declaration of Sentiments* signed at Seneca Falls Convention in New York

1851 Sojourner Truth gave "Ain't I a woman?" speech at Women's Convention in Akron, Ohio

1865 The Reconstruction Amendments (the 13th–15th amendments to the U.S. Constitution) abolished slavery, and granted equal protections clauses to "all persons"

1873 Founding of the Woman's Christian Temperance Union (WCTU), the oldest feminist organization in the U.S.

1890 Peruvian writer Clorinda Matto de Turner published *Aves Sin Nido (Birds without a Nest)*, which revealed the poor treatment of indigenous people

1893 Women gained the right to vote in New Zealand, the first self-governing country where all women had the right to vote in parliamentary elections

Members of the Congressional Union (later named the National Women's Party) worked toward the passage of a federal amendment to give women the vote by picketing the White House and engaging in other forms of civil disobedience **1913**

Margaret Sanger opened first birth control clinics in the U.S. **1916**

Charlotte Manye Maxeke was active in the campaigns against "Pass laws" in South Africa **1919**

U.S. Congress passed the Nineteenth Amendment, guaranteeing women the right to vote **1920**

Birth Control Council of America formed, which later became Planned Parenthood **1937**

1800s | 1900 | 1910 | 1920 | 1930 | 1940

Key Dates in Feminist Ethnography

1940s Anthropologists recruited by the U.S. government to assist with war efforts

1941 Elsie Clews Parsons became the first female president of the American Anthropological Association (AAA)

1947 Ruth Benedict served as president of the AAA for 6 months

1949 The Society of Applied Anthropology adopted the first Code of Ethics in a social science organization under the direction of Margaret Mead

Margaret Mead became president of the AAA **1960**

Anthropologists recruited by the U.S. Army to participate in Project Camelot, a counterinsurgency study in Latin America **1964**

The Waves of Feminism and Other Social Movements

"2nd Wave" of Feminism

Labor Movement

Civil Rights Movement

Anti-Vietnam War Movement

American Indian Movement (AIM)

Abortion Rights Movement

Key Dates in Feminisms and Social Movements

1942 "We Can Do It!" posters featuring a woman who later became known as "Rosie the Riveter" encouraged American women to work in factories and shipyards during World War II producing munitions and war supplies; during this time, nearly 19 million women held jobs, but many were fired when men returned from the war

1949 Feminist journalist, Black Nationalist, and member of the Communist Party U.S.A. Claudia Jones published "An End to the Neglect of the Problems of the Negro Woman" in *Political Affairs*

1954 U.S. Supreme Court case *Brown v. Board of Education* ruled that establishing separate public schools for Black and white students was unconstitutional, a major victory for the Civil Rights Movement

Activist Yuri Kochiyama meets Malcolm X and joins the Organization of Afro-American Unity **1963**

Betty Friedan published *The Feminine Mystique*, which some credit as sparking "Second Wave" Feminism in the U.S. **1963**

The U.S. Civil Rights Act outlawed discrimination based on race, color, religion, sex, or national origin **1964**

U.S. Voting Rights Act extended the right to vote to all adult citizens **1965**

Griswold v. Connecticut made it unconstitutional to prohibit married couples from using birth control **1965**

National Organization for Women (NOW) founded with 300 charter members **1966**

U.S. Civil Rights Act signed, including the Fair Housing Act **1968**

The Redstockings and New York Radical Feminists protested the Miss America Pageant **1968**

Shirley Chisholm became the first Black woman elected to the U.S. Congress **1968**

The Stonewall Riots, following a police raid on a gay tavern in New York, are often cited as the beginning of the Gay Liberation or LGBTQ Movement **1969**

1940 **1950** **1960** **1970**

Key Dates in Feminist Ethnography

1970 Association of Black Anthropologists (ABA) established; ABA leadership has included Lee Baker (see Ch. 2), Whitney Battle-Baptiste (see Ch. 4), Lynn Bolles (see Ch. 3), Elizabeth Chin (see Ch. 5), Dána-Ain Davis, Faye Harrison (see Ch. 7), Leith Mullings (see Ch. 7), Cheryl Rodriguez (see Ch. 1), and Bianca Williams, among others

1972 Eleanor "Happy" Leacock was named chair of Anthropology at City College of New York, after teaching as an adjunct instructor for decades; she credited her appointment to pressure from feminist activists for institutions of higher education to diversify their faculty

1972 *Feminist Studies* established, the first journal in women's studies

1974 *Women, Culture, and Society* published

1974 Louise Lamphere (see Ch. 2) denied tenure at Brown University; she filed a successful Title VII Sex Discrimination Case the following year

Toward an Anthropology of Women published **1975**

Signs: The Journal of Women in Culture and Society established **1975**

National Women's Studies Association established to promote and support the production and distribution of knowledge about women and gender through teaching, learning, research, and service in academic and other settings **1977**

The Waves of Feminism and Other Social Movements

- "2nd Wave" of Feminism
- Anti-Vietnam War Movement
- AIM | Abortion Rights Movements
- Disability Rights Movement
- Gay Liberation Movement/LGBTQ Movement

Key Dates in Feminisms and Social Movements

1970s The first Rape Crisis Centers were established

1970 Comisión Femenil Mexicana Nacional founded to address issues of concern to Chicana women

1971 Anna Nieto-Gómez founded a women's group and feminist Chicana newspaper, both named *Hijas de Cuauhtémoc* after a Mexican women's underground newspaper published during the 1910 Mexican revolution

1971 The Boston Women's Health Book Collective published the first edition of Our Bodies, Ourselves, encouraging women's active engagement with their health and sexuality

1972 Shirley Chisholm became the first major-party Black candidate for President of the U.S. and the first woman to run for President of the U.S.

1973 *Roe v. Wade* legalized abortion during the first trimester of pregnancy

1973 Lesbian feminists attempted to exclude Sylvia Riviera, a Latina drag queen and transgender activist who had been part of the Stonewall riots, from speaking at a gay pride event commemorating Stonewall

1973 COYOTE (Call Off Your Tired Old Ethics), a prostitutes' rights organization, formed to repeal prostitution laws and end the stigma associated with sex work

1974 Equal Rights Advocates (ERA) was founded as a nonprofit women's rights organization dedicated to protecting and expanding economic and educational access and opportunities for women and girls

1974 Native American civil rights activists, including Lorelei DeCora Means, Madonna Thunderhawk, established Women of All Red Nations (WARN)

The first United Nations (UN) World Conference on Women held in Mexico City to inaugurate the Decade of Women (1976–1985) **1975**

Women Against Violence Against Women (WAVAW) formed to end all forms of violence against women **1976**

Combahee River Collective Statement published (see Ch. 1) **1977**

National Center for Lesbian Rights (NCLR) was founded by lesbian feminist activists who were members of ERA **1977**

1970 **1972** **1974** **1976** **1978** **1980**

Key Dates in Feminist Ethnography

Association of Feminist Anthropology (AFA) established; AFA leadership has included Florence Babb (see Ch. 2), Dorothy Hodgson (see Ch. 7), Susan Hyatt (see Ch. 7), Louise Lamphere, Ellen Lewin, Sandra Morgan (see Ch. 5), Cheryl Rodriguez, and Beth Uzwiak (see Ch. 7), among others **1988**

The Association for Queer Anthropology (AQA), formerly known as the Society of Lesbian and Gay Anthropologists (SOLGA) established; SOLGA/AQA leadership has included Evelyn Blackwood, Tom Boellstorff (see Ch. 7), Christa Craven, Naisargi Dave (see Ch. 4), Mary Gray (see Ch. 3), Bill Leap, Ellen Lewin, Scott L. Morgensen (see Ch. 1), Esther Newton (see Ch. 2), David Valentine, Marcia Ochoa, Margot Weiss, Shaka McGlotten, among others **1988**

Judith Stacey's (see Ch. 3) article "Can There Be a Feminist Ethnography?" published **1988**

Annette Wiener (see Ch. 2) became president of the AAA **1991**

The conference "Black Women in the Academy: Defending Our Name 1894–1994" was held at the Massachusetts Institute of Technology (MIT), the first national conference focusing on issues pertaining to Black female scholars **1994**

The Waves of Feminism and Other Social Movements

"2nd Wave" of Feminism

"3rd Wave" of Feminism

AIM | LGBTQ | Abortion Rights | Disability Rights Movements

Racial Justice Movement

Reproductive Justice Movement

Key Dates in Feminisms and Social Movements

1980 Kitchen Table: Women of Color Press was cofounded by Barbara Smith, Audre Lorde, Cherríe Moraga, Hattie Gossett, Helena Byard, Susan Yung, Ana Oliveira, Rosie Alvarez, Alma Gomez, and Leota Lone Dog

1980 The UN 2nd World Conference on Women held in Copenhagen, where the Convention on the Elimination of All Forms of Discrimination against Women (CEDAW) was approved; over fifty countries have ratified the convention, although the U.S. signed, but never ratified the treaty

1983 International Conference, "Common Differences: Third World Women and Feminist Perspectives" organized by Chandra Talpade Mohanty (see Ch. 1) and Ann Russo

1985 The UN 3rd World Conference on Women was held in Nairobi, Kenya, closed the Decade of Women

Americans with Disabilities Act was passed, prohibiting discrimination based on disability and affording similar protections against discrimination as the Civil Rights Act of 1964, as well as requiring employers to provide reasonable accommodations to employees with disabilities, and accessible public accommodations **1990**

Chandra Talpade Mohanty's *Third World Women and the Politics of Feminism* published **1991**

Planned Parenthood vs. Casey nearly overturned *Roe v. Wade* to outlaw abortion, reigniting feminist concerns about maintaining access to abortion **1992**

Rebecca Walker coined the term "Third Wave Feminism" in an article in *Ms.* Magazine **1992**

Intersex Society of North America (ISNA) was founded by Cheryl Chase to protest genital surgery on infants born intersex; Chase has been critical of feminist writers, such as Alice Walker and Katha Pollitt, for not including intersexuality on the feminist agenda, despite their condemnation of female genital cutting **1993**

Feminist activists, including Loretta Ross (see Ch. 5), coined the term "reproductive justice," an approach that links sexuality, health, and human rights to social justice **1994**

1980 **1985** **1990** **1995**

TIMELINE, continued

Key Dates in Feminist Ethnography

1995 The Committee on the Status of Women in Anthropology (COSWA), which later became the Committee on Gender Equity in Anthropology (CoGEA) was established to monitor the status of gender equity in the discipline and the AAA, and annually awards the CoGEA Award (formerly known as the Squeaky Wheel Award), which has gone to Louise Lamphere and Sandra Morgen, among others

1996 Race, Gender and Class Section of the American Sociological Association (ASA) established; Mignon Moore and Nancy Naples (see Ch. 3) have served as president in 2011 and 2015, respectively

1999 Louise Lamphere became president of the AAA

AAA issued a statement opposing President George W. Bush's call for a constitutional amendment banning gay marriage as a threat to civilization **2004**

Anthropologists began to be recruited to serve on Human Terrain Systems, embedded with U.S. military personnel in Iraq and Afghanistan **2007**

The Waves of Feminism and Other Social Movements

"3rd Wave" of Feminism

AIM | LGBTQ | Abortion Rights | Disability Rights | Racial Justice | Reproductive Justice Movements

Anti-Globalization Movement

Key Dates in Feminisms and Social Movements

1995 The UN 4th World Conference on Women in Beijing, China endorsed "women's right to control [their] sexuality"

1995 Riki Anne Wilchins founded transgender advocacy group GenderPAC on explicitly feminist principles to lobby against hate crimes and employment discrimination

1996 President Bill Clinton signs the Defense of Marriage Act (DoMA) which establishes marriage as an institution between one man and one woman

1997 Loretta Ross cofounded the SisterSong Women of Color Reproductive Justice Collective

1997 The Audre Lorde Project opened in New York, a community center for lesbian, gay, bisexual, two spirit, and transgender (LGBTT) people of color

1997 NOW passed a trans-inclusion resolution in consultation with GenderPAC

The Netherlands became the first country to legalize same-sex marriage **2001**

The Consensus Statement on Treatment of Intersex Individuals was revised to prioritize psychosocial support for children and families due to activism by the INSA and the Accord Alliance **2006**

1995 **1998** **2001** **2004** **2007**

2009 Patricia Hill Collins, author of *Black Feminist Thought,* became president of the ASA

2009 Network for the Anthropology of Gender and Sexuality (NAGS) formed in the European Association of Social Anthropology (EASA)

2011 Leith Mullings became president of the AAA

AFA issued a statement regarding American University assistant professor Adrienne Pine, who had been censured for breastfeeding in her class (ironically in feminist anthropology); the statement called upon academic institutions to provide better services for employees who are parents of young children **2012**

AFA, ABA, and AQA supported a AAA resolution opposing the trend toward contingent labor in academia, often female faculty, with recommendations for establishing more equitable employment practices **2013**

European Network for Queer Anthropology (ENQA) was cofounded by Elisabeth Engebretsen (see Ch. 4) in EASA **2013**

Faye V. Harrison became president of International Union of Anthropological and Ethnological Sciences **2013**

Annette Lareau (see Ch. 5) became president of the ASA **2014**

Bianca Williams organized a "die-in" at AAA in honor of Black Lives Matter and against racialized repression and state violence **2014**

Alisse Waterston became president of the AAA **2015**

Key Dates in Feminist Ethnography

"3rd Wave" of Feminism

AIM | LGBTQ | Abortion Rights | Disability Rights | Racial Justice | Reproductive Justice | Anti-Globalization Movements

Occupy Movements against economic inequality

Black Lives Matter Movement

The Waves of Feminism and Other Social Movements

2009 Rep. Barney Frank introduced a transgender-inclusive version of the Employment Non-Discrimination Act (ENDA), which has yet to pass out of the U.S. Congress

2009 Mokgadi Caster Semenya, a South African runner, was subjected to "gender testing" after she won the gold in the women's 800 meters at the International Association of Athletics Federation's World Championships

2011 First Slutwalk rally and protest held in Toronto, Canada (see Ch. 1)

Transgender rights groups asked Planned Parenthood to remove reference to gender in their advertising (i.e., "women's health" and "women's reproductive choice") **2013**

Black Lives Matter (BLM) began as an online campaign against violence toward Black people started by community activists Alicia Garza, Patrisse Cullors, and Opal Tometi and evolved into an international movement to address racial profiling and police brutality **2013**

More than a million people participated in the March for Women's Lives in Washington, DC, making it the largest protest march in U.S. history; Loretta Ross was instrumental in changing the original name, March for Freedom of Choice, to March for Women's Lives, indicating that women's lives are threatened by more than the attack on the legality of abortion, but also human rights abuses, from poverty to lack of immigrant rights **2014**

Same-sex marriage legalized in the U.S. **2015**

Laws banning anti-discrimination protections based on sexual orientation and requiring transgender people to use bathrooms that match the sex on their birth certificates passed in several U.S. states **2016**

Key Dates in Feminisms and Social Movements

2007 **2010** **2013** **2016**

Introduction

Feminist Ethnography: Thinking through Methodologies, Challenges, and Possibilities (FE) was designed with the hope that feminist ethnography can play an integral role in your thinking about activism, theory, and research from a feminist perspective. Thinking through, in this case, has two meanings. First, we hope you will use the discussions in the book to arrive at some understanding of how feminist frameworks and writing can be useful as a critical approach to everyday experiences. The other meaning is to consider carefully, or think through, aspects of planning and the implementation of a project. To facilitate your ability to learn about feminist ethnography we use a problem-based approach, which is based on inquiry. Problem-based learning is an opportunity to ask and respond to critical questions, as well as complete assignments or tasks to enhance the integration of the ideas presented.

FE was written expressly with students in mind. Why? Because feminism and feminists—and consequently academic inquiry associated with feminism—have gotten a very bad rap in recent years, particularly in popular media. "Third Wave" feminism—often describe as a diverse resurgence of young feminists that emerged in the 1990s demanding attention to a range of issues addressing not only gender equity, but also antiracism, anticolonialism, queer rights, reproductive justice, and antiviolence initiatives—came on the heels of the conservative political environment of the 1980s and 1990s, which has led to public resistance to the term feminism. As recently as 2014, *Time* magazine included the word "feminist" in a readers' poll inquiring which words should be banned in 2015. Although *Time* later recanted and apologized, their contrition was the result of public outcry.[1] Despite the magazine's apology, the fact remains that feminism is often viewed as a "dirty word," as evidenced by the sheer number of blogposts that make and/or refute the claim. As a nonscientific test, we googled "Feminist a Dirty Word" . . . in September 2015 and received 568,000 results, and by January 2016 it had doubled to 1,170,000! Given the negative public perception and the ways in which the lives of women, lesbian, gay, bisexual, transgender, queer, and intersex people (LGBTQI+),[2] and those and those of Indigenous and People of Color are under attack, we want to impress upon you the possibilities that exist within feminist ethnography, which may serve as an important response to these inequities.

Drawing from feminist writer Gloria Anzaldúa's concept of "*un choque,*" or "cultural collisions" introduced in her groundbreaking book on feminist and Chicana Studies, *Borderlands/La Frontera: The New Mestiza,*[3] we present ideas that are sometimes contradictory or challenging within feminist thinking. The ability to work through tensions and contradictions, as we see it, is itself a source of knowledge and part of the production of feminist ethnography and ideology. For example, across race and ethnicity there are no uniform perspectives about the role, or even the meaning, of feminism. Nor will you find singular feminist analyses of issues within transnational politics or across political perspectives. This text then not only reveals the challenges within feminism but also positions those challenges as the *work* of feminism; in other words, parts of this text and the discussions and contradictions herein represent the concept of *un choque*.

Our point is to expose you to the breadth and history of feminist ethnography and the application of feminist ethnographic methods. Feminists have examined many issues that expand our thinking on contemporary political and social concerns. Political scientist Cathy Cohen, for example, is the principal researcher on the Black Youth Project,[4] which produces research about the ideas, attitudes, decision-making, and lived experiences of Black youth, aimed at encouraging civil engagement and mobilizing communities of color beyond electoral politics. Anthropologist Daisy Deomampo's research conducted on the global surrogacy industry in Mumbai, India, looks at the complex transnational issues surrounding gestational surrogacy, egg donation, and in vitro fertilization.[5] Sociologist Katherine Cross studies online harassment and gender in virtual worlds and writes regularly for the blog Feministing.org on topics such as gaming culture, Europe's "refugee crisis," transgender politics, sexual shaming, and the #sayhername Campaign.[6]

An important thing that we noticed in our research for this book is that although feminists across across a range of disciplines embraced feminist ethnography, some have admitted to being unfamiliar with ethnographic work outside of their own disciplines.[7] It is our goal to highlight the strong tradition of feminist ethnography that began (largely) in anthropology, but to also consider the contemporary application of feminist ethnography across a variety of disciplines—including communications, education, human geography, political science, psychology, sociology, and in a range of **interdisciplinary** fields such as American studies, critical race studies, ethnic studies, Africana studies, **Chican@/Latin@** studies, and women's, gender, and sexuality studies, among others.[8] We also want to speak to broader audiences that interface with academia, such as activists and transformative education efforts like the Inside-Out Program that offers pedagogical approaches for teaching and learning among college students and people who are incarcerated.

This book is your guide to feminist ethnography. You will come to understand its history and its varied methodologies. You will see how it has been produced and circulated, and you will explore the challenges and possibilities that open up when you engage feminist ethnography as a theoretical, empirical, political, and potentially activist project.

How We Got Here: Serendipity and Collaboration

Students often ask us how we came to write this book, which is really embedded in the story of how we met and have embarked upon several scholarly projects together. We met, quite by accident, at an American Anthropological Association (AAA) conference in the early 2000s. We were both sitting in the back of the room during a panel discussion interrogating globalization and transnational labor politics. Dána-Ain had recently been hired in a tenure-track position following a career in public health and activist work; Christa was a graduate student in anthropology. Sitting a few seats away from each other, we were both taken aback as we watched the panel unfold. After a noted feminist anthropologist articulated how insights from Black feminism could contribute to rethinking transnational labor politics, she was summarily dismissed by the white male anthropologists and activists on the

Coauthors Christa Craven and Dána-Ain Davis. *Photo*: Zenzile Green

panel, as well as the predominantly white male audience. We both intermittently sighed, exasperated by the male panelists' disregard. We were each keenly aware of the vibrant history of feminist ethnography and the ways in which that research had contributed to feminist, antiracist, and anticolonial efforts far beyond the academy. Frustrated, and looking around the room to see how others were bearing witness to the devaluation of Black feminist research, we caught each other's glance, exchanged a few muffled comments, and quickly agreed that grabbing coffee together would be a far better use of our time. Over coffee we found that we had much in common as both activists and scholars, which led to conference panel proposals and eventually larger collaborations, more often than not centered around issues and ideas related to feminist ethnography.

It was our most recent project—an edited volume incorporating the work of other feminist ethnographers, titled *Feminist Activist Ethnography: Counterpoints to Neoliberalism in North America*—that inspired us to write this textbook, a more historical, cross-cultural, and interdisciplinary discussion of feminist ethnography.[9] Our disciplinary training in anthropology led us to approach this textbook with keen attention to its particular history. But despite our training we situate ourselves as interdisciplinary feminist scholars and have been influenced by feminist scholarship, ethnography, and practice that spans many academic and activist spaces. This sense of ourselves infuses our approach to exploring the scope and application of feminist ethnography.

We worked collaboratively on this textbook over the course of several years, via innumerable phone calls, texts, emails, and back-and-forth chapter drafts. We also had an opportunity to work together in person for a few weeks during this time. During Christa's visit to New York, we took a break from writing to attend an exhibit at the Brooklyn Museum: "Kehinde Wiley: A New Republic." The exhibit featured Wiley's impressive portraits, which foreground people of color, particularly Black men. His artwork fuses classical representations of European heroes and elite men—in styles ranging from French Rococo to Baroque of the European Renaissance to Islamic architecture to West African textile design—with contemporary images of young men he has seen on the street. Dressed in their everyday common attire—jeans, T-shirts, sneakers, et cetera—the men assume the heroic poses of classical paintings. Wiley describes his work as "interrogating the notion of the master painter, at once critical and complicit." The exhibit also displays Wiley's reflection on the importance of representation in his work:

> Painting is about the world that we live in. Black men live in the world. My choice is to include them. This is my way of saying yes to us.
>
> —Kehinde Wiley, American, born 1977

As we moved through—and were moved by—the exhibit, we also noted the number of people of color in attendance, especially young Black men, Black families, and multiracial groups of patrons. The attendance at the exhibit is a stark contrast to First Lady Michelle Obama's important observation in a speech at the dedication of the Whitney Museum of American Art in New York, when she underscored how museums are often seen as "white spaces." Yet the Brooklyn Museum, which has become well known for featuring work by artists of color over the past few decades, reports that 40 percent of its visitors are minorities.[10] Visiting this exhibit reinforced what can happen when you bring people's lives to the center as subjects, artists, and authors—whether in museums, ethnographic texts, or other creative spaces. Being critically attuned to issues of representation—who and what is represented and who decides—is central to our discussions. We have consciously modeled this commitment throughout the text.

Thinking Through This Text

Before we tell you about the structure of the book, we want to offer a brief note on terminology. We follow scholars such as anthropologist Leith Mullings, sociologists Maxine Baca Zinn and Bonnie Thornton Dill, and Native American activist and environmentalist Winona LaDuke who capitalize particular terms that represent historically marginalized groups, such as Indigenous, Aboriginal, Native, Black, Chican@, Latin@, et cetera. However, we strategically utilize lowercase for the term "white" in an aim to decenter whiteness, the racialized identifier that has long served as the norm in disciplines that employ ethnography.

FE is organized into eight chapters. Chapter 1 provides an introduction to feminist perspectives and their meanings over time. It establishes the importance of feminist ethnography and offers our working definition of the term. Chapter 2 is an historical overview of feminist ethnography, noting that the feminist ethnographic approach is not always identified as such by authors. Chapter 3 enumerates recent debates among feminist ethnographers as the field expanded from the 1980s through the present. Chapter 4 examines feminist methodologies. It answers the question, how does one *do* feminist ethnography? While we do not cover every possible method for feminist ethnography, we explore participant-observation, oral history, narrative analysis, and participatory action research, among others. Chapter 5 investigates the challenges of doing and producing feminist ethnography, including the ethical dilemmas and logistical constraints faced during fieldwork and writing. In chapter 6, we further explore the production and distribution of feminist ethnography with attention to both traditional and creative ways that ethnography can be circulated, including ethnographic texts, blog posts, novels, film, and performance. Chapter 7 discusses what it means to be a feminist activist ethnographer and highlights strategies for integrating scholarly and activist work through contributions to advocacy efforts and public policy. In the final chapter, we engage in "conversation," based on our interviews with other feminist ethnographers at various stages in their careers, about their visions and advice for the future of feminist ethnography.

We incorporate a range of people whose contributions to feminist ethnography are often overlooked, particularly those from groups who have not always been featured prominently in collections on feminist ethnography. Over half are scholars of color, several are international scholars trained outside the United States, others identify as queer, some are activists, or activist-scholars. In addition, in contrast to many earlier texts on feminist ethnography, feminist anthropology, and feminist methods, we interviewed male scholars who identify as feminist ethnographers or have a feminist sensibility and view their scholarship to be heavily influenced by feminists. By feminist sensibility we mean the ability to appreciate and respond to the complex intellectual and theoretical influences of feminist theory, thought, practice, and politics. We recognize that this may appear controversial to some who wish to emphasize the ways that sexism has marked women's scholarship historically and in the present—a fact that we are not inured to, and also highlight in the text. Yet, as we look toward the future of feminist ethnography, we find many students and colleagues across the gender spectrum (or gender polyhedron, a three-dimensional shape, as one of Christa's students, Maram Ghanimeh, aptly described"the mess that is gender identity and expression") are deeply inspired and influenced by feminist ethnographic work. Indeed, as we conducted our interviews and historical research for this book we focused our inquiry on ethnographers who articulate a feminist sensibility in their research and writing, regardless of gender.

Unique Features of This Book

As we prepared this textbook, the process was much like a feminist ethnographic project. Between the two of us, we conducted informal fieldwork—participant-observation and informal conversations about the field—at nearly 40 conferences over 10 years (such as the annual meetings of the American Anthropological Association, National Women's Studies Association, American Psychological Association, and several smaller interdisciplinary conferences). We also interviewed over 30 feminist ethnographers about the intricacies of their work, assisted by students in Dána's graduate seminar "Feminist Ethnographies."[11] These interviews introduce into the text the perspectives and reflections of seasoned feminist ethnographers who have participated in the field's growth since the 1970s, those who witnessed the debates that emerged during the 1980s and 1990s, and newer scholars inspired to incorporate feminist ethnography in their work, including several students.

Each chapter is influenced by a "problem-based" approach guided by several critical questions. These will also be useful to return to after reading the chapter, particularly in the context of the *Spotlights* and *Essentials* highlighting a broad range of ethnographers and issues. Each chapter features three or four *Spotlights*, excerpts from interviews conducted to explore the meaning and practice of feminist ethnography. *Spotlights* include a photograph and a brief introduction of the speaker (including their interests, academic and/or activist training and affiliations, and major publications). Chapters also include four or five *Essentials*, excerpts of texts that we consider "classics" or influential texts to give you a deeper sense of the history and practice of feminist ethnography. *Essentials* include a photograph and brief background on the author(s). You will also find activities labeled *Thinking*

Through . . . that encourage you to further engage the concepts that we have presented. It is the "doing" of feminist ethnography that offers the best opportunity to learn, and urges you to reflect on the challenges and possibilities of feminist ethnographic approaches. At the close of each chapter, we provide a list of additional *Suggested Resources* for those of you who wish to pursue the topics we present in more depth. These are largely new materials, ones that we do not explore elsewhere in the textbook. We also recommend reading the materials highlighted in the *Essentials* and *Spotlights,* and other ethnographies that we profile in each chapter. Throughout the text, you will find words and phrases in **bold** that are defined on the first mention in the text and included in the Glossary of definitions. Finally, we have included a timeline of events, related to feminism and feminist ethnography. It reflects the issues we cover in the textbook and highlights important people and events in movements for social justice.

We believe that feminist ethnography offers valuable contributions to both scholarship and activism. This textbook will engage you in critical thinking about its production and circulation. Ultimately, it is your reactions, responses, and projects that will shape what lies in its future.

Notes

1 Katy Steinmetz, "Which Word Should Be Banned in 2015?" *Time Magazine*, November 12, 2014, http://time.com/3576870/worst-words-poll-2014/.

2 We use + to include non-Western and non-EuroAmerican understandings of gender and sexuality, as well as emerging identities, such as pansexual, omnisexual, asexual, etc. We use different acronyms throughout the text to indicate particular historical moments, for instance where LGBT politics and identities have been foregrounded.

3 Gloria Anzaldúa, *Borderlands/La Frontera*, 1987.

4 Cathy J. Cohen, "Black Youth Project." *Black Youth Project.* Accessed October 4, 2015. http://www.blackyouthproject.com/. Cohen is also the author of *Democracy Remixed: Black Youth and The Future of American Politics*, 2010.

5 Daisy Deomampo, "Transnational Surrogacy in India: Interrogating Power and Women's Agency," *Frontiers: A Journal of Women Studies*, 2013.

6 Feministing. "Katherine Cross Archive," accessed October 4, 2015. http://feministing.com/author/katherinecross/.

7 For example, see Annette Lareau, "Common Problems in Fieldwork," in *Journeys Through Ethnography*, eds. Annette Lareau and Jeffry Shultz, 1996, 225.

8 In our discussion, we frequently mention the disciplinary background of authors we cite, not to instantiate them in a single field (indeed, many are decidedly interdisciplinary in their approaches), but to highlight the multiple disciplines that constitute and contribute to the field of feminist ethnography.

9 Christa Craven and Dána-Ain Davis, eds. *Feminist Activist Ethnography: Counterpoints to Neoliberalism in North America*, 2013.

10 Arun Venugopal, "Museums as White Spaces," accessed May 5, 2015, http://www.wnyc.org/story/museums-white-spaces/?utm_source=sharedUrl&utm_medium=metatag&utm_campaign=sharedUrl.

11 Most interviews were recorded in person, by phone, or by Skype, and in a few cases, interview questions were exchanged via email.

CHAPTER 1

What Is the "Feminist" in Feminist Ethnography?

This chapter provides an overview of feminism and feminist ethnography. You will learn definitions, histories, and categorizations using the following questions as your guide:

- What is feminist ethnography?
- What contributed to the history of feminisms?
- How are feminist perspectives categorized?

***Spotlights** in this chapter:*

- Cheryl Rodriguez on Feminist Thinking
- Talisa Feliciano on Challenging Established Theories
- Scott L. Morgensen on the Influence of Feminist Ethnography
- Gayle Rubin's Influence

***Essentials** in this chapter:*

- Rosemarie A. Roberts, "Doing Feminist Ethnography"
- Susan B. Anthony, "Declaration of Sentiments"
- Combahee River Collective Statement
- Chandra Talpade Mohanty, "'Under Western Eyes' Revisited"

*You will also be **Thinking Through . . .***

- Foremothers of the Feminist Movement
- Feminist Perspectives and Key Texts

This chapter is designed to orient you to feminism and the shifts it has undergone, as well as how feminists have engaged in an internal critique of their own work over time. Feminist ethnographic research is generally understood to have emerged during the women's movement of the 1960s and 1970s. It is important to understand what led up to the development of feminist ethnography, frequently referred to as the "waves" of feminism. We acknowledge that the notion of waves focuses upon a Euro-American history of feminism, and that feminist activism has occurred at various times in many locations. We only utilize this metaphor (and related timeline) as a structure to make a feminist influence on ethnography legible, not to situate "waves" as the sole lens through which to view feminist activism.

We use an interdisciplinary approach to explore the influence of many different strands of feminism. Therefore, following a broad introduction of feminist ethnography, we consider the emergence of feminist thinking as it intersects with critical race, disability, gender, sexuality, and class analyses. The phases of feminism we identify represent time periods in which particular issues were raised. This is followed by a discussion of the political inclinations of several different feminist perspectives. We distinguish between the waves and perspectives because perspectives do not always overlap with a single time period. For example, although liberal feminism emerged during the First Wave (in the 1800s), one can see liberal feminism in many contemporary feminist struggles. Further, one could have been a socialist feminist in the First Wave, although this perspective became more common during the Second Wave in the 1960s and 1970s. So it is important to keep in mind that waves and perspectives are not necessarily congruent.

Despite the different strands that have been important to the development of feminism, many would argue that the simplest definition of being a feminist is someone who is committed to the idea that there should be equality between women and men. For feminist ethnographers, this would entail scoping out specific projects to make women's experiences visible as the political imperative. Yet the feminist project has come to mean more than solely focusing on women's experiences—it also encompasses prioritizing projects that impact those who are marginalized, including people of color, differently-abled people, LGBTQI+ people, and poor or low-income people. Thus, feminist thinking is organized around supporting the struggles of people whose lives are marked and marred by structural inequalities.

SPOTLIGHTS

Cheryl Rodriguez on Feminist Thinking

Cheryl Rodriguez *received her PhD in anthropology from the University of South Florida. She now chairs the USF Department of Africana Studies and is director of the USF Institute on Black Life. As a feminist ethnographer, her research focuses on the intersection of race, gender, poverty, and place. She is the co-editor of the recent edited collection,* Transatlantic Feminisms: Women and Gender Studies in Africa and the Diaspora *(2015) with Dzodzi Tsikata and Akosua Adomako Ampofo. The following interview excerpt is her response to the question: What is feminist ethnography?*

I think that feminist ethnography is a method of writing, a method of telling a story, and a perspective that is grounded in a theory of feminist politics and a feminist reality. It is not just about women, of course, it is about gender and the ways in which gender intersects with race, class, experience, human rights, and all kinds of other social realities of our daily lives.

It is a way of telling a story about gender and all of its intersections. For instance, if I am trying to talk about the impact of how poverty affects women's ability to have secure housing, the best way for me to talk about it is to describe real women and all the experiences they have as they go through the process of trying to find a place to live. And not just the story, but also an analysis of relationships of power that tries to understand how different policies affect women and how sometimes these policies are grounded in histories of oppression and often they are not really meant to help women. It is important that it's mostly women that are affected by these things. But again, poverty is pervasive and poverty is also a family issue.

Feminist ethnography is layered and I think it is important that we, as feminist ethnographers, tell stories that add depth to some of the simplistic analyses that people want to believe, or that may be easy for people to embrace. We try to add another perspective to those stories, to those beliefs. An important part of feminist ethnography is dismantling stereotypes. . . .

I had to learn how to conduct research in that way. My research wasn't focused on those issues at first. I didn't understand what it meant to be a feminist ethnographer. I had to learn it.

What Is Feminist Ethnography?

A common question about feminist ethnography is: what is it that makes feminist ethnography different from just good ethnography? Our answer is laid out more comprehensively below and woven throughout the text, but in essence, feminist ethnography attends to the dynamics of power in social interaction that *starts* from a gender analysis. By gender analysis, we mean that a feminist ethnographic project takes into account all people in a field site/community/organization, and pays particular attention to gender by honing in on peoples' statuses, the different ways in which (multiple) forms of privilege allow them to wield power or benefit from it, and the forces and processes that emerge from all of the above. For instance, in Christa's book, *Pushing for Midwives: Homebirth Mothers and the Reproductive Rights Movement* (2010) she chose to foreground the voices of homebirth mothers and midwives over the opposition to midwifery, which consisted mostly of physicians and public health officials (largely, though not entirely men) who were well positioned to be heard by legislators and the public through lobbyists, newspaper op-eds, as experts in court cases, et cetera. Within the midwifery movement, made up primarily of women, Christa was attentive to power dynamics, highlighting the socioeconomic class tensions that emerged between wealthy and middle-class organizers who promoted advocacy for access to midwives as a "consumer's right," and low-income homebirthers who did not identify as "typical midwifery consumers" who had a choice of options for childbirth providers. Her feminist commitment as an ethnographer led her to look at inequities and power dynamics—first through gender, and then within it. Really, *any* good ethnographer should be examining power dynamics and inequities in their research; what sets feminist ethnographers apart, however, is their focus on a feminist framework for gendered analysis at the outset and throughout their projects, analyses, and choices concerning the production and circulation of their work.

This leads to the question: What are the ways that activists and scholars define "feminist" and how do those definitions fit into a discussion of feminist ethnography? There is an old joke that if you ask 10 feminists to define feminism, you'll get 11 answers. Scholars across academic disciplines, activists engaged in social justice work, and public policy makers who sometimes utilize our work to justify political change, use the term feminist, and often feminist ethnography. Some say that feminist ethnography is a framework that influences the kind of research that one undertakes or that it reflects a feminist **epistemology**, an examination of how knowledge is produced from a feminist standpoint. Others present feminist ethnography as a range of methods—including, though hardly limited to, participant-observation, in-depth or life history interviewing, and participatory research. Still others would say that feminist ethnography is a research practice informed by a politics of social justice and that it must be accompanied by a social justice project. So, is it a research project? Is it a way of doing research? Is it an ideology or theory? Is feminist ethnography a way of writing or performing scholarship? Is it an activist engagement? It can be all of these! Feminist ethnography produces knowledge about people and situations in specific contexts with attention to power differentials and inequities that emerge from the various strands of feminism we introduce later in this chapter.

Like feminism, ethnography also has a long history, as well as disputed definitions—though we would argue less so than the term feminism. Ethnography has long been considered the primary research method in anthropology, employed across other social sciences such as sociology, and more recently by journalists. The difficulty in defining ethnography is that it has been used in an unsystematic way, including by some who claim to be ethnographers after only brief stints interviewing and/or living for a few days among a particular group of people. Most social scientists would agree that ethnography is a form of qualitative research that centers on studying people and what they do and the contexts in which they live *over time*.

Ethnography typically involves long-term interactions through **participant-observation.** While its history dates back to Herodotus in the fourth century BCE,[1] ethnography assumed prominence across a range of disciplines in the twentieth century and involves becoming immersed in a situation and/or among a group of people to understand society from the point of view of those being studied—what contemporary ethnographers have come to call the **emic** perspective. Ethnographic description, including the **etic** or analytical point of view of the ethnographer, is thus a researcher's primary tool to convey knowledge about a particular cultural group. Ethnography was recognized more formally as a field of study in the mid- to late 1800s.[2]

One of the first social documentarians, or observers, of the conditions of the working class was Peruvian-born French feminist and socialist Flora Tristan (1803–1844), who recorded workers' exploitation in London. Although less well known than Friedrich Engels's often-cited *The Condition of the Working Class in England* published in 1845, Tristan's research on workers was published in 1840 under the title *Promenades dans Londres*.[3] Tristan was not an academic, but a socialist feminist who sought to bring attention to the impact of capitalism, the treatment of workers, and the links between the working class and women's rights. One of her primary arguments was that it was absolutely necessary to highlight the needs and experiences of women workers in order to address the needs of all workers. Tristan's work is a thread in the **intellectual genealogy** of contributions to (feminist) ethnography that emphasizes solution-based goals of documentary research.

Many academic disciplines and professions use participant-observation as a data collection method, but in anthropology, the origins of participant-observation are traced to Bronislaw Malinowski. Malinowski used participant-observation to generate anthropological knowledge among the Trobriand Islanders in 1914 and was among the first anthropologists to advocate using detailed descriptions of everyday life to understand societies. Across disciplines, practitioners now use ethnography to examine and understand how groups and people live their lives. The ethnographic account that results is a detailed description of that interaction and the product is also referred to as an ethnography. Far from being notable solely as a methodological choice, ethnography is as much as about bridging theory and practice—**praxis**—grounded in an effort to explore situations from the perspective of those living the experiences being researched. In fact, one of the insights offered by early feminist ethnographers, that continues to be reiterated today, is that it challenges theories and ideas that are made to seem like the only possibility for understanding culture and that privilege dominant groups.

Feminist ethnography originally emerged in the 1970s in an effort to correct women's absence from previous scholarship. Much of the previous male-centered research focused primarily on understanding culture, history, and everyday life from men's point of view. Women ethnographers in the field (and some men) made a concerted effort to correct this disparity by focusing on how life, politics, and sociocultural institutions were gendered and they sought to understand those issues by seeking out women's perspectives through the use of ethnographic methods. Sociologist Beverly Skeggs notes:

> The first location for feminist ethnography is in anthropology where ethnography is the central methodology. Here it has been strongly framed by colonialism and heterosexuality. The tradition of the heterosexual couple—him the distinguished anthropologist, her the interested and helpful wife, traveling to distant

SPOTLIGHTS

Talisa Feliciano on Challenging Established Theories

Talisa Feliciano *is a doctoral candidate in cultural anthropology at the Graduate Center, City University of New York. Her dissertation research is on the policing of youth of color in public space. Feliciano comes to this project as an Afro-Boricua woman, a native New Yorker of Puerto Rican descent, who has worked with activist organizations, such as the Ecuadorian International Center, the movement against police brutality, and the Audre Lorde Project. Here, she discusses the possibilities for feminist ethnography to challenge established theories about the policing of Black and brown bodies and promote analyses that foreground creative responses aimed at social justice.*

Feminist ethnography has always represented a challenge of supposedly established theories, whether it be the universal superiority of men over women, the idea that capitalism is the best or most free labor system, the racial superiority of whites and white supremacy, or that heterosexuality is natural and other forms of sexuality are deviant. So first, feminist ethnography will guide me to challenging established ideas about my work. In particular, studying and reading on youth, race, policing, and urban public space, there are anxieties present about the "natural" deviancy of youth, hyper-aggressiveness associated with young men of color and simultaneous hypersexuality associated with young women of color. These behaviors become naturalized through the State and formal police institutions. These ideas also become naturalized in the geographies of public space, public opinion of the types of people occupying these places, and policies implemented to regulate public space. Feminist ethnography opens up, for me, tools that have often been overlooked. It allows me to center art, literature, expression, and people's own accounts of themselves rather than hegemonic accounts of people made by others in the name of preservation, keeping order, and policy. Feminist ethnographies lean towards social justice, which propels my project forward out of the realm of just an interest, but takes seriously how people express themselves creatively in order to resist hegemonic white supremacist state policies enforced through hyper-aggressive policing.

continents to spend years living in a "culture" in order to understand it—has led to the production of some exceedingly reflexive accounts.[4]

Ultimately, feminist ethnography does not have one single definition, nor can "doing" feminist ethnography be confined to a single scholarly trajectory. Just as important is the fact that feminist ideologies have shaped and been shaped *by* ethnographic processes. We offer you this working definition of feminist ethnography, which:

1. involves a feminist sensibility, and commitment to paying attention to marginality and power differentials; these include not only gender, but also race, class, nation, sexuality, ability, and other areas of difference
2. draws inspiration from feminist scholarship—in other words, our feminist intellectual genealogy is important
3. challenges marginalization and injustice
4. acknowledges and reflects upon power relations within the research context
5. aims to produce scholarship—in both traditional and experimental forms—that may contribute to movement building and/or be in the service of organizations, people, communities, and issues we study.

Our goal is not to dispute multiple meanings and definitions, but rather to examine the ways that feminist ethnography is practiced, and how feminist research is produced and circulated. We also draw inspiration from dance scholar Rosemarie A. Roberts, who shared the following set of injunctions, or rules, that she attempts to follow in her own work at the 2014 National Women's Studies Association's annual meetings.[5]

ESSENTIALS

Commentary on Doing Feminist Ethnography by Rosemarie A. Roberts

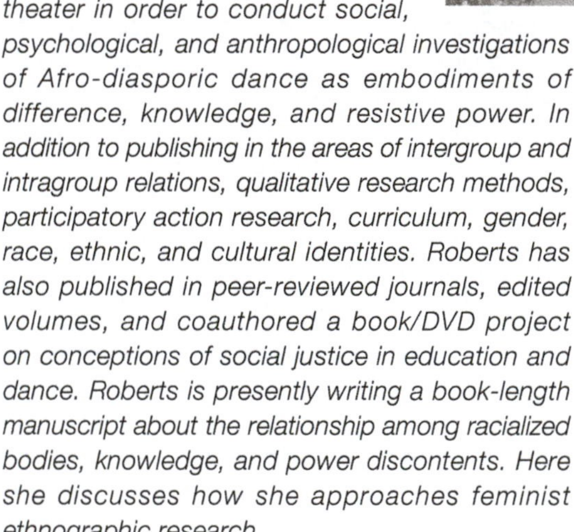

***Rosemarie A. Roberts** is a dance studies scholar, dancer, and educator with an interdisciplinary background including a PhD in social personality psychology and training in traditional and folkloric Cuban, Haitian, Puerto Rican, and Brazilian dance. Her artistic and scholarly work blends history, dance, and theater in order to conduct social, psychological, and anthropological investigations of Afro-diasporic dance as embodiments of difference, knowledge, and resistive power. In addition to publishing in the areas of intergroup and intragroup relations, qualitative research methods, participatory action research, curriculum, gender, race, ethnic, and cultural identities. Roberts has also published in peer-reviewed journals, edited volumes, and coauthored a book/DVD project on conceptions of social justice in education and dance. Roberts is presently writing a book-length manuscript about the relationship among racialized bodies, knowledge, and power discontents. Here she discusses how she approaches feminist ethnographic research.*

Number 1: Build on knowledge that has come before your work. Don't knock down others in the interest of promoting one's own work as new or original. I know this goes against what I think so many of us have been trained to do—we have to show our projects as new and original, and we have to put somebody else down, or we have missed the main point. Building on and collaborating WITH is about changing the academy.

Number 2: Don't pay lip service to writing in accessible language. Actually write in accessible language that illuminates rather than obscures what you have come to say.

Number 3: Make sure your argumentation is carefully constructed and supported by evidence. For me, that means invoking qualitative data for the insights they offer, and using quantitative data for the trends and patterns they might suggest. The difference between qualitative and quantitative data is not a contest between subjective and objective, but it's about determining the methodologies that work best to get me to the understandings and nuances that I'm seeking.

Number 4: Practice Holism. That includes appreciating that intellectual reason is a part of, but is not the whole story. Practicing holism includes appreciating that the kinesthetic, affective, and emotional is also part of the whole. I tell myself, "Don't privilege reason over emotion, and don't privilege emotion over reason."

Number 5: Look for and cite those who continue to be marginalized, acknowledging their important contributions to our collective knowledge base.

Number 6: Remind yourself that self-promotion is problematic if you put yourself forth as the one who has developed a new philosophy or theory when actually, you haven't. Especially when the theory or approach comes from the communities you are studying. But, if you have created a work or developed new something, embrace it! Recognize and remind yourself that . . . it is not self-promotion in a negative way to let others know about your work and activities. That's good to do. After all, if you don't do it, who will?

Source: Roberts, Rosemarie. Roundtable Discussant Commentary, "Interdisciplinary Perspectives on Feminist Ethnography & Activism." National Women's Studies Association Annual Meetings, San Juan, Puerto Rico. 2014.

We explore the production of knowledge through the lens of feminist ethnography. When we talk about how knowledge is produced, that means we consider the sources of explanation. Historians can produce knowledge by searching through archival material. In the natural sciences, knowledge may be acquired through a series of experimental steps known as the scientific "method" that relies on **empirical**, or verifiable, knowledge. Feminists often produce knowledge by reconsidering how power operates differentially, prioritizing women's experiences and those of others who have been historically sidelined. Feminist knowledge is also important in identifying not only oppression, but resistance as well.

Of course, it is important to recognize that the history of any research practice—and, as Morgensen highlights in the next Spotlight, our political perspectives—will often be told through the lens of dominant members of society. The history of feminist ethnography is no different. Some scholars have noted that feminist ethnography emerged in the United States at the same time as Second Wave feminism, in response to the eye-opening writings of liberal feminist Betty Freidan. Freidan's 1963 book *The Feminine Mystique* lamented the seeming destiny of suburban housewives—women whose lives, according to those Friedan interviewed, were almost devoid of meaning beyond shopping, decorating, and chauffeuring children to a host of activities.[6] Their displacement and sense of exclusion became a battle cry for what became known as the Second Wave of feminism in the 1960s and 1970s. But there were other influences as well . . .

SPOTLIGHTS

Scott L. Morgensen on the Influence of Feminist Ethnography

Scott L. Morgensen *received his PhD in anthropology and women's studies at the University of California, Santa Cruz, and teaches in the Department of Gender Studies at Queen's University. He is the author of* Spaces between Us: Queer Settler Colonialism and Indigenous Decolonization *(2011). Morgensen's scholarship works the intersections of queer, feminist, Indigenous, and critical race studies to explain how*

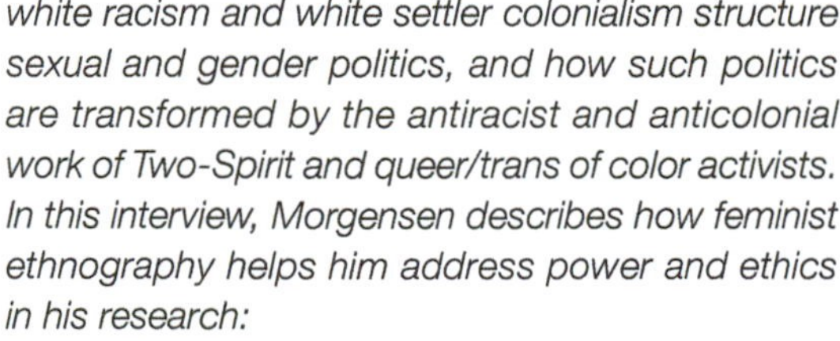

white racism and white settler colonialism structure sexual and gender politics, and how such politics are transformed by the antiracist and anticolonial work of Two-Spirit and queer/trans of color activists. In this interview, Morgensen describes how feminist ethnography helps him address power and ethics in his research:

Paying attention to what people are telling me about themselves forces me to hold my own political investments in a critical light: not to let go of my politics, but to expose that they carry a culture and a history too. Feminist ethnography shows me how to have political stakes and also expose their situatedness. I think doing this makes research and writing better. I don't hesitate to get involved in politicized research because feminist ethnography checks my desires to control what I will learn or know. Feminist ethnographers aren't afraid of confronting the ways we are situated in relation to our subjects or topics of study. And when complex issues arise, feminist ethnography models ethical ways to address them. By this, I don't mean a bullet point list of "do this" and "don't do that," but the sensitivity to address how power is shaping everyone in every research relationship.

If we keep doing research in the future and all forms of oppression aren't gone yet, then we're going to keep confronting ethical problems. So, let's just be more clear about them—and thank you, feminist ethnography, for setting the bar!

What Contributed to the History of Feminisms?

The "Waves"

History is a funny thing. It can be told from many points of view and that is the case with both the history of feminism and feminist ethnography. Typically, when people discuss Euro-American feminism they do so in terms of phases or waves beginning in late-nineteenth-century Europe and the United States, although the term "waves" may not be the most appropriate way to capture the shifting moments of various histories of feminist thinking. As feminist activist organization INCITE: Women of Color Against Violence asserts in their slogan "Feminist since 1492," a single "History of Feminism" that privileges Euro-American Global North contributions loses sight of the important contributions of Indigenous feminist thinkers and women of color (WoC). And even within a European context, historians cite feminist figures before the late nineteenth century, such as lyric poet Sappho of ancient Greece who wrote about passion and love for both women and men in ~600 BCE. Others born in or before the eighteenth century include writer and philosopher Mary Wollstonecraft (1759–1797) of Britain, who is considered to be one of the foremothers of the modern women's movement.

Thinking outside of a Euro-American framework demands consideration of women who made contributions to what might now be considered feminism. For us, this would include figures such as poet and nun Sor Juana Inés de la Cruz (1651–1695) of Mexico who promoted the right for women to have an education and African American preacher Jarena Lee (1783–?) who supported equality for women and was the first woman authorized to preach by the African Methodist Episcopal (AME) church. Through their writing and public speaking, these and other women, paved the way for the First Wave of feminism in the nineteenth century.

First Wave feminism had international dimensions in Europe, Latin and South America, and Africa, as well as in North America. For example, in France we may look to socialist feminist Flora Tristan, discussed earlier in this chapter. In Latin and South America, there was a strong tradition of women involved in journalism who advocated for women's rights, such as Clorinda Matto de Turner, born in Peru (1852–1909), who, although she was white, advocated on behalf of Incan Indigenous rights. Matto de Turner also authored *Aves Sin Nido* (*Birds Without a Nest*)—a book that ultimately led to her be excommunicated from the Catholic Church because it revealed the atrocious treatment of Peruvian natives. She was a formidable supporter of women's education and her work has been compared to Wollstonecraft's (1792) *A Vindication of the Rights of Woman* because, like Wollstonecraft, she argued that marital egalitarianism could be achieved through educating women.

Another example from the late nineteenth and early twentieth century can be found in the work of South Africa's religious leader Charlotte Manye Maxeke (1871–1918). Maxeke was active in the campaigns against pass laws that restricted Black South African's movement. She founded the Bantu Women's League of the South African Native National Congress (SANNC). As leader of SANNC, Maxeke led the first demonstration against passes and was active in protests against low wages. Maxeke is likely to have been the first African woman to graduate university in the United States, Wilberforce University in Ohio, where she took courses under Pan-Africanist, W. E. B. Du Bois.[7]

What we find compelling across these biographies is that cumulatively the women represent a varied history that in some cases predates and in other cases disrupts the more widely accepted history of the First Wave of feminism. The following sections trace the developments of feminism primarily in the United States, but we situate the foundation of these developments, acknowledging that other histories can also contextualize the emergence of feminism.

The First Wave

In the United States, the First Wave of feminism was connected to two other movements: the **abolitionist** and **temperance movements**, in that many of the members of the women's movement were also working toward abolition of slavery and encouraging moderation in the consumption of alcohol. The "Women's Liberation" movement is generally understood to have been a nineteenth-century project that coalesced in 1848 at the Seneca Falls Convention in New York where 300 men and women came together to call for women equality. It was there that Elizabeth Cady Stanton drafted the Seneca Falls *Declaration of Sentiments*, which laid out the movement's ideas and political strategies. Due to fear of retribution, the Declaration was only signed by 100 of the 300 participants. This declaration ultimately gave rise

 ESSENTIALS

A Portion of the Seneca Falls Declaration of Sentiments, July 19, 1848

When, in the course of human events, it becomes necessary for one portion of the family of man to assume among the people of the earth a position different from that which they have hitherto occupied, but one to which the laws of nature and of nature's God entitle them, a decent respect to the opinions of mankind requires that they should declare the causes that impel them to such a course.

A group of life-size bronze statues is the iconic signature piece of art at the Women's Rights National Historical Park in Seneca Falls, New York. The statues depict Elizabeth Cady Stanton, Frederick Douglass, Lucretia Mott, and other attendees to the 1848 Women's Rights Convention held in Seneca Falls, at which 100 women and men signed a Declaration of Sentiments modeled after the 1776 Declaration of Independence.

We hold these truths to be self-evident: that all men and women are created equal; that they are endowed by their Creator with certain inalienable rights; that among these are life, liberty, and the pursuit of happiness; that to secure these rights governments are instituted, deriving their just powers from the consent of the governed. Whenever any form of Government becomes destructive of these ends, it is the right of those who suffer from it to refuse allegiance to it, and to insist upon the institution of a new government, laying its foundation on such principles, and organizing its powers in such form as to them shall seem most likely to effect their safety and happiness. Prudence, indeed, will dictate that governments long established should not be changed for light and transient causes; and accordingly, all experience hath shown that mankind are more disposed to suffer, while evils are sufferable, than to right themselves by abolishing the forms to which they are accustomed. But when a long train of abuses and usurpations, pursuing invariably the same object, evinces a design to reduce them under absolute despotism, it is their duty to throw off such government, and to provide new guards for their future security. Such has been the patient sufferance of the women under this government, and such is now the necessity which constrains them to demand the equal station to which they are entitled.

Source: http://womensrightsfriends.org/pdfs/1848_declaration_of_sentiments.pdf.
Photo: National Park Service Photo.

to the U.S. women's suffrage movement, advocating for women's right to vote and women's political participation. These two issues initiated important conversations about the differences between men and women, and the resulting rhetoric of equity was based on an assumption of women's moral superiority.

Of course, others contributed to the development of feminism during this time. Frederick Douglass, who escaped enslavement in 1838, was one of the most outspoken proponents of women's rights in the nineteenth century, supporting Elizabeth Cady Stanton and Susan B. Anthony in their quest for women's suffrage. Another formative moment for the First Wave was when Sojourner Truth, a Black abolitionist and Methodist preacher, walked into the predominately white Women's Convention in Akron, Ohio, in 1851, three years after the first Women's Rights Convention in Seneca Falls, New York. The white women at the conference did not want their struggle for suffrage to be mixed in with the issue of race, despite the fact that a Black man, Douglass, had kept the controversial issue of women's suffrage central at the first convention in Seneca Falls. Yet, when Truth rose to enter into the conversation, her speech, known as "Ain't I a Woman?" in which she recounted the pain of having her 13 children sold into slavery and enduring slavery herself, she drew strong admiration. Truth subsequently spoke with many audiences about the importance of linking abolition and women's rights.

Suffrage is a widely accepted context for understanding First Wave feminism in the United States. It took from 1848, the Seneca Falls Convention, to 1920, to ratify women's right to vote with the passage of the Nineteenth Amendment. Yet this exposes a significant problem with the "waves" metaphor. Globally, there has been uneven realization of women's suffrage. Women had been voting in New Zealand since 1893 and in Australia since 1894. Women could not vote until 1944 in Jamaica, 1954 in Belize, 1945 in Italy, 1963 in Iran, and 1978 in Zimbabwe. Thus, women's access to the political arena has been uneven.

One issue that divided First Wave feminists was expectations for women regarding childbearing. Many nineteenth-century feminists were involved in the temperance movement and strong supporters of the "womanly duty" to bear children. Indeed, Stanton described abortion as "the degradation of women," though she argued that voluntary motherhood—through access to birth control and the legal ability to say no to her husband's sexual demands—was key to women's salvation. Some U.S. feminists, however, became ardent proponents of birth control during the early 1900s and Margaret Sanger opened the first birth control clinics in the United States in 1916. Sanger, who founded the American Birth Control League (which later became known as Planned Parenthood), advocated for women's control over their fertility as a means of social mobility, albeit not without problems, as you will see shortly.

Feminist ideas, such as voting and birth control, were initiated as broad and bold political agendas ostensibly capable of encompassing the intersection of sexuality, gender, race, and class. But the "victories" of change brought about by these political struggles and agendas often ended up supporting white, elite, and heterosexual women. A case in point were the clinics founded by the American Birth Control League (ABCL). Initially, some U.S. clinics reserved services for white women. It was only after pressure from African American women for birth control that the ABCL expanded access. Then, **eugenics** proponents became primary funders for fertility control clinics in the United States, leading to controversial alliances between feminists and eugenicists who hoped that these technologies would limit births among poor and nonwhite women. Sanger herself promoted certain eugenicist ideas, in particular that "the unfit" should be eliminated. As a result, many African American women began to organize through their own community networks, both for access to fertility control and against the compulsory sterilization of many African American women.[8] Support for fertility control was not unanimous, however, and some African American and Native American women continued to resist birth control into the 1900s, arguing that it was an attempt at **genocide**, a policy designed to reduce the size of their populations. Thus, although there is some evidence of multiracial feminist activism during the early to mid-twentieth century, white women and women of color often worked in separate organizations toward suffrage, community reform, antisterilization efforts, and access to birth control and abortion.

As scholars and activists Jael Silliman, Marlene Gerber Fried, Loretta Ross, and Elena Gutiérrez emphasize in *Undivided Rights: Women of Color Organize for Reproductive Justice*, in 1920, following the achievement of women's suffrage, feminist activist campaigns quieted during the mid-1900s, though local struggles continued to demand access to education and reproductive services on a community level.[9] It became increasingly evident, however, that universal equality for women had not been achieved through suffrage alone. Women's rights—to equal pay, educational equity, and reproductive rights—had not been fully achieved, and remained significantly stratified by race and class.

The Second Wave

The Second Wave of feminism in the United States spanned from the 1960s to the 1990s, named for the resurgence of feminist activism during this time. It is often described as a "radical" movement, in part because of one event that precipitated its expansion: the Miss America Pageant in 1968. Radical groups, such as the Redstockings and New York Radical Feminists, staged a joint protest to expose the ways that women in these pageants were paraded like cattle. Down the Atlantic City boardwalk they engaged in a number of theatrical events to make their point, such as ceremoniously crowning a sheep as a pageant queen, and throwing bras, high heels, and other oppressive items in garbage cans. The Second Wave refracted multiple national tensions that were emerging during this time.

Inspired by the civil rights, lesbian and gay, and antiwar movements of the 1960s and 1970s—each of which critiqued capitalism and imperialism—feminists in this wave also critiqued **patriarchy**, systems in which men hold the power from which women are generally excluded. Differences between and among women caused various constituencies—including women of color, poor women, and lesbians—to challenge Second Wave organizing among what some call "mainstream feminists" for their tendency to **essentialize** womanhood—which is the reduction of womanhood to a set of basic characteristics. The critique was based on the fact that mainstream feminists modeled their understanding of feminism on issues affecting middle-class, white women. Women of color, poor women, lesbians, and "Third World"[10] women viewed mainstream feminists as presumptuous regarding the idea that being a woman was enough to unite women in struggle. In fact, many argued that in order to understand women's experiences of oppression, feminists needed to acknowledge the different ways women—because of their particular histories and circumstances—had been subjugated. For example, whereas some white feminists argued that being in the home was repressive, there were many women who had traditionally worked—or been forced to work under slavery, or because of financial insecurity—outside the home. Their oppression did not come from having to stay home; rather it came from having to engage in forced or wage labor *and* **reproductive labor**, which includes the social and household work that sustains society. A second example is the alienation African American women experienced both within male-led civil rights organizations and in primarily white feminist groups, leading many to participate in local organizations to make demands that emerged from their unique experiences of gender, race, and class oppression.

Another schism in feminist organizing during this time centered on the emergence of lesbian feminism, which emphasized efforts against **heteronormativity**, the assumption that society should be structured around heterosexual relationships. Although many lesbians were active in feminist organizing in the U.S., they were excluded from prominent organizations like the National Organization for Women (NOW), founded in 1966. Then-president of NOW, Betty Friedan, courted the ire of prominent lesbian feminists—such as Charlotte Bunch, Adrienne Rich, Audre Lorde, and Marilyn Frye—after firing several lesbian staff members, including Rita Mae Brown, and allegedly referring to the growing lesbian visibility within feminist organizing as the "lavender menace." Lesbian feminism intensified during the 1970s as a part of mainstream feminist organizing, as well as within the Gay Liberation movement, which encouraged "coming out" as a form of public activism, as well as community events such as pride marches, which remain popular internationally.

As anthropologist David Valentine has written in his extensive history and ethnography of the category "transgender," Second Wave feminism intersected with transgender activism in pivotal ways.[11] For instance, historians have engaged in debates over who started the Stonewall riots during a 1969 police raid of the Stonewall Inn, a gay tavern in Greenwich Village, New York: a multiracial coalition of drag queens or an implicitly white group of "fluffy sweater boys, dykes, sissies, college students, boys in chinos and penny loafers"?[12] Contradictions also arose for feminists and LGB activists when lesbian feminists attempted to exclude Sylvia Rivera, a Latina drag queen and transgender activist, from speaking at a gay pride event in 1973 commemorating the Stonewall riots. Following the publication of radical lesbian feminist Janice Raymond's *The Transsexual Empire: The Making of the She-Male* in 1979,[13] which controversially described transsexualism as a "patriarchal myth" that reinforced traditional gender stereotypes, transgender rights groups formed throughout North America. For example, the Transexual Menace was the first direct action group for transgender rights cofounded by transgender feminists Riki Ann Wilchins and Denise Norris. Hermaphrodites With Attitude became the first direct action group for the rights of intersex people, founded by Executive Director of the Intersex Society of North America (ISNA) Cheryl Chase. GenderPAC emerged as the first national transgender advocacy group, founded on explicitly feminist principles by Wilchins. Wilchins is also the author of *Read My Lips: Sexual Subversion and the End of Gender*, which is notable for linking trans* liberation to feminist ideology and politics.[14]

Another concern centered on issues of inclusion. Beatrice Medicine, for example, who was also a feminist anthropologist, conducted path-breaking work on Indigenous women and inspired a generation of Indigenous feminist scholars.[15] Medicine, in her 1988 article "Native American (Indian) Women: A Call for Research,"[16] emphasizes that there was no research agenda addressing Native American women. Medicine's argument existed within a Second Wave framework in terms of inclusion. Without the perspective Medicine calls for, Native women are frequently represented in stereotypical ways and the dominant context of their existence is often considered pathological. For instance, when male anthropologists conducted much of the initial research on Native Americans and Aboriginal people, research focused primarily on dropout rates, alcoholism, suicide, and homicide rates. Medicine advocated ethnographic research by Indigenous women on Indigenous women to highlight the importance of gender variation in Native communities and different roles among Native women that could influence feminist theory.

The Second Wave is also associated with struggles for sexual freedom, reproductive rights, and the development of disability rights and studies. As a result, some parochial ideas and norms about sex and sexuality shifted and the institution of marriage was no longer a requirement for sexual interactions. Medical advances, in particular the birth control pill, made it possible for people to pursue the pleasure of intimacy without linking it to pregnancy. Thus, controlling one's reproduction, particularly access to birth control and abortion, became an important feature of women's organizing. In the United States, the right to obtain legal access to birth control and abortion was achieved through a series of legal decisions that culminated in the 1973 U.S. Supreme Court decision in *Roe v. Wade* to legalize abortion. Legal challenges since that time have added substantial waiting periods, parental consent, and other restrictions that have curtailed women's access to reproductive services. Similarly, as the legalization of abortion has become more common globally, access varies widely and is frequently limited by restrictive and complicated laws. This exemplifies once again the concept of *un choque* discussed in the introduction—a contradiction whereby abortion is legal in many areas, but inaccessible.

We also see tensions surrounding abortion and disability rights. For example, bioethicist Adrienne Asch both supported abortion in general as a woman's right, but opposed it as a means of preempting the birth of disabled infants. Asch and Michelle Fine's article, "Shared Dreams: A Left Perspective on Disability Rights and Reproductive Rights,"[17] makes the argument that women have a right to an abortion and newborns have the right to medical treatment and that those rights, although unequivocal, are contested by politics. The rights are viewed separately, whereby some conservatives take a pro-family position arguing against abortion and a woman's right to control her own body. Some progressives have taken the position that abortion should be accessible if a woman determines that the fetus has a disability. The legitimacy of abortion, they argue, should not be in competition with the provision of treatment or the right for a disabled newborn to survive. On the other hand, the authors point out that the right of a disabled newborn should not be used as the "strawman" in arguing against women's rights to have an abortion. Emerging within these contradictions and internal disputes, in the 1990s, a new generation of feminists inaugurated what has become known as Third Wave feminism.

The Third Wave

It was a response to the Second Wave that, according to authors Jennifer Baumgardner and Amy Richards in *Manifesta: Young Women, Feminism, and the Future*,[18] grew out of a need for the feminist movement to speak to a generation of young women who had the confidence and intellectual legacy bestowed upon them by Second Wave feminists. Many attribute the organizational structure of Third Wave feminism to Rebecca Walker, the daughter of prominent Second Wave feminist novelist Alice Walker, who won the Pulitzer Prize for her 1982 novel *The Color Purple*. Rebecca Walker wrote an article for *Ms. Magazine* in 1992, "Becoming the Third Wave," articulating the anger and desire for action in response to, among other things, the confirmation of Clarence Thomas as Supreme Court Justice amidst controversy over allegations of sexual harassment by Anita Hill, an attorney who had previously worked for Thomas.

Third Wave feminists collaborated with many feminists of color from the Second Wave in articulating a global alliance among women. They have placed greater emphasis on multiracial links among women and positioned inclusivity—with regard to economic disparities, transnational coalitions, and work for LGBTQ rights—at the center of organizing efforts. The Third Wave also emerged out of the "sex wars" among feminists in the 1980s—heated debates over pornography, prostitution, BDSM,[19] and transgender rights/identities—encouraging "sex-positive" feminism that promotes sexual freedom. The emergence of queer theory in the 1990s reignited controversies over the prominence of sexuality within feminist organizing efforts. With an emphasis on embracing gender fluidity, queer activists criticized essentialist understandings of gender, while a small group of radical feminists have maintained a vocal opposition to transgender liberation politics and denied intersections between feminist and queer activism. Mainstream LGBT efforts, such as the promotion of same-sex marriage and the expansion of adoption laws, have become widely supported by many women's rights organizations. This was despite earlier feminist critiques of marriage as a patriarchal institution that served primarily to limit women's autonomy. Recent efforts to promote transgender inclusion, such as appeals to Planned Parenthood and the National Abortion and Reproductive Rights Action League (NARAL) in 2013 to remove reference to gender (i.e., "women's health" and "women's reproductive choice") in the names of their health clinics and reproductive justice campaigns, have continued to meet resistance among some feminist organizers.

Efforts to combat violence against women—including domestic violence, rape, and sexual harassment—that were central to feminist organizing in the 1970s when rape crisis centers were first established, have taken new forms in the twenty-first century. The highly publicized Slutwalk protest marches, for instance, emerged in response to a Toronto police officer's admonishment that women should not dress like "sluts" so they do not become victims of (presumably) male sexual violence. In 2011, the first rally and protest occurred in Toronto and subsequent marches have been organized throughout Asia, Europe, Latin America, and North America. Prominent feminist pundits and bloggers have accused the movement of trivializing women's experience and excluding women of color, reigniting concerns about racialized divisions in contemporary mainstream feminist organizing. On the other hand, we would argue that the influence of Third Wave feminism has helped to shape the intersectional politics of predominantly women-led movements like Black Lives Matter.

Thinking Through . . .

Foremothers of the Feminist Movement

Choose a person who was influential to the development of feminism. Building on what you have read so far, pretend that you will conduct an interview with that person about their contribution to feminism. Develop a set of questions and fashion what you think would be likely "responses."

How Are Feminist Perspectives Categorized?

In the previous section, you see that feminists generally hold the view that people are treated differently in society and have uneven access to resources and power. Feminists also believe that this inequity can be changed through social movements and by challenging cultural practices and norms. Holding a feminist perspective can encourage one to examine the roles that marginalized people in general, but women in particular, have in society and explore the ways in which inequalities are expressed in peoples' everyday lives. Generally then, contemporary feminists pay attention to how people are stratified, or **hierarchized** in terms of gender, race, class, ability, and other markers or categories of difference. Hierarchizing occurs when people are treated differentially in society allowing some people access to more power, control, and privilege than others.

There are many ways to explore these inequities and people often view the **etiology**, or cause, of stratification as having different sources. Thus, there are different variations of feminisms. If one were to ask, "How and why are women (or racial minorities, or poor lesbians, among other groups) less privileged and have less power?" there would be different starting points to answer the questions. There might even be different ways of asking the question because of how various feminists even *understand* a problem. For instance, would they highlight social, economic, political, or other factors in their answer? Some of the more typical ways that feminisms are categorized are Liberal, Radical, Cultural, Marxist, Socialist, Black, "Third World," Postcolonial and Transnational, and Postmodern. In this section, we include brief explanations of these perspectives. Although they are presented as unique forms of feminism, the lines between them are often blurred and the distinctions are not mutually exclusive.

Liberal Feminism centers on the argument that while women may be universally subordinate, they are not inferior to men, and can assert power within particular spheres. Mary Wollstonecraft, the eighteenth-century author of the book *A Vindication of the Rights of Women,* argued in 1792 that women are not inherently inferior to men. Writing in the liberal tradition, she promoted individual rights. Liberal feminists believe that all people are equal and oppression exists because of the way that people are conditioned or socialized. Since it is societal norms that orchestrate how women and men are expected to act, the society must be changed. That change comes by making institutions accountable, not by eliminating the institutions themselves (as some other feminists suggest). Thus, liberal feminists argue that gender equality can be attained by working *within* institutions. The kinds of rights liberal feminists would seek to secure have included voting rights, protection of women under the law, and equal funding for girls' education and sports. Since liberal feminists identify equal opportunity at the center of their analysis, they tend to hold the view that discrimination and barriers can be resolved through government reforms. They work within existing structures to create opportunities and use legislative and electoral politics to ensure equity. International efforts toward women's suffrage are associated with the liberal feminist efforts of the nineteenth and early twentieth centuries. A more contemporary example of liberal feminism would be the promotion of same-sex marriage legislation, aimed at alleviating legal inequities between heterosexual couples and lesbian and gay couples.

Radical Feminism is a perspective that emerged during the Civil Rights Movement in the 1960s. Radical feminists argue that women's oppressed status cuts across race, culture, and class and uses an analysis of the structure of sex/gender to understand women's oppression. Thus, all women are oppressed and oppression stems from male dominance. If the root of oppression lies in male dominance, it is that structure that needs to be dismantled. Radical feminists support movements that are about direct social change and even cultural revolution. Many radical feminists view violence against women and sexual violence as the primary reasons for women's subjugation. Therefore, understanding women's oppression would come from examining and analyzing violence in all of its forms as one of the most important strategies that facilitate the perpetuation of patriarchal society in which women are oppressed. Radical feminism has focused on how deeply entrenched the male/female division is across cultures, arguing that women have been oppressed and discriminated against in all areas and their oppression is primary. Radical feminists are generally skeptical of a reformist (liberal feminist) approach to address women's oppression. For example, they do not believe that antiviolence laws will end male supremacy. Yet they use the law as a protective strategy while seeking other avenues to end male supremacy.

Cultural Feminism is a perspective that some say followed a decline in radical feminism, representing a historical progression, but a particular formulation of feminism based on biological distinctions. It is rooted in the perspective that differences between men and women are primarily biological. These biological variations result in different behaviors. For example, cultural feminists might argue that women are inherently more nurturing than men because of their capacity to give birth. From the point of view of psychoanalytical sociologist Nancy Chodorow, women's domestic and nurturing work should be compensated and recognized as productively important. Cultural feminists are less interested in equality per se and instead argue for there to be greater societal value placed on women's roles and work. Following radical feminists, cultural feminists reify the characteristics that they argue make men and women different. They advocate for a system of governing based on women's virtues and ways of being, which they consider more peaceful, nurturing, and collaborative, in contrast to male tendencies toward violence and competition. Chodorow's work, as well as that of other cultural feminists, was featured in some of the earliest publications in feminist anthropology, such as *Woman, Culture, and Society* in 1974. Although this perspective has since been heavily critiqued—by later feminist anthropologists, as well as many of those who published initially in the volume as graduate students—the influence of cultural feminism remains important to the genesis of feminist ethnography.

Marxist Feminism attributes women's oppression to the capitalist and private property system. Under the capitalist system, the **means of production** are controlled by those who have power, and in the process, women's labor is exploited. In other words, the rewards for production—be it the social reproduction of inequalities or manufacturing production of commodities—do not exist for those engaged in labor. The reward comes to those who *own* the means of production. For Marxist feminists, it is this form of oppression, the structure of class, to which all other forms of inequity are linked. Capitalism then is the reason for female oppression. Many Marxist feminists also link capitalist oppression to other spheres such as race, class, and sexual identity, which are all subordinated in the interest of capital gain. Marxist feminists would view women's oppression in exponential terms, because capitalism oppresses women, often based on gender, race, and class. Like radical feminists (and in contrast to liberal feminists), Marxist feminists tend to be skeptical about the chances of achieving substantive change by working within "the system." Marxist feminist perspectives were also well represented in early publications in feminist anthropology. One of the most widely cited articles from that time period is anthropologist Gayle Rubin's "The Traffic in Women: Notes on the 'Political Economy' of Sex," which has been called "a tour de force of Marxism, structuralism, and Freudo-Lacanian theory, [as it] draws on analogies with political economy to hypothesize a universal 'sex-gender system.'"[20]

Socialist Feminism is an elaboration of Marxist feminism, but primarily with regard to the need to integrate a historical materialist analysis. A historical materialist perspective interrogates the causes of societal change and the development of society by examining the economic system that operates at particular moments. Socialist feminists depart from the Marxist focus on class oppression as the sole or

SPOTLIGHTS

Gayle Rubin's Influence

__Gayle Rubin__ completed her PhD in anthropology from the University of Michigan and now teaches there in anthropology and women's studies. She is best known as a feminist and queer activist and theorist of sex and gender politics. Along with "The Traffic in Women," discussed in this interview, her influential 1984 article, "Thinking Sex: Notes for a Radical Theory of the Politics of Sexuality," argues that there were different systems of stratification, and that certain kinds of sexual oppression (such as that of gay people) were not necessarily or uniquely attributable to gender stratification. Although Rubin's work was influenced by Karl Marx's work on class oppression, she argues against a sort of "theoretical monomania"—a single theory of everything (Marxism, feminism, etc.), or a single set of primary causal relationships at the root of all social problems. Here she addresses the legacy of her article "Traffic in Women" for feminist ethnographers:

I think it is important for emerging scholars to understand what questions earlier generations were trying to address, and what tools were available with which to tackle them. "Traffic in Women" emerged out of a very specific time and set of circumstances. Second Wave feminism was trying to establish the legitimacy of very basic claims to improved social status for women, and for its demands to redress a whole panoply of political and economic grievances. This was in the context of very pervasive assumptions that women were intrinsically different from men in ways that justified impaired civil status, lesser pay and other economic limitations, and a punitive sexual double standard. Male privileges—and their access to better jobs, more respect, greater physical mobility, and a vast range of personal and sexual services—were largely unquestioned. So intellectually, one of the pressing tasks was to dismantle the ideologies that reinforced these durable structural liabilities based on gender.

As for academic disciplines at the time, anthropology was probably among the more progressive, not only in terms of gender, but also race and class (for which many anthropologists had been considered subversive and harassed during the course of the twentieth century). But it was still riddled with sexism and male privilege, both in its social relationships and substantive contents. So as Second Wave feminism took hold in the field, one task was a kind of ground clearing to challenge these assumptions. Another was efforts to collect more primary data on women cross-culturally to redress the skewed ethnographic focus on males. And another was to construct alternative theoretical frameworks and generate new models for human societies and behavior that did not project assumptions from the mid-twentieth-century United States onto the rest of human history.

CC: What drew you to Marxist critique in your analysis of "the political economy of sex," and how have you found it useful in your subsequent work on sexuality?

GR: The tool kit with which to approach all these issues was limited, although feminist anthropologists were extremely creative in figuring out how to use the existing intellectual resources of the field to do so. One of these was Marxism, which was then enjoying a kind of political and intellectual renaissance in parts of U.S. academia. Women's Liberation largely grew out of what was then the "New Left," in which many strains of Marxism were percolating. But in addition to its political aspects, Marx's oeuvre was one of the great bodies of early social science analysis. Many of the basic concerns of emerging late-nineteenth-century social science—especially anthropology and sociology—were generated as various thinkers attempted to understand social stratification and how it operated in different times and places. Marx had always been among the most important of these. Moreover, there was actually a lot of Marx embedded within anthropology already, although not always explicitly or in recognizable forms. One problem with Marx, however, is that his work also tended to be treated as a rigid set of canonical beliefs, rather than as a collection of supple theoretical tools. So those of

(continued)

us working with Marx had to disentangle what was useful from accretions of stale and often mandatory dogmas. In some ways, this intellectual project was parallel to the political project of the differentiation of second wave feminism out of the New Left. Women's Liberation owed a great deal to the social and intellectual movements of the period, but had to establish its own claims, analytic frameworks, and organizational structures. My work at the time was part of this broader process.

Photo: Michael Rosen

primary way to view society. Rather, they argue that gender and class operate simultaneously creating particular forms of oppression and privilege for women and men in different classes. Socialist feminists view the intersection of sexism, racism, and classism as forms of oppression that need to be addressed concurrently. The solution they propose is socialism, a societal organization that encourages more social ownership rather than individual ownership, resulting in cooperative and more socially and economically equitable management of the economy.

Black Feminism emerged in the 1970s in response to white feminist efforts that failed to incorporate the simultaneous struggles for Black liberation in the Civil Rights Movement. In England, Black feminism was the term used to include Asian and African women as a way to capture the fact that women from these locations had been subjected to colonization in their countries of origin and to racism in England. A Black feminist perspective is usually linked to socialist feminism in that it pushes for political analyses that incorporate race, gender, and class oppression along with heterosexism, as intersecting or intersectional issues. Black women's political participation—from abolition and suffrage movements to efforts for reproductive justice—have always engaged with intersectional analysis and resulting politics, even when organizers did not identify explicitly as feminists.

One of the most important—and enduring—outcomes of the Black Feminist framework is the Combahee River Collective Statement, a document that lays out the importance of attending to sexism, racism, classism, and heterosexism as part of political organizing. Many feminists have drawn upon this statement as inspiration for intersectional scholarly work. An influential Black feminist thinker was Audre Lorde, whose creative writing, activism, and scholarship, has influenced two generations of feminist scholars, artists, and activists. Lorde's contributions are the result of her complex analyses of systems of oppression and the relevance of her work on sexism, racism, heterosexism, classism, and imperialism that resonate both inside and outside the academy. Her work provides a grammar that gives durability to theorizing across disciplines, and has contributed to Black feminist, literary, queer, and postcolonial theories, and transnational feminisms.

"Third World," Postcolonial, and Transnational Feminisms were emboldened in the 1980s by the critical work of Black feminists. Postcolonial feminist theorists began to critique Western feminist analyses of "Third World" women in homogenizing and derogatory ways without considering the context of their lives. Postcolonial and transnational feminist theorist Chandra Talpade Mohanty's groundbreaking essay in 1991, "Cartographies of Struggle: Third World Women and the Politics of Feminism," defines "Third World" as including Black, Latino, Asian, and Indigenous peoples in the United States, Europe, and Australia, as well as those from Latin America, the Caribbean, sub-Saharan Africa, South and Southeast Asia, East Asia, South Africa, and Oceania.[21] Although the terminology of "Third World" has given way to other articulations, and postcolonial feminism is used less frequently than transnational feminism among contemporary feminists, the history of the terms

ESSENTIALS

Excerpt from the Combahee River Collective Statement

The Combahee River Collective *was a group of Black, lesbian, socialist feminists in Boston who gathered from 1974 to 1980. The Combahee River Collective Statement, excerpted below, was inspired by abolitionist Harriet Tubman's leadership in the Combahee River Raid in South Carolina on June 2, 1863, during the Civil War, which freed 750 slaves. This statement exemplifies the commitment of many feminist ethnographers to combatting oppressions based not only on gender but also on multiple axes of inequality.*

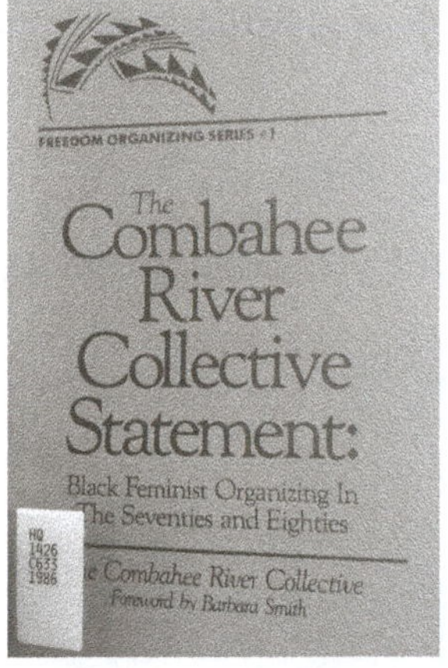

Above all else, our politics initially sprang from the shared belief that Black women are inherently valuable, that our liberation is a necessity not as an adjunct to somebody else's but because of our need as human persons for autonomy. This may seem so obvious as to sound simplistic, but it is apparent that no other ostensibly progressive movement has ever considered our specific oppression as a priority or worked seriously for the ending of that oppression. Merely naming the pejorative stereotypes attributed to Black women (e.g., mammy, matriarch, Sapphire, whore, bulldagger), let alone cataloguing the cruel, often murderous, treatment we receive, indicates how little value has been placed upon our lives during four centuries of bondage in the Western hemisphere. We realize that the only people who care enough about us to work consistently for our liberation are us. Our politics evolve from a healthy love for ourselves, our sisters and our community which allows us to continue our struggle and work.

This focusing upon our own oppression is embodied in the concept of identity politics. We believe that the most profound and potentially most radical politics come directly out of our own identity, as opposed to working to end somebody else's oppression. In the case of Black women this is a particularly repugnant, dangerous, threatening, and therefore revolutionary concept because it is obvious from looking at all the political movements that have preceded us that anyone is more worthy of liberation than ourselves. We reject pedestals, queenhood, and walking ten paces behind. To be recognized as human, levelly human, is enough.

We believe that sexual politics under patriarchy is as pervasive in Black women's lives as are the politics of class and race. We also often find it difficult to separate race from class from sex oppression because in our lives they are most often experienced simultaneously. We know that there is such a thing as racial-sexual oppression which is neither solely racial nor solely sexual, for example, the history of rape of Black women by white men as a weapon of political repression.

Source: Cherríe Moraga and Gloria Anzaldúa. *This Bridge Called My Back: Writings of Radical Women of Color*. New York: Kitchen Table: Women of Color Press, 1983, 212–213. (This source is also available full text on multiple websites, such as http://circuitous.org/scraps/combahee.html.)

contribute to understanding the importance of the sustained influence of feminist perspectives that have emerged outside of a primarily white, Global North, colonialist framework. Closely aligned with Black feminism, postcolonial feminism emerged as a critique of Western feminists and postcolonial theorists, drawing critical attention to the impact of colonialism and imperialism on gendered oppression.

Several factors ushered in what has become known as transnational feminism, as distinct from the international women's movement from the 1970s, which was organized around the principle that "sisterhood is global"—a phrase coined by Robin Morgan in the 1980s. The general idea is that all women are linked through a *common bond of being women*. However, most transnational feminists vehemently resist a universalized vision of feminist solidarity. Rather, they address the intersections between nation, race, gender, sexuality, and economic exploitation in relation to global capitalism. A transnational feminist approach questions inequities that have resulted from centuries of colonialism and racism, as well as new forms of inequalities as a result of globalization. It emphasizes interconnections among

ESSENTIALS

Excerpt from "Under Western Eyes Revisited" by Chandra Talpade Mohanty

Born and raised in India, ***Chandra Talpade Mohanty*** *received her PhD in education from the University of Illinois at Urbana-Champaign and is currently chair and distinguished professor of women's and gender studies at Syracuse University. She became widely known as a postcolonial feminist scholar after the 1984 publication of "Under Western Eyes: Feminist Scholarship and Colonial Discourses," which she wrote as a graduate student. Subsequent publications included* Feminist Genealogies, Colonial Legacies, Democratic Futures *(1996) with M. Jacqui Alexander,* Feminism Without Borders: Decolonizing Theory, Practicing Solidarity *(2003) and* Feminism and War: Confronting US Imperialism *(2008), with Robin Riley and Minnie Bruce Pratt. The following excerpt is Mohanty's reflection on her first publication, which highlighted the colonization of the experiences of so-called "Third World" women within western feminist theory.*

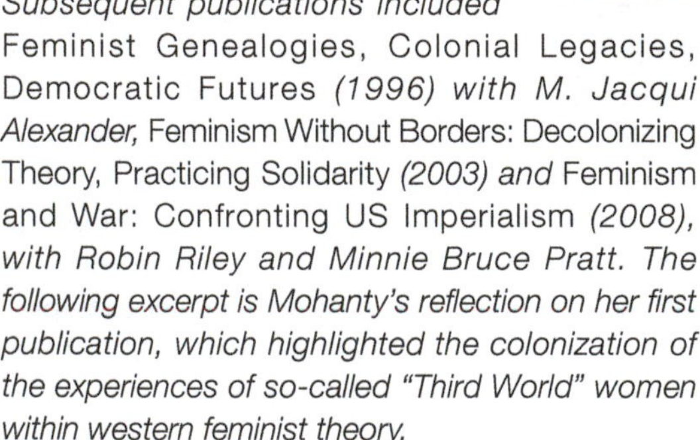

I wrote "Under Western Eyes" to discover and articulate a critique of "Western feminist" scholarship on Third World women . . . I also wanted to expose the power–knowledge nexus of feminist cross-cultural scholarship expressed through Eurocentric, falsely universalizing methodologies that serve the narrow self-interest of Western feminism. As well, I thought it crucial to highlight the connection between feminist scholarship and feminist political organizing while drawing attention to the need to examine the "political implications of our analytic strategies and principles." I also wanted to chart the location of feminist scholarship within a global political and economic framework dominated by the "First World." My most simple goal was to make clear that cross-cultural feminist work must be attentive to the micropolitics of context, subjectivity, and struggle, as well as to the macropolitics of global economic and political systems and processes. . . .

After almost two decades of teaching feminist studies in U.S. classrooms, it is clear to me that the way we theorize experience, culture, and subjectivity in relation to histories, institutional practice, and collective struggles determines the kind of stories we tell in the classroom. If these varied stories are to be taught such that students learn to democratize rather than colonize the experiences of different spatially and temporally located communities of women, neither a Eurocentric nor a cultural pluralist curricular practice will do. In fact narratives of historical experience are crucial to political thinking not because they present an unmediated version of the "truth" but because they can destabilize received truths and locate debate in the complexities and contradictions of historical life. [This approach suggests] the complexities of the narratives of marginalized peoples in terms of relationality rather than separation. These are the kinds of stories we need to weave into a [discussion of] feminist solidarity [which focuses] on mutuality and common interests... It requires one to formulate questions about connection and disconnection between activist women's movements around the world. Rather than formulating activism and agency in terms of discrete and disconnected cultures and nations, it allows us to frame agency and resistance across the borders of nation and culture.

Source: Chandra Talpade Mohanty. "'Under Western Eyes' Revisited: Feminist Solidarity through Anticapitalist Struggles." *Signs: Journal of Women and Society* 28, no. 2 (January 1, 2003): 222–223.

seemingly disparate communities (such as interrogating global flows of labor and commodities), rather than the comparison of gender relations between cultures (that was popular among radical/cultural feminists in the 1970s). It is also important to note that more recently, scholars identify as anticolonialist, rather than postcolonial, indicating a political position that colonialism has not passed.[22]

Postmodern Feminism developed in the 1980s out of a critique of ideological **binaries.** This form of feminism argues against binarisms as the primary organizing structure of society, such that categories like male/female or Black/white need to be rethought. Postmodern feminists draw on the intellectual legacies of theorists, such as Hélène Cixous, Simone de Beauvoir, Jacques Derrida, Franz Fanon, Michel Foucault, Luce Irigaray, Julia Kristeva, and Jacques Lacan, in an attempt to deconstruct and blur the boundaries of binaries to critique structures that dominate our ways of thinking. In other words, there are many ways of being "a woman," which makes the man/woman binary useless. How can there be an essence or an essential way of being, if there are, in fact, a range of ways of being? Postmodern feminism was a key influence on feminist ethnography in the 1980s, in part because postmodern feminists view the use of language and writing as crucial. The primary technique employed by postmodernists is discourse analysis with attention paid to the fact that discourse and language are neither neutral nor objective. While maculinistist language can reinforce the dominant social order, postmodern feminists believe that feminist/feminine approaches to writing promote alternative ways of seeing.

Conclusion

In this chapter, we have provided a general overview of feminisms that we see as most significant in their contribution to the production of feminist ethnography. We recognize that there are other feminist perspectives that have influenced particular feminist ethnographers. In the next chapter we focus on the lineage of feminist ethnography, providing a window into how feminism(s) contributed to women's entré into ethnography in the 1800s and ultimately the development of feminist ethnography as a practice in the late twentieth century.

Thinking Through . . .

Feminist Perspectives and Key Texts

Identify a contemporary social issue, such as same-sex marriage or birth control, and apply what you have read to analyze the issue from two feminist perspectives. Write a brief comparison of how feminists with these different leanings might understand and approach the contemporary issue.

Suggested Resources

Angela Y. Davis (2011 [orig. 1981]) *Women, Race, & Class.*

Cherríe Moraga and Gloria Anzaldùa (1983) *This Bridge Called My Back: Writings of Radical Women of Color.*

bell hooks (1984) *Feminist Theory: From Margin to Center.*

Jennifer Nelson (2003) *Women of Color and the Reproductive Rights Movement.*

Judith Lorber (2011) *Gender Inequality: Feminist Theories and Politics*, 5th Ed.

Notes

[1] Before Common Era (BCE) is commonly used by anthropologists as an alternative, secular naming of the Christian Calendar. See Robin Patric Clair's "The Changing Story of Ethnography," in *Expressions of Ethnography*, ed. Robin Patric Clair, 1992.

[2] Henry R. Schoolcraft (1793–1864) was one of the first in the United States to publish information in an ethnographic style. Schoolcraft was a geographer and ethnologist who studied Native Americans. Married to a woman who was part Ojibwa, he learned the language and began documenting Indian lore. Franz Boas, a German anthropologist, contributed to the further development of ethnography in the late 1800s. Boas's students, which included Margaret Mead, Ruth Benedict, Zora Neale Hurston, and Ruth Landes, among others, dominated the field of ethnography in the early 1900s.

[3] Friedrich Engels, *The Conditions of the Working Class in England,* 1845; Flora Tristan, Promenades dans Londres, 1840.

[4] Beverly Skeggs, "Feminist Ethnography," in *Handbook of Ethnography*, 2001, 428.

[5] The panel, "Interdisciplinary Perspectives on Feminist Ethnography & Activism," was organized by Christa Craven, moderated by Dána-Ain Davis, and included Nancy Naples, Lynn Roberts, Rosemarie Roberts, and Alisse Waterston at the 2014 annual meeting of the National Women's Studies Association.

[6] Betty Freidan, *The Feminine Mystique*, 1963.

[7] South African History Online, "Charlotte (née Manye) Maxeke," Text, February 17, 2011. http://www.sahistory.org.za/people/charlotte-n%C3%A9e-manye-maxeke.

[8] Jennifer Nelson, *Women of Color and the Reproductive Rights Movement*, 2003.

[9] Jael Miriam Silliman et al., *Undivided Rights,* 2004.

[10] "Third World" was a term that referred to nonwestern "developing" countries. See the section in this chapter on Third World Feminism for more detail.

[11] David Valentine, *Imagining Transgender*, 2007.

[12] Eric Marcus, "Stonewall Revisited," in *Independent Gay Forum*, 1999; David Valentine, *Imagining Transgender*, 2007, 45.

[13] Janice G. Raymond, *The Transsexual Empire: The Making of the She-Male*, 1979.

[14] Riki Anne Wilchins, *Read My Lips*, 1997.

[15] We use the term Native American, Aboriginal and Indigenous not to summarily lump together women, but in Medicine's article, she uses all three.

[16] Beatrice Medicine, "Native American (Indian) Women: A Call for Research," *Anthropology and Education Quarterly*, 1988.

[17] Adrienne Asch and Michelle Fine, "Shared Dreams: A Left Perspective on Disability Rights and Reproductive Rights," in *Radical America,* 1984.

[18] Jennifer Baumgardner and Amy Richards, *Manifesta: Young Women, Feminism and the Future,* 2000.

[19] The term BDSM includes erotic practices such as bondage, discipline, sadism, and masochism.

[20] Micaela di Leonardo and Roger Lancaster, "Gender, Sexuality, Political Economy," *New Politics*, 1996.

[21] Revisiting her initial work, in *Feminism Without Borders,* Mohanty (2003) later rejected the term "Third World" in favor of "Two-Thirds World" to highlight the social majority of those in the "Third World" or "Global South" and move away from misleading geographical and ideological binarisms. As discussed further in chapter 3, we follow the more recent usage the terms "Global North" and "Global South" by transnational feminists.

[22] Njoki Wane, Jennifer Jagire, and Zahra Murad, eds. *Ruptures: Anti-Colonial & Anti-Racist Feminist Theorizing*, 2013.

CHAPTER 2

Historicizing Feminist Ethnography

In this chapter you will explore the early formation of feminist ethnography. The questions below will help you identify how feminist ethnography was used as a "corrective" to earlier studies by and about men, and explain the range of contributions feminist ethnography has made for social issues:

- Who were some of the early contributors to feminist ethnography?
- How did feminist ethnography mature between the 1920s and 1960s?
- What impact did the women's movement of the 1960s have on the next phase of feminist ethnographic production? (1960s–1980s)
- What are the contributions of feminist ethnography from the 1990s through the present?

***Spotlights** in this chapter:*

- Florence Babb on the Impact of *Woman, Culture, and Society* and *Toward an Anthropology of Women*
- Louise Lamphere on the Legacy of *Lamphere v. Brown*
- Lee Baker on Feminist Histories

***Essentials** in this chapter:*

- Alice Fletcher and Francis LaFlesche, *The Omaha Tribe*
- Zora Neale Hurston, *Mules and Men*
- Esther Newton, "Too Queer for College" in *Margaret Mead Made Me Gay*
- Gina Pérez, "Methodological Gifts in Latina/o Studies and Feminist Anthropology"

*You will also be **Thinking Through . . .***

- Restudying Culture
- Faculty Composition at Your Institution
- Critiques and Reviews of an Ethnography

Attention to issues of gender and inequality has a long history in some disciplines. For example, extending back the early 1900s, anthropology and sociology have foregrounded concerns with social, political, and economic inequities and power differentials. In the previous chapter we discussed the Second Wave of feminism and the women's movement of the 1960s and 1970s. During that time, feminists viewed women's oppression as the thread connecting women's experiences across the globe. Yet if one was searching for research on women's lives, there was little to be found. Feminist ethnography emerged out of an effort to correct women's absence from scholarship. Much of the previous **androcentric**, or male-centered, research focused primarily on understanding culture, history, and everyday life from men's perspective. So, the question many asked was: Where was women's point of view?

The beauty of working in the present is that one can go back in time and rethink scholars' interpretations, which were limited by the contexts and ideologies of the time. The development of feminist ethnography is not a simple story. There are twists and turns. For example, sometimes the people identified in the **canon** as feminist ethnographers may not have used the label "feminist" to describe themselves. In some cases, a person may have identified as a feminist who conducted ethnography, but may not have used what contemporary feminist ethnographers would consider to be a feminist methodology.

There are several ways to sort out any history. One can focus on particular people, or categorize particular moments, such as musical periods of Rhythm and Blues (1940s–1950s), Funk (1960s), Deep Funk (late 1960s), Hip-Hop (1970s), and NeoSoul (1980s–1990s). Usually the categories roughly correspond to particular dates. This is called periodization. This chapter **periodizes** anthropological contributions to feminist ethnography; that is, it is divided into particular portions of time. Below, we use anthropologist Kamala Visweswaran's periodization, which she devised in her 1997 article "Histories of Feminist Ethnography" in the *Annual Review of Anthropology*. She proposes four time periods 1880–1920, 1920–1960, 1960–1980, and 1980–1996 as "rough approximations, not absolute chronological markers" of feminist ethnographic production.[1] It may be useful to connect the histories of feminist ethnography to the "waves" discussed in chapter 1, to get a sense of how the development of feminist ethnography intersects with the sociopolitical and historical contexts in which the waves are situated. To assist with this, we have provided a timeline of key dates and periods in feminism and the development of feminist ethnography located after the Preface.

Who Were Some of the Early Contributors to Feminist Ethnography?

To understand the history of what became feminist ethnography, we begin by looking at several female anthropologists in the United States who were influential in the social sciences, and innovative in their scholarship on women. Many of these scholars represent a generation of women ethnographers, who given the privileges of whiteness and wealth were able to attend university and work at a time when Victorian mores proscribed more restrictive roles for women. These women were among those who viewed themselves as achievers, but were in many ways still constrained by the parochial conventions of women's expected roles.[2]

Edward B. Tylor, one of the founding figures of British anthropology, viewed women's contribution to anthropology as merely an addition to male anthropologists—not as one that could be legitimately produced on their own. He appears to have come to this conclusion while visiting James and Matilda Coxe Stevenson, the first ethnographers sent by the Bureau of American Ethnology to visit Zuni Pueblo in New Mexico in 1884.[3] In Tylor's estimation, some of the best results for anthropological work occurred when male anthropologists teamed up with their wives who could collect information from women, a group to which the male anthropologist typically had little access.[4] Thus, women's role as anthropologists was viewed as something to be achieved through marriage, not formal training. Ironically, by Tylor's own admission, he recognized a more diverse ethnographic production when the team of researchers was "male and female."

Indeed, Matilda Coxe Stevenson's (1849–1915) work took place primarily with Zuni women, in an effort to better understand domestic life and children's experiences. There are two ways in which one may consider Stevenson as part of a feminist ethnographic tradition. She was the first woman to study the American Southwest, albeit initially as an adjunct to her husband's work. An interesting point to consider in this discussion is, in whose interpretation was she an adjunct? Tylor's? James Stevenson's? Ours? Additionally, if we cast feminist ethnographic production in terms of prioritizing gender as a category of analysis, then Stevenson's work offers one of the earliest examples, as she was the first American ethnologist to acknowledge the cultural importance of women and men.[5]

Whereas Stevenson fit the mold described and proscribed by Tylor, she did not have a PhD and she was the wife of the anthropologist. On the other hand, Alice Fletcher (1838–1923) offers a different experience of a female ethnographer in the Victorian era. Fletcher pursued archeology late in life, and ultimately lived with and studied the Omaha Indians of Nebraska. By 1889 she was living on the Nez Percé reservation with Jane Gay, a childhood friend and presumed lover. Working in Indian policy for the Bureau of Indian Affairs, like many of her eras, Fletcher developed and helped to implement controversial land reform policies on Indian reservations. Fletcher was a founding member of the American Anthropological Association in 1902. As was the case with Stevenson, gender was a significant category of analysis for Fletcher and she ultimately lived and studied among several Native groups, including Sioux women on the Rosebud Reservation. Her commitment to autonomy and gender equity may be viewed through her work with the Women's National Indian Association, where she—well ahead of her time—introduced the concept of microloans, that is small loans enabling the purchase of land and homes. Her achievements may be considered part of the history of feminist ethnography for several reasons, including that she was not married and carried out research as an independent woman unattached to a male anthropologist. Fletcher also supported women. One of her assistants on the Rosebud Reservation was Susan LaFlesche, an Omaha woman and the sister of Francis LaFlesche, a longtime collaborator of Fletcher's. Fletcher helped Susan LaFlesche secure a loan to attend medical school, which allowed her to become the first Native American doctor in the United States.

Many would argue that one of the most influential female ethnographers of her time was Elsie Clews Parsons (1875–1941). Parsons was born into a wealthy New York family. She obtained her MA and PhD at Barnard where she trained under the tutelage of evolutionary sociologist Franklin H. Giddings. His theoretical leanings were evident in her first work *The Family* (1906), which discusses the family as a social structure, focusing on familial and marriage patterns. While the theoretical focus of the work has been critiqued, Parsons also became known for her controversial advocacy that women and men should enjoy "trial marriage, divorce by mutual consent, access to reliable contraception, independence and elasticity within relationships, and an increased emphasis on obligations to children rather than to sexual partners."[6]

Her feminist inclinations are most apparent in her work examining how marriage, the family, religion, and social mores act to constrain women. A self-identified feminist, Parsons wrote a text unpublished during her life, *Journal of a Feminist*, in which she argued for women's liberation.[7] Increasingly, she became interested in anthropology, and was Franz Boas's first female student,[8] going on to conduct an ethnographic study at Zuni and Laguna.

Parsons was involved with various political groups and participated in a number of organizations composed of upper-middle class and wealthy women who

ESSENTIALS

Excerpt from *The Omaha Tribe* by Alice Fletcher and Francis LaFlesche

***Alice Fletcher** trained with anthropologist Frederic Ward Putnam at the Peabody Museum of Archaeology and Ethnology, Harvard University. She was made assistant in ethnology at the Peabody Museum in 1882. She served as president of the Anthropological Society of Washington and was the first woman president of the American Folklore Society in 1905. She also served as vice president of the American Association for the Advancement of Science. Francis LaFlesche was the first professional Native American ethnologist (Omaha). He worked for the Smithsonian Institution and served as Alice Fletcher's translator and researcher. Fletcher and LaFlesche's book was based on 29 years of study and many consider it the most comprehensive study ever written about a Native American group.*

Avocations of Women

The avocations of women all pertained to the conservation of life. She transmuted the raw material provided by the man into food, raiment, and shelter; the home was a product of her labor and all its duties belonged to her.

Bringing the wood for the fire was a part of a woman's task. For this purpose she used the burden strap; the broad band was worn across the chest and the long thongs were used to tie the wood in a bundle at her back . . .

The care of the garden has already been mentioned. This was the principal outdoor work of the women, not that their labors were otherwise confined to the house, for during warm weather everything that could be done out of doors was performed under a shade set up outside the dwelling. Cooking, sewing, and the eating of meals all took place under this temporary structure.

Source: Alice Cunningham Fletcher and Francis A. LaFlesche. *The Omaha Tribe*, Volume 2. Bison Book Edition reproduced form the 27th Annual Report of the Bureau of American Ethnology to the Secretary of the Smithsonian Institution, 1905–1906. Washington: Government Printing Office, 1911, 339–340.

Photo: Courtesy of the National Anthropological Archives, Smithsonian Institution via Library of Congress.

scorned the subservient role ascribed to motherhood (yet many reinscribed certain forms of subservience by hiring domestic help). While opposing the constraints women experienced, Parsons simultaneously universalized male dominance and it is for the latter that she has been critiqued. However, she has been widely praised by later scholars for her patronage of other female anthropologists, probably more than any other person. Parsons funded the research of many women, including Ester Goldfrank, Ruth Bunzel, and Ruth Benedict.

In contrast to Parsons, ethnographer Daisy Bates, born in Ireland in 1863, did not identify herself as a feminist, but her research was important because she addressed culture, household, and family. Her major contribution was in the area of kinship systems in Australia among Aborigines.[9] She articulated a new understanding of kinship systems in the early 1900s, which was only parenthetically acknowledged by Alfred Radcliffe-Brown, a well-known social anthropologist from Britain who claimed "the discovery of the Kariera system by myself in 1911."[10] Bates later accused Radcliffe-Brown of stealing her idea. Based on the timing of her research (several years prior to Radcliffe-Brown's) and his admission that he had access to her work prior to his, her claims seem quite plausible. While she was critiqued for her maternalistic attitude toward her informants, exemplified by the title of her book *My Natives and I*[11]—an impulse not that different from other Victorian-era U.S.-based anthropologists—Bates's near absence from the anthropological record illustrates how women's intellectual contributions have been silenced.

Recovering the histories of all female anthropologists and ethnographers is beyond the scope of this textbook, but a final anthropologist we wish to highlight, who remains largely hidden in the annals of anthropological history, is Eslanda Goode Robeson, an African American anthropologist. Although she was not a contemporary of the women discussed above, Robeson was born in 1895, the Victorian era—the time during which Stevenson, Fletcher, Parsons, and Bates were conducting research. Robeson, a chemist, journalist, activist, and scholar was married to Paul Robeson[12] and received her degree in anthropology from the London School of Economics under Bronislaw Malinowski. Historian Barbara Ransby authored the book *Eslanda: The Large and Unconventional Life of Mrs. Paul Robeson,*[13] which chronicles Robeson's contributions as an antiracist, anticolonial intellectual who advocated women's rights on an international level are an important addition to the hidden histories of the field.

These women represent—although not exhaustively—both the origins and development of early feminist ethnography and activism. Some could be challenged for the ways they universalized women's circumstances and because some of them fostered mother/child-like dynamics with their informants. Yet, we celebrate them for contributing to the development of feminist ethnography, problematizing patriarchy, supporting or living a version of women's autonomy, and contributing to a feminist intellectualism and institutionalization of the category gender as a legitimate field of inquiry. A charitable interpretation might position some of them as having had feminist sentiments or inclinations, although they were unable to achieve the kind of democratic intellectualism that allowed them to embrace class or racial differences. What these women did in studying Native Americans in the Southwest, Aboriginal groups, and challenging racism and colonialism, respectively, was to open up intellectual dialogues about social structure and patriarchy, as well as forge a path for women ethnographers to be visible and recognized.

How Did Feminist Ethnography Mature Between the 1920s and 1960s?

The previous section points out that the antecedents for the intellectual project of feminist ethnography began in the late nineteenth century and the turn of the twentieth century. While that time period serves as foundational, it was during the 40-year period from the 1920s through the 1960s, that female ethnographers elaborated on earlier work and themes, and more feminists engaged in ethnography and attended to gender issues in their scholarship. This literature reflects a formal articulation of purpose and perspective, highlighting: the rethinking of the categories sex and gender, ethnographic work by and with Indigenous women, stylistic innovations, and narrations of race through the lens of gender.

During this time, there was a robust production of ethnographies by and about women. Although many of these authors did not explicitly identify as feminists, some aimed to correct the androcentric bias that had existed in earlier ethnographic work, an important thread in the trajectory of feminist ethnography. Their work positions gender as a central category of analysis and as Visweswaran points out "oscillated between the empiricist assumptions of Tylor and Parsons (studying women for a complete picture of society) and vindicationist approaches that sought to refute cultural or gender stereotypes."[14]

Societal shifts in thinking about sexuality opened the door for women to begin studying sexual behavior and same-sex sexuality during the early-to-mid-1900s. Social scientists across the disciplinary spectrum came to understand a range of sexual practices as "normal," and feminist ethnographers took up these issues with vigor. Anthropologists Gladys Reichard and Ruth Benedict adopted more inclusive language to describe sexual behaviors than previous writers. In political science, Katherine Bement Davis, the first female commissioner of corrections in New York who also worked at the Bureau of Social Hygiene, facilitated a study of sexual practices, frequency, and interest in the early 1900s.

Anthropologist Margaret Mead, well known for her work on adolescence and sexuality, is most often identified as one of the first feminist ethnographers. Ironically, this is not because she claimed that label for herself (she did not), but because of the major contribution (although subject to criticism) that she made to elaborating on the difference between sex and gender and her analysis of gender as socially constructed. Her first major work was *Coming of Age in Samoa* in 1928, challenging the notion of a universally difficult adolescence. Her later work took up the subjects of childbirth and child-rearing norms, and she was often called the "popularizer" of anthropology (most often as a critique), because of her regular column in the popular women's magazine, *Redbook*, and her work with high-profile childcare experts, such as Dr. Spock.

There were also a number of women who identified as feminists prior to attending university. They continued the tradition of conducting work with Native groups, such as the Pueblo (Ruth Benedict), Navajo (Ruth Benedict and Gladys Reichard), and Piman (Ruth Underhill). They worked with female informants contributing to the nascent scholarship on women across different cultures. Ruth Underhill's *Papago Woman* in 1934,[15] for example, was the first substantial document on a Southwestern Indian woman. In the late 1930s, Phyllis Kayberry, who conducted ethnographic research with Aboriginal women in Australia—resulting in her book *Aboriginal Woman*[16]—used her work to challenge negative stereotypes about Native women as unimportant by presenting the significance of Aboriginal women's contributions to societal development and organization.

Some scholars also engaged in writing ethnographies that were stylistically innovative toward these ends. Ethnographic work was published in various forms, including novels, autobiographies, life histories, and travel narratives. Trained under Boas, Zora Neale Hurston was the first Black student at Barnard College in the 1920s and graduated in 1928 with a BA in anthropology. Her contributions have often been minimized in the discipline, but she has been widely recognized for her work as a novelist, journalist, and playwright. A variety of factors contributed to this trend—not the least of which was the racism that permeated the discipline at the time. In addition, at a time when ethnographic research focused primarily on native North Americans in the United States and non-Western cultures, Hurston's ethnographic work centered on her hometown of Eatonville, an African American community in Florida, although she also drew from her fieldwork on the African diaspora in Haiti and Jamaica.

Hurston remains well known for her prolific contributions to literature, in particular the novel she is best known for, *Their Eyes Were Watching God* in 1937, and *Mules and Men* in 1935, the first major work on Black folklore by an African American.[17] In this text, Hurston blends genres and voice using a unique narrative style to document songs, conversations, and slave tales in African American communities of Eatonville and Polk County, Florida, and New Orleans, Louisiana. Anthropologist Graciela Hernández in her article "Multiple Mediations in Zora Neale Hurston's *Mules and Men*," argues that Hurston's work elevates folklore to a form of literature, weaving it with ethnographic narrative.[18]

Also trained under Boas, Ella Deloria wrote the novel, *Waterlily*, in the 1940s based on her ethnographic research that chronicled Dakota Sioux life prior to American expansionism and settler colonialism (see more on this in chapter 6).[19] Deloria's fictional work presented the contributions of Great Plains women. Exemplifying the devaluation of both stylistic innovation and gendered analysis, Deloria's fiction was not published until 1988, over a decade after her death.

Feminist anthropologists are noted for illuminating and reflecting upon their own gendered and raced positions to narrate or mediate issues of race in the mid-twentieth century. Hortense Powdermaker in *After Freedom* (1939) examines how race and gender confounded her research in Mississippi, exploring her role as a white woman interviewing "negro" men. Ruth Landes's *City of Women* (1947), based on fieldwork from 1938 to 1939 in Bahia, Brazil, describes the challenges of negotiating sexist and racial ideologies as a white woman both in the United States and at her field site. A cadre of women of color feminists, such as Johnetta Cole, Vera Green, Diane K. Lewis, and Niara Sudarkasa (born Gloria Marshall) trained as ethnographers in anthropology programs the 1950s and 60s. Cole and Sudarkasa moved into important leadership roles in the academy over the next few decades, Green contributed significantly to human rights work, and Lewis conducted pivotal analyses reinterpreting sex role socialization in Black families. By the end of this period, anthropology had gained more of a public face and contributed to movements for sexual freedom, civil rights, antiwar organizing, and the burgeoning women's movement.

 ESSENTIALS

Excerpt from *Mules and Men* by Zora Neale Hurston

The following excerpt offers a beautiful example of ***Zora Neale Hurston****'s attention to African American folklore, language, and culture, and is evocative of her unique narrative style.*

I thought about the tales I had heard as child. How even the Bible was made over to suit our vivid imagination. How the devil always outsmarted God. . . When I was rounding Lily Lake I was remembering how God had made the world and elements and people. He made souls for people, but he didn't give them out because he said:

Folks ain't ready for souls yet. De clay ain't dry. It's de strongest thing Ah ever made. Don't aim to waste none thru loose cracks. And then men got to grow strong enough to stand it. De way things is now, if Ah give it out it would tear them shackly bodies to pieces. Bimeby, Ah give it out.

So folks went round thousands of years without no souls. All de time de soul piece, it was setting 'round covered up wid God's loose raiment. Every now and then de wind would blow and hist up de cover and then de elements would be full of lightning and de winds would talk. So people told one 'nother that God was talking in de mountains.

Source: Zora Neale Hurston. *Mules and Men*. New York: Harper Perennial Modern Classics, 2008 [orig. 1935], 3. *Photo*: Courtesy of the Library of Congress, New York World-Telegram & Sun Collection.

Thinking Through . . .

Restudying Culture

Many anthropologists have restudied topics that offer a different, more holistic gender, race, and class analysis of the subject. Can you identify an early ethnographic work (1800s–1950s) that is limited in its view and does not account for gender, racial, ethnic, sexuality, or class dynamics? Then identify a later ethnographic text that attempts to correct the absence of those dynamics. (One good example of the concept of corrective is the revision of Bronislaw Malinowski's *Argonauts of the Western Pacific* (1922) done by Annette Weiner in her 1988 restudy, *The Trobrianders of Papua New Guinea*, which offered a gender analysis of the Trobrianders.)

What Impact Did the Women's Movement of the 1960s Have on the Next Phase of Feminist Ethnographic Production? (1960s–1980s)

Ethnographies by and about women written during the 1960s and 1970s were produced in part as a result of the women's movement of this time, the Second Wave of feminism discussed in chapter 1. In the 1960s, feminist ethnography became part of the larger challenge that feminism posed to **positivist** social research, in which researchers presume to approach the setting logically, objectively, and with predetermined criteria for measurement. But feminist philosophers of science, such as Sandra Harding and Donna Haraway, have challenged these notions as *always* situated and have critiqued positivism as reproducing a privileged perspective. One of the major accomplishments attributed to feminist ethnography is that it validated the epistemological importance of women's contributions to society. Feminist ethnography first sought to do research about women, by women, and for women. It was organized around the belief that women were universally oppressed by patriarchy—a central tenet of cultural feminism during the 1970s—that is, the systems of power that stabilized men's control over social, economic, and political life. In the 1960s and 1970s feminist ethnography came to involve "giving voice" to marginalized groups whose experiences had rarely been represented or understood. This notion was not without critique, in that it reinforced a hierarchy of the researcher over the researched, and assumed a sort of victimhood and lack of **agency** among marginalized women.

In anthropology, where ethnography had become most common, this meant that the anthropological record had to be corrected and the missing story of women had to be included. At first, this "corrective project" was the result of research that had been conducted by the wives of male anthropologists, who told the stories their husbands did not. Later the corrective took on a new agenda, revisiting the fieldsites where men had done their research, but had omitted a gender, race, and/or class analysis.

Women's experiences as ethnographers also became an important subject during this time, particularly as more and more women trained in ethnography and entered the field. Anthropologist Peggy Golde's groundbreaking collection *Women in the Field: Anthropological Experiences*, published in 1970, was among the first to address "subjective aspects of field work," particularly how gender can directly or inadvertently affect the ethnographic process. With chapters by pioneering female anthropologists, such as Ruth Landes, Ernestine Friedl, and Margaret Mead, the volume highlighted the vulnerabilities, misconceptions, and possibilities for North American women conducting ethnography in various contexts.

Two other texts stand out as foundational from the 1970s: *Woman, Culture, and Society* edited by Michelle Rosaldo and Louise Lamphere (1974) and *Toward and Anthropology of Women* edited by Rayna (Rapp) Reiter (1975). Both volumes attempted to answer questions about women's status cross-culturally. *Woman, Culture, and Society* grew out of a course taught at Stanford University in 1971 where various faculty gave lectures, and was organized around three explanations about women's status: structural analysis, cultural analysis, and psychological analysis.[20] Some critics viewed the volume as essentialist because it had "Woman" in the title, which seemed to mark that there was only one way in which a woman could be a woman. The issue of whether or not scholars could make broad or universal claims about the category of woman created tension both within and beyond feminist anthropology.

Toward an Anthropology of Women addressed similar concerns, but came at those issues from a distinctly Marxist feminist perspective. This collection emerged from a student-initiated women's studies course at the University of Michigan for which—in an effort to find relevant readings—Reiter (Rapp) and Norma Diamond solicited colleagues to write pieces, which became the "backbone of the network in *Toward an Anthropology of Women.*"[21] The intentions of the text were very clear; in the introduction, it states that the goal of the volume was to help feminists in the struggle against sexism and inequality through an examination of how women experienced equality and inequality cross-culturally. The chapters place women at the center of analysis and locate the origins of women's subordination and oppression in capitalism, and consider how various cross-cultural data inform analyses of the resulting inequities. For example, anthropologist Karen Brodkin Sacks's work explores state and class formation as instrumental in creating unequal spheres in which women and men operate. What is crucial about both texts is that they set the stage for the many directions that subsequent women in anthropology have taken, as well as led to a robust feminist inquiry in ethnography more broadly.

Many of the contributors to these volumes were also active in the burgeoning Women's Movement in the United States and Britain. As Lousie Lamphere recalls in her reflection on the relationship between theory, ethnography, and activism in feminist anthropology during the 1970s:

> Through participating in demonstrations for women's liberation, legislative hearings on abortion rights, and especially consciousness raising (CR) groups, women anthropologists came to the view that "the personal is political" and began to bring a feminist sensibility to their research and teaching as well as to their own personal lives. At this stage, activism in the public sphere brought changes to anthropology, but feminist advocacy on issues of importance to women (abortion rights, child care, job discrimination, etc.) tended to be segregated from anthropological endeavors or at least treated through conventional research methodologies . . .
>
> [For instance,] in Boston, Bread and Roses, a socialist-feminist ("politico") organization, advocated for a broad range of changes in women's lives from equality in the workplace, to control over their bodies, and free child care. Michelle Rosaldo joined a Bread and Roses CR group composed of Radcliffe graduates in October 1969. She later participated in another group at Stanford. I joined a small group at Brown that emerged from our chapter of the New

SPOTLIGHTS

Florence Babb on the Impact of *Woman, Culture, and Society* and *Toward an Anthropology of Women*

Florence Babb *received her PhD in anthropology from the State University of New York (SUNY) at Buffalo and is the Harrington Distinguished Professor of Anthropology at the University of North Carolina. She has conducted ethnographic research in Peru, Nicaragua, Mexico, and Cuba. She is the author of* Between Field and Cooking Pot: The Political Economy of Marketwomen in Peru *(1989, revised edition 1998),* After Revolution: Mapping Gender and Cultural Politics in Neoliberal Nicaragua *(2001), and* The Tourism Encounter: Fashioning Latin American Nations and Histories (2011).

I was a student during the 70s. It was a really important time for me. I went to grad school in 1974, that was the year when Rosaldo and Lamphere's book came out (*Woman, Culture, and Society*). A year later Rayna Rapp Reiter's book came out (*Toward an Anthropology of Women*). To this day I still remember discovering those books on the bookshelves. I found the first, Rosaldo and Lamphere, at our bookstore the summer before I started grad school at SUNY Buffalo. And the following year I was doing research in Cornell University's archives, and I discovered Rayna's book at the campus bookstore. Both of them were hugely important to my thinking during that time—as they were for so many others. I have to say that those readings were very inspiring to me in my own work. I was bringing together strands of feminist theory and feminist studies along with my anthropology. And in fact Bill Stein, my advisor, helped make me a charter subscriber to the feminist journal *Signs*. So I would say that he was a feminist influence as well. And as you know, during the mid-70s it was the beginning of the UN conferences on women and attention to gender and development. I was going with that current and my MA project in the mid-70s was on gender and development.

> University Conference (NUC), a university and college-based anti-war organization and from activities that grew out of the Brown campus-wide May 1970 strike. We shared an interest in addressing our personal concerns in relation to men and to the larger power structure; these CR groups offered us a safe environment for exploring such issues.
>
> Female anthropologists in Michigan and New York were also part of similar CR groups. In Michigan, Rayna Rapp and Gayle Rubin joined a consciousness-raising group that had spun off from "Resistance," the draft resistance and anti-war movement group active on the University of Michigan campus. In New York, the Ruth Benedict Collective (RBC), brought together senior anthropologists (June Nash, Eleanor [Happy] Leacock, and Ruby Rohrlich-Leavitt), recent PhDs, and graduate students, including Leni Silverstein. In its early years (1969–71), some of the 25 or so anthropologists in the RBC met in small consciousness-raising groups that provided personal, intellectual and professional support.[22]

Importantly, ethnographers of this time were also deeply influenced by the feminist fiction of the 1970s, including writers such as Toni Morrison (author of *The Bluest Eye* in 1970 and *Song of Solomon* in 1977), Maxine Hong Kingston (author of *Warrior Woman* in 1976), and Alice Walker (author of *Meridian* in 1976).[23] As Asian and Asian American literary scholar Karen Su writes in her chapter on ethnographic authority in *Feminist Fields: Ethnographic Insights*, "[The position of] ethnic women writers parallel the positions of 'native' women anthropologists. [They have] had to write under the constraints of the 'ethnographic gaze.'"[24] Some ethnographers were inspired by the different representations of women's experiences in literary works, leading them to analyze the challenges that they, as scholars, faced having "ethnographic authority" and exploring the importance of translating cross-cultural experiences.

Other collections of writing contributed to rethinking the different ways that women lived their lives. They raised questions about how women related to other women, to themselves, and to society. One of the most important collections that influenced feminists and feminist academics was the 1981 edited volume, *This Bridge Called My Back: Writings by Radical Women of Color*, which has become "one of *the most* cited books in feminist theorizing."[25] *This Bridge Called My Back* provided an important challenge to white feminists who drew upon the idea of sisterhood to make claims of solidarity. The volume brought together women who were Native American, Latina, Chicana, Asian, and Black not only creating one of the most profound examples of writing about how it feels to be non-white, but was also a major factor in the creation of women of color coalitions. One of the most notable moments for feminists in the 1980s was the international conference "Common Differences: Third World Women and Feminist Perspectives," held in 1983. This conference was organized by a multiracial, international group of women and one of the first times that women of color and white women in the United States and women from what we would now call the Global South, but then was referred to as the Third World, came together around their common differences. The conference fundamentally challenged the definition of feminism to include a much broader concern with equity.[26]

The Chicana movement also emerged in the 1970s, responding to female and maternal archetypes that limited Chicana women's agency. According to feminist educator and historian Barbara J. Love's book *Feminists Who Changed America 1963–1975*,[27] the Comisión Femenil Mexicana Nacional was founded in 1970 to address issues of concern to Chicana women and initially focused on ending the compulsory sterilization of women. By 1985, they had expanded their scope to include issues related to teenage girls involved in the criminal justice system. It was this kind of organizing that contributed to academic production on and by Chicana women. For instance, anthropologist M. Patricia Fernández-Kelly examined the gendered and human rights dimensions of multinational manufacturing in Cuidad Juarez on the U.S.-Mexico border where maquiladoras, or assembly plants, exist. Her book, *For We Are Sold, I and My People*,[28] uncovers the realities of "Third World women's" exploitation in manufacturing plants.

In the 1970s and 1980s several ethnographies drew from dependency theory and gendered analyses of women's labor. For example, anthropologist June Nash's influential ethnography *We East the Mines and the Mines Eat Us: Dependency and Exploitation in Bolivian Tin Mines*[29] is but one example of the role she played in establishing gender as a crucial analytic for scholars of Latin America. Later, feminist ethnographers who did work in Latin America, such as anthropologist Kay Warren, documented gender roles among indigenous communities in the Andes and Peru. Political scientist, Susan Bourque (with Kay Warren) wrote *Women of the Andes: Patriarchy and Social Change in Two Peruvian Towns*,[30] offering an analysis of women's subordination.

Through the 1980s we find tremendously diverse efforts and scholarship shaping the production of feminist ethnography. But it was not a simple path toward gaining respect for feminist analysis. In fact, it was a rough and challenging road.

ESSENTIALS

Excerpt from "Too Queer for College" by Esther Newton

Esther Newton *received her PhD in anthropology at the University of Chicago and is now an emeritus professor at Purchase College, SUNY, and term professor of women's studies at the University of Michigan. Her first book,* Mother Camp: Female Impersonators in America *(1972), was the first major anthropological study of a homosexual community in the United States. Her second ethnographic book,* Cherry Grove, Fire Island: Sixty Years in America's First Gay and Lesbian Town *(1993) documented the changing dynamics of the beach resort Cherry Grove, one of the oldest and most visible predominantly LGBT communities in the United States. Most recently, she published a collection of essays, her "intellectual autobiography,"* Margaret Mead Made Me Gay *(2000). In the following excerpt from "Too Queer for College," Newton discusses the challenges she faced not only as a butch lesbian in the field, but also as a feminist, and among feminists:*

In 1968, after I got my first job, I became a passionately committed feminist. . . . The movement also attracted many straight women. Some have been staunch allies; others have capitulated under straight male pressure to get rid of the queer perspective my person and my work have represented.

I was denied tenure on my first job. The rejection felled me like a dumb ox. The process was secret, but privately and as a favor, the woman department head told me some people had trouble with my "personality." There was also a question about my "commitment to anthropology." It was like the menacing encounter I'd had with the college dean [who had threatened Newton with expulsion as a graduate student after seeing her in a phone booth with a friend, who ironically was not even her lover]: You're doing something wrong and I won't say what, but we *know* about it.

[Ultimately, Newton was also denied tenure at her second job, with the committee citing "feminist bias" in her work. More savvy and sophisticated, however, Newton fought and won her tenure case. Shortly afterward, she felt comfortable "coming out" on her job, as well as writing about her experiences as a butch lesbian feminist in academia.]

Source: Esther Newton. "Too Queer for College: Notes on Homophobia 1987." In *Margaret Mead Made Me Gay: Personal Essays, Public Ideas*, 1st Edition, 219–24. Durham, NC: Duke University Press Books, 2000, 221.

Because of the projects and feminist commitments that women had, some were denied tenure, and others were unable to secure a full-time teaching job for many years.

Probably the most well-known and successful case against employment discrimination by a feminist ethnographer—indeed by a female faculty member in the 1970s—was that of anthropologist Louise Lamphere. Lamphere was denied tenure by her all-male senior colleagues in the department of anthropology at Brown University in 1974. She filed a **Title VII** Sex Discrimination Case in 1975 that the university settled out of court, awarding her tenure in 1977. The case also required Brown to enter into what became known as the Lamphere Consent Decree, which governed the university's faculty hiring and tenure decisions between 1977 and 1992, and promoted a significant increase in women on the Brown faculty.[31] Upon her retirement from the University of New Mexico (where she took a position in 1986), Lamphere sought to preserve the legacy of feminist scholarship at Brown by ensuring that courses on gender and sexuality would be accessible to students; she created the Louise Lamphere Visiting Assistant Professorship in Gender Studies a two-year rotating teaching and research position in both the Brown Anthropology Department and the Pembroke Center for Teaching and Research on Women. Marking the 40th anniversary of the lawsuit's filing in 2015, the Pembroke Center hosted an exhibition and two-day conference, "The Legacy of *Louise Lamphere v. Brown University*." Lamphere was awarded an honorary degree in May 2015.

In light of these legal changes, the conflation of research and identity work in the academy continues to plague young feminist scholars, especially as denials of

SPOTLIGHTS

Louise Lamphere on the Legacy of *Lamphere v. Brown*

Louise Lamphere *received her PhD from Harvard University and is distinguished professor emeritus from the University of New Mexico. In addition to her early contributions to feminist anthropology through* Woman, Culture, and Society, *she coauthored* Sunbelt Working Mothers *(1974)*: Reconciling Family and Factory *(1993) with Patricia Zavella, Felipe Gonzales, and Peter B. Evans, and coedited* Situated Lives: Gender and Culture in Everyday Life *(1997) with Helena Ragoné and Patricia Zavella. Her most recent book* Weaving Women's Lives *(2007)*: Three Generations in a Navajo Family *is the result of five decades of fieldwork and collaborative scholarship. We had the pleasure of speaking with Lamphere about her experiences with the case and its legacy. When Lamphere met with her Department Chair in May 1974 and discovered that she was being denied tenure, she was shocked:*

I was pretty shaken. I was very committed to my career and thought I had excellent qualifications. It was like a rug had been pulled out from under me. I didn't know how to respond when he told me that my teaching was "poor but not so much worse than others" and that my research on women was "theoretically weak." A man would have gotten angry, but like many women I felt angry but with a dose of self-doubt. I thought, "Maybe my Chair was right, maybe I wasn't good enough." Still when I left his office, I felt I had to do something.

[Ultimately, Lamphere filed a lawsuit.]

The reason I was able to make an impact was that it became a Class Action suit. It took a year to certify the class, but ultimately three other women who had worked at Brown, including two who had also been denied tenure, joined the suit. If I had filed an individual lawsuit, I would have had to prove discrimination by the Department. Brown University could have said, "We'll give you a cash settlement, and you can go away." And that's what happened with a batch of these [kinds of cases] because any lawyer will tell you that most cases get settled out of court. The way they get them settled is to say, "We'll pay you this" and by that time, you're so tired you don't pursue further action.

The one thing that's good about discrimination law is that if the University or the Company loses then they do have to pay the lawyers. Of course, the other thing is that you might have to pay their legal fees if you lose, so it's a risk. I had what I would consider to be a perfect storm. I had lots of information from the Anthropology Department's correspondence. I was the first woman to come up for tenure in Sociology and Anthropology. The man that came up the year before me . . . had fewer publications than I did. And of course, they claimed that the standards were being raised because they were in this terrible financial crush because of the decline of oil prices in '73 and the heating bills were escalating. They were creating a staffing plan that they put into effect in about 1973. The law is a little [fuzzy on this. Some contended] that you couldn't raise the standards without telling anybody, suddenly in the middle of somebody's probationary period. I don't know how that would have played out in court. They could have argued, "Well, we had to raise the standards." And I would have said, "You didn't tell me!"

(continued)

and [laughter]. I had a stronger case than the last male [who received tenure in anthropology], because that's the way a lot of cases went. You sort of compared yourself to other men in equal positions, and if they had fewer publications than you did, then you could make a case for discrimination.

Despite the success of my case, it became harder to win these cases after the 1980s, when the burden of proof was shifted from the institution to the plaintiff. One of the things about Title VII, in the beginning, was that the burden of proof was with the university or the company or whatever, so they had to prove that they didn't discriminate. When they re-did the law they shifted the burden of proof to the plaintiff, so that meant that the person has to show that the university did discriminate. That's very hard. The burden of proof is where the toughest deal is. You know, I can say, "Prosecute somebody for a murder!" The burden of proof is on the state to prove that the person did it. In these civil cases, they can go either way, depending on how the law is written. . . .

Photo: Margaret Randall

tenure and promotion are typically couched in language about "fit" with the program or institution. In an article in the journal *Cultural Anthropology*, anthropologists Tami Navarro, Bianca Williams, and Attiya Ahmad, underscore this point, especially its relevance for women of color faculty.[32]

> Invocations of diversity made in many university mission statements, and the attention now paid to critical race and gender studies within disciplines such as anthropology would suggest that this is a new moment—a different time in which the academy has presumably ended explicit racism and begun seriously addressing questions of inclusion and exclusion . . . .We argue that despite these seeming improvements, the difficulties experienced by female faculty of color have not only continued, but have intensified in recent years. We partly tie this change to the increasing corporatization of the academy, particularly the decline in tenure-track appointments in favor of non-secure, contract-based positions . . . . Female professors of color . . . are confronted with students' preexisting raced, classed, and gendered understandings of what constitutes a "professor" (Agathangelou and Ling 2002). These understandings often come to light in student evaluations, which institutions take more and more seriously given their increased dependence on tuition and their focus on student satisfaction. In these evaluations, disappointed students who feel they have been cheated out of a "real" (i.e., neutrally positioned/objective/white male) professor, often vent their frustrations. To compound these difficulties, women of color (WoC) continue to shoulder disproportionate amounts of affective labor in the academy, work that goes systematically unrecognized and remains undervalued. Finally, the conflation of WoC with their research agendas—that is, the assumption that these scholars are necessarily speaking from a "native" position—continues to be a problem for female anthropologists of color.[33]

Navarro, Williams, and Ahmad suggest not coddling or holding the hands of faculty of color—as they say, "an insulting notion, at best"—but rather make practical suggestions like hiring scholars of color in clusters so that they can support one another, connecting junior WoC with senior mentors for early feedback on publications, and offering opportunities for coteaching that can illuminate racialized and gender dynamics in the classroom, as well as foster interdisciplinary engagement among students and faculty. What is clear from this article, and our interviews with a variety of feminist ethnographers, is that—as we so often document in feminist ethnographic work in a variety of communities—equity has yet to be achieved in

Thinking Through . . .

Faculty Composition at Your Institution

Locate the most recent edition of the American Association of University Professor's (AAUP) Faculty Salary Survey (this is conducted bi-annually and searchable data can be found at the Chronicle of Higher Education's website, www.chronicle.org). Search the data for your college or university. Compare salaries for female and male faculty across salary ranks. (In the United States, assistant professors are often called "junior faculty," once a faculty member receives tenure—when they are asked to stay at the institution in a permanent position, they are associate professors, and may become full professors, the highest rank for faculty, based on further scholarly achievements.)* Consider also the number of full-time versus part-time or adjunct faculty. What gender disparities does your research suggest?

**Unfortunately, at the time we published this book, AAUP provided no information about the race and ethnicity of faculty across ranks.*

the academy, and the important work that feminist faculty began in the 1970s must continue into the future.

What Interventions Came Out of Feminist Ethnography from the 1990s Through the Present?

By the 1990s feminist ethnographic production had grown and matured across various intellectual terrains. This scholarship included, but was not limited to, feminist ethnographies produced by women of color offering new epistemological narratives, the incorporation of gender analyses in global and transnational processes, research exploring the complexities of various domains of gender including masculinity and LGBTQI+ experiences.

From the 1990s until the present, feminist theorizing and feminist ethnographic production has been robust, having been influenced by social movements, tensions that arose within the feminist community in earlier decades, as well as economic shifts. Although we will cover ethnographic work from this period in many of the subsequent chapters, here we highlight feminist ethnography in these recent decades more broadly.

We start with the progressive scholarship by women of color, which had at its core an articulation of **intersectionality** regarding race, class, and gender dynamics and oppression. Conceptually, an intersectional analysis argues that all categories of identity and existence operate at the same time in a person's experience of oppression and subordination. One example of an intersectional analysis can be found in exploring the twitter responses to Ms. Nina Davuluri, who won the Miss America contest in 2014. After her win, people tweeted that "Miss Al-Qaeda" won, or said that Davuluri should not have won. These oppressive comments exemplify how racism, sexism, and xeonophobia operate at the same time against Ms. Davuluri being the contest winner. The hate-filled response to her win and the ways in which people analyzed that hatred is an example of an intersectional analysis accounting for how race, nationhood, and gender operate to demonize groups of people. On what basis was she despised more? Because she was brown woman? Because she was presumed to not be a citizen of the United States? It was none of these in isolation, rather the intersection of them.

The analytic category of gender as the dominant way in which women's experiences were both researched and produced was insufficient, thus women of color's scholarship was crucial. We flag the broad ways in which work by women of color created a scholarship that influenced the production of feminist ethnography. This is accomplished by focusing on the frameworks and interdisciplinary critical perspectives offered by women of color scholars and writers.

Women of color scholars in the 1980s and 90s not only acknowledged differences among women but also produced scholarship that "reshaped basic concepts and theories of the discipline," according to sociologists Bonnie Thornton Dill and Maxine Baca Zinn.[34] The Inter-university Research Group Exploring the Intersection of Race and Gender was the site of discussion and comparative research on women of color and members of the group used the analytic framework of intersectionality to explain both their lives as women of color scholars and the exclusion of women of color in research. *Women of Color in U.S. Society*,[35] edited by Dill and Zinn, was instrumental in showing how the lives of women of color are structured by race, class, and gender hierarchies. Importantly, these dynamics were analyzed and written by women of color. Another scholar noted for using intersectional analysis was anthropologist Patricia Zavella, whose ethnography *Women's Work and Chicano Families: Cannery Workers of the Santa Clara Valley*[36] merges Chicana labor history with the canning industry in California. The ethnography explores a range of workplace and kin networks, in which Chicana women circulate and strategize their survival. Psychologist Aída Hurtado's *The Color of Privilege: Three Blasphemies on Race and Feminism*[37] offers a different assessment of intersectionality as a response to critiques of Second Wave feminist essentialization of women. Hurtado makes the argument that women of color's responses to feminism are orchestrated not so much by the differences between women, but by the differentially subordinate relationship women have with white men. Anthropologist Leith Mullings's *On Our Own Terms* explores racial and gendered difference in order to theorize women's work in the family, community, and in wage labor. In this collection of essays, Mullings reveals how her own experiences serve as a foundation from which she can analyze inequalities in the lives of African American women drawing from her over two decades of ethnographic engagement. Finally, sociologist Yen Le Espiritu's book *Asian American Panethnicity: Bridging Institutions and Identities* was the first to explore the conflicts and benefits of the construction of Pan-Asian identities in the mid-1990s.[38]

Postcolonial feminist theorizing, like women of color theorizing, became central to feminist ethnography as a corrective to the orientation of feminist thinking based on Western experience. The intersection between globalization, gender, and labor are underscored in ethnographies such as Aihwa Ong's *Spirits of Resistance and Capitalist Discipline: Factory Women in Malaysia*.[39] Ong's ethnography demonstrates the assertion of global capitalism on culture, the economy, and gender in South East Asia. Anna Lowenhaupt Tsing's *In the Realm of the Diamond Queen: Marginality in an Out-of-the-Way Place*, analyzes gender, power, and the politics of identity among Meratus Dayaks, a marginal and marginalized group in the Indonesian rainforest.[40] These and other works from the 1980s and early 1990s paved the way for more feminist ethnographic attention to the gendered effects of globalization.

 ESSENTIALS

Excerpt from "Methodological Gifts in Latina/o Studies and Feminist Anthropology" by Gina Pérez

Gina Pérez *is an associate professor of comparative American studies at Oberlin College. She received her PhD in anthropology from Northwestern University. Before coming to Oberlin, Pérez was a research associate at the Center for Puerto Rican Studies at Hunter College, CUNY. Pérez is the author of the award-winning* The Near Northwest Side Story: Migration, Displacement, and Puerto Rican Families *(2004).*

In the 1980s feminist anthropologists conducted pioneering research focusing on women and work, and women and development, as well as gender and the international division of labor. Studies by feminist anthropologists that focused on global division of labor were an important reminder of the ways in which local economies, gender ideologies, kin relations and household arrangements are shaped by global capital and uneven power relations among nations. Lynn Bolles' work in Jamaica, for example, demonstrated how Jamaican women workers, their local communities and households were shaped by International Monetary Fund structural adjustment programs, reminding us that what happens in local communities is indelibly shaped by global forces. Helen Safa's research on shifting gender relations in Puerto Rico highlighted how industrial policy and industrialization programs had a profound impact on shifting gender relations on the island. This analytical framing shares much with critical new directions in Latina/o studies scholarship employing a transnational lens for understanding gender, sexuality, cultural production and community development among Latina/o communities in the United States. In addition to the pioneering work of Juan Vicente Palerm, Patricia Zavella, Carlos Velez-Ibanez and Lynn Stephen, such scholarship has inspired a new generation of anthropologists whose work explores the various dimensions of transnationalism in the lives of migrants both in the United States and abroad. . . .

Finally, as Rayna Rapp noted in her contribution to this series, feminist anthropology is simultaneously found at the place where theory and practice meet. The scholarly, political and activist engagements defining feminist anthropology also inform Latina/o Studies scholarship, like Leo Chavez's work on the impact of immigration reform on immigrant communities; Ana Ochoa O'Leary's research highlighting migrant women's border crossings and the gendered experiences of border enforcement; as well as Latina/o anthropologists concerns with increasing militarization of Latina/o communities and shifting notions of citizenship. Luis Plascencia's investigation of the implications of posthumous citizenship for Latin American immigrant soldiers and Ana Yolanda Ramos Zayas' work exploring issues of citizenship and notions of "deficient citizenship" among Puerto Rican youth are examples of the continued salience of anthropological praxis in this post 9-11 world. My own work within Puerto Rican communities reflects many of these methodological questions and commitments. My first book provides a gendered reading of Puerto Rican migration and transnational practices, and locates the lives of Puerto Rican women and their families within the historical political economies of San Sebastian, Puerto Rico and Chicago. A particularly striking finding within my work was how military service often served as an important survival strategy for many poor and working-class Puerto Rican families and how a growing number of Puerto Rican and Latina/o youth participate in a growing number of JROTC* programs in American public high schools. The expansion of JROTC is concomitant with an explicit targeting of Latina/o youth for military service, and in both instances a powerful discourse of the military's ability to provide discipline for "at risk" youth, including young women at risk of becoming unwed mothers, justifies millions of dollars of government spending to support such efforts. Feminist and Latina/o scholarship in

(continued)

anthropology deeply inform my work, strengthen my methodological approaches and provide invaluable analytical tools in order to pursue anthropological research that seeks not only to continue to raise new questions about how research should proceed, but also how to use our research to build a more just world.

Source: Gina M. Pérez, "Methodological Gifts in Latina/o Studies and Feminist Anthropology." *Anthropology News* 48, no. 7 (October 1, 2007): 6–7.

*JROTC stands for the Junior Reserve Officers' Training Corps and is designed to ostensibly teach high school students the value of citizenship, personal responsibility, self-esteem, community service among other characteristics that seem to be important to the U.S. Army. It states that its mission is "to motivate young people to be better citizens."

Significant political events, such as the end of the Cold War in 1989 and the Soviet Union's collapse in 1991 further influenced the work of feminist ethnographers on globalization. On the one hand, some believed that with the end of "Communist threat," the United States would be the dominant superpower able to espouse and spread values of democracy, free markets, and peace. Others argued that there emerged a much greater potential for ethnic, political, and economic conflict. Economic shifts, such as the consolidation of **economic liberalism** and the signing of the North American Free Trade Agreement (**NAFTA**) in 1992, brought about divisions of labor and new economic and political arrangements.

The outcome of these new arrangements influenced the gendered dimensions of the international division of labor and social movements. For example, anthropologist Carla Freeman's *High Tech and High Heels in the Global Economy: Women, Work, and Pink-Collar Identities in the Caribbean*[41] discusses how processes of transnationalism impact Afro-Caribbean women's lives in Barbados. The gendered dimensions of social movements are the subject of such work as *After Revolution: Mapping Gender and Cultural Politics in Neoliberal Nicaragua*[42] by anthropologist Florence Babb, who examines agrarian reform on the lives of working class and poor women in Nicaragua.

Another significant influence on feminist ethnography during the 1990s and beyond was the interventions offered in LGBT and queer scholarship. We do not mean to suggest that all scholarship on LGBTQI+ issues exemplifies feminist thinking, but many scholars who do fieldwork in LGBTQI+ communities define themselves as feminist. This research contributed significantly to the feminist ethnographic enterprise in that it moved theorizing away from a gender-specific domain. In other words, rather than solely a focus on women, queer scholarship pushes forward analyses that examine differentially and differently gendered bodies. We limit our discussion primarily to the influences of queer ethnographers who articulate a feminist perspective in their work, acknowledging that much queer theory and early queer ethnographic inquiry was dominated by (white) male scholars.

It was only in the mid-twentieth century that ethnographic research began to focus explicitly on homosexuality, bisexuality, and transgender experiences. The first book-length ethnographies on gay and transgender life was *Mother Camp: Female Impersonators in America* published in 1972 by anthropologist Esther Newton.[43] This classic text had no contemporaries until the later part of the 1970s and early 1980s when Deborah Goleman Wolf and Gilbert Herdt published *The Lesbian Community* and *Guardian of the Flutes: Idioms of Masculinity: A Study of Ritualized Homosexual Behavior,*[44] respectively. Evelyn Blackwood's *The Many Faces of Homosexuality: Anthropological Approaches to Homosexuality* was groundbreaking in 1986 because it was the first collection to examine diverse manifestations of homosexuality in various historical periods and across a variety of non-Western cultures.[45]

By the 1990s there were a number of theoretically sophisticated ethnographies examining LGBTQI+ issues. For example, anthropologist Kath Weston's *Families We Choose: Lesbians, Gays, Kinship* looks at the ways sexuality and identity reframe the biological meanings of family.[46] Anthropologists Ellen Lewin and William Leap coedited a volume considering the debates around gay and lesbian ethnography, with a focus on the positionality of the ethnographer, *Out in the Field: Reflections of Lesbian and Gay Anthropologists*.[47] Lewin's influential ethnography *Lesbian Mothers: Accounts of Gender in American Culture* and her edited collection *Inventing Lesbian Cultures in America*[48] also contributed to broader understandings of how female sexuality is shaped by culture, and the imagined communities that lesbians create. Further, Blackwood's feminist ethnographic study of tombois and femmes in Indonesian lesbi communities since 1989 was revolutionary in its attention to female desire and masculinity.[49]

The range of queer ethnographic scholarship produced in the late 1990s and early 2000s has been influential in moving scholars into directions of inquiry that interrogate the possibilities and limitations of queer theory, as well as among communities that were previously neglected in ethnographic research. For example, anthropologist Erica Lorraine Williams, in her ethnography *Sex Tourism in Bahia: Ambiguous Entanglements*,[50] points out that queer theory was important in her methodological, data collection, and interpretive choices—allowing her to question assumptions that all of the women involved in Brazilian sex tourism were straight. When we interviewed her, she explained how feminist ethnography benefits from the insights of queer ethnography:

> The literature on sex work was very heterosexual: American men, locals, Dominican women. But I saw more than that going on in Bahia. I really pushed back against having to be focused on just straight women. For example, one of the women I talk about who identified as a lesbian and had a female partner, but in her sex work she had relationships with older European men. Just because people are sex workers does not mean they are straight. I found Black Queer studies, for example E. Patrick Johnson and Jafari Allen, to be a rich literature.

Likewise, Surinamese-Dutch anthropologist Gloria Wekker's *The Politics of Passion: Women's Sexual Culture in the Afro-Surinamese Diaspora* challenged Western stereotypes about identity-based sexuality in her study of the mati work among women in Suriname.[51] Wekker's ethnography examines the complex and historically constituted creation of family among working-class women that goes beyond **consanguinity**, or relation by blood, and beyond the choice of hetero- or homosexual family making. Wekker's reflexive discussion of her relationship with one of her informants, Mis' Juliette, also marks an important moment in queer feminist ethnography where, as Wekker writes, "It behooves us who do (cross-cultural) sex research to be transparent, accountable, and reflective about our own sexualities."[52]

In the twenty-first century, there has been a proliferation of interdisciplinary scholarship on sexuality both within and outside North America. Here we underscore an example of the interrogation of Black queer experiences. As Shaka McGlotten and Dána-Ain emphasize in their edited collection *Black Genders & Sexualities*,[53] too often the Black body is a site of pathology, difference, and hypersexualization. Yet a central goal of many collections and ethnographies is to move the conversation about Black genders and sexualities beyond merely normative heterosexualities toward critical approaches to activism and performativity within the field of Black queer studies. African American Studies scholar Marlon M. Bailey's

Butch Queens Up in Pumps: Gender, Performance, and Ballroom Culture in Detroit provides an combination of ethnography and memoir chronicling how over three decades of ballroom culture have provided a space of resistance for many Black gay men, a space where people who are marginalized build alternative communities.[54]

It is also important to note the influence of queer theory on spaces beyond solely or ostensibly LGBTQI+ communities. Anthropologist Margot Weiss's *Techniques of Pleasure: BDSM and the Circuits of Sexuality* explores San Francisco Bay Area's pansexual BDSM community (which included mostly heterosexual men and bisexual, lesbian, and heterosexual women, including two transwomen).[55] Weiss argues against the notion that BDSM is inherently transgressive. Rather, she highlights how economic shifts contribute to the development of commodity-oriented sexual communities, predicated on the eroticization of gendered, racialized, and national inequalities. Understanding sexuality as a circuit, she connects sexual desire and pleasure to the reproduction of raced and gendered social norms. Weiss's work offers an important intervention in the possibilities for the incorporation of queer theory into feminist ethnography.[56]

A final important thread in this discussion has to do with how masculinity has been mapped onto feminist thinking and ethnographic production over the past few decades. Anthropologist Matthew Guttman's *Meanings of Macho: Being a Man in Mexico City,*[57] for instance, pluralizes the meaning of Mexican masculinity thereby challenging the stereotypical legacy of machismo. Sociologist C. J. Pascoe's *Dude, You're a Fag: Masculinity and Sexuality in High School* addresses youth sexuality and masculine identities, including female masculinity.[58] Medical anthropologist Marcia Inhorn's work since the 1990s, and most recently in *The New Arab Man: Emergent Masculinities, Technologies, and Islam in the Middle East*, has addressed masculinity in the context of new reproductive technologies and infertility.[59] Another recent example is an article by Osmunco Pinho, "Ethnographies of the Brau: Body Masculinity and Race in the Reafricanization in Salvador,"[60] which explores masculinity as it is racially constructed. Outside of anthropology we can look to geographer Rashad Shabazz, who works on masculinity and spatiality. In particular, he examines categories of race, gender, and class and how they are mapped, considering how power is located spatially and what forms it takes. Shabazz's work is articulated within a feminist framework, as he enters into his "discussion of masculinity through the prism of Black feminism."[61] His historical ethnography charts the "architecture of black masculinity," through maps, memoirs, and historical documents, as well as analyzing contemporary texts and spatial relationships.

One of the things we wish to underscore in this text is that regardless of the gender identity of the ethnographer or whether their topic centers on analyses of women or gender, it is the feminist sensibility—the commitment to paying attention to previous feminist scholarship, and both respond to and integrate the complexities of feminist intellectual influences—that produces feminist ethnographic inquiry. In our interview with anthropologist Lee Baker, whose work focuses primarily on the history of anthropology, he discusses the importance of the feminist perspective and avoiding tokenism.

Conclusion

Clearly, although feminist ethnography began as a project by, for, and about women, it has transitioned into broader explorations of gender and sexuality through a feminist lens. The theoretical sophistication evidenced in the historical trajectory of feminist ethnography elucidates important connections to intersectional, critical

SPOTLIGHTS

Lee Baker on Feminist Histories

Lee Baker *received his PhD in anthropology from Temple University and currently serves as Dean of Academic Affairs and Associate Vice Provost of Undergraduate Education at Duke University. He is the author of* From Savage to Negro: Anthropology and the Construction of Race, 1896–1954 *(1998),* Life in America: Identity and Everyday Experience *(2003), and* Anthropology and the Racial Politics of Culture *(2010). Although Baker's work has focused on the history*

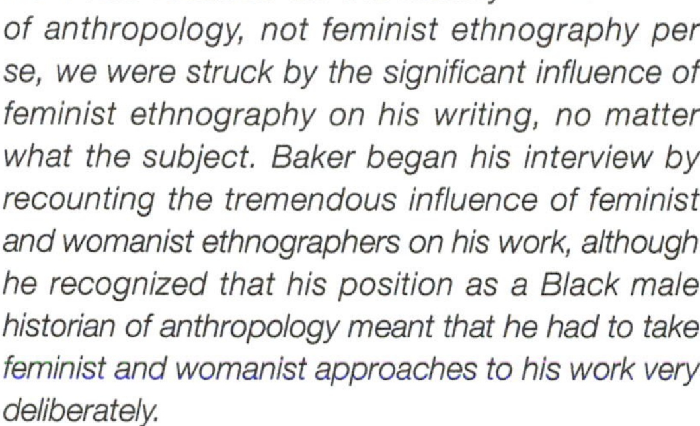

of anthropology, not feminist ethnography per se, we were struck by the significant influence of feminist ethnography on his writing, no matter what the subject. Baker began his interview by recounting the tremendous influence of feminist and womanist ethnographers on his work, although he recognized that his position as a Black male historian of anthropology meant that he had to take feminist and womanist approaches to his work very deliberately.

My work is informed politically by a particular subject position, a perspective even, and I try to embrace that. What's a little different for me is that I don't have a community. It's just dead white guys who I do research on . . . For me then, I think about my readers, that's my community and I want to make sure that students who are reading the history of Anthropology understand that it was not just a bunch of dead white guys, but that there were plenty of women and underrepresented folks. Lots of people contributed and moved the discipline forward in important ways. That's why my more recent work on Margaret Mead is important because Margaret Mead played a huge role in the fight against racism. While you can be critical of Margaret Mead, especially her crusade of population control that leaned toward eugenics, what she did with regard to bringing the American Association for the Advancement of Science together with the American Anthropological Association was very significant. She was pivotal in the way she organized the scientific societies to figure out that there was no difference between the races, which was an important support for Civil Rights leaders. . . .There were a lot of scientists that were trying to say that IQs were different for different races, that they are really different species, and so that "race science" got recycled again in the mid-60s, right in the middle of the Civil Rights Movement. But it was Margaret Mead, as a woman, who organized with all the men.

My feminist perspective is committing to really hunting down and uncovering her story, the history when women had a big impact, but . . . don't have a large footprint in the historical record. I think you have to work harder, at least for me, when you're doing historical work. You have to dig deeper, because if you just research the usual suspects and the stuff that's been written before, you are going to just reproduce a sexist, heteronormative history.

It is particularly important though to avoid tokenism . . . It's not like, "Oh I found a couple of women, and throw them in there" . . . but you dig a little deeper and go into sources that are not the more traditional ones and start making connections . . . . It takes a lot of work to tell history from an empowering perspective.

race, and queer scholarship. For us, the importance of writing this chapter was to uncover some of the complex, and often hidden histories of those who contributed to feminist ethnography. We can look back to critique this canon, but also to make meaning of the contemporary articulations of the field. This history is not finite, but it is a beginning. We offer you our set of **interlocutors**, those who shaped our thinking about feminist ethnography, as a starting point from which to engage as you begin to grapple with feminist ethnography.

Thinking Through . . .

Critiques and Reviews of an Ethnography

Whenever a scholar publishes their work, they open themselves to critique. This often serves as an elaboration of key issues in their discipline (or the disciplines of those reviewing their work) when they publish their research. We have mentioned many ethnographies in this chapter, but did not have the space to discuss them in depth. Read one of these ethnographies—preferably on a topic or time period of particular interest to you. Make note of the theoretical, methodological, and/or ethical issues that the ethnographer emphasizes. Then, find at least three book reviews written about the ethnography. What critiques do they level? Do they engage in debate on topics in the book? Are they in agreement, or do you see differences of opinion across the reviewers?

Suggested Resources

Henrietta Moore (1989) *Feminism and Anthropology.*

Michaela di Leonardo, ed. (1991) *Gender at the Crossroads of Knowledge: Feminist Anthropology in the Postmodern Era.*

Evelyn Blackwood and Saskia Wieringa, eds. (1999) *Same-Sex Relations and Female Desires: Transgender Practices Across Cultures.*

The Latina Feminist Group (2001) *Telling to Live: Latina Feminist Testimonios* (especially chapters by Patricia Zavella, Iris López, and Ruth Behar).

Ellen Lewin (2006) *Feminist Anthropology: A Reader.*

Notes

[1] Kamala Visweswaran, "Histories of Feminist Ethnography," *Annual Review of Anthropology*, 1997, 594.

[2] There were also many individuals who moved across gender boundaries, such as Herculine Barbin, an intersex French individual who was designated female at birth but later considered male after an affair with a woman and physical examination, George Sand who was born Armandine Aurore Lucille Dupine, and many others who have gone unacknowledged.

[3] Zuni is a significant site in the development of professional anthropology and the location of fieldwork for Franz Boas's and other prominent anthropologists' students, such as Ruth Benedict and Elsie Clews Parsons.

[4] Nancy O. Lurie, "Women in Early American Anthropology," in *Pioneers of American Anthropology*, ed. June Helm, 1966.

[5] Nancy J. Parezo, "Matilda Coxe Stevenson: Pioneer Ethnologist," in *Hidden Scholars*, ed. Nancy J. Parezo, 1999.

[6] Desley Deacon, *Elsie Clews Parsons*, 1997, xii.

[7] Elsie Clews Parsons, *The Journal of a Feminist*, 1994.

[8] Many consider Franz Boas to be the "Father of American Anthropology."

[9] Antoinette T. Jackson, "Daisy M. Bates: Ethnographic Work among the Australian Aborigines." Unpublished Paper, 1998.

[10] A. R. Radcliffe-Brown, "The Social Organization of Australian Tribes," *Oceania*, 1930, 46.

[11] Daisy Bates (edited by Peter J. Bridge), *My Natives and I*, 2004.

[12] Paul Robeson was a twentieth-century athlete, lawyer, and performer. As a student at Columbia University's school of law, he supported himself by playing professional football on the weekends. His career began as a lawyer, but racism and the support of his wife, Eslanda pushed him to the stage.

He is most well known for his roles in *The Emperor Jones* by Eugene O'Neill and *Showboat* during which he sang *Ol' Man River*, his signature song. His political passions included antiracism, anti-imperialism, and communism.

[13] Barbara Ransby, *Eslanda: The Large and Unconventional Life of Mrs. Paul Robeson*, 2013.

[14] Kamala Visweswaran, "Histories of Feminist Ethnography," *Annual Review of Anthropology*, 1997, 602.

[15] Ruth Murray Underhill, *Papago Woman*, 1985 [orig. 1936].

[16] Phyllis Mary Kaberry, *Aboriginal Woman*, 2004 [orig. 1939]. See also, Christine Cheater, "Kaberry, Phyllis Mary (1910–1977)," in *Australian Dictionary of Biography*. Accessed October 4, 2015. http://adb.anu.edu.au/biography/kaberry-phyllis-mary-10654.

[17] Zora Neale Hurston, *Their Eyes Were Watching God*, 2013 [orig. 1937], 3; *Mules and Men*, 1978 [orig. 1935].

[18] Graciela Hernández, "Multiple Mediations in Zora Neale Hurston's *Mules and Men*." *Critique of Anthropology*, 1993.

[19] Ella Cara Deloria, *Waterlily*, Reprint edition, 1988.

[20] Louise Lamphere, "Anthropologists are Talking about Feminist Anthropology," *Ethnos*, 2007.

[21] Ibid., 415.

[22] Louise Lamphere, "Feminist Anthropology Engages Social Movements: Theory, Ethnography and Activism," in *Mapping Feminist Anthropology in the Twenty-First Century*, edited by Ellen Lewin and Leni M. Silverstein, forthcoming 2016.

[23] Toni Morrison, *The Bluest Eye*, 1999 [orig. 1970] and *Song of Solomon*, 2014 [orig. 1977]; Maxine Hong Kingston, *The Woman Warrior: Memoirs of a Girlhood among Ghosts*, 2010 [orig. 1976]; Alice Walker, *Meridian*, 2011 [orig. 1976].

[24] Karen Su, "Translating Mother Tongues: Amy Tan and Maxine Hong Kingston on Ethnographic Authority," *Feminist Fields, 1999*, 34.

[25] Rebecca Aenerud, "Thinking Again: *This Bridge Called My Back* and the Challenge to Whiteness" in *This Bridge We Call Home*, eds., AnaLouise Keating and Gloria E. Anzaldúa, 2002, 71.

[26] Chandra Talpade Mohanty, Ann Russo, and Lourdes Torres, eds., *Third World Women and the Politics of Feminism*, 1991.

[27] Barbara J. Love, ed., *Feminists Who Changed America, 1963–1975*, 2006.

[28] Maria Patricia Fernández-Kelley, *For We Are Sold, I and My People*, 1984.

[29] June Nash, We Eat the Mines and the Mines Eat Us, 1979.

[30] Susan Bourque and Kay Warren, Women of the Andes, 1981.

[31] "Exhibit—The Lamphere Case: The Sex Discrimination Lawsuit That Changed Brown | Pembroke Center for Teaching and Research on Women." Accessed October 4, 2015. http://www.brown.edu/research/pembroke-center/archives/christine-dunlap-farnham-archives/louise-lamphere-vbrown-university/exhibit-lamphere-case-.

[32] Tami Navarro, Bianca Williams, and Attiya Ahmad, "Sitting at the Kitchen Table: Fieldnotes from Women of Color in Anthropology," in Cultural Anthropology, 2013.

[33] Ibid., 443–44.

[34] Bonnie Thornton Dill and Maxine Baca Zinn, Women of Color in U.S. Society, 1994, 3.

[35] Ibid.

[36] Patricia Zavella, Women's Work and Chicano Families, 1987.

[37] Aida Hurtado, The Color of Privilege, 1997.

[38] Leith Mullings, On Our Own Terms, 1997; Yen Le Espiritu, Asian American Panethnicity, 1993.

[39] Aihwa Ong, *Spirits of Resistance and Capitalist Discipline*, 1987.

[40] Anna Lowenhaupt Tsing, *In the Realm of the Diamond Queen*, 1993.

[41] Carla Freeman, *High Tech and High Heels in the Global Economy*, 2000.

[42] Florence Babb, *After Revolution*, 2001.

[43] Esther Newton, *Mother Camp*,1972.

[44] Deborah Goleman Wolf, *Lesbian Community*, 1979; Gilbert Herdt, *Guardians of the Flutes*, 1981.

[45] Evelyn Blackwood, *The Many Faces Of Homosexuality*, 1986.

[46] Kath Weston, *Families We Choose*, 1991.

[47] Ellen Lewin and William L. Leap, eds., *Out in the Field*, 1996. See also their subsequent volumes: *Out in Theory*, 2002 and *Out in Public*, 2009.

[48] Ellen Lewin, *Lesbian Mothers*, 1993; and Ellen Lewin, ed., *Inventing Lesbian Cultures in America*, 1996.

[49] Evelyn Blackwood, "Tombois in West Sumatra: Constructing Masculinity and Erotic Desire," in *Cultural Anthropology*, 1998; and later, Evelyn Blackwood, *Falling Into the Lesbi World: Desire and Difference in Indonesia*, 2010.

[50] Erica Lorraine Williams, *Sex Tourism in Bahia*, 2013.

[51] Gloria Wekker, *The Politics of Passion*, 2006.

[52] Ibid., 134.

[53] Shaka McGlotten and Dána-Ain Davis, *Black Genders & Sexualities*, 2012.

[54] Marlon M. Bailey, *Butch Queens Up in Pumps*, 2013.

[55] Margot Weiss, *Techniques of Pleasure*, 2011.

[56] It would be impossible to name all of the innovative queer feminist ethnographies that have emerged over the past two decades—for some of the highlights, see the Association of Queer Anthropologist's (AQA) Ruth Benedict Prize winners (http://queeranthro.org/awards/), the proceedings of the Yale University Queer Anthropologies conference in 2015 (http://lgbts.yale.edu/event/conference-queering-anthropology), the proceedings of the "Queer Kinships and Relationships" Conference organized by the Institute of Psychology, Polish Academy of Sciences, in Zalesie Mazury, Poland (http://queerkinship.systemcoffee.pl), and the special issue of *lambda nordica*, a journal of LGBTQ Studies in Sweden on Queer Kinship and Reproduction (Ulrika Dahl and Jenny Gunnarsonn Payne, eds., "Special Issue: Kinship & Reproduction," *lambda nordica*, 2014).

[57] Matthew Guttman, *The Meaning of Macho*, 1996.

[58] C. J. Pascoe, *Dude, You're a Fag*, 2011.

[59] Marcia C. Inhorn, *The New Arab Man*, 2012.

[60] Osmundo Pinho, "Ethnographies of the Brau: Body, Masculinity and Race in the Reafricanizatin in Salvador," *Estudos Feministas*, 2006.

[61] Rashad Shabazz, *Spatializing Blackness*, 2015.

CHAPTER 3

Debates and Interventions in Feminist Ethnography

In this chapter, you will examine debates in feminist ethnography from the 1980s through the present by considering the following questions:

- Who should be claimed as a feminist ethnographer?
- Can there be a feminist ethnography?
- How have feminist ethnographers approached the insider/outsider dilemma?
- What is the role of citational politics in feminist ethnography?
- How involved or engaged should a feminist ethnographer be?

***Spotlights** in this chapter:*

- Shannon Speed on Fieldwork and Identity
- Ishan Gordon-Ugarte on the Power and Potential Drawbacks of Challenging Positivism
- Mary L. Gray on the Labor of Feminist Ethnography

***Essentials** in this chapter:*

- Linda Tuhiwai Smith, *Decolonizing Methodologies*
- Judith Stacey, "Can There Be a Feminist Ethnography?"
- Nancy A. Naples, *Feminism and Method*
- María Amelia Viteri, *Desbordes*
- Lynn Bolles, "Telling It Straight"
- Sara Ahmed, Feminist Killjoys, "Making Feminist Points"

*You will also be **Thinking Through . . .***

- An Intellectual Genealogy
- What Would A Feminist Ethnographer Do (WWFED)?

The histories of feminist ethnography have included several debates and interventions. In this chapter we present, in roughly chronological order, issues as they have influenced research and production in the field of feminist ethnography. Beginning with the emergence of feminist ethnography as a field in the 1970s, scholars have questioned whose voices should be claimed from the historical canon. In the 1980s feminist ethnographers queried, in the context of concern about power inequities in feminist ethnography (and feminist research more generally): can there even be a feminist ethnography? Feminist ethnographers became active in debates about what Patricia Zavella in the 1990s called the insider/outsider dilemma. Another significant concern in the 1990s was citational politics—that is, whose work is being cited more or less often than others. Yet citational inequities continue into the twenty-first century. Finally, debates over activist scholarship have emerged in many fields over the past few decades, and feminist ethnographers have been instrumental in these discussions.

Who Should Be Claimed as a Feminist Ethnographer?

Early in the feminist ethnographic enterprise, as we noted in the last chapter, the cadre of feminist ethnographers that emerged in the 1980s and 1990s struggled to "reclaim" earlier female researchers who had inspired the development of this field, but may not have identified their work as "feminist." Generally, women scholars of the early and mid-1900s did not use the word feminist in the titles of their work, although their work contributed to feminist goals and some participated in feminist movements. Conceptually, women's scholarship, especially in anthropology, was organized around traditional subjects such as family, politics, religion, and subsistence. However, those traditional anthropological inquiries, when viewed through the lens of women's roles represented a deliberate departure from earlier studies focused on men. We also see evidence of a convergence of gender politics and scholarship in what anthropologist Micaela di Leonardo has called the "bibles" of feminist anthropology: Michelle Rosaldo and Louise Lamphere's edited collection *Woman, Culture, and Society* and Rayna (Rapp) Reiter's *Toward an Anthropology of Women.*[1] These texts formed the underpinnings of Second Wave feminist anthropology, and in both, the authors of the various chapters theorize and analyze women's lives. Yet it took nearly fifteen years after the publication of both collections for the Association for Feminist Anthropology to be established in 1988.

Feminist ethnography came into existence in the context of struggle and it was not an easy road. In order to contextualize this history, we first want to take into account cross-cultural examples of the types of challenges faced in gender-based research. For example, in areas such as Southern Africa, in particular Namibia—where Dána-Ain worked with Richard Lee, Ida Susser, and Karen Brodkin, research on gender is often commissioned by **donor agencies** or governments. What this meant at the time was that gender-based research was guided by funders' interests, a situation which can compromise an ethnographer's research agenda. Additionally, feminist ideology, theory, and practice have developed differentially. In other words feminist ethnography did not necessarily correspond to the timeline of the emergence of feminism in the West. For example, as discussed in chapter 1, if one uses suffrage as a marker for the emergence of feminist thinking and organizing and thus writing, the development of feminist ethnography was (and remains) uneven in light of this differential political positioning. Finally, although not limited to women in the Global South, but certainly important there, is that while women may be involved in political organizing they may not necessarily consider themselves to be feminists. For example, consider the Committees of the Mothers of the Disappeared across Latin America in the 1970s. During this time, right-wing military and paramilitary dictatorships, which governed much of Latin America, used tactics such as "forced disappearances" of people who opposed their regimes. As this issue surfaced as a global concern, many Latin American women were at the forefront of the movement against state-sanctioned violence, highlighting their roles as mothers, wives, sisters, grandmothers, daughters, and aunts of disappeared men, but not necessarily counting themselves as feminists. Consequently, we must recognize that some scholars

 ESSENTIALS

Excerpt from *Decolonizing Methodologies: Research And Indigenous Peoples* by Linda Tuhiwai Smith

***Linda Tuhiwai Smith** is a professor of education and Māori development at the University of Waikato in Hamilton, New Zealand, and currently serves as the Pro-Vice Chancellor Māori. She affiliates to the Māori iwi (tribes) Ngāti Awa and Ngāti Porou. She is the author of* Decolonizing Methodologies: Research and Indigenous Peoples *originally published in 1999 and reissued in 2012. Below is an excerpt from the introduction, and Smith discusses the 15-year anniversary of her book in a YouTube video, "Decolonizing Knowledge," offered as a suggested resource at the end of this chapter.*

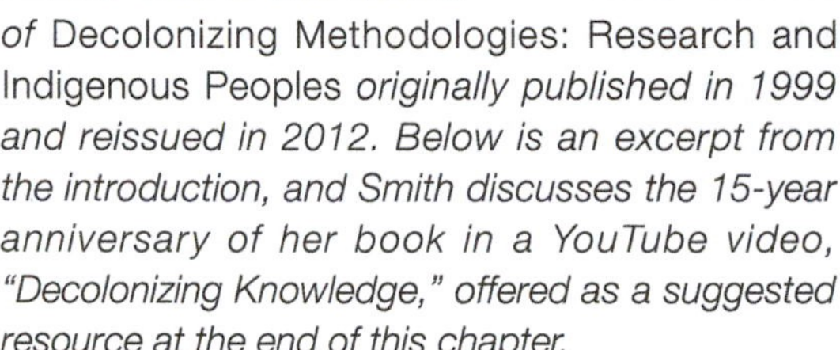

From the vantage point of the colonized, a position from which I write, and choose to privilege, the term, "research" is inextricably linked to European imperialism and colonialism. The word itself, "research," is probably one of the dirtiest words in the indigenous world's vocabulary. When mentioned in many indigenous contexts, it stirs up silence, it conjures up bad memories, it raises a smile that is knowing and distrustful. It is so powerful that indigenous people even write poetry about research. The way in which scientific research is implicated in the worst excesses of colonialism remains a powerful remembered history for many of the world's colonized peoples. It is a history that still offends the deepest sense of our humanity. Just knowing that someone measured our "faculties" by filling the skulls of our ancestor with millet seeds and compared the amount of millet seed to the capacity for mental thought offends our sense of who and what we are. It galls us that Western researchers and intellectuals can assume to know all that is possible to know of us, on the basis of their brief encounters with some of us. It appalls us that the West can desire, extract and claim ownership of our ways of knowing, our imagery, the things we create and produce, and then simultaneously reject the people who created and developed those ideas and seek to deny them further opportunities to be creators of their own culture and own nations. It angers us when practices linked to the last century, and the centuries before that, are still employed to deny the validity of indigenous peoples' claim to existence, to land and territories to the right of self-determination, to the survival of our languages and forms of cultural knowledge, to our natural resources and systems of living within our environments.

This collective memory of imperialism has been perpetuated through the ways in which knowledge about indigenous peoples was collected, classified and then represented in various ways back to the West, and then, through the eyes of the West, back to those who have been colonized.

Source: Linda Tuhiwai Smith. *Decolonizing Methodologies: Research and Indigenous Peoples* (Second Edition). London: Zed Books, 2012 (orig. 1999), 1.

have strategically avoided the term "feminist" viewing it as a Western imperialist and elitist term. Yet other scholars, including an advocate for Indigenous feminist research Linda Tuhiwai Smith, have directly challenged Western feminist attitudes toward "the Other" and proposed alternative forms of feminist knowledge gathering.

Smith proposes Indigenous research projects, such as Claiming, Testimonies (which she links to *testimonios*, the Latin American tradition of narratives of collective memory), Intervening, (Critical) Reading, Writing and Theory Making, Gendering, Envisioning, Networking, and Sharing Knowledge among Indigenous people from throughout the world.[2] Smith also highlights New Zealand Māori scholar and lesbian activist Ngahuia Te Awekotuku's set of ethical responsibilities that researchers have to Māori people, based on the code of conduct for the New Zealand Association of Social Anthropologists, which in turn is based on the American Anthropological Association's Code of Ethics.

1. *Aroha kit te tangata* (a respect for people).
2. *Kanohi kitea* (the seen face, that is present yourself to people face to face).
3. *Titiro, whakarongo* . . . (look, listen . . . speak).
4. *Manaaki kit te tangata* (share and host people, be generous).
5. *Kia tupato* (be cautious).
6. *Kaua e takahia te mana o te tangata* (do not trample over the *mana* of people).
7. *Kia mahaki* (don't flaunt your knowledge).[3]

We began this section by asking who should be claimed as feminist? But maybe the question is not who should be considered a feminist, but rather who and what has contributed to feminist knowledge production and in what ways? Reframing the question this way suggests that feminist knowledge production can rely on contributions by people who do not necessarily claim or are able to claim being feminists. Nor does making the claim have to be linked to individual feminist declarations. Like the example of the Māori Code of Ethics above, which embodies a set of principles, the same may be said for other principles and theories such as critical race, disability, and queer studies.

Can There Be a Feminist Ethnography?

A central question raised in the 1980s by sociologist Judith Stacey and anthropologist Lila Abu-Lughod, is whether there can even be such a thing as a feminist ethnography.[4] It may well be accurate that the relationship between feminism and ethnography can be "awkward," as anthropologist Marilyn Strathern has emphasized.[5] Strathern questions whether or not feminist research is capable of transforming anthropology. Some contemporary scholars would agree with anthropologist Kamala Visweswaran that ethnography is not inherently feminist, in the sense that it could avoid all inequity between researcher and participant.[6] But like many other contemporary feminist ethnographers, we believe ethnographic research is not a project feminists should give up. For instance, feminist ethnography has charted new terrain on the challenges of power dynamics within fieldwork. This impels us (and others) not to abandon our work, but to approach it with heightened care and awareness.

Stacey's now-classic article "Can There Be a Feminist Ethnography?" raised questions about feminist ideals of equity in the research encounter at a vital point in the development of feminist principles for research and ethnography. Stacey challenged the notion that feminist ethnography was somehow egalitarian—that there could be fewer, if any, power distinctions between the researcher and her informant because of women's shared identity *as women*. As Stacey saw it, feminist ethnography is faced with several problems: that of interventions, the inherently unequal relationship with informants, and feminist reporting quandaries.[7] One of Stacey's arguments was that contradictions exist between feminist principles and feminist ethnography. Although one goal of feminist ethnography is to produce nonhierarchical, collaborative research, the data a feminist ethnographer collects can compromise a participant's integrity.

Stacey argued that the feminist ethnographic process places subjects in a position of exploitation because the lives, loves, and tragedies they share with a researcher are, "ultimately data, grist for the ethnographic mill, a mill that has a truly grinding power."[8] Her point was that despite the equitable intentions of feminist ethnography, there are numerous fieldwork experiences that generate a conflict of interest and emotion between the ethnographer and the participant because of *the things that we cannot tell*. To illustrate, Stacey describes a situation in which she cultivated a close relationship with two women who were key informants. The first of the two women shared very personal information about the second: although the second woman was married and a fundamentalist Christian, at the time of her conversion just prior to being married, she was in a closeted lesbian relationship with the first. The

 ESSENTIALS

Excerpt from "Can There Be a Feminist Ethnography?" by Judith Stacey

Judith Stacey *received her PhD in sociology from Brandeis University and is an emeritus professor of New York University's Department of Social and Cultural Analysis. In addition to her classic article on feminist ethnography, excerpted here, Stacey is the author of* Brave New Families: Stories of Domestic Upheaval in Late-Twentieth-Century America *(1990) and* Unhitched: Love, Marriage and Family Values from West Hollywood to Western China *(2011).*

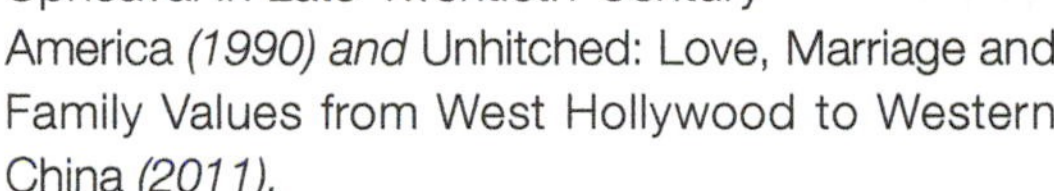

Although there is no uniform canon of feminist research principles, and many lively debates about whether there should be, and, if so, what one should contain, still it is possible to characterize a dominant conception of feminist research currently prevailing among feminist scholars. Most view feminist research as primarily research on, by, and especially for women and draw sharp distinctions between the goals and methods of mainstream and feminist scholarship. Feminist scholars evince widespread disenchantment with the dualisms, abstractions, and detachment of positivism, rejecting the separations between subject and object, thought and feeling, knower and known, and political and personal as well as their reflections in the arbitrary boundaries of traditional academic disciplines. Instead most feminist scholars advocate an integrative, trans-disciplinary approach to knowledge which grounds theory contextually in the concrete realm of women's everyday lives. . . .

Ethnography emphasizes the experiential. Its approach to knowledge is contextual and interpersonal, attentive like most women, therefore, to the concrete realm of everyday reality and human agency. Moreover, because in ethnographic studies the researcher herself is the primary medium, the "instrument" of research, this method draws on those resources of empathy, connection, and concern that many feminists consider to be women's special strengths and which they argue should be germinal in feminist research. Ethnographic method also appears to provide much greater respect for and power to one's research "subjects" who, some feminists propose, can and should become full collaborators in feminist research. . . .

[Yet] precisely because ethnographic research depends upon human relationships, engagement, and attachment it places research subjects at a grave risk for manipulation and betrayal by the ethnographer. . . . [Additionally,] ethnographic method appears to (and often does) place the researcher and her informants in a collaborative, reciprocal quest for understanding, but the research product is ultimately that of the researcher, however modified or influenced by informants. With very rare exceptions it is the researcher who narrates, who "authors" the ethnography. In the last instance an ethnography is a written document structured primarily by a researcher's purposes, offering a researcher's interpretations, registered in a researcher's voice. Here too, therefore, elements of inequality, exploitation, and even betrayal are endemic to ethnography. Perhaps even more than ethnographic process, the published ethnography represents an intervention into the lives and relationships of its subjects.

Source: Judith Stacey. "Can There Be a Feminist Ethnography?" *Women's Studies International Forum* 11, no. 1 (1988): 21–24.

awkward situation for Stacey was twofold. First, there was the potential betrayal to both women if she shared the "intimate" information publicly in her book. Second, the conundrum raised the possibility of being inauthentic as a researcher, if Stacey did not.

Nearly twenty years later, Dána-Ain revisited Stacey's questions in "Border Crossing: Intimacy and Feminist Activist Ethnography in the Age of Neoliberalism."[9] The motivation for reengaging with the self-revelatory narrations that women shared with her during oral and life history interviews, was to explore how those self-disclosures could be understood in terms of power, as articulated by Stacey, and within the context of **neoliberalism.** The question became, what insights did feminist ethnography generate about the relationship between intimacy (or self-disclosure) and neoliberalism? In revisiting her research, she realized that Black women who were battered and needed public assistance had expectations of her. Dána-Ain faced having to decide whether or not to reciprocate after women shared their desperate needs and some very personal details about their lives. Whereas one of Stacey's concerns was that there was an unequal relationship between researcher and informant because of our power to use women's stories as we saw fit, Dána-Ain dealt with women mobilizing their stories to get something from her to mitigate their experiences of scarce resources. And while Stacey was concerned about what not to say for fear of betraying women's "secrets," the women Dána-Ain interviewed were more likely to *want* her share their stories with people in powerful positions, who they believed might be able to facilitate helping the women access to housing and services they required. Women's interests in having their lives narrated by the researcher to people they presumed had power, differed across race. No white woman requested that Dána-Ain share her experiences with others, because access to resources was differently situated across race, ethnicity, and citizenship status.

Writing during the same period as Stacey, Lila Abu-Lughod's article, also (inadvertently) entitled "Can There Be a Feminist Ethnography?" critiqued feminist ethnographers who assume a universal "women's experience" that erases power differentials between the most privileged ethnographer and her research subjects.[10] Abu-Lughod's work was a response to radical feminists, such as Robin Morgan, who argued in the introduction to *Sisterhood Is Global* that a latent global women's culture exists that could be activated by women examining their common experiences with patriarchal oppression.[11] The majority of contemporary feminist ethnographers join Abu-Lughod in rejecting this claim. In *Feminism and Method*, for instance, sociologist Nancy A. Naples frames feminist ethnography as emerging from diverse perspectives, as well as the unique personally, politically, and academically significant experiences of feminist ethnographers.

Following debates over whether there could even be a feminist ethnography, which were largely resolved through increased attention to power differentials in research (albeit, with the admission that this would always be imperfect), feminist ethnographers have continued to debate the limitations of some theoretical proclivities guiding ethnographic research and their ensuing outcomes. One such debate has been over the theoretical frameworks of **postmodernism** and **post-structuralism,** which in broad strokes seek to shift away from what is perceived as reductionist generalizations, to analyses that reveal fluidity and **polyvocality**, analyses that could have multiple, contestable meanings. A popular cultural example of polyvocality can be seen in performer Janelle Monae's album *The Electric Lady,*[12] where Monae uses her music to showcase a powerful consolidation of **Afrofuturism** and **cyberfeminism.** To get a sense of how she accomplishes exemplifying polyvocality through music/gender/feminism/race/technology, look at the multiple levels of meaning in the videos from her album.

 ESSENTIALS

Excerpt from *Feminism and Method* by Nancy A. Naples

***Nancy A. Naples** received her PhD in sociology from The Graduate Center, City University of New York, and holds degrees in education and administration and social policy. She is a professor of Sociology and Women's, Gender and Sexuality Studies at the University of Connecticut. Author of numerous books, including* Grassroots Warriors: Activist Mothering, Community Work, and the War on Poverty *(1998),* Women's Activism and Globalization: Linking Local Struggles and Transnational Politics *(2002),* Feminism and Method: Ethnography, Discourse Analysis, and Activist Research *(2003), and* Border Politics: Social Movements, Collective identities, and Globalization, *coedited with Jennifer Bickman Mendez (2014); she has also served as president of Sociologists for Women in Society (2004) and is the recipient of the Sociologists for Women in Society's 2011 Distinguished Feminist Lecturer award.*

Feminist theoretical perspectives were developed in the context of diverse struggles for social justice inside and outside the academy. In their various formulations, feminist theories emphasize the need to challenge sexism, racism, colonialism, class, and other forms of inequalities in the research process. . . . Like many feminist scholars, I address questions in my research that are simultaneously personally, politically, and academically significant. From my earliest memories I have been concerned with understanding and fighting inequality and injustice. Not surprisingly, my academic work focuses on examining the reproduction of, and resistance to, inequalities in different communities, as well as identifying strategies that foster social and economic justice. My growing sensitivity to the formal and informal ways domination is manifest in different research settings helped me negotiate discrimination, sexual abuse, and the relations of ruling that infuse my own life. In light of my activist goal of challenging inequality in all its complex guises, I was drawn to feminist efforts to conduct research that minimizes exploitation of research subjects.

Source: Nancy A. Naples, *Feminism and Method: Ethnography, Discourse Analysis, and Activist Research*. New York: Routledge, 2003, 13.

One of the main critiques feminist ethnographers have leveled against the "post-" discussions within academia is that they are depoliticized, offering little, if any, analysis of power, race, class, and gender dynamics. A major corrective to that work is Micaela di Leonardo's *Gender at the Crossroads of Knowledge: Feminist Anthropology in the Postmodern Era*.[13] Expanding upon previous work in feminist anthropology that had focused primarily on sociocultural analyses of gender, di Leonardo's volume is grounded in political economy across all four subfields within anthropology, including archaeology, biological anthropology, and linguistic anthropology. Although authors were influenced by postmodern debates, such as an enhanced attention to reflexivity, they contended that material realities cannot be disconnected from the ways that meaning and knowledge are constructed. Specifically, the collection emphasizes how knowledge production is always political, as well as historically embedded in political, economic, and social processes. di Leonardo offers one of the most comprehensive discussions of feminist anthropology's history from the 1970s through the 1990s, when feminist texts proliferated.

From the 1980s onward, the increasing engagement with reflexivity and attention to relations of power in the research encounter lead feminist ethnographers to (re)consider their own identities as "insiders," "outsiders," and often both, in their fieldwork. The position of the ethnographer vis-à-vis the research participants involves not only their own position in terms of how they perceive themselves, but also how participants respond to and perceive them—which can include many different experiences even within a single community or field site.

How Have Feminist Ethnographers Approached the Insider/Outsider Dilemma?

The insider/outsider dilemma concerns the researcher's relationship to those being studied. Specifically, it suggests that an "outsider" might lack strategic knowledge of those under investigation, and presumes that the "insider" knows the perspective of the group under study. This debate is concerned with whether or not being an outsider "guarantees" a more objective view or interpretation of the group or situation under investigation. Is the insider/outsider dichotomy a definitive way to understand the researcher/researched relationship? Does the insider role establish legitimacy for the researcher? Does being familiar with the group make it easier to interview or conduct extended fieldwork with them?

Earlier discussions of this debate were framed as emic versus etic perspectives. An emic perspective is that taken by a researcher who is part of the community being studied, or the perspectives of those within the community. Alternatively, an etic perspective assumes that a researcher is not part of the community being studied. Another question is: to what degree can an ethnographer become immersed in a community given their (assumed) group membership? Another way the insider/outsider debate has been cast is in terms of the problems posed for researchers who straddle both an insider and an outsider role.

Ethnographers have discussed the pros and cons of this issue at length. For instance, being an insider may help the researcher understand the contexts in which people do things because they know the history of the community and the meaning people give to some aspects of life. They are able to explain, describe, and interpret their experiences with a degree of authority. Another benefit may be that the researcher knows participants, and having access to individuals within the community can facilitate the research process. Yet, some suggest that knowing "too much" about a community or an individual's circumstances creates bias in the data one collects, and how one interprets it. This last point leans toward the view that being an outsider is advantageous because the researcher is presumed to have more distance and is therefore capable of being more objective. One question to ask, however, is whether it is possible to maintain strict objectivity throughout any research project? And why is objectivity considered an advantage? Most feminist researchers, including feminist ethnographers, would argue that all scholarly inquiry is subjective—in the questions we choose, how we gather data, as well as our positions as we encounter participants in fieldwork.

A further critique of the feminist insider/outsider dilemma is that it sets up a dichotomy related to a researcher's position that is too simplistic, emphasizing either that one is *only* an insider *or* an outsider. This construct suggests there is a degree of absoluteness in sameness or difference. Let us presume that you are a Senegalese ethnographer conducting research among Senegalese factory workers. The insider/outsider construct could ostensibly position you as a person who would be successful in conducting research among Senegalese workers employed in a groundnut/peanut oil factory *because* you are Senegalese. Or the insider/outsider construct could locate you as a person who might be biased in your data collection *because* you are Senegalese. What if more detail was available? For instance, what if you were a university-educated, Christian from a Wolof-speaking community, and most workers were poor, Muslim Wolofs, who had not completed elementary school? The presumed similarity of a Wolof-speaking researcher and participants in your research would obscure the fact that there are differences among Senegalese that can create more research challenges than opportunities.

Anthropologist Patricia Zavella wrote about a similar problem in her classic 1996 article, "Feminist Insider Dilemmas: Constructing Ethnic Identity with 'Chicana' Informants."[14] Here, she reflexively explores research she conducted with Chicana working mothers. As a Chicana woman herself, Zavella was an insider who had participated in the Chicano movement. Being part of the movement meant acknowledging pride in pre-Columbian heritage and celebrating **mestizo** culture, as well as rejecting the influence of Spanish colonizers. Being Chicana also meant trying to achieve self-determination and controlling various institutions within the Chicano community. Zavella hoped that sharing her own heritage with informants would facilitate their ability to express their ethnicity openly. But instead of identifying as Chicana, most of her informants identified as Spanish or Spanish American, and Zavella struggled with their self-identification with colonizers in contrast to her own sense of identity.

This example makes it clear that shared membership in a group does not automatically mean there is complete sameness within that group. Likewise, not being a member of a group does not denote complete difference. It seems interesting that the poles of this discussion are set in an absolutist way, offering a narrow range of experience and understanding. Anthropologist Kirin Narayan highlights in her widely read article, "How Native Is a 'Native' Anthropologist?,"[15] that **hybridity**—being both insider and outsider—reveals the challenge of the native/anthropologist dichotomy. When anthropologists return to study their culture of origin, particularly in postcolonial contexts where their communities were colonized, colleagues often problematically position the "native" anthropologist's knowledge as authentically "native." Assuming that the ethnographer is automatically an insider obscures the relations of privilege that they may have as an outsider as well, particularly vis-à-vis their education and/or class status.

Feminist ethnographers, indeed researchers in general, typically recognize the fluidity and complexity of human experience and know that the spaces between the poles of insider and outsider are far more complicated. This is demonstrated in the experiences of ethnographers whose positionality is ambiguous, which also has pros and cons. One researcher, for instance, communication studies scholar Anastacia Kurylo who studies interpersonally communicated stereotypes, says that she is "visually ambiguous." The fact that she could be a member of a variety of ethnic or racial backgrounds means she could be viewed as an insider. However, among some groups she would also be perceived as an outsider. Kurylo thinks that having an ambiguous cultural identity makes people cautious about saying anything they might deem "too offensive" out of fear that they will insult her. She also points out that even ambiguous positionality can be useful, because if people do not identify her as a minority, then they may be less cautious about describing stereotypes.[16]

The experience of feminist geographer Lorena Muñoz in her research on Latina street vendors is also instructive in this debate. During an interview, Muñoz told a participant, Herminia, that she was also "gay," and noticed a profound change in Herminia's demeanor toward her. In fact, Herminia had many questions for Muñoz about how her family responded to her sexuality, whether she had a partner, and admits "*Huy si hubiera sabido esto desde antes, te hubiera invitado a mi casa desde hace mucho* [Well, if I had known that from the beginning, I would have invited you to my house a long time ago]."[17] Ultimately, Muñoz notes that her "queer" feminist identity often conflicted with her identity as a "cross-border Chicana." Her ability to speak Spanish with a "Mexican" accent had initially positioned her as a community member with many of the vendors, although she notes that it took her longer to establish relationships with vendors from Central America. Yet, identifying herself as "queer," as someone who usually "embodied [a] straight Chicana immigrant identity" in heteronormative spaces, became not only a potential barrier, but also an opening to multiple ways of seeing the lives of the women she studied.[18]

With regard to the conundrums that arise in the insider/outsider debate, Shannon Speed, notes that, "A fundamental premise of participant observation—anthropology's primary ethnographic research method—is that viewing a culture from an outside perspective allows one to 'see' aspects of its workings that for insiders are naturalized and thus invisible. At the same time, the presumption that prolonged field work and some measure of cultural participation is needed to get inside of a cultural context in order to understand it, is also built into the discipline." Speed offers insights from her perspective as an Indigenous feminist ethnographer.

Many of the questions that emerged around insider/outsider concerns during the 1980s coincided with the intervention of **feminist standpoint theories.** Feminist standpoint theorists, such as sociologist Dorothy E. Smith, claim that knowledge is socially situated: the knowledge that one has is affected by where they stand (their subject position) in society.[19] Sociologist Patricia Hill Collins emphasizes that

SPOTLIGHTS

Shannon Speed on Fieldwork and Identity

Shannon Speed *earned her PhD in anthropology and Native American studies at the University of California, Davis. She teaches gender studies and anthropology at UCLA, where she also serves as director of the American Indian Studies Center. Speed is a citizen of the Chickasaw Nation. Her ethnographic work has been primarily in Mexico, on topics including indigenous politics, human rights, neoliberalism, gender, indigenous migration, and activist research. She has published books in both English and Spanish, including* Rights in Rebellion: Human Rights and Indigenous Struggle in Chiapas *(2007),* and Dissident Women: Gender and Cultural Politics in Chiapas *(2006) edited with R. Aída Hernández Castillo, and Lynn Stephen.*

The question of emic and etic, or insider and outsider, perspectives is crucial to the anthropological undertaking of ethnographic research. A fundamental premise of participant observation—anthropology's primary ethnographic research method—is that viewing a culture from an outside perspective allows one to "see" aspects of its workings that for insiders are naturalized and thus invisible. At the same time, the presumption that prolonged field work and some measure of cultural participation is needed to get inside of a cultural context in order to understand it is also built into the discipline. A variety of critical perspectives have been brought to bear on these premises, perhaps most notably feminist critiques challenging both the bipolar nature of the insider/outsider dichotomy and the relations of power between researcher and researched that this dichotomy simultaneously occludes and reinscribes.

One important line of this critique has highlighted the fundamental arrogance of presuming that a researcher can or should come from outside to tell the people involved what they are actually doing, rather than what they think/say they are doing (most often a Western, first-world academic deciding the "truth" of what non-Western/non-first-world/less formally educated people are doing). This led to a period of reflection on "home work" by

(*continued*)

"insider" ethnographers—many of them feminists of color—working with/in their own communities, however defined. Yet, home work also generated contradictions and tensions, as researchers confronted their own "outsiderness" as their university educations altered their positionalities within their communities, and many struggled to rectify theoretical frameworks learned in academia with the lives of their friends and family members as research "subjects." Following on the insights this work provided, feminist ethnographers have been interested in exploring the ways in which one is simultaneously an insider and an outsider, and how different aspect of these relational concepts come to the fore in different moments.

These insights were crucial for me as an indigenous feminist ethnographer. As a tribal citizen of the Chickasaw Nation I am a Native American, though tribal belonging in the United States brings its own complex set of insider/outsider issues based on enrollment, residence, language ability, blood quantum, and phenotype, just to name a few. The fact that I grew up in Los Angeles and my anglo-leaning phenotype have led some to question my right to claim insider status as a Native American. These questions—at least the ones I took seriously—came from a "people of color" perspective which rightly noted that I do not suffer racial bias as a person of color. Due to the history of imposed assimilation and colonization of this country, the fact is that many Native Americans who have legitimate relationships with their tribal nations do not "look Indian," particularly to non-Indians bearing their own unexamined stereotypes about what an Indian looks like. However, at least for the federally recognized tribes (another can of worms), tribal sovereignty dictates that tribal governments have the right to define their membership, not the racial -stereotype bearing general public. That said, while my tribal membership was clear, my field research relationships in Oklahoma were likely to raise significant issues of difference and my perspective could hardly be simply defined as an "insider" one in this regard.

These blurrings of the dichotomous line between insider and outsider became even more muddied when I decided to shift my field research to Chiapas, Mexico, where an important indigenous uprising was occurring. I was drawn there because as a Native person, I was interested in indigenous oppression and indigenous rights, and because I saw the tremendous shared experience of oppression and resistance of Native peoples that the Zapatista movement embodied. Nevertheless, to arrive in Chiapas and present myself to communities of impoverished Maya as "one of them" or our experience as one of "shared oppression" would have been incongruous. The racial privilege I enjoy based on my phenotype in the United States was amplified in Chiapas, where as a *gringa* (person from the United States) and a *güera* (white girl), as well as a university researcher in a context where few indigenous people have access to a university, I was as alien as anyone else stepping into those communities. The extraordinary levels of poverty, marginalization, and violence that characterize the lives of indigenous communities of Chiapas are not part of my experience, or that of most Chickasaws. I do not wish to underestimate the poverty and violence suffered by Native communities in the United States, which in some cases approximates that of the Mayan communities of Chiapas, but in this case it would have been preposterous for me to assert an insider positionality. Yet, my research was inevitably shaped by my own perspective as an indigenous person and my experience as a Native American in a distinct context. Indeed, my analysis of identity formation, the role of different states and social movements in relation to indigenous identity, and the ways these played out for indigenous women, was undoubtedly a product of my own positionality as a Native researcher, though many I worked with never identified me as such.

I venture this brief reflection on my field experience to support the fundamental feminist insight that dichotomies such as insider/outsider, based in the first instance on positivist impulses to codify social reality, simplify to a point of occluding most of what is interesting about a given social situation. As positionalities, insider and outsider are fluid and porous categories, and are experienced differently by people at distinct points in time and as they move through different subject locations. Most importantly, attempts to impose insider/outsider distinctions can do violence to our research subjects by masking the power differentials and experiential differences between the researcher and the researched.

ESSENTIALS

Excerpt from *Desbordes* by María Amelia Viteri

***María Amelia Viteri** holds a PhD in cultural anthropology from American University in Washington DC, with a concentration on race, gender, and social justice. She is currently a professor of anthropology at Universidad San Francisco de Quito (USFQ) in Ecuador. Her research bridges citizenship, belonging, and identity within a transnational and intersectional framework. Sexuality and gender are at the core of her work. Moving between the geopolitical spaces of the United States and Ecuador through research and teaching, she speaks from a situated space as a transnational scholar herself. She has incorporated visual arts as additional tools that bring academia closer to local communities. Below is an excerpt from a section of her book* Desbordes: Translating Racial, Ethnic, Sexual and Gender Identities across the Americas *(2004) reflecting on her identity, entitled "Geography Matters."*

I was born in the Andean capital city of Ecuador, Quito, to an upper-middle-class family whose recent history was shaped by our internal migration to the capital city as a result of lost haciendas in the province of Imbabura. Class in Ecuador is defined by proximity to Spain—in terms of phenotype, family name, and inheritance of material or social capital—rather than affluence. As such, there could be significant discrepancies between families who would be considered "upper middle class." Regardless of differences in income, their privilege was defined by access to privileged entertainment and social places in addition to a network of support that guarantees a social circle that will mostly help a person navigate with more ease the bureaucracy of a classist society. Being upper middle class in Ecuador does not necessarily mean that your income would match an upper-middle-class income in the United States. One's family name and the class one descended from usually matter more than one's income. For example, a darker wealthy person born into a working-class family has fewer privileges than one born within the names acknowledged as closer to Spain, read as "white." The bilingual Catholic school I attended as a child was known at that time for not accepting darker girls and girls with indigenous last names. The country club my father founded was also known at that time to screen out applicants who were not from the traditional upper-middle-class families. Again, skin color and last name were major factors in this decision. . . .

Being nonheterosexual in Ecuador can inflict a serious wound on one's family's image, and it is highly discouraged. People are rigidly compartmentalized into categories according to class, "race," ethnicity, and gender. It was only in 1997 that Article 516 in the Ecuadorian constitution penalizing homosexuality was repealed, thanks to the successful mobilization of "trans" women supported by other organized gay and lesbian organizations. Nevertheless, sharp variations are found across the country. Manabí Province, located on the coast, is known as a "queer paradise" . . . The title "queer paradise" was applied there because of the perception that families are less punitive toward same-sex couples than in other parts of the coast and the Andes. There is also at least one beach known as an LGBT-friendly place where the community cruise and hang out, particularly on Sundays. This is subject to further research as Manabí is also known for a masculine-dominant "machete" culture where *montubios* are highly sexualized. . . .

As a Latina myself, I have experienced the reflexive process through which subjectivity and identity are dialogically constituted using different positionalities to render visible the array of LGBT "Latino" discourses around race and sexuality which tease out the rather contradictory politics of lived sexual citizenship and belonging. I am arguing that this subject positioning as a "queer" immigrant, anthropologist, scholar, and Latina is in constant negotiation, disjuncture, and conversation with understandings of "Latino" and "queer" community involvements.

Source: María Amelia Viteri. *Desbordes: Translating Racial, Ethnic, Sexual, and Gender Identities across the Americas.* Albany: State University of New York Press, 2014, 90, 91, 94.

marginalized groups are socially situated in ways that make it more possible for them to be aware of things and ask questions than it is for nonmarginalized groups and that research should be particularly focused on power relations and begin with the lives of marginalized people.[20] Among feminist standpoint theorists, the idea is that particular positions occupied by women and people without societal privileges are a good source of knowledge making because they have different views of a situation. Yet, others have argued that understanding the powerful relations and structures that orchestrate one's life is but one way to survive the reality of being dominated or controlled. Standpoint has been an important theoretical position for feminists. However, critics have questioned an "automatic epistemic privilege" such that one's social location is enough to give one an advantage of knowledge. Instead, they argue that the standpoint of subordinated group members is achieved through history, economic status, and through the process of political consciousness.

What becomes clear is that a key aspect of feminist ethnographic inquiry is the interrogation one's **positionality**, how one is situated in relation to participants in their work. Some feminist ethnographers rely on the position and experience offered by standpoint theory, which can serve as an important epistemological location. A significant aspect of standpoint theory is the role **reflexivity** plays in guiding the critical review of the feminist insider/outsider dilemma. This requires that researchers position themselves in terms of the research being conducted by identifying who they are and their relationship to the project or community. A well-crafted example of such reflexivity is anthropologist María Amelia Viteri's detailed discussion of how her personal background influenced her research on how migration status, gender, sexuality, class, race, ethnicity, and nationality impact the lives of LGBT Latinos in the United States, El Salvador, and Ecuador.

What Is the Role of Citational Politics in Feminist Ethnography?

A crucial part of conducting any feminist ethnographic project is developing a feminist intellectual genealogy. Who you read and *how* you read that material is a significant part of how one develops, organizes, and embarks upon a project. This encourages you first to ask questions informed by a feminist sensibility and perspective, and then to choose research methods that will allow you to collect the information most necessary to answer them. Many of those interviewed for this book acknowledged the important intellectual debts they owe to other feminist scholars, as we have done in the previous chapters. They are also keenly aware of the need to prepare for new projects by reading the work of feminist scholars to think through the subject and to frame their projects.

In his book on race, gender, and revolution, *¡Venceremos?: The Erotics of Black Self-making in Cuba*, anthropologist Jafari Allen draws on the influence of Black feminist scholars to address how some Cuban women he interviewed engaged in liberatory actions and organizing, but did not necessarily identify as "feminist":

> As Barbara Smith reminds us "Black women were never fools, we could never afford to be" (1998: xxvii). That is, black women's participation, from the abolition and suffrage movements to anti-lynching activism, civil rights efforts, and HIV prevention, for example, has had long and deep engagement in intersectional analysis and action. The same is true for Cuban women, whether or not they used the term "feminist." In "A Black Feminist Statement" the Combahee River Collective, including Smith, connects socialist political activism in transnational communities of black women with the most intimate and personal political areas of everyday life. Moving precipitously beyond the sort

> of feminism that Espín [a participant in Allen's study] and others eschew, this speaks directly to the current struggles and triumphs of my Cuban respondents and friends.[21]

Allen's work exemplifies how one can draw from a Black feminist vocabulary to analyze a range of gendered experiences. His strategy illustrates that we can connect our participants to those we cite, generating parallel as well as integrative voices, which can be a key facet of feminist scholarship.

Although the issue of citational politics is not restricted to gender, it has been well documented that publications with women authors (whether as sole authors or coauthors) are cited less frequently than those attributed to male authors.[22] Anthropologist Lynn Bolles stresses (see excerpt) that African American women's publications are significantly undercited by other scholars, including feminists. It is important to keep in mind that who we cite—and equally important, who we do *not* cite—shapes our projects in important ways. We generate ideas and knowledge in the context not only of our own life experiences, as feminists have long argued, but also in relation to the scholars, activists, and others who influence our work.

As a brief personal aside, Lynn Bolles and her work on citational politics was a crucial reason that Christa entered the field of anthropology. When Christa went to her first American Anthropological Association conference as an undergraduate in 1995, the first panel she attended was a retrospective honoring the 20-year legacy of the feminist anthropological canons, *Toward an Anthropology of Women* and *Woman, Culture, and Society*. It was there that she heard Bolles deliver a paper in which she strategically cited only women of color to underscore the ways in which their work was so often omitted from the (feminist) anthropological canon. It was an epiphany of sorts when Bolles shifted the focus from critiquing whom we do not cite (though certainly acknowledging the importance of this) to becoming actively engaged with locating diverse scholarship in order to influence our work and knowledge development.

ESSENTIALS

Excerpt from "Telling It Straight: Black Feminist Intellectual Thought in Anthropology" by Lynn Bolles

Lynn Bolles *received her PhD in anthropology from Rutgers University and taught in women's studies, anthropology, African American studies, American studies, comparative literature and the Latin American Studies Center at the University of Maryland until her retirement in 2015. Her research focuses on women, organized labor, and gender relations in globalization in the African Diaspora concentrating in the Caribbean, Latin*

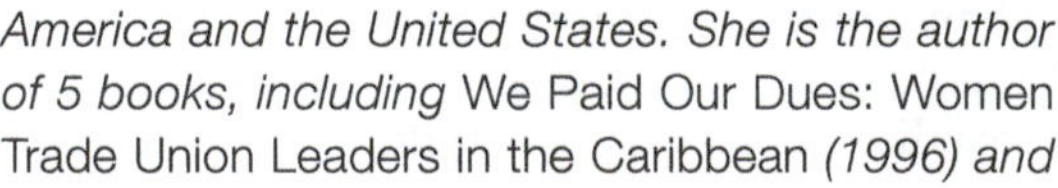

America and the United States. She is the author of 5 books, including We Paid Our Dues: Women Trade Union Leaders in the Caribbean *(1996) and* Sister Jamaica: A Study of Women, Work and Households in Kingston *(1996). Bolles is a past president of the Caribbean Studies Association (1997–1998), the Association for Feminist Anthropology (2001–2003), the Society for the Anthropology of North America (2009–2011), and the Association of Black Anthropologists (ABA, 1983). She also served on the cultural seat of the executive board of the American Anthropological Association (2012–2015). In 2013, Bolles received the "ABA Legacy" award for outstanding mentorship, contributions to anthropology, and unswerving service to the ABA.*

(continued)

The important work of Black feminist anthropologists is not only marginalized or made invisible by the canon-setting White men, who, until quite recently, controlled anthropology and are its primary practitioners, but as I emphasized earlier, also by their European American feminist counterparts. . . Many of the writers of the key canonical texts in feminist anthropology reproduced the practices of exclusion practiced by the discipline at large. A quick review of six major texts of women, gender, and feminist anthropology provides a clue to the answer.

The two foundational texts in feminist anthropology were published within months of each other, *Woman, Culture, and Society* (1974) edited by Michelle Rosaldo and Louise Lamphere and *Toward an Anthropology of Women* (1975) edited by Rayna Rapp (then Reiter). Between the two, [none] of the contributors [were] African American. At the same time, Black women anthropologists, as graduate students, untenured and the few tenured ones were working toward building the Association of Black Anthropologists as their research on women was embedded in the struggles of colonialism, neo-colonialism, and racism at home and abroad. They knew each other's names and supported one another. [Yet] they were not invited to join the feminist anthropological publishing collaborations of that time. . . .

The point still remains clear . . . that even though African American feminist anthropologists publish, their works fail to be adequately recognized and cited by anthropologists, including those who count as allies and colleagues. The verification of the merit of the work—the citations that references to the original work—is absent in the majority of those six influential texts. Anthropologists, like other scholars cite authors whose opinions they concur with, or are of use value to them in their research. This is a practice learned in graduate [and undergraduate] training . . . In that setting . . . students learn who is "good," become skilled at presenting evidence to the contrary, and become critical in their analysis of methodology, theory, and other aspects of research and scholarship. Without exposure, there is no scholarly location to provide evidence for assessment. . .

Citation indices are an important source for documenting the differential rates of citation of anthropologists, including feminist anthropologists. By and far, anthropologists of color, especially those of African descent, have been out of this citation loop. As mentioned earlier, African American feminist anthropologists tend to cite each other, particularly in similar subfields, but often their contributions to the wider field are not recognized—virtually absent. If the citation wars have meaning in the modern academy, as Lutz and others who have carried out similar research claim, then in both short and long runs African American scholars are/will be faceless and voice-less in the anthropological record.

Consider this a challenge to young scholars. Expand your list of whom you cite on a particular topic and the politics of that decision. Black women anthropologists are productive and are in need of all the support they can garner by their peers and colleagues. If feminist anthropology is going to learn from the past, it must maintain a constant vigilance of the process. The cost of not doing so continues the practice of miseducation and omission in the field and the invisibility of Black women's intellectual thought in the field of anthropology.

Source: A. Lynn Bolles, "Telling the Story Straight: Black Feminist Intellectual Thought in Anthropology." *Transforming Anthropology* 21, no. 1 (2013): 65, 66, 69.

Ultimately, Bolles puts the onus on each of us as feminist scholars and writers to make it *our business* to seek out, and incorporate, innovative research from scholars whose work is often ignored because of structural inequities. This allows us to produce the best (feminist) ethnographic work possible. In fact, we don't believe that this should only be a feminist project, but rather all scholars should look for diverse interlocutors as they approach their research. Anthropologist Elizabeth Chin (see spotlight in chapter 5) once half-joked that we should have photos next to the authors' names in every work cited, reference, or bibliography. Although it is easy to challenge the politics of using visual identification—being both an imperfect way to identify people, as well as problematic that people would need to be identified in any way—this would offer a startling "**taxonomy**" of how identity can, and so often does, shape those who are credited in scholarly work. Ultimately, citation is quite an effective "reproductive technology," as media and communications scholar Sara Ahmed points out on her research blog, "Feminist Killjoys."

We argue that being insistent about developing a diverse intellectual geneaology is key to feminist ethnography. But it need not be done in isolation. It should, in fact, involve reaching out to others who conduct similar work—whether they be peers in class, your professors, other feminist scholars you connect with through hearing campus talks, attending conferences, et cetera. It also involves looking at those you admire and seeing who they cite in their research: who has influenced them? Being attentive to the politics of citation is also an important reminder that

 ESSENTIALS

Excerpt from "Making Feminist Points," on the Feminist Killjoys Blog by Sara Ahmed

***Sara Ahmed** teaches in the department of media and communications at Goldsmiths' University of London. She is the author of seven single-authored books, including* Cultural Politics of Emotion *(2004),* Queer Phenomenology: Orientations, Objects, Others *(2006), and* The Promise of Happiness *(2010). She is the co-convenor of the MA in Gender, Media and Culture, the convenor of the Feminist Postgraduate Forum, and the director of the Centre for Feminist Research. She is currently writing a book,* Living a Feminist Life, *which, draws on everyday experiences of being a feminist, in particular experiences of being a feminist killjoy, as a way of doing feminist theory. Ahmed is also the author of* Feminist Killjoys, *her research blog, where she wrote the excerpt below about the politics of citation:*

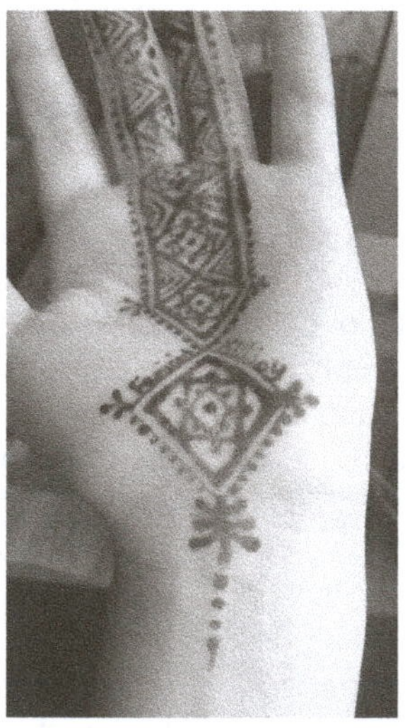

Feminist Killjoy henna tattoo by Roxie Freeman, a double major in women's, gender, and sexuality studies and psychology at the College of Wooster, who is completing their undergraduate thesis on Ahmed's *The Promise of Happiness*, exploring how "happiness" is represented in women's magazines such as *Ebony, Lesbian News*, and *Cosmopolitan*.

I would describe citation as a rather successful reproductive technology, a way of reproducing the world around certain bodies.

These citational structures can form what we call disciplines. I was once asked to contribute to a sociology course, for example, and found that all the core readings were by male writers. I pointed this out and the course convener implied that "that" was simply a reflection of the history of the discipline. Well: this is a very selective history! The reproduction of a discipline can be the reproduction of *these techniques of selection*, ways of making certain bodies and thematics core to the discipline, and others not even part.

I have noticed as well that these citational practices can occur even when the topic is one that feminists have written extensively about. I recently attended a conference in which there was a panel on reproductive justice, a topic that feminists have written rather extensively about, and two of the three papers were entirely framed around the work of male philosophers! Indeed men can even cite only men when critiquing male privilege. . . .

We are not just talking about citation within academic contexts. We are talking about what I think of as screening techniques: how certain bodies take up spaces by screening out the existence of others. If you are screened out (by virtue of the body you have) then you simply do not even appear or register to others. You might even have to become insistent, wave your arms, even shout, just to appear. And then of course how you appear (as being insistent) means you still tend not to be heard.

Source: feministkilljoys. "Making Feminist Points." Feministkilljoys, September 11, 2013. http://feministkilljoys.com/2013/09/11/making-feminist-points/.

feminists must broaden their intellectual circles of influence, which means making the work of historically marginalized authors more visible and valued. In that way, we contribute to revising and shaping broader ethnographic canons.

Thinking Through . . .

An Intellectual Genealogy

Select a contemporary ethnographer and trace that person's intellectual genealogy. You should begin by researching the ethnographer's training (mentors, advisors, and dissertation committee members), as well as reading their work to see which theorists and other ethnographers that person cites. Do you see any of the trends noted above?

How Involved or Engaged Should a Feminist Ethnographer Be?

There are debates about positivist expectations that ethnographic work must be objective and neutral rather than humanistic that, for some, would certainly foreclose being an engaged scholar. Feminists have disputed the accusation that their position sacrifices objectivity. Some feminist scholars, in fact, have challenged the virtues of objectivity over subjectivity. Others argue that rejecting objectivity in favor of subjectivity means scholars succumb to radical **cultural relativism**, often critiqued as an "anything goes" philosophy, which clearly falters when one considers some complex cultural and political issues. For instance, even the most staunch radical cultural relativist would be hard pressed to argue for the validity or legitimacy of genocide or rape. Nevertheless, the specter of positivism continues to be a concern for many feminist ethnographers. Ishan Gordon-Ugarte's discussion underscores the continued necessity of engaging with critiques about subjectivity in feminist ethnographic work.

SPOTLIGHTS

Ishan Gordon-Ugarte on the Power and Potential Drawbacks of Challenging Positivism

***Ishan Gordon-Ugarte** is a doctoral student in cultural anthropology at the Graduate Center, City University of New York. Inspired by Black feminist ethnography, Gordon-Ugarte's dissertation research examines the social tensions around the sexuality of young Afro-Latina "Creole" women in Bluefields, Nicaragua. Here she tells us about the goals of her feminist ethnographic research, as well as her lingering concerns about balancing her feminist objectives of challenging power structures and gaining access to support and resources for her study.*

Afro-Latina "Creole" women's sexuality is contested terrain. These young women are caught between their families who seek to control the shame of their premarital sexuality, the young and older men who covet them sexually and romantically, and the state and state-like institutions, such as

(continued)

churches and schools, that seek to regulate their sexuality. The central thesis of my project is that race, gender, and class structure these women's lives, critically regulating their sexuality and compromising their reproductive rights. . . . By centering women in their struggles for agency in relationship to their own sexuality in the context of patriarchal institutions and interpersonal relations, I want to create a feminist ethnography that destabilizes the patriarchal structures that frame their lives.

Thanks to our feminist ancestors who exposed the fallacy of "value-free science," feminist ethnographers often use prescriptive ethics to examine power dynamics between subjects and researchers to ensure that research subjects are not exploited. This includes methodologically assaulting the exploitative and hierarchical relations of standard research that have been hallmarks of participant-observation in anthropology, and that created a persistent binary of Western Norm/non-Western Other anthropological authority over the object of study. While always mindful of the unavoidably exploitative nature of aspects of the ethnographer's practices, I will still use feminist ethics and methodologies in an attempt to rupture the power of the ethnographer. Following the praxis of feminist ethnographers I seek to create a relationship between researcher and researched that is equitable and reciprocal to ensure an interactive means of studying women and their sexuality in order to help to end exploitation of women in general, and as research subjects in particular.

I am a young woman who, like all young women of color, experiences quotidian hypersexualization. However, structures of race/sexuality not only shape our experiences, but provide us with the basis for contestation. Moreover, I was born in Bluefields on the Caribbean Coast of Nicaragua to a "Bi-racial Black" father born in Harlem, New York and a Creole mother born in the mines of Rosita and raised in Bluefields. Bluefields is my home. I identify nationally as Nicaraguan, ethnically as Afro Latina Creole, and racially as Black.

Feminist Anthropology has helped us to understand how differently positioned researchers, particularly those who are women, and specifically those of us who are Black women, can use the methodologies that an insider perspective allows. [This enables us] to grasp the multiple "truths" of any particular social reality, thus contributing to our understanding of social phenomena and our ability to transform them. In addition, the sum of my experiences in Bluefields culminates in my position as a loving insider (daughter, sister, cousin, friend, neighbor) that transforms a field work/community into a homework/family with potential for transformative practice.

Yet I have fears about the project too. Other ethnographers have told me horror stories about their inability to find funding because their work was too "radical" and too threatening to the existing powers that be. But how can my work truly be feminist if I do not question existing structures of oppressions that insidiously exclude, exploit, and maintain gender and racial stratification? Because of this, I worry about what intellectual sacrifices I will have to make in my work in order to find the resources to support my research.

In sociologist Ann Oakley's critical discussion of feminism and the social sciences, she challenges the feminist case against quantitative methods in favor of qualitative methods, and argues that positivism is ultimately a search for social facts that predict behavior.[23] The adequacy of positivist social science is guaranteed by objectivity, the absence of bias, and distance or removal of the researchers' values and experiences to ensure validity of the knowledge being understood and produced. Oakley is suggesting that positioning the debate as one of positivism versus anti-positivism takes away the gray area where positivist research, such as quantitative research, may be useful to activists and/or activist-scholars. She advocates the value of mixed-methods research, since creating a dichotomy between quantitative and qualitative approaches shuttles away the possibilities for one, and reifies the other. Given Gordon-Ugarte and Oakley's arguments, what do you think about the role of positivism in feminist ethnography?

SPOTLIGHTS

Mary L. Gray on the Labor of Feminist Ethnography

Mary L. Gray is a senior researcher at Microsoft Research and an associate professor in the Media School at Indiana University. She studied anthropology before receiving her PhD in communication from the University of California, San Diego. Her research explores how media access and everyday uses of technologies transform people's lives. Gray is the author of Out in the Country: Youth, Media, and Queer Visibility in Rural America *(2009).*

Last month [in 2015] someone sent me an email, cc'ing it to the entire faculty of the Media School, my home academic department. The person addressed it to me because I had been in the newspaper talking about LGBTQ issues and they wanted my peers and university administration to know their contempt for me as a scholar and the institution that supported such work. It was a screed about how homosexuals should not have legal rights and people like me should never be allowed to teach. I responded to the individual and the entire faculty, acknowledging the email and letting the person know that I would contact them directly. I then emailed the Media School faculty and asked that they not engage with the person, fearing that someone might decide to take on this hater and I would be left to clean up the mess. People have no idea what you have to deal with when you take a position as an activist ethnographer. Vitriolic emails like this are the clearest reminder of the cost that comes with being public. While they can be personally hurtful, they also underscore the yawning divide between those of us who can imagine being targeted by hatred and peers who cannot. But the experience can also be validating, showing others the need for our work. Another challenge may be the added weight if students identify with you and see you as a safe harbor on campus for issues around sexuality, race and class. But also, we run the risk of becoming the tokenized, resident person for whom both faculty and students rely on for support. So much happens through the bodies of scholars doing this work. It's not measureable and we don't feel entitled to ask for support. Peers who do work that is not as politically charged struggle to understand the vitriol and political work that activist scholars take on.

Additionally, Mary L. Gray underscores the labor associated with doing feminist work, particularly research that does not stem from a positivist framework, from within the academy. This labor, she argues, needs to be visible because, for some, it is just as fundamentally important and part of an academics' praxis as the other roles a researcher plays. Any ethnographer's research stands the chance of being misinterpreted, but when one has a long-term engagement or commitment to a community, those stakes may be higher.

What we find in Gray's case is that a scholar runs the risk of becoming the laser focus of a disaffected group or person who now have a place to deposit their hostility. This may make some scholars question the practicalities of being an engaged scholar. But Gray's commitment to activist work and public scholarship is an important intervention that calls into question the idea of positivist neutrality that is so often expected in knowledge production. But if a feminist researcher is committed to being an activist and does not claim neutrality, does that mean the scholarship is compromised? What does being "neutral" accomplish for a researcher? Is neutrality even possible in the context of feminist critiques of positivist research? For many feminist ethnographers, writing about these issues and debates has become a crucial part of their ethnographic work.

And for some feminist ethnographers, such as anthropologist Faye V. Harrison (see spotlight in chapter 4), engagement remains central to their work, not "an appropriated buzzword."[24] Deeply influenced by feminist and Pan-Africanist scholars Louise Lamphere, George Houston Bass, St. Clair Drake, Bridget O'Laughlin, and Michelle Rosaldo, Harrison has challenged the lines between activist engagement and academic production throughout her career. In an interview with Gina Athena Ulysse, Harrison envisions a field that centralizes engaged scholarship:

> Those of us who wish to align our scholarly endeavors with activism, advocacy, policy reformation and reaching wider audiences should be encouraged to do so. Moreover, the organizational means should exist to facilitate those pursuits. I don't want my students and my son, who is also a cultural anthropologist, to replicate the disciplinary alienation and negation that generations before them experienced. I'm working toward the anthropology I optimistically envisioned when all those years ago, I decided that I wanted to be an anthropologist when I grew up.[25]

Toward this end, Harrison's 1991 classic *Decolonizing Anthropology: Moving Further Toward an Anthropology for Liberation* was a key theoretical intervention in the field, emphasizing the political responsibility of intellectuals to interrogate "race and class disparities, which anthropologists are too prone to neglect or ignore . . . with gender to assume their rightful place at the center of political as well as theoretical deliberation."[26] Harrison's goal was and continues to be encouraging more ethnographers to become committed to liberating the discipline and engaging in scholarly inquiry aimed at transformation and liberation.

Conclusion

As with all decisions in practicing and producing feminist ethnography, it is crucial for the feminist ethnographer to critically think through their engagement. Exploring some of the debates and deliberations in feminist thinking and feminist

Thinking Through . . .

What Would A Feminist Ethnographer Do (WWFED)?

Identify a feminist ethnographer among the faculty at your school or at another school who you can interview in person, via online chat, or phone.* Develop a set of questions that will allow you to explore how they became a feminist ethnographer, and how they situate themselves with regard to one (or more) of the debates above. Some of the things you want to be sure to find out are: What is their discipline? How did they come to identify themselves as a feminist ethnographer? Who influenced their thinking about feminism? What does being a feminist or feminist ethnographer mean to them? How does being a feminist influence their research? Write a short essay discussing the feminist ethnographer's perspectives on the field. Ideally, you can share these, and note comparisons, with other class members.

**If they are unavailable, email questions, but understand that written responses are far less dynamic than verbal interactions.*

ethnography offers a window into how raising questions, and engaging in debate and deliberation can destabilize what may be considered resolved. One can certainly argue that feminist theorizing and feminist ethnography have grown from these debates. The questions we raise among ourselves and what influences our understandings of knowledge production can contribute to a feminist ethnographic literacy. In the following chapters, we take up some of the methods, methodologies, and styles of production that feminists have used to pursue these goals.

Suggested Resources

Begoña Aretxaga (1997) *Shattering Silence: Women, Nationalism, and Political Subjectivity in Northern Ireland.*

Richelle D. Schrock (2013) "The Methodological Imperatives of Feminist Ethnography," in *Journal of Feminist Scholarship.*

Decolonizing Knowledge: A Conversation between Dr. Linda Tuhiwai Smith, Dr. Michelle Fine, and Dr. Andrew Jolivette on community-based research within Indigenous communities (2013) https://www.youtube.com/watch?v=7lb7edhWghY.

Mary Maynard (2013) *Researching Women's Lives from a Feminist Perspective.*

Kamala Visweswaran (1994) *Fictions of Feminist Ethnography.*

Notes

1 Micaela di Leonardo, "Introduction: Gender, Culture and Political Economy: Feminist Anthropology in Historical Perspective," in *Gender at the Crossroads of Knowledge*, 1991, 7; Michelle Rosaldo and Louise Lamphere, eds., *Woman, Culture, and Society*,1974; Rayna Reiter (now Rapp), *Toward an Anthropology of Women*, 1975.

2 Linda Tuhiwai Smith, "Twenty-five Indigenous Projects," in *Decolonizing Methodologies*, 2012, 143–164.

3 Ngahuia Te Awekotuku and Manatu Maori, *He Tikanga Whakaaro: Research Ethics in the Maori Community*, 1991.

4 This section is adapted from Dána-Ain Davis, "Border Crossing: Intimacy and Feminist Activist Ethnography in the Age of Neoliberalism," *Feminist Activist Ethnography*, eds. Christa Craven and Dána-Ain Davis, 2013.

5 Marilyn Strathern, "An Awkward Relationship: The Case of Feminism and Anthropology," *Signs: Journal of Women and Society*, 1987.

6 Kamala Visweswaran, *Fictions of Feminist Ethnography*, 1994.

7 Judith Stacey, "Can There Be a Feminist Ethnography?" *Women's Studies International Forum*, 1988, 26.

8 Ibid., 24.

9 Dána-Ain Davis, "Border Crossing: Intimacy and Feminist Activist Ethnography in the Age of Neoliberalism," in *Feminist Activist Ethnography*, eds. Christa Craven and Dána-Ain Davis, 2013.

10 Lila Abu-Lughod, "Can There Be A Feminist Ethnography?" *Women & Performance: A Journal of Feminist Theory*, 1990.

11 Robin Morgan, *Sisterhood Is Global*, 1996, 1.

12 Janelle Monae, *The Electric Lady*, Wondaland Arts Society and Bad Boy Records, released 2013.

13 Micaela di Leonardo, ed., *Gender at the Crossroads of Knowledge*, 1991.

14 Patricia Zavella, "Feminist Insider Dilemmas: Constructing Ethnic Identity with Chicana Informants," *Feminist Dilemmas in Fieldwork*, ed. Diane L. Wolf, 1996.

15 Kirin Narayan, "How Native Is a 'Native' Anthropologist ?" *American Anthropologist*, 1993.

16 Anthothy Naaeke et al., "Insider and Outsider Perspective in Ethnographic Research," Proceedings of the New York State Communication Association, 2011. Available at: http://docs.rwu.edu/nyscaproceedings/vol2010/iss1/9.

17 Lorena Muñoz, "Brown, Queer and Gendered: Queering the Latina/o 'Street-Scapes' in Los Angeles," in *Queer Methods and Methodologies*, 2010, 55.

18 Ibid., 60.

19 Dorothy E. Smith, *Writing the Social*, 1999.

[20] Patricia Hill Collins, *Black Feminist Thought*, 2009.

[21] Jafari Allen, *¡Venceremos?: The Erotics of Black Self-making in Cuba,* 2011, 117.

[22] Virginia Dominguez, Matthew Guttman, and Catherine Lutz, "Problem of Gender and Citations Raised Again in New Research Study," *Anthropology News*, 2014.

[23] Ann Oakley, "Gender, Methodology and People's Ways of Knowing: Some Problems with Feminism and The Paradigm Debate in Social Science," *Sociology*, 1998.

[24] Gina A. Ulysse, "Faye V. Harrison and Why Anthropology Still Matters," in *The Huffington Post*, 2013.

[25] Ibid.

[26] Faye V. Harrison, *Decolonizing Anthropology: Moving Further Toward an Anthropology for Liberation*, 1997 [orig. 1991], 9.

CHAPTER 4

How Does One *Do* Feminist Ethnography?

This chapter covers the process of developing and doing a feminist ethnographic research project. You will learn how to design a feminist methodological approach to, and employ a variety of methods in, a feminist ethnographic project by examining the following questions:

- How should a feminist ethnographer choose a topic?
- Can an ethnographer's personal experience be a part of a study?
- What methods have been useful to feminist ethnographers?

Spotlights *in this chapter:*

- Elisabeth Engebretsen on Choosing Methods and Shifting Knowledge
- Tracy Fisher on Using Oral/Life History to address Feminist Ethnographic Questions
- Whitney Battle-Baptiste on Historical Archaeology & Literary Fiction

Essentials *in this chapter:*

- Faye V. Harrison, "Feminist Methodology . . ." in *The Gender of Globalization*
- Lila Abu-Lughod, *Veiled Sentiments*
- *Naisargi Dave, Queer Activism in India*
- Caroline C. Wang and Mary Ann Burris, "Photovoice"

You will also be ***Thinking Through . . .***

- Three Options to Explore Methodological Possibilities

This chapter explores the creation of a feminist methodology and the kind of methods that feminist ethnographers can use to carry out their research. In part, it offers a "how to" guide with the goal of introducing you to basic principles and methods that have been useful to ethnographic researchers and fruitfully employed by feminist ethnographers. Yet this is also a theoretical chapter, in the sense that conducting ethnography involves far more than the successful application of particular research methods. In fact, as visual sociologist Alison Rooke notes in her ethnographic project exploring the interconnections of spatiality and subjectivity for working class lesbian and bisexual women in Britain, "Ethnography [including feminist and queer ethnography] is undoubtedly methodologically untidy."[1]

By focusing on methods and methodology, this chapter also invites you to imagine (and possibly develop) your own project, consider how to create feminist research questions, choose research methods suitable for a feminist ethnographic project, and begin to think through how choices about method and methodology influence the production of feminist ethnography. As you read this chapter, remember that many examples and issues will resurface in subsequent chapters (and we'll return to a few briefly introduced before). Indeed, it is ultimately the ways that feminist theory and methodology can contribute to scholarly aims and activist possibilities for feminist ethnography that we hope you will engage in as you move through the rest of this book.

In order to do this, differentiating between one's research methodology and one's methods is essential. Developing a feminist methodology—a body of methods

ESSENTIALS

Excerpt from "Method and Methodology" by Faye V. Harrison

Faye V. Harrison *received her PhD from Stanford University in 1982 and currently teaches in anthropology and African American studies at the University of Florida-Gainesville. Harrison is the editor of* Decolonizing Anthropology: Moving Further toward an Anthropology for Liberation *(2010[1991]) and author of* Outsider Within: Reworking Anthropology in the Global Age *(2008). She discusses the importance of not conflating method and methodology in "Feminist Methodology as a Tool for Ethnographic Inquiry on Globalization" in* The Gender of Globalization: Women Navigating Cultural and Economic Marginalities *(Nandini Gunewardena and Ann Kingsolver 2007). Expanding on philosopher Sandra Harding's distinction between epistemology, method, and methodology in her classic 1987 edited collection* Feminism & Methodology,* *Harrison writes:*

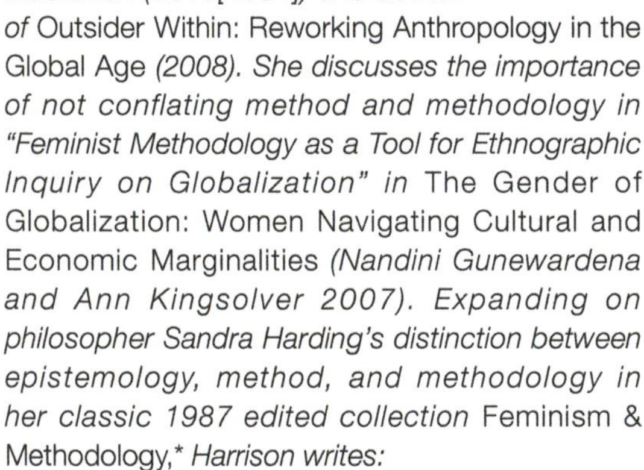

Methods are specific procedures, operations, or techniques for identifying and collecting the evidence necessary to answer research questions. In and of themselves, they are not feminist or non-feminist. Therefore, there are no "feminist methods" per se. However, there are "feminist methodologies," because methodologies articulate conceptual, theoretical, and ethical perspectives on the whats, whys and hows of research and the production of knowledge. . . . Methodologies provide the philosophical or logical rationale for the links researchers make among theory, pragmatic research strategies, evidence, and the empirical world. . . . A feminist methodology clues us in on which combination of methods is likely to be most suitable for meeting the pragmatic and ethical objectives of a feminist research project. . . .

Although ethnography is typically characterized principally in terms of qualitative methods, its methodological repertoire may indeed include quantitative techniques, particularly those appropriately and meaningfully triangulated with the styles and procedures that are ethnography's traditional cornerstones—participant-observation and various kinds of intensive interviewing. . . .

We might even claim that ethnographic methodologies cover the range of research theories that consider experience-near participant-observation or participatory-immersion approaches central to the process of asking researchable questions, finding the best answers by some combination of techniques, and producing new layers of knowledge from analyzing and theorizing the research results. . . . [In this way,] ethnography has been conceptualized and deployed as a feminist methodology.

Source: Faye V. Harrison. "Feminist Methodology as a Tool for Ethnographic Inquiry on Globalization." In *The Gender of Globalization: Women Navigating Cultural and Economic Marginalities*, edited by Nandini Gunewardena and Ann Kingsolver, 23–31. Santa Fe, NM: School for Advanced Research Press, 2007, 25.

*Sandra G. Harding, *Feminism and Methodology*, 1987, 2–3.

that allows us to create knowledge by engaging with feminist theoretical and ethical perspectives—is the crux of getting at the business of *doing* ethnography. As Harrison emphasizes, methods themselves are neither inherently feminist nor nonfeminist. However, they offer important tools to aid in gathering data that is then subject to feminist analysis and interpretation. It is important to remember that two ethnographers could use the very same methods—say participant-observation and in-depth interviews—to study prostitution, but approach it from very different theoretical and methodological orientations. Thus, it is *how* a feminist ethnographer utilizes and contextualizes various methods that enable them to contribute to feminist ethnographic research.

Recall, for instance, Cheryl Rodriquez, who is spotlighted in chapter 1. In our interview with her, she too discussed the methodological approaches to her work as what makes it explicitly feminist. She notes:

> First of all, I rely on the work of feminist thinkers. Sometimes that feminist thinker is not necessarily an ethnographer, but that person's theoretical perspective can contribute in some way to my own thinking and to what I am trying to accomplish. The first thing is the literature, being grounded in feminist literature. And then in terms of methodology, I just think that many of us, even those who don't call themselves feminists, have tried to transform what we think of as ethnographic work into a much kinder, gentler, more compassionate type of research where we understand our role as researchers and where we know that we are in the way. We know that we are changing things just by being there. In other words, [we must think] about the implications of our presence as researchers. Because our work involves situating ourselves in some place, in some institution, [that] affects people's lives. Typically, we are not just sitting in a room—we are not supposed to be anyway—just making stuff up. So for me, my methodology is about self-awareness and being caring, and understanding the threatening aspects of my asking questions and having a real solid sense of what I am trying to get at.

As a part of this awareness, it is important for feminist ethnographers to think carefully about how they refer to those who participate in their research. It should already have become apparent (we hope) that when it comes to the language that feminist ethnographers employ, our words, their histories and connotations, and their (sometimes multiple) meanings, are very important. Ethnographers have referred to those who participate in their research in many different ways: as subjects, informants, participants, contributors, respondents, interpreters, interlocutors, and those with whom they had especially close relationships as key informants, gatekeepers, coauthors, and collaborators. Although we do not wish to anoint any one of these terms as appropriate for all feminist ethnographic projects, we do believe that thinking through the meanings and connotations of each is important as we consider research topics and develop our methodological choices. For instance, what type of relationship do you hope to develop with those who participate in your research (this may be different for short- and long-term projects)? Does the term you choose suggest a hierarchical relationship between you, the researcher, and the researched (is this your intent? could inequities be minimized?)? How much shared work does the term suggest? Are those involved in your research prepared to make this commitment of time and energy? What connotations might the term have outside of your discipline, and outside of academia? For instance, "respondent" and "subject" have a long history of use in psychology to describe those who fill out surveys or are involved in experiments—will your research aim to replicate, or differ from, such studies?

We choose to use "participant," a more neutral term, acknowledging that feminist ethnographers have used others in their publications (and we maintain their usage when citing or referring to their work). Beyond naming those involved in our ethnographic work, how we phrase and frame our research questions and how we describe and implement our methods (i.e., contemporary feminists avoid terminology like "giving voice to" those in their research) should be subject to the same types of preliminary interrogation as we begin our projects. It is beyond the scope of this text to discuss all of these possibilities, but the points we wish to emphasize here are that (a) feminist ethnographers must think about language to describe their research *as they design their study* and (b) as feminist ethnographers approach their writing, it is important to explain how and why particular choices were made (or why and how changes occurred during or after the research encounter).

Doing feminist ethnography requires significant practice, and how methods are employed is (or at least should be) a result of reading about the experiences of many previous ethnographers. Their pitfalls and successes have influenced the ways that these methods have been practiced over time. In our interview with sociologist Jennifer Bickham Mendez (see Spotlight in chapter 7), for instance, she likened the methodological process for each feminist ethnographer to practicing yoga: it is a life-long exploration, and what it looks like—what comes easily and what is particularly challenging—will be different for each person.

How Should a Feminist Ethnographer Choose a Topic?

Choices about where and with whom to conduct research are necessarily riddled with basic and sometimes mundane questions: Where do you live or have the ability to travel? What will it cost to go to your research site and what funding is available for your research? Do you know people in the community you hope to access? How might your identity, your personality, your similarity and/or difference to those you will interact with impact your research? What potential logistical or ethical challenges can you foresee in your fieldwork? Are there precautions you can take ahead of time to mediate these concerns?

Beyond these basic questions (relevant for any ethnographic project), feminist anthropologist Margery Wolf says, "Choosing a research topic sounds rather like a chapter title in an elementary methodology textbook, but it could also be one in a book of feminist ethics."[2] Indeed, feminist researchers have a long history of challenging inequalities—both in their application of research methods, and through their research objectives. A principal priority in feminist ethnographic work, since its inception, is to honor what is important to the people you are working with. This is true both in terms of topic, as well as how they participate in your work.

In the following Spotlight, Elisabeth Engebretsen discusses the way she developed her methodology for her feminist ethnographic work with queer Chinese women, and how it ultimately shifted her "Western" assumptions about gender and sexuality as a Norwegian ethnographer trained in Europe and the United States.

Feminist ethnographers often engage in projects reflecting particular political commitments, or develop research agendas that highlight gender dynamics/issues and intentionally employ methods in feminist ways. In some cases a feminist ethnographer may be asked by a community or organization to work on a particular project. Remembering what makes an ethnographic project feminist is when it is in the hands of a feminist—someone who pays attention to gender and power dynamics—who is intentional in their research design, and draws from previous feminist scholarship to conduct feminist ethnography. It is also true that a

SPOTLIGHTS

Elisabeth Engebretsen on Choosing Methods and Shifting Knowledge

Elisabeth Lund Engebretsen *received her PhD in anthropology from the London School of Economics and Political Science. She is a senior lecturer in gender studies at the Centre for Gender Research in the University of Oslo, Norway, and an affiliated researcher with the Amsterdam Research Centre for Gender and Sexuality, at the University of Amsterdam in the Netherlands. She is the author of* Queer Women in Urban China: An Ethnography *(2013) and coeditor of* Queer/Tongzhi China: New Perspectives on Research, Activism and Media Cultures *(2015). She is a co-convener of the European Network for Queer Anthropology.*

The methodological specifics of my work have been shaped by the fact that lesbianism was and is relatively invisible in society, and homosexuality remains taboo even though it is not criminalized as such. In my initial study, I wanted to focus specifically on women because there was, at the time, no work being done on "queer women"; Chinese homosexuality was by default focusing on men. Few women were "out," and managing confidentiality—also within community settings—was essential. Conventional interviews, focus groups and other structured research methods would not have worked in this context. Instead, I came to rely on unstructured, semi-casual conversations with women in social and community spaces of their choice. I did eventually conduct and digitally record 15 semi-structured interviews, but they served a complimentary function. As I came to know more people and get a sense of the concerns that shaped their everyday lives, I revised my initial topic guide, to focus on three broad themes: (1) personal life, including intimate experiences and sex, romantic relationships and desires, and the process of coming to terms with same-sex desires; (2) negotiating family and social life, including marriage pressure and children; and (3) community experience, including activism and politics. Whereas I initially imagined my research to concern identity politics and activism, I learned from my research participants about the ways that broader issues shape queer lives. This insight profoundly altered my understanding of how to study sexual and gender subjectivities transnationally, relativized my "Western" knowledge of these matters, and it continues to inform my work.

Photo: Uni You

person may shape a feminist project on a topic that does not have an inherently feminist focus. For instance, anthropologist Matthew Gutmann's now-classic discussion of changing male identities and practices with respect to fathering, sexuality, housework, alcohol, violence, and the cultural history of machismo in *Meanings of Macho: Being a Man in Mexico City*, offered a feminist approach to gender images, practices, and beliefs about *machismo*. The topic of masculinity or *machismo* could be approached from many perspectives—indeed it has often been approached from a decidedly patriarchal perspective—but the theoretical insights and analytical techniques Gutmann employed, as well as collaborative methodologies such as returning to participants with their initial answers to questions and continuing discussions, mark his approach as a feminist one.[3]

Feminist ethnographers must also consider the desires of participants regarding how they engage with ethnographic work. At times, feminist ethnographers develop collaborative projects that fully involve participants in designing, implementing, analyzing, and producing research. At other times, feminist ethnographers make strategic choices to involve participants (or select participants) in generating questions for the project, reading and discussing interview **transcripts** (typed copies of recorded interviews), participating in focus groups for data analysis, et cetera. Many feminist ethnographers have considered the benefits and the challenges of collaborative work. When anthropologist Karen Brodkin Sacks conducted fieldwork with African American hospital workers for her book, *Caring by the Hour: Women, Work, and Organizing at Duke Medical Center*, for instance, she positioned her work as part of a feminist and radical tradition:

> It takes sides and challenges the idea that there is a privileged, objective, and neutral point of view, that observer and observed, analyst and subject are unrelated. Among other things, this involved sharing my interpretations with activist workers and submitting prepublication drafts for criticism. Each of these activities had its own consequences, and facing them with more or less success has in turn shaped the final work. To ask those with whom I was working to share in my research was easier and democratic in theory than it was in practice. Such participation demands more work from people than the most thoughtful interview. It also contains a hidden constraint: that the co-analyst [must] either approach the issues guided by my assumptions and questions, or challenge them.[4]

Another example of choosing a topic with collaborative intention is Swedish anthropologist Ulrika Dahl's collaborative "femme-on-femme" ethnographic research. What she terms a "femme-inist" ethnography calls into question "the dichotomy between the theorizing academic and her 'informants'."[5] Her collaborative ethnography with gender variant queer visual artist Del LaGrace Volcano, *Femmes of Power: Exploding Queer Femininities*,[6] provides an example of feminist efforts to include participants as coresearchers and coproducers of research, both as objects and subjects of research.

> Through sharing many moments of making images with femmes, I was able to follow how collaboration works in the production of representation, and learn about the intimacy of photographic art and about the mutual trust that is required in order to produce a carefully framed image with many layers. Through "participant-observation" in the photographic sessions, I gained a tremendous respect for the femmes who were willing to partake in the project and for the labour it takes to make images under what at times were rather difficult conditions of cold, rain, snow, crowd intervention and so on. In many cases, the very production of the image turned into a public spectacle, which in and of itself contributed to the reconfiguration of public representations of femininity.[7]

In an effort to create a collaborative "queer archive," Dahl includes performative and written work by the authors, performers, and artists that she researches into her publications.[8]

Ultimately, there is no one "right" way to make choices about a topic, research design, or potential collaboration in feminist ethnographic projects. But feminist ethnographers must be deliberate in thinking through the relationships they hope to build with participants, as well as attending to the power dynamics inherent to social research. There is no completely equitable ethnographic encounter (see chapter 3 on Debates), but we believe that feminist ethnographers should work toward as balanced an exchange as possible with those involved in their research. Florence Babb, who conducts her anthropological work in Latin America and the Caribbean (see Spotlight in chapter 2), says she actualizes her feminist practice by spending sufficient time with a group of people to build a relationship and trust, enabling her to deepen her understanding of their lives and of the questions she wants to address in her research. It is important, she argues, to remain flexible so that she can revise her research plans as things move along, taking her cues from the people she is working with and remaining mindful of their differences. Babb points out that these may or may not be feminist methods:

> I think they reflect my desire to respond to those I work with and to try to produce work that they would deem worthy of their time and collaboration. I make an effort to be sensitive to differences of power between myself and my collaborators, and seek out individuals who might not be the customary spokespeople in their communities. Women and others who may be socially marginal are often central to my interest.

Can an Ethnographer's Personal Experience Be a Part of a Study?

We begin this section with the often-quoted feminist slogan: the Personal is Political. When it comes to feminist ethnographic research, this could not be truer. Feminist sociologists Dorothy E. Smith and Patricia Hill Collins have emphasized that an individual's knowledge and opinions develop from one's experiences in different social locations. One's perspective always involves multiple, intersecting factors. Feminists have a long history of valuing personal experience, and how it informs and often becomes part of our scholarship.

Feminist ethnographers often discuss personal aspects of their lives that motivated them to embark on particular projects, or compelled them to approach a project in particular ways. Anthropologist Rayna Rapp, whose research centers on gender, science, and technology studies, opens her feminist ethnography *Testing Women, Testing the Fetus: The Social Impact of Amniocentesis in America* with a chapter entitled "How Methodology Bleeds into Daily Life," in which she intimately interlaces her own experience with prenatal diagnosis with those of participants in her study, alongside a broader review of biomedical and feminist research on new reproductive technologies.[9] Sharing those experiences can legitimate ethnographic inquiry. But it can also highlight the differences that may become apparent because of other aspects of identity and privilege. For Rapp, this necessitated having what she calls an "open-ended methodology," meaning that she followed opportunities to interview people on the "outer reaches" of her sample (which originally included women undergoing—or opting out of—prenatal diagnostic tests), including disability rights activists, pregnant friends seeking advice, and an even younger reporter sent to interview Rapp about her research. In many settings, she noted, it became increasingly difficult to tell who was interviewing whom.

Sharing cultural connections with participants can also shape ethnographers' experiences, sometimes in quite unexpected ways. Palestinian-American anthropologist Lila Abu-Lughod has written about her experiences with what she calls "halfie anthropology," fieldwork conducted by bicultural or multicultural anthropologists who share a partial belonging with those involved in their research. In her first book, *Veiled Sentiments: Honor and Poetry in a Bedouin Society*,[10] Abu-Lughod discusses how she began her fieldwork among the Awlad 'Ali Bedouin in the Western Desert of Egypt in 1978 with her father as intermediary.

Abu-Lughod's experience offers an important reminder of how our identities as "insiders" and "outsiders," and all the shades of in-between that these seemingly exhaustive terms elide, always matter in the ethnographic encounter. It is our job as feminist ethnographers to be attentive to positionality as we embark on our research, and discuss the inevitable (and sometimes multiple) impacts of our identity

ESSENTIALS

Excerpt from *Veiled Sentiments* by Lila Abu-Lughod

***Lila Abu-Lughod** trained at Harvard University and teaches in anthropology and women's and gender studies at Columbia University. She has published seven books drawing on her experiences with long-term participant-observation in Egypt and the Middle East. Her most recent,* Do Muslim Women Really Need Saving? *(2013) offers a scathing critique of popular images of victimized Muslim women that are often used to justify U.S. militarization toward their "rescue." Here, we highlight an excerpt from her first book,* Veiled Sentiments: Honor and Poetry in a Bedouin Society, *published in 1986 and reissued in 2000, which remains widely assigned in courses on ethnography:*

I suspect that few, if any, fathers of anthropologists accompany them to the field to make their first contacts. But my father had insisted that he had something to do in Egypt and might just as well plan his trip to coincide with mine. I had accepted his offer only reluctantly, glad to have the company but also a bit embarrassed by the idea. Only after living with the Bedouins for a long time did I begin to comprehend some of what had underlain my father's quiet but firm insistence. As an Arab, although by no means a Bedouin [he had grown up in Jaffa, Palestine], he knew his own culture and society well enough to know that a young, unmarried woman traveling alone on uncertain business was an anomaly. She would have been suspect and would have a hard time persuading people of her respectability.

[Abu-Lughod had been convinced that her half Arab heritage, having lived in Egypt for four years as a child and having spent summers with her family in Jordan, would allow her to overcome any suspicions by behaving properly, but] What I had not considered was that respectability was reckoned not just in terms of behavior in interpersonal interactions but also in the relationship to the larger social world. I had failed to anticipate that people as conservative as the Bedouins, for whom belonging to tribe and family are paramount and the education of girls novel, would assume that a woman alone must have so alienated her family, especially her male kin, that they no longer cared about her. Worse yet, perhaps she had done something so immoral that they had ostracized her. Any girl valued by her family, especially an unmarried girl whose virginity and reputation were critical to a good match, would not be left unprotected to travel alone at the mercy of anyone who wished to take advantage of her. By accompanying me, my father hoped to lay any such suspicions to rest.

Source: Lila Abu-Lughod, *Veiled Sentiments: Honor and Poetry in a Bedouin Society*. Updated ed. with a new preface. Berkeley: University of California Press, 1999 (orig 1986), 11–12.

in our writing. Abu-Lughod experience also reminds us that there is much that an ethnographer can learn about one's location through fieldwork—as she did about Bedouin understandings of gender and sexuality, the importance of family and community, and respectability—that can never be taught in books, or even by previous ethnographers who do not share one's particular identity.

Life-altering events may also have significant impacts on the ways that feminist ethnographers are accepted (or not) in the field, as well as the ways they think about their work. For some, this has been a diagnosis of a life-threatening illness or the death of a parent or spouse. For anthropologist Elise Andaya having children profoundly shifted her approach to analysis and writing her ethnography, *Conceiving Cuba: Reproduction, Women, and the State in the Post-Soviet Era*:

> Still childless when I conducted the bulk of this fieldwork, the fact of becoming a mother (twice over) during the long process of analysis and writing has inevitably meant that I have reread the material collected for this book in the context of my own U.S.-centered experiences of prenatal care, gendered labor and household economies, and the home/work balance, heightening my appreciation for both the difficulties and the benefits of mothering under Cuban socialism of the twenty-first century. This has also entailed grappling with a central tension: as a feminist, I applaud the Cuban state's commitment to the provision of services such as subsidized childcare and free and accessible abortion and prenatal care. Also as a feminist, however, I am compelled to critically examine the often unintended consequences of state policies as they shape women's lives in post-Soviet Cuba.[11]

For communications scholar Ahmet Atay, his identity as a queer diasporic Turkish Cypriot man and his use of the Internet to establish a diasporic community influenced his cyberethnography of diasporic masculinity. In *Globalization's Impact on Cultural Identity Formation: Queer Diasporic Males in Cyberspace*, Atay writes that self-awareness was integral throughout his study from choosing what to observe, what methods to use, what data to collect, and how to write about a cultural group that defied geospatial boundaries. Reflecting on his own identity, he writes:

> Reflexivity was a central part of my research process on diaporic queer bodies. In order to make sense of my own life and in-between experiences, I turned outwards to study cultural groups, particularly diasporic queer bodies, and their cultural identity formation through mediated forms, particularly through the Internet and cyberspace technologies. Therefore, I had to be constantly aware of my own positionality in this research. Understanding my reasons to select particular web pages and Internet-based social networks as part of my cyberfield, realizing how emotional and intellectual states interfered with my data collection, selection, and finally the writing process helped me to reflect on my own involvement in this research. For me, reflexivity became a way of finding my own voice in this research, while I reflected on others who are similar and also different, in terms of lived queer diasporic experiences and positionalities.[12]

Feminist ethnographers' commitment to reflexivity may also extend to the relationship an ethnographer has with particular participants. For example, Alisse Waterston describes her work, *My Father's Wars: Migration, Memory, and the Violence of a Century* as "intimate ethnography," where she centers the narrative around his life (not her own, as an autoethnographic account would) through her interviews with him and those who knew him, archival research, and participant-observation in the areas he lived. As Waterston writes:

> The dual daughter-anthropologist role makes it difficult to place this book in an established genre. It is not just my father's biography, not just his narrated memoir; it is not about the anthropologist, not about the daughter, nor is it only about cultural framework or national histories or the violence that wreaked havoc during my father's lifetime. It is about all these things at once.[13]

Most contemporary ethnographers engage in some form of reflexivity in their work, though considering the ethics of fieldwork encounters in relation to an ethnographer's positionality has been important for feminist ethnographers with their attention to power and privilege.

What Methods Have Been Useful to Feminist Ethnographers?

Feminist ethnographers can use traditional and/or experimental methods. These typically include participant-observation—often considered the hallmark of ethnographic research—and many have integrated life history and in-depth interviewing, surveys, the analysis of archival or cultural materials, participatory research, and interpretive communities in their work. In fact, **mixed-methods** approaches, using several research methods together for a particular project, are common in feminist ethnographic work. Many feminist ethnographers, such as anthropologist Leith Mullings in her article "African American Women Making Themselves: Notes on the Role of Black Feminist Research," have made compelling arguments for blending feminist ethnographic approaches, including participant-observation and in-depth interviewing, with multidisciplinary collaborative community research, particularly toward political aims and efforts to shape public policy.[14] Mullings worked with anthropologist Alaka Wali on their book *Stress and Resilience: The Social Context of Reproduction in Central Harlem*. They partnered with the New York Urban League's Harlem Birth Right project, which sought to understand and combat the high rates of infant mortality in the Harlem Community. By partnering with the project, Mullings and Wali included community members in the design of questions and methods and in the implementation of the ethnographic research.[15] The result is that the book incorporates the voices of women in the community who document their own experiences in words and participatory engagement with the study.

Ultimately, however, it is the feminist practice of paying attention to power differentials that should guide methodological choice. As the quote by Faye V. Harrison in the first Essential in this chapter underscores, research methods themselves are neither feminist nor nonfeminist. They offer us tools through which to collect data, and are used in a variety of scholarly projects. Rather, it is our methodology—the rationale we create for the links we make among feminist theory, our research strategies and ethical decisions, the data we collect, and its relevance to the world—that is what marks our research as feminist ethnography. Nevertheless, the choices we make to utilize and/or combine specific methods are critical to the success of feminist ethnographic research and should be both pragmatic and political. Pragmatically, we must ask ourselves: what methods will give us the data we need to answer our research questions? What limitations exist for particular methods and will this undermine our research goals? What possibilities are there for combining methods (and perhaps collaborating with other researchers and/or participants) to broaden the net we cast for data that can inform our project?

In this section, we introduce some of the most common ethnographic research methods, particularly those that have been used in innovative or particularly effective ways by feminist ethnographers. Our list of methods is not exhaustive, but there really are a limited number of ways to collect data. Feminist methodologies, however, can deeply influence how we *use* those methods. For example, interviewing is one ethnographic method. A feminist interpretation of that technique might result in the researcher allowing interviewees to ask them questions, as Christa did with LGBTQ people in her interview-based project on reproductive loss. The project grew out of her desire to make more resources available for LGBTQ families. Christa begins each interview by telling participants that they are also welcome to ask her questions about her experience as a queer woman who had a second-trimester loss. Another example is when Dána-Ain conducted interviews with battered women. Acknowledging their difficult circumstances and experiences, she was open to conducting the interviews in nontraditional ways. One woman did not want to tell the story of her life on tape, so instead, she drew a timeline. Another woman wanted to be given the questions so she could answer them in the privacy of her own space with Dána-Ain's recorder.

What we do here is offer an overview of several key methods and at least one practical example of their use by a feminist ethnographer. You may explore this further in the Thinking Through . . . activity listed at the conclusion of this chapter.

Participant-Observation

Participant-observation is the most common method employed in ethnographic fieldwork. It involves intensive involvement with a group of people over an extended period of time (often a year or more). Ethnographers take detailed fieldnotes and frequently conduct informal interviews during participant-observation. They often pair this method with others, such as in-depth interviewing, life history, or surveys. Although some journalists have adopted the term participant-observation to refer to spending a few days or a week with a group, most scholars find this usage problematic, since the goal of participant-observation is to gain a deep and intimate familiarity with a community. Many students conduct what some professors' call "mini-ethnographies" over the course of a semester-long class.

Participant-observation is often considered the mainstay of cultural anthropology, but is also commonly used in sociology, communication studies, social psychology, religious studies, and human geography, among other disciplines. Some critics have argued that participant-observation is merely an "awareness" of things around you, but participant-observation relies upon detailed, recorded observations and reflection upon one's own participation in ways that allow for the collection of a large body of data for ethnographic analysis.

Feminist ethnographers conduct participant-observation in many ways—in fact, most feminist ethnographic projects center on this research method. The following excerpt offers an example of multisited participant-observation in anthropologist Naisargi Dave's research on queer activism in India.[16] She describes how she carried out her research and how the relationships that ethnographers forge can complicate, but also deepen our research. Anthropologist Aimee Meredith Cox describes engaging in her work as what she calls an "observing participant," underscoring the intention with which one approaches a project, and the longevity that allows for physical relationships to develop.[17] Although this method has most often been used in actual spaces, recently ethnographers have turned to virtual communities for fieldwork.

In *Coming of Age in Second Life: An Anthropologist Explores the Virtually Human*,[18] for example, anthropologist Tom Boellstorff argues that ethnographers need to take the spaces of virtual communities, and their inhabitants, seriously, conducting fieldwork in much the same way as ethnographers do so in the "actual" world. Boellstorff set aside fieldwork time at regular intervals, developed a presence in Second Life, and interacted with other participants in much the same way as an ethnographer would do in any field site. For Boellstorff, this means he was particularly attentive to the ways that power and inequities form in virtual locations, as well as ways in which they reflect, replicate, or challenge those that participants may experience in "actual" worlds. Although he never made an effort to meet any participants outside of their virtual community, his own virtual experience (as well as theirs) reflected "a complex transaction between the designers [of virtual worlds], who have certain goals and desires about what people will do, and the denizens of the virtual worlds themselves who exercise individual and collective agency."[19] His analysis focused on themes such as personhood, intimacy, community, and inequality in virtual communities.

ESSENTIALS

Excerpt from *Queer Activism in India* by Naisargi Dave

Naisargi Dave *earned her PhD in anthropology at the University of Michigan and now teaches in anthropology and the Centre for South Asian Studies at the Asian Institute at the University of Toronto. She is the author of* Queer Activism in India: A Story in the Anthropology of Ethics *(2012). The following excerpt discusses the questions and process that led to her participant-observation.*

There is no one setting from which to write an ethnography of lesbian activism in India: queerness has a way of moving about. Gay lovers escape oppressive regimes, lesbians run away from small towns, women leave their villages to become men, hijras move to the city, and nonresident Indians come looking for their roots, perhaps founding an NGO while they are at it. But this is not just an ethnography of the movement of people and things; it is also an ethnography of how queer people came to be, how they imagine, transform, and are transformed. These are questions that require both physical location and conceptual mobility. My methodology was thus multi-sited. I accompanied activists as they traversed the network of their associations across India and also conducted short periods of research on my own in Bangalore, Bombay, and Pune. My place of everyday engagement, though, was Delhi. . . .

I lived and conducted fieldwork in this remarkable city between December 2001 and December 2003. My work began smoothly through a snowballing of acquaintances. . . . I made friends and accompanied them to meetings, or gay nights at a local club. I could soon move comfortably through this world on my own.

I write in this book not only about my friends, but about people whose work I believe in. As a queer woman, these are also the people who have made my own life fuller, easier, and better. To write critically in such a context has been a source of trouble—for my conscience and, occasionally, my relationships. . .

Although I have strived to be careful and accurate, and to honor my relationships of care and politics through a practice of critical solidarity (Chari and Donner 2010), my perspective, like anyone's, remains utterly partial. As I say again later on, I spent more time, and shared more deeply with some than others. Often this was rooted in politics—I was drawn, for example, toward groups with strong feminist connections and, sometimes rather conflictingly, with feminists who sought radical, explicit queer transformations. An ethnographer with different priorities, passions, and education who sat through the same meetings as I did at the same period in history would surely have tracked different debates and offered other conclusions.

Source: Naisargi N. Dave, *Queer Activism in India: A Story in the Anthropology of Ethics*. Durham: Duke University Press, 2012, 21–22, 26–27.

Ethnographic Interviewing

In the same way that participant-observation is more than just "awareness" of people, things, and settings an ethnographer encounters, ethnographic interviewing is more than just asking a predetermined set of questions. Interview questions are usually generated from ethnographic fieldwork that involves other methods, such as participant-observation and informal interviewing. Further, ethnographers conduct open-ended interviews, in the sense that they frequently depart from predetermined questions to get more information using probes, such as, "Can you tell me more about that?" when a participant strays from the focus of the ethnographer's questions to more specific ways: "I heard you sigh when you spoke about that. Can you share more about why?" In many cases, ethnographic interviews become more like conversations than one-sided questioning, and the ethnographer frequently learns more about their projects by fielding questions from participants in this context. Going "off-topic" also allows ethnographic interviews to delve further into things that are important to participants. Feminist ethnographers have found this useful as a guide to how their project unfolds, and what elements of it become central to their analysis.

Claire Sterk's *Tricking & Tripping: Prostitution in the Era of AIDS*,[20] has become a "classic" ethnography on prostitution and drug use in the 1980s and 1990s when HIV/AIDS was becoming a pandemic. Trained as both a sociologist and medical anthropologist in the Netherlands, Sterk engaged in participant-observation over ten years, ultimately conducting in-depth interviews with 180 women. This is a *far* greater number of interviews than most ethnographic projects, which oftentimes rely on between 25 and 50, and sometimes ethnographers write their accounts primarily about a single individual. The sheer quantity of interview data Sterk collected underscores the importance of this method to her project. Particularly since Sterk left the field daily (vs. an ethnographer who lives with a population for extended periods of time), she found it essential to collect in-depth stories from the women she met during fieldwork to get a fuller picture of their lives. In her ethnography, she quotes extensively from many participants—sometimes including two or three excerpts per page—which serves her goal of humanizing the women she interviewed, in contrast to many dismissive portrayals of prostitutes' lives. Utilizing direct quotes also allows participants to speak for themselves, versus an analytical paraphrase by the ethnographer. Of course, the ethnographer is usually the one choosing the excerpts (though not always), so it is important to always be thinking about how an ethnographic account is shaped, even if the words of participants make up the bulk of it.

Oral History/Life History

A style of ethnographic interviewing that is often associated with feminist ethnography is what many historians and archaeologists call "oral history" and many social researchers term "life history" interviewing. This method involves multiple planned interviews with individuals, during which they are encouraged to document key moments, or a particular aspect of their lives that has developed over their life course. Many ethnographers begin with in-depth interviewing of various community members, but encounter a particular individual whom they believe can accurately or eloquently capture experiences within a culture or community.

Probably the best-known ethnography featuring extensive life history interviewing is *Nisa: The Life and Words of a !Kung Woman* by anthropologist Marjorie Shostak. Although Shostak interviewed many !Kung San women in the Kalahari desert of Botswana about "what being a woman meant to them and what events had been important in their lives" she developed a particularly close bond with a middle-aged woman she calls Nisa.[21] Nisa was an accomplished storyteller and over the course of 15 interviews conducted during a two-week period, and six more during a second fieldwork trip four years later, Shostak amassed nearly 30 hours of recorded interviews in the !Kung language that produced hundreds of pages of literal translations once transcribed. Although Shostak focuses on Nisa's life story in her ethnography, she notes that it is just one view of !Kung life, because Nisa's interview represented only 8 percent of the total hours she spent conducting interviews with !Kung women. Drawing from her participant-observation and interviewing, Shostak begins each chapter with an overview of !Kung life to contextualize Nisa's stories. Nisa's stories are then included verbatim, though organized by Shostak to flow chronologically. *Nisa* has been widely read in introductory Cultural Anthropology courses, and is one of the books that has continued to popularize feminist ethnographic approaches since its publication in 1981. Shostak wrote a second book based on later interviews with Nisa as Shostak was battling breast cancer in the 1990s, *Return to Nisa*, which was published posthumously in 2000.[22] The poignancy of this second book, especially Nisa's efforts to heal Shostak's cancer through a traditional !Kung ceremony, offers a moving example of the power of life history to teach readers about unfamiliar cultural and political contexts.

The politics of memory and whose stories are valued is a critical question that anthropologist Tracy Fisher poses in producing life histories.

SPOTLIGHTS

Tracy Fisher on Using Oral/Life History to Address Feminist Ethnographic Questions

Tracy Fisher *earned her PhD in anthropology from the Graduate School and University Center of the City University of New York (CUNY). She has an interdisciplinary background in political science, Africana studies, anthropology, and women's studies. She is the author of* What's Left of Blackness: Feminisms, Transracial Solidarities, and the Politics of Belonging in Britain *(2012) and a coeditor of* Gendered Citizenships: Transnational Perspectives on Knowledge Production, Political Activism, and Culture *(2009). Her research areas are influenced by anthropological and political-economic approaches to the study of gender, race, ethnicity, and class particularly in Britain and in the United States.*

I am interested in life histories and oral histories as feminist ethnographic methods. I find life histories and oral histories fascinating. People can have recollections, but in the (re)telling of events, situations, and circumstances, they can recreate, reshape, and interrupt history and normative narratives. Thus, life histories and oral histories can disrupt master narratives, while at the same time serve as important sources of knowledge. Life histories and oral histories can illuminate people's every day experiences shaped by race, class, gender, and sexuality. The key is to couple these histories—because they have value and meaning—with other methods so one can obtain the most accurate interpretations of an event or history. The data gathered from life histories or oral histories can fill in the gaps that may occur by using a different ethnographic method. There are lots of different methods that one can employ to gather data, but the key for me is the kinds of questions one asks, the methodologies.

The kinds of questions asked in feminist projects are marked by their connection to justice-based visions for transformation. For example, what kind of power is embedded in gender? What are the ways in which we can challenge systems of knowledge and knowledge production? How can we talk about an oppositional consciousness? Can we imagine a world free from gendered racial and sexual exploitation and oppression? How might we imagine liberation and freedom in the broadest sense? What new tools are needed to combat inequality and injustice in the context of globalization?

Survey

The use of survey research—a predetermined set of questions that are given to a particular sample of a population—is by no means unique to ethnography. In fact, applied statistics and survey research have long dominated government censuses, health and marketing research, political and public opinion polls, and academic fields like psychology, political science, and quantitative sociology. Yet, many ethnographers have found surveys to be a useful complement to fieldwork in order to offer a broader picture of the communities and groups they study. Some feminist ethnographers have also adopted the use of surveys with strategic political intent. Anthropologist Iris López, for instance, used a combination of participant-observation, survey, and interviews in *Matters of Choice: Puerto Rican Women's Struggle for Reproductive Freedom.*[23] She used quantitative data on Puerto Rican women's reproductive health strategically to make the experiences of individuals and communities with sterilization more likely to be heeded by policy analysts and other academic researchers concerned with "scientific objectivity." For instance, as a result of her survey, López was able to document that 47 percent of Puerto Rican women in Brooklyn that she surveyed were surgically sterilized, one of the highest rates of sterilization in the world. Although generating quantitative data is not typical of most ethnographic research; in this case, it served as a useful mechanism to demonstrate the importance of López's interview data in documenting trends among the women she interviewed.

A second example, where survey was central to an ethnographic project, is sociologist Mignon Moore's *Invisible Families: Gay Identities, Relationships, and Motherhood Among Black Women.*[24] Moore paired her survey with long-term participant-observation, attending social gatherings among Black lesbians in New York for 12 months before beginning formal fieldwork. After an additional 12 months of participant-observation, during which she hosted weekly dance parties, she administered a 14-page survey. Although survey response rates vary greatly, it is testament to Moore's long-term involvement with the community and the trust she was able to build that participants returned 100 of 131 surveys, an impressive response rate of 76 percent. Moore used these surveys, along with other methods, to gain insight into the ways that Black women negotiate sexuality, family, and identity, and they guided the questions she then generated for individual interviews and focus groups around key topics, such as gender identity and religion. Surveys in and of themselves can never replace the ethnographic emphasis on close interactions with communities and individuals, but these examples show the utility of survey both to complement and aid in generating additional data for feminist ethnographic studies.

Analysis of Cultural Material

The analysis of cultural materials spans a wide array of possible records, including archives, museum collections, and caches of virtual material, to name but a few. What is important is that cultural materials are different from other ethnographic data, in that someone other than the ethnographer collects them. They can represent an individual's collection or a historical record made to preserve particular information. Ethnographers frequently look at archival materials for what they can reveal about the group they are studying—history, changes over time, cultural norms (which may also change over time), representations of particular groups or actors. It is important to consider not only who compiled the materials but also for whom they were/are intended. Some cultural materials may be promotional (for instance, in advertising for a political candidate) or critical in nature (for example, and op-ed piece). Additionally, keep in mind that cultural material of any kind, but particularly those collected digitally (for instance, through data capture), can be overwhelming to any researcher! It is important to develop meticulous labeling and categorization when preparing cultural materials for analysis.

Many feminist ethnographers employ cultural materials in their analyses, and one example is anthropologist Catherine Lutz and sociologist Jane Collins's *Reading National Geographic.*[25] The authors engaged in participant-observation at the National Geographic headquarters, conducted extensive interviews with editors, photographers, and writers, and provide a detailed history of the publication. However, the bulk of their analysis centers on a systematic analysis of the photographs in the magazine and their captions (how they are presented to the reader). Lutz and Collins used extensive coding to categorize photos. They enlisted a group of graduate students to **code** all photos that included people by skin tone: black, bronze, and white. Some photos included multiple people or could not be categorized, but overall there was 86 percent agreement among themselves and their coders. They were also particular about choosing their timeframe for analysis, 1950–1986, citing key historical changes as a result of social movements. Ultimately, their analysis addresses the ways that the "ethnic other" is created in the pages, and how race and gender are presented to exoticize Black people and "civilize" whites.

One of the biggest logistical challenges of analysis of cultural materials is to narrow down ones sources, but still come away with meaningful results that can elucidate cultural patterns accurately. While Lutz and Collins, and their team of graduate researchers, were able to analyze over 400 full issues of *National Geographic*, let's use their project as an example to consider how a student ethnographer might further narrow their focus if they had less time and resources. Ethnographers aiming to look at changes in the representation of gender and race over several decades might choose to analyze all magazines from a single year of publication at regular intervals (i.e., 1951, 1961, 1971, 1981, or 1950, 1955, 1960, 1965, etc.). Alternatively, if a researcher aimed to look at changes over a shorter period of time, say a single decade, they might look at the publication during a single month—to account for seasonal changes that might be effected by holidays or special issues—of each year (such as every March edition between 1965 and 1975). The bottom line is that any good ethnographer assessing inequities or prejudice in their analysis must find ways to systematically categorize their materials for meaningful analysis.

Ethnohistory

Ethnohistory combines ethnographic work with historical analysis. It is used by ethnographers tracing the history of communities in many disciplines, as well as a common technique among historical archaeologists. It produces a cultural history by examining—but moving beyond—existing historical records, such as documents and archives. Ethnohistory often includes an analysis of folklore, archaeological materials, music, language, museum collections, and may incorporate life history interviews. As Lee Baker discussed in chapter 2 on historicizing feminist ethnography, uncovering historically marginalized voices is challenging, and can require intensive work for the feminist ethnographer. One must also consider how these power differentials play out, not only in social interactions but also in how materials were produced, and for what audiences.

A poignant example of the use of ethnohistory in feminist ethnography is Janice Boddy's *Civilizing Women: British Crusades in Colonial Sudan*, which examines British efforts to eliminate Sudanese practices such as female genital cutting (FGC, which some also term female genital mutilation or FGM) through health and education projects. Boddy draws on a broad range of archival sources to produce a nuanced ethnohistorical context for her analysis, including government materials published by British midwives and teachers, advertisements, novels, memoirs, and both scholarly and popular histories, especially during the period from 1920 to 1946, when British colonial efforts were most intense. The second half of her book relies on her participant-observation among Arab Sudanese women in Hofriyat conducted in the 1970s and 1980s to analyze the effects of post-coloniality on notions of agency, Islamic piety, and gender identity. Ultimately, she underscores that feminism is not a homogenous movement, nor do Sudanese women all agree about circumcision. She argues that those who oppose FGC must move beyond a framework of judgment toward one of mutual respect, attentive to the social and historical contexts of African lives. Further, they must consider the work of Sudanese feminists who address FGC not in isolation, but alongside issues of reproductive health more generally, as well as the negative effects of structural adjustment on food security and health services. The power of ethnohistory as a primary method in Boddy's work is that it offers important context for what is often construed by international anticircumcision activists and politicians as merely a contemporary ethical and cultural debate.

As a second—quite different—example of the use of ethnohistory, we include an interview with feminist historical archaeologist Whitney Battle-Baptiste, who although she does not conduct ethnography, has found feminist ethnographic approaches essential to her historical archaeological analysis. Battle-Baptiste's work pays particular attention to the intellectual legacy of African American literary fiction as it directly documents the lives of African Americans. While some historical documents exist from this time period, they are written primarily by white men and some white women; there is little recorded in African American women's voices. Thus, although literary fiction is not typically incorporated into archaeological analysis, in reconstructing the past, fictional accounts shape Battle-Baptiste's feminist analysis and interpretation in important ways. Feminist archaeologists have long critiqued the androcentric focus of the archaeological record,[26] but Battle-Baptiste's attention to contemporary ethnographic work on African Americans, as well as historical literary fiction offers new methodological possibilities for feminist ethnographic approaches within archaeology.

In her book, *Black Feminist Archaeology*, Battle-Baptiste delves into how she utilized a Black feminist framework to conduct her archaeological research.[27] In addition to the literature of Zora Neale Hurston, she also drew upon Black literary fiction writers Toni Morrison and Gayl Jones. Her analysis is also informed by feminists including the Combahee River Collective, Audre Lorde, and feminist anthropologists, such as Johnetta Cole, Irma McLaurin, Lynn Bolles, and Maria Franklin, among others. The point of her methodological approach is to use a Black feminist framework as a lens to examine race, class, and gender in the past. Battle-Baptiste's reading and engagement with Black feminist theory, ethnography, and literature shaped her interpretations of the domestic sphere of both female and male enslaved Africans. In this case, it influences research questions and opens up spaces to generate new theories. As new interpretations of a site become possible, different ways of viewing the space are inevitable. Battle-Baptiste's work inspires an expanded interpretive lens. For example, one could go to an archaeological site of an antebellum home and ask questions such as: Did the homes of women of African descent mimic the consumption patterns of white women? What Battle-Baptiste's discussion demonstrates is how a methodological strategy of engaging with Black feminist texts activates the conceptual framework or methodology (as Harrison discusses earlier in this chapter) that she draws upon to develop her project.

SPOTLIGHTS

Whitney Battle-Baptiste on Historical Archaeology and Literary Fiction

Whitney Battle-Baptiste *describes herself as "a Black Feminist (who happens to be an archaeologist)." She received her PhD in anthropology at the University of Texas, Austin, in the African Diaspora Program and now teaches anthropology at the University of Massachusetts Amherst, where she was recently named director of the W. E. B. Du Bois Center. A historical archaeologist of African and Cherokee descent, she has done fieldwork at Colonial Williamsburg, the Hermitage, the W. E. B. Du Bois homestead, and other sites in the Southern United States and the Bahamas. She is the author of* Black Feminist Archaeology *(2011), which argues for the centrality of the tenets of Black feminist thought in reshaping contemporary historical archaeology.*

Battle-Baptiste began the interview by highlighting how archaeologists are typically concerned with "materials and landscapes. In historical archaeology, we move back and forth between artifact and . . . oral histories." She started her work during the 1990s when there was a disciplinary move toward public archaeology. As she emphasizes, however, "Public archaeology was still about taking the knowledge as an expert and presenting it to the public. So it is still a presentation, a distance model." When she began her own research, she admits that she "was still using that archaeological tool kit that separates you from living people because we are dealing with the past," but she soon began to see the intersections of her work and Black women's fiction. Zora Neale Hurston was an important influence: "It was through [her] fiction that I began to open my eyes and see that Black women were writing in ways that seemed relevant [to the materials I was researching]."

Literary fiction became increasingly important to her project.

"Because I started out looking at slavery and plantations I did not have the benefit of talking with women or being a participant-observer in a particular society or culture or place. . . . I didn't have the people to speak to, but I still had to figure out how patriarchy worked in a society that is different [for those that were] captive people. How is it different? How is gender functioning in these spaces? Because captive African men are not benefiting from patriarchy in the same ways white land-owning men are. Even though I don't have people to speak to, that's where I look to literature, I hate the term but, at the neo-slave narrative of how people who are remembering the past [are constructing it]."

*This interview was conducted by Ishan Gordon as part of her final project for Dána-Ain's course in *Feminist Ethnographies* at the Graduate Center, CUNY.

Participatory Research

Many feminist ethnographers engage with participants before, during, and/or after their research, and discuss these decisions in their publications. They often seek guidance on issues of importance to the community and/or return transcriptions of interviews to participants for edits, comments, and to inspire further conversation. Some also engage in analysis with participants. Sociologist Shulamith Reinhartz describes collaborative research as a model, "Designed to create social and individual change by altering the role relations of people involved in the project. . . . Differences in social status and background give way as shared decision-making and self-disclosure develop."[28] We would argue, in the spirit of Judith Stacey, that while this may be the *ideal*, collaborative researchers must be especially attentive to these relationships and reflect critically on their limits.

One collaborative strategy that has been used productively by feminist ethnographers is **Participatory Action Research (PAR)**. PAR aims to better understand a community not only through participation in it (as all ethnographers do) but also through working collaboratively with participants to make social change. PAR is predicated upon collaborative reflection and collectively inquiry. One example is education scholar Patricia Maguire's research with a group of battered women in Gallup, New Mexico, which she chronicles in *Doing Participatory Research: A Feminist Approach*.[29] Maguire draws on educator and philosopher Paulo Freire's emphasis on learning as a dialogical process,[30] working with formerly battered women in a cycle of reflection and action with the intention of moving forward after living with abusive partners.

An innovative example of PAR was orchestrated by faculty and students in the social psychology program at the Graduate Center, City University of New York. The project examined the impact of access to college classes in prison on women and their children, ultimately assessing the outcomes after their release from prison. The report, "Changing Minds: The Impact of College In a Maximum-Security Prison," is recognized as the basis for supporting the College in Prison movement and is a powerful example of feminist ethnography using a participatory, multimethod approach with the goal of creating social change.[31]

One genre of PAR is photovoice, a technique that has been used by feminist ethnographers to engage with participants to record and reflect upon their community. After participants take photos centered on a particular theme or topic (which may simply be about their lives), photographs are often displayed publically or to small groups to promote critical dialogue about challenges and concerns they face. Additionally, photovoice—through photographs and critical responses by participants—may be used to lobby policy makers or others in positions of power. Public health researcher Caroline C. Wang's provocative work, "Worker Self-Narrative through Photography" (http://photovoicechina.com/) drew from participants who experienced common challenges in Chinese factories, such as low worker morale, lack of job satisfaction, and poor communication among workers and between workers and management. Wang presented these stories publically and engaged with companies to improve the conditions for workers.

The possibilities for photovoice and PAR in feminist ethnography are exciting, and something that has become popular in recent years. Another example of a feminist ethnographic project that includes photovoice was the New York State Scholar Practitioner team directed by anthropologist Leith Mullings.[32] In 1996, the W. K. Kellogg Foundation developed a multiyear initiative that sought to understand the effects of welfare reform and health care in five states across the country: Wisconsin, Florida, Washington, Mississippi, and New York. Working with community members and employees of community-based organizations in Harlem and the Lower East Side of New York, the team invited people to use a camera to capture their community on film. This had the effect of allowing people to record and reflect on their community's strengths and concerns as they related to the passage of the Personal Responsibility and Work Opportunity and Reconciliation Act (PROWORA) of 1996. It promoted critical dialogue and knowledge about personal and community issues. One team member facilitates group discussions with photographers to develop captions and analyze the meaning of the images as they related to the impact of welfare policy on people's lives and to reach policy makers. The flexibility, innovation, and emphasis on participation that characterize this methodology made it ideal for the New York State Scholar Practitioner team to use as a strategic engagement with community participants.

ESSENTIALS

Excerpt from "Photovoice" by Caroline Wang and Mary Ann Burris

Photovoice was developed by ***Caroline Wang*** *from the department of health behavior and health education at the University of Michigan School of Public Health. Initially, Wang and her research partner* ***Mary Ann Burris*** *used the method in 1992 as a way to empower rural women in the Yunnan Province of China, and to influence the policies and programs that affected them. Photovoice has become widely used in participatory research to promote participant engagement and empowerment. The following is an excerpt from "Photovoice: Concept, Methodology, and Use for Participatory Need Assessment" (1997):*

Photovoice is a process by which people can identify, represent, and enhance their community through a specific photographic technique. It entrusts cameras to the hands of people to enable them to act as recorders, and potential catalysts for change, in their own communities. It uses the immediacy of the visual image to furnish evidence and to promote an effective, participatory means of sharing expertise and knowledge. In previous instances, we have called this methodology *photo novella*. But the terms *photo novella, foto novella,* and *photonovel* have also been commonly used to describe the process of using photographs or pictures to tell a story or to teach language and literacy. . . .

Photovoice has three main goals: (1) to enable people to record and reflect their communities' strengths and concerns, (2) to promote critical dialogue and knowledge about important community issues through small and large discussion of photographs, and (3) to reach policymakers. In line with these goals, people can use photovoice as a tool for participatory research.

Source: Caroline Wang and Mary Ann Burris. "Photovoice: Concept, Methodology, and Use for Participatory Needs Assessment." *Health, Education & Behavior* 24, no. 3 (1997): 369.
Photo: Courtesy of the University of Michigan School of Public Health

Interpretive Communities

All ethnographers engage in some form of thematic analysis of the data they collect, which involves the identification of recurrent themes. Narrative analysis, using texts, such as transcriptions of interviews and cultural materials, can allow the ethnographer to construct a story from the data that can be a useful way of presenting it to an audience. How ethnographers locate such themes, however, has generated important conversations among feminist ethnographers. Creating interpretive communities is one strategy that some feminist ethnographers use, allowing them to be direct conversation with research participants.

When research participants are involved in analysis, they assist in shaping the ethnographic project by identifying themes that are salient and meaningful, often encouraging researchers to rethink, revise, and develop new thematic frameworks. Dána-Ain's book *Black Battered Women and Welfare Reform*,[33] for instance, benefited immeasurably from the Interpretive Community she formed among some participants to consider themes that were emerging in her research. In this case, Dána-Ain gave copies of oral history interviews back to the women for both approval and ideas about emerging themes. One theme that several women identified was how they use talking to get resources (such as apartments, jobs, and housing). Because several women noted the same phenomenon, Dána-Ain expanded upon this theme in her work, calling it "Speech Acts," which became a subtopic in one of the chapters of her ethnography.

Interpretive communities may also be a collective endeavor undertaken by scholars committed to fostering feminist ethnographic work *among themselves*. For instance, the collection *Interpreting Women's Lives: Feminist Theory and Personal Narratives* began as a collective project among scholars in the Personal Narratives Group, a research group affiliated with the Center for Advanced Feminist Studies at the University of Minnesota in 1984. The interdisciplinary group met to facilitate and coordinate feminist scholarship and conduct research that placed personal narratives at its core. As a result of meeting regularly over several years, the group of historians, anthropologists, and literary scholars implemented several related projects: co-teaching courses on women's autobiography, organizing a conference on autobiography, biography and life history, and eventually publishing *Interpreting Women's Lives*. As they write in the introduction:

> [Ongoing] discussions . . . made us increasingly aware that we were seeing women's personal narratives from new perspectives. We were repeatedly reminded of the importance of the narrator's own self-definitions as they talked about their lives, in contrast to the definitions imposed by interpreters of personal narratives and by the narrators' own society. The importance of the political and institutional contexts of both the narrator and the interpreter of a personal narrative became increasingly obvious. We began to question the relationship between the form of a narrative and the interpretation of the life story told. These issues exemplify our own intellectual transformation.[34]

Conclusion

Whatever methods or analytical techniques you choose, our aim in this chapter is to have gotten you thinking critically and creatively about the research process. Inevitably, just like two ethnographers could do research in the same area and have very

Thinking Through . . .

Three Options to Explore Methodological Possibilities

1. Select any one of the methods discussed above. Using 3 or 4 different sources, prepare a brief critical discussion of how a range of researchers have utilized that method. The focus of this assignment is for you to understand the possibilities for, but also limits and critiques of, particular methods.
2. Read a feminist ethnography of your choice and take note of what methods the author uses, how they explain their methodology, and their strategies for analysis. Write a brief essay summarizing their methods, the challenges they faced, and what methods you might consider using if you were working on the same research topic.
3. Select a topic that you are interested in—maybe incarceration, Black Lives Matter, access to birth control, heritage studies—whatever you like. Then in a brief essay discuss first your methodological strategy and how at least three of the methods described would be effective (or not) in researching your topic.

different experiences based on their positionality and the topics that interest them, ethnographers use the methods and analytical techniques outlined above in very different ways, toward very different ends. Our intent is to get you thinking about and experimenting with a variety of possibilities and reflecting on how to choose the methods that will be most fruitful for your project. Indeed, the feminist practice of being attentive to marginality and reflecting critically upon power differentials within the research context is an important first step toward conducting feminist ethnography.

Suggested Resources

Rae Bridgman, Sally Cole, and Heather Howard-Bobiwash, eds. (1999) *Feminist Fields: Ethnographic Insights.*

Kath Browne and Catherine J. Nash, eds. (2010) *Queer Methods and Methodologies: Intersecting Queer Theories and Social Science Research.*

Sharlene Nagy Hesse-Biber (2014) *Feminist Research Practice: A Primer.*

Nancy A. Naples (2003) *Feminism and Method: Ethnography, Discourse Analysis, and Activist Research.*

Michelle Téllez (2005) "Doing Research at the Borderlands: Notes from a Chicana Feminist Ethnographer," *Chicana/Latina Studies.*

Diane L. Wolf, ed. (1996) *Feminist Dilemmas in Fieldwork.*

Any of the feminist ethnographies profiled in this chapter would also make for useful further reading.

Notes

1 Alison Rooke, "Queer in the Field: On Emotions, Temporality and Performativity in Ethnography," in *Queer Methods and Methodologies*, 2010, 28.

2 Margery Wolf, *A Thrice Told Tale*, 1992, 124.

3 Matthew C. Gutmann, *The Meanings of Macho,* 1996, 9.

4 Karen Brodkin Sacks, *Caring by the Hour,* 1988, vii.

5 Ulrika Dahl, "Femme on Femme: Reflections on Collaborative Methods and Queer Femme-inist Ethnography," in *Queer Methods and Methodologies*, eds. Kath Browne and Catherine J. Nash, 2010, 145.

6 Ulrika Dahl and Del LaGrace Volcano, *Femmes of Power*, 2009.

7 Ulrika Dahl, "Femme on Femme: Reflections on Collaborative Methods and Queer Femme-Inist Ethnography," in *Queer Methods and Methodologies*, eds. Kath Browne and Catherine J. Nash, 2010, 156.

8 Ibid., 161, 174.

9 Rayna Rapp, *Testing Women, Testing the Fetus: The Social Impact of Amniocentesis in America*, 1999.

10 Lila Abu-Lughod, *Veiled Sentiments: Honor and Poetry in a Bedouin Society*, 1999 [orig. 1986].

11 Elise Andaya, *Conceiving Cuba*, 2014, 22.

12 Ahmet Atay, *Globalization's Impact on Cultural Identity Formation*, 2015, 54–55.

13 Alisse Waterston, *My Father's Wars: Migration, Memory, and the Violence of a Century,* 2014, xv–xvi.

14 Leith Mullings, "African American Women Making Themselves: Notes on the Role of Black Feminist Research," *Souls,* 2000, 21.

15 Leith Mullings and Alaka Wali, *Stress and Resilience,* 2001.

16 Naisargi Dave, *Queer Activism in India: A Story in the Anthropology of Ethics*, 2012.

17 Aimee Meredith Cox, *Shapeshifters*, 2015, 31–32.

18 Tom Boellstorff, Bonnie Nardi, Celia Pearce, and T. L. Taylor, eds. *Coming of Age in Second Life*, 2015 (orig. 2008).

19 Tom Boellstorff, ed., *Ethnography and Virtual Worlds,* 2012, 1.

20 Claire Sterk, *Tricking & Tripping: Prostitution in the Era of AIDS*, 2000.

21 Marjorie Shostak, *Nisa*, 1981, 7.

[22] Marjorie Shostak, *Return to Nisa*, 2000.

[23] Iris López, *Matters of Choice: Puerto Rican Women's Struggle for Reproductive Freedom*, 2008; see also, Iris López, "Negotiating Different Worlds: An Integral Ethnography of Reproductive Freedom and Social Justice," in *Feminist Activist Ethnography: Counterpoints to Neoliberalism in North America*, Christa Craven and Dána-Ain Davis, eds., 2013.

[24] Mignon Moore, *Invisible Families: Gay Identities, Relationships, and Motherhood Among Black Women*, 2011.

[25] Catherine Lutz and Jane Collins, *Reading National Geographic*, 1993.

[26] Joan M. Gero and Margaret Conkey, eds., *Engendering Archaeology*, 1991; Janet Spector, *What This Awl Means*, 1993.

[27] Whitney Battle-Baptiste, *Black Feminist Archaeology*, 2011.

[28] Shulamit Reinharz, *Feminist Methods in Social Research*, 1992, 181.

[29] Patricia Maguire, *Doing Participatory Research*, 1987.

[30] Paulo Freire, *Pedagogy of the Oppressed*, 2000.

[31] Michelle Fine, et al., "Changing Minds: The Impact of College In a Maximum-Security Prison," A Collaborative Research Project by the Graduate Center of the City University of New York and the Women in Prison at the Bedford Hills Correctional Facility, 2001.

[32] CUNY Graduate Center, PhD Program in Anthropology, "The Impact of Welfare Reform on Two Communities in New York City," W. K. Kellogg Foundation, 2003, accessed January 15, 2016. http://www.wkkf.org/resource-directory/resource/2003/01/the-impact-of-welfare-reform-on-two-communities-in-new-york-city.

[33] Dána-Ain Davis, *Black Battered Women and Welfare Reform: Between a Rock and a Hard Place*, 2006.

[34] Personal Narratives Group, *Interpreting Women's Lives: Feminist Theory and Personal Narratives*, 1989, 12.

CHAPTER 5

Challenges for Feminist Ethnographers

In this chapter, you will investigate how to address challenges in fieldwork, and production of feminist ethnography by considering the following questions:

- What logistical constraints arise in feminist ethnographic research?
- How do ethical concerns shape the research encounter?
- (How) Should you "give back" to research participants?
- How can we assess the (potential) impacts of feminist ethnography?

Spotlights *in this chapter:*

- Elizabeth Chin on Envisioning a Feminist IRB Process
- Loretta Ross on Working with Former Skinhead White Supremacists
- Tanya Erzen on the Politics of Reciprocity and Mediation
- Kiersten Downs on "Feminist Curiosity" and Stamina
- Sandra Morgen on Movement Building

Essentials *in this chapter:*

- Susan Erikson, "Global Ethnography: Problems of Theory and Method"
- Delores Walters, "Cast among Outcastes" in *Out in the Field*
- Diane Wolf, *Feminist Dilemmas in Fieldwork*
- Alma Gottlieb and Philip Graham, *Parallel Worlds*

You will also be ***Thinking Through . . .***

- Difficult Ethnographic Experiences
- Ethical Dilemmas

Ethnography is a challenge. It is a challenge for a number of reasons, not the least of which is that it is difficult to define. Ethnography has historically been both the process and product of anthropology and other disciplines. Ethnographic research is often conducted to capture and tell the stories of people's lived experiences. As such, it can—among other things—be helpful in challenging stereotypes. An ethnographic project may also be used to examine the interconnectedness of communities or peoples to broader structures and processes, especially (though not exclusively) by residing in communities for extended periods of time and presenting data through the eyes of those living there. Questions regarding how one engages in long-term involvement with a community are germane to any study, but particularly when a feminist ethnographer is attentive and reflexive about power relationships that may emerge within (and beyond) the research encounter.

Nearly every social science discipline has a Code of Ethics within their professional organization(s) that offer guiding principles for conducting research (see a partial list in the Suggested Resources). Although professional organizations are not **adjudication boards**, meaning that they do not prosecute or punish members, they do investigate breaches of ethics on the part of researchers and, in some cases, remove the researcher from the organization. The primary goal of such codes is the welfare and protection of the individuals and groups that researchers study. Central issues are **confidentiality**, keeping the identity of participants from being disclosed beyond the researcher, and **informed consent**, confirmation that participants are taking part in the study willingly and not being coerced to participate.

For feminist ethnographers, however, ethical concerns go far beyond those described in the disciplinary Codes of Ethics, such as the debates over inequities in the research encounter detailed in chapter 3. For example, the issue of ethics and the **Institutional Review Board** (IRB) process is one that anthropologist Elizabeth Chin has pointedly critiqued in "The Neoliberal Institutional Review Board, or Why Just Fixing the Rules Won't Help Feminist (Activist) Ethnographers."[1] Chin's polemic argument encourages feminist ethnographers to be diligent in challenging IRBs in their uneven application of restrictions—often judging projects, like feminist ethnography, which contest positivist research aims, more harshly. Further, she argues that feminist ethnographers should challenge the structural role of the IRB as it reinforces the neoliberal transformation of the academy. In our interview with Chin, she reflects on the possibilities of a feminist IRB.

What we explore in this chapter are some of the challenges that have emerged out of our reading of feminist ethnographic texts and the interviews we conducted

SPOTLIGHTS

Elizabeth Chin on Envisioning a Feminist IRB Process

Elizabeth Chin *is an anthropologist whose practice includes collaborative ethnography with children, performative knowledge production, and a range of writing experiments. A founding member of the Media Design Practices/Field track at Art Center College of Design, she created the Laboratory of Speculative Ethnology in 2014. She is author of Purchasing Power: Black Kids and American Consumer Culture (2001), and* The Consumer Diaries *(Forthcoming). In addition she is editor of* Katherine Dunham: Recovering an Anthropological Legacy, Choreographing Ethnographic Futures *(2014).*

In my imagination the IRB would use feminist principles to do its work. The review process would be a dialogue, engaging the members of the IRB with the researcher and, if possible, including representatives of the group to be researched. Rather than being the closed and oppositional process that typify IRB workings currently, the IRB would focus on supporting researchers in doing the most creative and ethically rigorous work possible. Indemnification of the institution, the current focus of most IRBs, would be strictly a by-product of the work, not its core. In my dream process, the expertise of the IRB members would be used to productively challenge researchers to consider the best interests of those participating in research, and could further assist researchers in accessing resources necessary to meet these interests in a timely and rigorous way. People would sit together

(continued)

and really talk about the work. At present, you submit an application and you get a decision, it's a kind of black box process and everybody hates everything about it. You have people from a variety of disciplines on these panels, but too often people are imposing their own disciplinary values onto other people and this is especially difficult for feminist ethnographers who tend to use methods that stray quite significantly from the positivist approaches used in the best-funded of the social sciences, much less in the hard sciences and in medicine. It's a problem, of course, to assert that because we're "down with the people" we can skirt things like informed consent, but the problem for many of us is that the very form of informed consent—particularly a piece of paper covered with legalistic writing—inserts itself as a kind of violence into the delicate and intimate relationships we form in the field. We need other ways to communicate to people about what we are doing and what the implications are. Now that I work in a design department, I can imagine visual ways to explain our work and to get consent. Perhaps there are other media and technologies we could develop that would allow us to effectively communicate our research while securing the safety and dignity of our interlocutors all at the same time satisfying institutional needs.

with feminist ethnographers. We take up concerns about the particular gendered dimensions of being in the field, ethical concerns that move far beyond the IRB, the politics of doing research with groups with which you are not politically aligned, how feminist researchers approach issues of reciprocity with participants, and consider the potential for broader contributions of feminist ethnographic work.

What Logistical Constraints Arise in Feminist Ethnographic Research?

Although conducting research in a community for an extended period of time was a prerequisite for early ethnographers, some contemporary researchers do not live with the people they study. For feminist ethnographers, it is important to think about how and where we can best collect data for feminist analysis. All ethnographers face logistical concerns, including access to a site and the constraints of **geopolitics**. Geopolitics includes such issues as diplomacy, security, global economics, financial markets, and sometimes civil disruption. The following is one example of a feminist ethnographer (who we do not name to protect her identity) who faced logistical constraints that ultimately compromised her ability to conduct research.

> [A feminist ethnographer] who conducted dissertation fieldwork in a Middle Eastern country was forced by her home institution (an Ivy league University) to create a relationship with an IRB in her host country. This requirement is indeed best practice and uncontested by the American Anthropological Association (AAA) on principle. The problem was that in her host country there was no such thing as the IRB, but there was a highly repressive political regime. My colleague had arrived in her host country intending to conduct research on women and politics. As her work progressed, her interlocutors told her over and over again that the real thing she needed to look into was sexual revolution. In the meantime, members of her host country IRB were spying on her and those with whom she spoke. What her home institution had failed to account for was that the host country might not have an understanding of ethics commensurate with that in the United States. My colleague was forced to conduct a huge amount of "red herring" research in order to protect her research subjects; needed to send her field notes via encrypted FTP to her advisor; and kept an entire computer full of field notes utterly unconnected to her project. The host

country ultimately placed her under house arrest for six weeks, bringing her field research to a close.[2]

Logistical constraints can also be experienced in less dramatic ways. For Dána-Ain's project on Black women who were battered, she did not live at the shelter where she worked because it was not feasible to do so; it was a shelter, after all, and the available beds were for staff, not researchers. In other cases, informants' mobility or multisited fieldwork means that it may not be possible to participate with and observe people in a single setting. Christa, for instance, could not have lived in every community that had midwives in Virginia. Instead, she traveled to multiple communities for weeklong stints to conduct interviews and participant-observation, and met many homebirth activists multiple times at legislative hearings in Richmond and at activist meet-ups throughout the state.

It has also become more commonplace that researchers will no longer spend years in one location doing research, but that an ethnographic project may be of a shorter duration, or involve research across a range of locations. A thoughtful discussion of conducting "global ethnography" in a feminist context is anthropologist Susan Erikson's research on global health. Her work in Germany and Sierra Leone explores how emerging global rationalities shape human well-being. In Erikson's work, she describes the challenges she faced pursuing a multisited ethnography across several continents and with various constituencies on the topic of reproductive imaging technologies (such as ultrasound and data). She suggests making strategic choices about where to conduct research, centered on the lived experiences of participants in the research.

Ultimately the issues raised above reflect shifts in the practice of ethnography responding to ways in which the temporal (time) and spatial (space) conditions of ethnography have changed. The challenges for all ethnographers include questions such as: Is what one observes typical of what happens in this culture? What if we only view people in one part of their lives (e.g., if we only view them at work, but not at home or in leisure time)? Do we miss something?

Cultures and communities transform in relation to global and political processes, which can pose challenges for the initiation and continuation of ethnographic research projects. One anthropologist, Andrea Queeley, conducted her research in Cuba among the descendants of early twentieth-century migrants from the English-speaking Caribbean to Cuba.[3] They were attracted to move there because of heavy U.S. economic investment. The children and grandchildren of those original immigrants had initiated a revitalization of the West Indian organizations that their parents and grandparents had established between the 1920s and 1950s but had been closed down due to the revolution. Queeley wanted to examine the dynamics around that revitalization. One challenge she faced was the inability to continue her research because the state of Florida passed a statute in 2008 that no faculty or students at Florida public institutions could travel or use state funds to travel to any country on the list of "Terrorist Sponsoring Nations." Although faculty throughout Florida waged a campaign to dispute the legislation, it did not result in a policy change. Queeley was informed that she would be unable to use any funds to go to conferences in Cuba, or travel to Cuba. Further, outside grants (those that were not from the university where she worked) could not be used for travel to Cuba either. In this case, the challenge was that Queeley was unable to continue her research due to geopolitics. However, the U.S. has adjusted its relationship to Cuba, and as of January 2015 the U.S. trade and travel restrictions have been loosened. As of this writing, it remains unclear if academics in Florida will be able conduct research in Cuba.

ESSENTIALS

Excerpt from "Global Ethnography: Problems of Theory and Method" by Susan Erikson

***Susan Erikson** is an associate professor of health sciences at Simon Fraser University who has worked in Africa, Europe, Central Asia, and North America. Her first career involved working with or for U.S. government agencies including the U.S. Congress, U.S. Departments of State and Agriculture, and the U.S. Agency for International Development. As an academic, Erikson combines her practical work experience with a critical study of the relations of power informing global health scenarios. She was the founding director of the Global Health Affairs Program at the Korbel School of International Studies at the University of Denver, and was voted Best Professor there in 2004.*

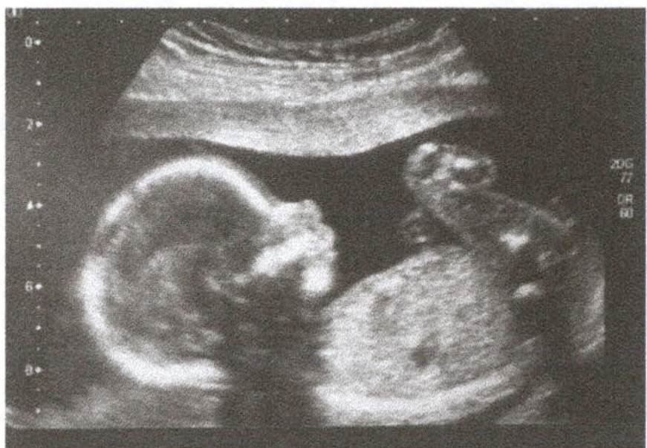

Ultrasound of a fetus, the subject of Erikson's newest book, *Scan: Ultrasound and the Biopolitics of Obstetrical Necessity.*

I have tried to move away from the binary of local and global that shaped globalization scholarship in anthropology in the 1990s. During the 1990s, when anthropologists contended with academics from other disciplines who insisted on the homogenizing effects of global forms, the local–global schema turned scholarly attention to more nuanced considerations of the heterodox ways in which global macro processes affected people's lived experiences at the local level . . . .

My research suggests that we treat global ethnography constitutively as an aggregating process. Start with people like Ingrid [a pregnant German medical student who is central to Erikson's account] and move through the various dimensionalities that *directly* affect their experiences. Move through the contexts of biomedicine, disability, politics, and the economy within which they live. Do research in those places. Follow the people, the thing, the conflict (Marcus 1998) and allow one site to lead to another. Pay attention to only those state and market sites that are actually relevant to lived experience. Using this approach, I met Ingrid and women like her in the hospitals, parents of children with disabilities, the German parliamentarians debating the ethics of prenatal diagnostic technologies in the Reichstag in Berlin, and vice presidents at Siemens Medical Solutions in California and Bavaria, interviewing almost 300 people. I moved from village-scale (hospital) research sites to national-scale (government bureaucracies) and global-scale (multinational corporations). This approach to ethnographic research is iterative, a kind of snowball sampling of sites rather than populations. . . .

Methodologically, such an approach has its challenges. It requires the relativity anthropologists have long employed in their research. Relativity is demonstrably more complicated for anthropologists, though, when the informants are bureaucrats, politicians, and corporate types. It also requires the flexibility to think about ethnography itself in more than one way, with multiple sets of design criteria. My research design included a large sample size at the lived-experience dimension (many women have ultrasound during pregnancy), but only a few people at the corporate level (there are only so many vice presidents). In the hospital stage of research, I could go and "take up residence" in conventional anthropological fashion (I lived in the hospital's fourth floor doctors' quarters), but the governance and corporate stages of research required that I traipse all over the country.

Source: Susan Erikson. "Global Ethnography: Problems of Theory and Method." In *Reproduction, Globalization, and the State: New Theoretical and Ethnographic Perspectives*, edited by Carole H. Browner and Carolyn Sargent, 23–37. Durham: Duke University Press. 2011, 28.
Photo: Thinkstock

The global politics of mobility also revises the notion that all ethnographic research takes place in single "bounded communities." For example, although Dána-Ain primarily conducted her research with women who were battered in "Laneville," New York, some of the women she encountered were from all over New York State and some women had immigrated from Mexico and Europe. Thus, their histories of violence and survival were linked to multiple places. In one case, Drita, a sixty-year-old woman, had experienced a range of forms of violence. In her country of origin, Serbia, Drita's husband had beaten her for forty years. In sharing her oral history, Drita positioned the Yugoslav Wars from 1991 to 2001, which centered on ethnic conflict, as another form of violence that she endured linking it to the violence she experienced at the hands of her husband. Finally, she and her husband left Serbia and came to the United States, where he continued to beat her, marking the reason she left him and came to the shelter. In this case, analyzing Drita's oral history had to take into account the multiple spatial locations that she had occupied. Consequently, understanding her cumulative incidents of violence had to be contextualized by the politics of Serbia, her immigration to the United States, and her ability to feel safe in upstate New York.

Going into the field posed a different kind of challenge for Delores M. Walters, a Black lesbian anthropologist, who describes what she had to deal with when she began her fieldwork on women, health care, and social reform in Yemen. Walters integrated her identification as a feminist and her desire to be "out" in the field as a lesbian into her preparation for fieldwork. Her reflection on the experience, and the challenge it posed for her, points toward one way in which feminist ethnographers may have to confront issues that more positivist researchers do not have to address.

Sociologist Annette Lareau, who conducted one of the first **longitudinal** ethnographic studies on childhood education, contends that researchers should be open about the logistical and ethical challenges that we face—in order to help students cope with their own fieldwork challenges and develop better skills in the field. Lareau has written extensively about feeling "unsure"—at many times—during her research and offers reflective, practical suggestions on how she would deal with particular challenges differently in future research.[4] For instance, she found herself unable to take detailed fieldnotes during many of her participant-observation sessions at schools, and with families in their homes. At first, she committed to writing detailed notes after each visit, but frequently found that she did not have the time to complete them because of other obligations outside of her field site. She advises students to be aware of this when making decisions about note-taking and fieldnotes. Time—for researchers, as well as the participants—is clearly an important practical consideration.

Several edited collections by feminist ethnographers have also sought to elevate the research process to more than a casual mention in an appendix or footnote. *Gendered Fields: Women, Men and Ethnography*, edited by anthropologists Diane Bell, Pat Caplan, and Wazir Jahan Karim considered the influence of gender in the ethnographic fieldwork encounter by incorporating the experiences of international scholars, including geographers, historians, philosophers, and sociologists.[5] Sociologist Diane Wolf edited *Feminist Dilemmas in Fieldwork* about the complicated dynamics inherent in fieldwork, as well as for feminist ethnographers in the academy.[6]

Feminist ethnographers often study marginalized groups, those with less social, political, or economic power than themselves. Yet in 1972, Laura Nader issued a clarion call for anthropology to reinvent itself and for researchers to "study up," given their unique position and focus on analyzing processes of power. In her still cogent article, "Up the Anthropologist: Perspectives Gained from Studying Up,"[7]

 ESSENTIALS

Excerpt from "Cast among Outcastes" by Delores Walters

***Delores Walters** was trained in anthropology at New York University and also holds degrees in liberal studies, biology, and nursing. She has served in various administrative/teaching capacities at the University of Rhode Island: director of recruitment and retention of faculty of color; associate dean for diversity; diversity consultant, and director of the Southern Rhode Island Area Health Education Center (sriAHEC) in the College of Nursing. She is the author of* Gendered Resistance: Women, Slavery and the Legacy of Margaret Garner *(2013), an anthology of papers from the Gendered Resistance Conference, coedited with historian Mary E. Frederickson. In this excerpt from her chapter in* Out in the Field: Reflections of Lesbian and Gay Anthropologists, *she discusses the challenges of being "out" in Yemen.*

In the summer of 1982, my partner at the time and I left the United States for nearly two years, most of which was devoted to conducting field-work in what was then known as the Yemen Arabic Republic. . . . One of the pressing questions for those about to embark on fieldwork is how to conduct or maintain one's personal life. To a group of graduate students who inquired how I managed, I remarked that I had taken my personal life with me. These students, whom I encountered at an American Anthropological Association meeting on my return from the field in 1984, were somewhat in awe at such a novel idea. I am not sure whether it was the public statement about having a same-sex partner in the field that was mildly shocking or the fact itself, because I know that among my sympathetic listeners there were other lesbians.

Anyone planning an extended stay in Yemen is required to pass a stringent security clearance. The question was how to get my partner, Lee into the country . . . Thus, one of my objectives when I visited Yemen the year before I began fieldwork was to determine whether a companion would be permitted to accompany me. Clearance through the proper Yemini authorities might be facilitated by a few options, according to my British and American Colleagues, then resident in the country. Couldn't I claim that Lee was my mother? they asked. To which I replied, "right age, wrong color," because she is White and old enough to be my mother. Little did I know that when they met us Yemeni women all over the country would immediately assume that Lee was my mother because they observed an appropriate age difference for this to be possible and ignored the fact that she is fair-skinned and blue-eyed while I, especially in the sunny climate of Yemen, am very brown. . . . Adoption was another option, but it would take too long and besides, my own mother would be eagerly awaiting my return . . . . Finally after exhausting all the possibilities, my colleagues and I simply inquired at the research center. I was assured that permission would be easily granted. Once we arrived in the country, I had only to write Lee into my project for their records. The way was clear for the two of us to work together as a team.

*This excerpt is dedicated to the memory of Lee Maher who was my valuable assistant and partner in Yemen.

Source: Delores Walters. "Cast Among Outcastes: Interpreting Sexual Orientation, Racial, and Gender Identity in the Yemen Arab Republic." In Ellen Lewin and William L. Leap, eds. *Out in the Field: Reflections of Lesbian and Gay Anthropologists*, 58–69. Urbana and Chicago, IL: University of Illinois Press, 1996, 58–59.
Photo: Michael Selerno

Nader argues that we need to examine the operationalization of power where it is wielded. Nader asked, "What if . . . anthropologists were to study the colonizer rather than the colonized, the culture of power rather than the culture of the powerless, the culture of affluence rather than the culture of poverty?"[8] Given that there was already a lot of scholarship on disadvantaged populations, we had much to

 ESSENTIALS

Excerpt from *Feminist Dilemmas in Fieldwork* by Diane Wolf

***Diane Wolf** received her PhD in rural sociology from Cornell University and teaches sociology at University of California, Davis. She is the author of* Beyond Anne Frank: Hidden Children and Jewish Families in Postwar Holland *(2007) but is probably best known for her groundbreaking collection,* Feminist Dilemmas in Fieldwork *(1996). In this text, Wolf argues that it was not only feminists who do what we call feminist ethnography but other progressive scholars as well. We would extend her complex positioning of power to all ethnographers who are guided by a feminist sensibility, many of whom may be differentially positioned within the academy for reasons other than, or in addition to, gender.*

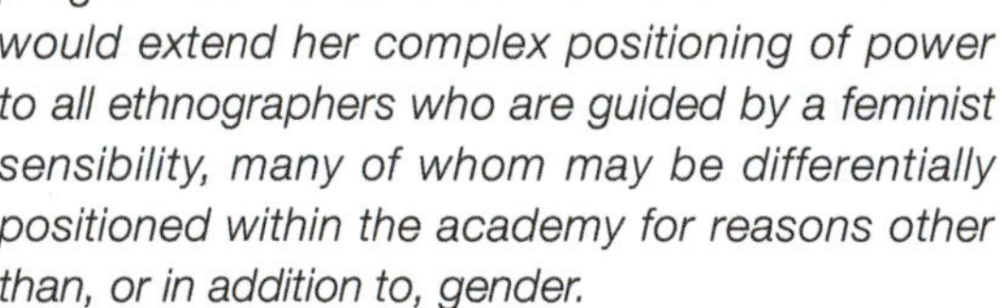

I think it is important to acknowledge and accept that when one is working with poorer and marginalized peoples, power differentials between feminist researchers and their subjects remain as such. Although feminist researchers may attempt to equalize relationships while in the field through empathetic and friendly methods, these methods do not transform the researchers' positionality or locationality. The "equality" is short-lived and illusory because the researcher goes home when she is finished, reflecting her privileged ability to leave. This does not mean that attempts at more egalitarian field relationships should be abandoned but rather they should be seen more realistically.

At the same time, I do not mean to portray research subjects as victims without agency or consciousness. Our subjects affect our research plans if they decide not to interact with us. But these microdynamics do not subvert the hierarchy of power when the positionality of the researcher is considered. Furthermore, subjects are often fully aware of this differential and the difference in benefits that will result from the research.

Although we confront the dilemma of power in our positionality, our research processes, and our post-fieldwork practices, many feminists, particularly feminists of color, confront their own sense of marginality when they return to academia. Although being an academic is a privileged position, feminists are usually not in positions of power within the academy. Thus, the dilemma of power in field relations is fraught with further contradictions—although we may be treated as privileged in the field, we have no power to alter policies that may affect our subjects' lives and usually very little power once we return to our own workplace and home.

Source: Diane L. Wolf, ed. *Feminist Dilemmas in Fieldwork*. Boulder: Westview, 1996, 10.

learn by putting a face on bureaucracy, institutions, and people who control others' lives. Nader's original call was for ethnographic studies of banks, realtors, law firms, insurance companies, manufacturing corporations, the communications industry, and government regulatory agencies—institutions at the center of capitalist processes leading to stratification. This appeal posed challenges, however. How was the ethnographer to gain access to bankers, CEOs, lawyers, and the like, who are often paid substantially for their time? Could the ethnographer offer critical perspectives on the workings of power without being silenced or sued?

Nader's call was answered by some feminist ethnographers and scholars such as former investment bank employee and anthropologist Karen Ho, who wrote *Liquidated: An Ethnography of Wall Street*, which addresses financial crises and booms, connecting the values and actions of investment bankers to the construction of markets and the restructuring of U.S. corporations.[9] Political theorist

Cynthia Enloe in her book *Seriously! Investigating Crashes and Crises as If Women Mattered*,[10] points out the importance of examining the gendered politics of institutions and notes that patriarchal privileging can be understood when one investigates women's experiences of how masculinity operates. According to Enloe, Ho's ethnography, which she situates as a feminist text, scrutinizes masculinity within the context of institutional power. Also, anthropologist Melissa Fisher's ethnography *Wall Street Women* examines the first cohort of women in finance and explores how they enacted market feminisms by incorporating tenets of liberal feminism, such as equal rights, into Wall Street institutions and practice.[11] Fisher faced challenges doing this work of studying up. In our interview with Fisher, she noted that "when you're looking at elites, there's an issue about . . . your relationship with powerful people." Arguably, ethnography, and feminist ethnography in particular, presumes a degree of authority over those whom researchers study. This is especially evident if one is studying people who occupy subordinate social spaces. Yet this asymmetrical relationship is either neutralized or inverted in a number of circumstances, such as with Fisher and Ho. Fisher's book was innovative because no one had previously followed a group of elite women over a long period of time. Fisher and Ho's work raise a question: if one goal of feminist ethnography is to reduce power differentials through the possibilities of cocreating the ethnography, how is that transformed when the power dimensions of your work are reversed? For instance, if an ethnographer were to coauthor a publication with a CEO or president of an organization, they might be significantly constrained in what and how they could write.

Finally, in the vein of studying up, anthropologist Sandra Morgen and social welfare scholar and activist Mimi Abramovitz probe what we might call an "up issue" in *Taxes are a Women's Issue: Reframing the Debate*.[12] One of the significant challenges that they faced was that no one, including feminists, had paid attention to taxes regarding their gendered dimensions and consequences. Morgen and Abramovitz show how the U.S. tax system, supported by the Internal Revenue Service (IRS), was created in—and still caters to—ideals of men as breadwinners with stay-at-home wives. In response to the challenge of addressing a complex tax policy system, their goal in writing this book was to demystify the tax system, foster tax literacy through accessible writing, and draw women more substantively into debates surrounding tax reform. In so doing, they make a complex system legible to readers. Although making complex systems comprehensible has been the intent of many ethnographers, what is notable here is that these authors include the demystification of political, legal, and economic systems as fundamentally essential for their vision of feminist ethnographic inquiry.

How Do Ethical Concerns Shape the Research Encounter?

Clearly, ethical concerns can—and do—arise in all research projects. Feminist ethnographers often have an awareness of such issues because of the attention they pay to gendered dynamics in the research encounter, which we frequently reflect upon in our writing. *Women Fielding Danger: Negotiating Ethnographic Identities in Field Research*, edited by sociologist Martha Huggins and anthropologist Marie-Louise Glebbeek,[13] addressed a range of logistical and ethical issues faced by feminist ethnographers across a range of disciplines, including anthropology, criminology, Latin American Studies, literary criticism, political science, psychology, sociology, and Women's and Gender Studies. The collection explores female ethnographers' experiences with threats of physical violence, the emotional toll of difficult fieldwork experiences, and the influence and negotiation of gender, as well as nationality, ethnicity, caste, and class, on ethnographic research. Authors also address ethical dilemmas, such as choices to conceal aspects of their identity, concerns about placing local interlocutors in danger through their research, conducting research with groups that the ethnographer does not respect or support (such as torturers or paramilitary members), and protecting sensitive field data. The question of ethics raised in these instances pose a significant quandary for ethnographers who study sensitive or controversial topics.

Depending upon the location of fieldwork, scholars may find themselves in situations when they observe something horrific or have participated in an event sanctioned by the community, or person being studied, with which they disagree. Deciding whether or not to participate is often fraught with tensions about acceptance in the field and concerns about maintaining respect within one's discipline. Ellen Gruenbaum's fieldwork in Sudan that resulted in the ethnography *The Female Circumcision Controversy: An Anthropological Perspective*,[14] drew her into complex emotional and ethical territory. Gruenbaum draws on five years of fieldwork to demonstrate the deep embeddedness of female circumcision in Sudanese cultural traditions and to critique simplistic (often feminist) Western efforts to summarily

 ESSENTIALS

Excerpt from *Parallel Worlds: An Anthropologist and a Writer Encounter Africa* by Alma Gottlieb and Philip Graham

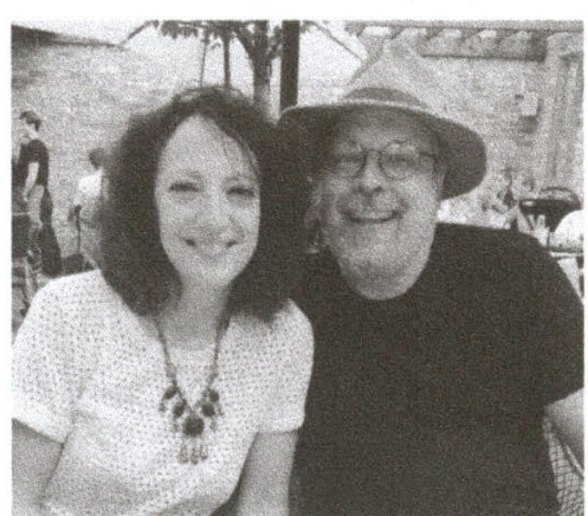

***Alma Gottlieb** and **Philip Graham** teach at the University of Illinois at Urbana-Champaign in anthropology and English, respectively. Both contribute to the Center for African Studies. Together, they have written two memoirs:* Parallel Worlds: An Anthropologist and a Writer Encounter Africa *(1994), excerpted below, and* Braided Worlds *(2012). Here, Gottlieb shares a harrowing experience they shared in a Beng village in Côte d'Ivoire.*

That night Philip and I were awaked by screams. Half dreaming, I thought I was back in Bongalo, Aya's mother wailing her sorrow, and the painful memory roused me. Philip and I dressed and hurried out anxiously. We recognized the voice: it was Nakoyan's.

We followed the sound of her cries. Already there was a small gathering outside the house in her family's compound. From inside a room came the howls of a woman in near hysteria.

"What could they be doing to Nakoyan now?" I asked Philip.
"Poor thing," he said, "god only knows."

[Gottlieb's difficult rendering of the scene follows, along with her debate with her husband—and herself—about whether to summon the police.]

Even if Philip and I did inform the police of the rape, the gendarmes might just shrug off the event as local village custom and laugh at our intrusion. Nor was I confident that Nakoyan herself would be grateful to me for interfering. Just last week Gaosu had told me that his father had consulted the diviner Lamine, who had pronounced that Nakoyan was possessed by a male spirit of her clan who was especially jealous of human rivals: If the spirit-husband were propitiated with a chicken sacrifice, he would release Nakoayn to Gaosu. Had she accepted this explanation? If so, perhaps tonight's rape was also an exorcism. . . Contemplating such question—unanswerable for the moment—sapped my will to take action. I turned to Philip and said, "I hate to say it, but I think we have to stay."

Philip nodded unhappily, unwilling to interfere in this crucial decision in my fieldwork. I forced myself to take out my notebook.

Source: Alma Gottlieb and Philip Graham. *Parallel Worlds: An Anthropologist and a Writer Encounter Africa*. University of Chicago Press, 1994, 151–153.

eradicate the practice. Gruenbaum's participant-observation spanned many events and spaces, but the one she reflects on most profoundly was when she observed a girl's genital surgery with a midwife she had come to know well. Despite planning to limit herself to observation in this setting, she found herself helping to hold the child steady for xylocaine injections.[15] Although this situation was ethically complicated (not to mention unexpected) for the ethnographer, those in the community saw it as part of her engagement with a cultural practice they deeply valued. This is a particularly shocking (for most Western readers) example of the ways that ethnographers often encounter unexpected events in their research. Part of the writing process for feminist ethnographers is to reflect upon these experiences, consider the ethical implication, and pay attention to how power manifests in the situation.

As the example of the previous page demonstrates, bearing witness to a difficult event is an experience Alma Gottlieb recounted after conducting extended fieldwork among the Beng in West Africa with her husband, creative writer Philip Graham. What they faced included witnessing a young bride being raped, among other ethically complicated events. Gottlieb notes that her graduate training had not prepared her, nor even mentioned, the possibility of witnessing (or experiencing) rape or violence in the field. It took her seven years after leaving the field to write about the situation she had experienced.

You may also wish to see examples produced by postgraduates and early career anthropologists on www.anthropologymatters.com, the official network of the Association of Social Anthropologists of U.K. and Commonwealth. This website stimulates discussion on a number of topics, including challenges researchers face and witness in fieldwork.

Thinking Through . . .

Difficult Ethnographic Experiences

Free Write and Conversation: Given what you have read in this textbook thus far, what tools do you think a feminist ethnographer should draw upon to navigate these situations? Do Gruenbaum and Gottlieb's experiences exemplify situations where you think an intervention must or should occur? Why or why not?

Ethical concerns begin as we start to conceive our projects and continue far beyond our fieldwork into our choices about writing, continued involvement with the people and communities we study, and our responses in the event of controversy that emerges from our research. People with various political perspectives conduct research of all types, even research that may seem to be counter to the researchers' politics. In this vein, imagine doing a research project that is at odds with your political perspective. For example, picture being a feminist who favors reproductive freedom and conducting research on right-wing pro-life efforts. Or how would it feel to study with people whose politics you disagree with? What might it be like to study racist groups if you are antiracist?

Anthropologist Faye Ginsburg, who wrote the ethnography *Contested Lives: The Abortion Debate in an American Community*,[16] faced a significant dilemma regarding her work. For this project, Ginsburg conducted research with pro-choice and pro-life activists in Fargo, North Dakota. Doing this ethnography forced her to confront what it meant to be a feminist engaged in this kind of study, as well as her decision not to share her convictions about the debate with either participants, or her academic colleagues. She writes that a "native's point of view" is fine when the "native" is from someplace else. It is another thing to describe the worldview of informants when they are from the same place as the researcher, and when they are presumed to be the enemy. Ginsburg was accused of having "gone native" and becoming a right-to-life advocate. Ultimately, her largely pro-choice academic colleagues struggled more with her decision than her participants, who were more comfortable with her role of neutrality.[17] In a project such as this one where participants span a wide range of beliefs about a subject, it is possible for the finding to be endorsed by all the members of the study group?

In her recent article, "Trying to be A Vulnerable Observer: Matters of Agency, Solidarity and Hospitality in Feminist Ethnography," anthropologist Tine Davids reveals that she struggled with the dilemma of having a different political perspective than her informants.[18] Her research explored elite Mexican women's engagement in politics. Davids reexamined the difficulty she had conducting research with right-wing, female politicians. She found herself rethinking the idea of feminist solidarity with someone whose politics diverged from her own. Focusing on Marina, whose political sympathies Davids found troubling, she wondered how the concepts of "vulnerable observer," a term coined by Ruth Behar and cultural diversities are managed in such a situation. Davids's commitment to feminism and her willingness to deploy a reflexive stance allowed her to listen and hear Marina's voice differently. By examining her own biases, Davids analyzes the processes whereby she opens herself up to locate agency in Marina's conservatism. What comes through in this reflexive analysis is that understanding the researcher's context as part of narrative interpretation is important, as is revisiting one's work to face interpretive challenges or differing perspectives. Davids suggests that in opting to critically examine our own roles and relationships to power in the construction of feminist research, we should make ourselves vulnerable and be hospitable to our informants. In this case, we must take risks in opening up our emotional door to strangers that could be "unsafe," instead of only opening our emotional door to those we already know. In other words, we can easily show or feel solidarity to those with which we agree. Managing interpretations of differing perspectives, Davids suggests that we integrate hospitality into our conceptualization of solidarity.

In some cases, researchers may choose to make their potentially conflicting identities or perspectives known to the communities they study. Others working from the assumption that an absolute eradication of bias is both impossible and unnecessary, opt instead to critically examine their own roles and relationships to power in the construction of feminist research.

This was the case with feminist sociologist Kathleen Blee, author of *Women of the Klan: Racism and Gender in the 1920s*.[19] In her work on women in the Klan, Blee indicates she had very little difficulty interviewing women who had been members of the Ku Klux Klan in Indiana in the 1920s. She points out that it was very easy to develop a rapport with her informants, in part because she was from Indiana and has white skin. Blee's initial recruitment of participants did not indicate her own political leanings opposing the Klan. In fact, it was her similarity to her informants that led them to assume that she had the same worldview they did. Blee also admitted she was prepared to hate her informants, in part because of her own progressive politics. Instead, she found the women "interesting and intelligent." Although cultural relativism is the stated goal of most ethnographers, this is not the same as **moral relativism**, often taken to mean that we should tolerate all cultural behaviors even when we disagree with them. It is important for feminist ethnographers to reflect on these challenges as they aim to gain a greater understanding of the communities they research.

Reproductive justice activist Loretta Ross's work with former white supremacists also offers an illuminating example. While Ross is not a feminist ethnographer within the academy, she has contributed to shaping national conversations about injustice and **reproductive justice,** a term that she coined along with 11 other women in 1994, attending a conference sponsored by the Illinois Pro-Choice Alliance and the Ms. Foundation for Women. Because her work dovetails with that of feminists and feminist ethnographers, such as sociologist Kathleen Blee, political scientist Marlene Gerber Fried, and others, we include her here. While her work researching

SPOTLIGHTS

Loretta Ross on Working with Former Skinhead White Supremacists

Loretta Ross *is a nationally recognized women's rights and human rights leader. She was a cofounder and the national coordinator, from 2005 to 2012, of the SisterSong Women of Color Reproductive Justice Collective, a network of women of color and allied organizations that organize women of color in the reproductive justice movement.*

I worked at the Center for Democratic Renewal (CDR), formerly known as the National Anti-Klan Network from 1990–1995 as their Program Director. One of my jobs was to work with people who had been in the hate movement who were seeking to defect. The challenge for me was working with the perpetrators instead of victims. That wasn't the first time I had to deal with this transposition. Back in the 1970s at the DC Rape Crisis Center, I worked with men who were incarcerated because they had raped women. But they were black men, so it felt like I was working with a portion of our community who were in jail. When I had to work with ex-neo-Nazis and Klansmen, they were not my "community." So it was a major paradigm shift that I didn't think I could handle.

My boss at the time was Rev. C.T. Vivian, who was an aide to Rev. Martin Luther King. He said to me "If you ask people to give up hate, then you must be there for them when they do," which I didn't necessarily want to hear. This led to me working with CDR's Research Director Leonard Zeskind and participating in the de-programming of people who had been in the hate movement. It was wonderful work. It blew my mind and made me rethink how I viewed people who had been in the hate movement. I tended to think of them as people who were like roaches who only came out in the dark. And because they practiced the politics of hate, they didn't have human rights that I needed to respect. But working with them humanized them for me. I no longer could maintain the anger I felt towards them individually or as a group. I began to feel sorry for their particular combination of fear and envy that propelled them into hate groups.

Someone who stood out for me was Floyd Cochran in 1992. He and I ended up together on the Jerry Springer Show as part of a road tour for Floyd to apologize for his previous behavior as a Nazi. Floyd was a national spokesman for the Aryan Nations and when his second child was born with a cleft palate, his Aryan brothers told him his child was defective and needed to be put to death. Aryans believe in a so-called "human perfectability." Floyd's epiphany was realizing that these people did not have his best interests at heart. He left the compound and asked CDR for help. (See *Up from Hatred*, *Los Angeles Times*, http://articles.latimes.com/1997/aug/10/magazine/tm-21338.)

With the assistance of churches and other anti-racists, CDR had a sort of underground railroad for people defecting from the white supremacist

(continued)

movement. People leaving these movements often do so with knowledge about crimes the group has committed, so they need protection. We've helped people who had to leave home in the dead of the night. There is no government program designed to help them reestablish a new life. Many want to leave. Some turn state witnesses, but most don't; they just want out.

Floyd's most painful story was that he had recruited two skinheads from Allentown, PA. Their last name was Freeman. These two brothers were church going boys, who became members of the Aryan skinhead movement. One evening, they came home and killed their entire family, mother, father, and 11-year-old brother. They were caught and convicted of murder. Floyd never confessed to any crimes he personally committed, but he did feel responsible for the murder of the Freeman family. (See *New York Times: 2 Skinhead Brothers Charged with Killing Family Members,* http://www.nytimes.com/1995/03/03/us/2-skinhead-brothers-charged-with-killing-family-members.html.)

Let's be clear, a lot of teen boys can be attracted to hate movements, not necessarily because of the ideology, but because they are bullied. When they join racist groups like skinheads or neo-Nazi groups, it is as a counter to being bullied. That was Floyd's experience. He became a Nazi because he was a rather small guy getting bullied, it was not the ideology of Nazism, he barely understood that as a teenager. A lot of people don't understand the psychological impulses that can cause people to join hate groups.

I never felt particularly unsafe doing this work until after the Oklahoma City bombing on April 19, 1995, by white supremacist and militia member Timothy McVeigh. After I was in some interviews in national newspapers, the Texas Militia managed to make contact with my mother who was wheelchair bound, suggesting that they wanted to talk to her about me. This tricked her into revealing a lot of personal information about me because my mother tended to brag about her children. They invited my mother to a meeting of the militia to prove that they weren't part of a racist movement, as I had said in the newspapers. When I called her on Mother's Day to ask if she received the flowers I sent, she told me she had had a two-hour phone call with the Texas Militia. Her number was unlisted, so this definitely scared me. It wasn't personally threatening to me but it was a not-so-veiled warning to me through my family.

hate groups was difficult, she felt that it was important to know how the "other side" thinks and works.

Identifying the "other side," however, can be difficult in projects that engage with activist movements. In Christa's research with midwifery advocates, for example, organizers frequently disagreed upon strategies to forward their cause. It would have been impossible to agree with, or support, each position. Christa had to bow out of particular debates—for instance, what type of licensure or certification the government should provide to midwives, a subject well beyond her area of expertise—and discuss other debates and conflicts in her published work.

A particularly thoughtful engagement with writing about conflicts and controversies is American Studies scholar Tanya Erzen's book, *Straight to Jesus: Sexual and Christian Conversions in the Ex-Gay Movement*, which investigates the lives of men and women living at New Hope Ministry, a residential ex-gay program. Erzen spent eighteen months volunteering at New Hope, while she conducted fieldwork.

Being uncomfortable is something that most ethnographers become intimately familiar with during—and in Erzen's case, also following—fieldwork. Researchers who conduct studies that address traumatic events must find ways to address discomfort throughout their fieldwork, and frequently for audiences who read or hear about their work. Sociologist Doug Meyer conducted research on violence against queer people, a topic that has attracted media attention in recent years, though the focus has been primarily on white, middle-class men.[20] Meyer conducted 47 interviews with LGBTQ people who had experienced violence to show that misogyny

SPOTLIGHTS

Tanya Erzen on the Politics of Reciprocity and Mediation

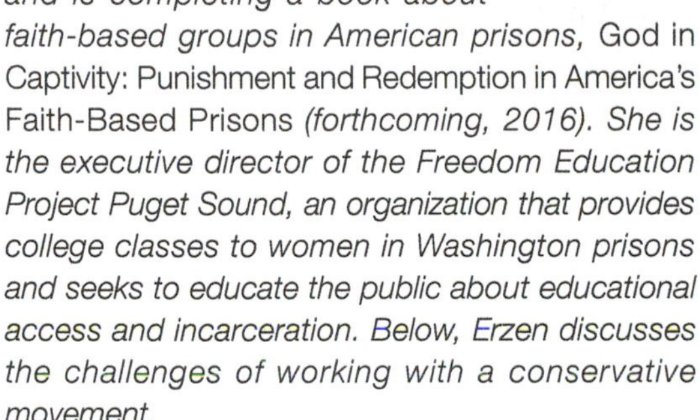

Tanya Erzen *received her PhD in American studies from New York University and now teaches religious studies at the University of Puget Sound. Her first book,* Straight to Jesus: Sexual and Christian Conversions in the Ex-Gay Movement *(2006), has received numerous awards, including the Ruth Benedict Prize from the Association of Queer Anthropology. She is also the author of* Fanpire: The Religion of Twilight *(2012) and is completing a book about faith-based groups in American prisons,* God in Captivity: Punishment and Redemption in America's Faith-Based Prisons *(forthcoming, 2016). She is the executive director of the Freedom Education Project Puget Sound, an organization that provides college classes to women in Washington prisons and seeks to educate the public about educational access and incarceration. Below, Erzen discusses the challenges of working with a conservative movement.*

One of the really practical things that happened when I first started doing the ex-gay research was that I was trying to find a reason to actually be at the ex-gay ministry, especially as a woman around men. In graduate school, I had made money doing HTML webpage work, and [the ministry] needed somebody to help them with their website, and I remember asking Faye [Ginsburg, my dissertation advisor], should I volunteer in their offices, so I can actually be in the office every day that I'm there? And she said, "oh absolutely," you have to do this. I said, "but then I'm helping them to create their website" [for a cause I didn't support]. And she said, "but I think if you're explicit about that in your research, then that's okay."

The other was there's this whole piece that I don't think is always talked about in feminist ethnography around religion and especially in a community that is a proselytizing community that very much saw me as a person, well, at the time I was single. I had moved across the country by myself. The woman who ran the ministry with her husband, said she saw herself in me at a younger age. And so there were all these strange dynamics with them feeling like they were taking care of me, but maybe hoping that in some way that this would alter me to a certain extent. I was sort of submitting myself to that process, even knowing it wouldn't happen.

I think that as time went on—and I spent a lot of time there—it became easier. I never hid my views. I mean we were always respectful, but I never pretended to think otherwise. I was very clear, I'm only here because I want to really understand what sort of motivations and rationale [you have], and daily life of how a place like this functions. If I were interested in just bashing you, I don't have to do this. And I think they really respected that, just the commitment to spend time. The people who I ended up being closest to were in some ways more marginal to the ministry, and the people who were much more stalwart believers in the mission of the ministry as Christians, I always knew them, but I didn't have the rapport I had with other people.

[After publishing my research, sometimes I've felt like a] mediator. It was really stark when the book came out because I did a lot of live radio shows—unexpectedly, since I didn't have any experience with that. They had call-ins, and you'd get people saying, "why do you hate gay people?" And then the next caller would say, "why do you hate Christians?" . . . . One other funny anecdote: the only time I was on TV was MSNBC, and the woman interviewing me, the anchor, I don't know who briefed her, but she introduces me, "It's Father's Day. Imagine your son says, 'Dad, Happy Father's Day, I'm gay.' Here's Tanya Erzen, a lesbian, a former lesbian who went through an ex-gay ministry to talk to us about her book." [laughter]

Also, I felt that initially when I would present about the work to academics, they felt I was too sympathetic to the group. When I gave a talk at [a prominent University in California, where I conducted my research, after] the book came out, one of the men in the book who lived there, and who I have remained close with, came to the talk, and in the Q&A he actually spoke up and identified himself to the audience. I knew he was planning to be

(continued)

there. It was a moment of the two worlds really colliding. There's always an expectation in those academic settings that the people [you research] aren't there, and yet here he was in that presence, and he actually now has a PhD. So, he started speaking back to that academic world. And that was a really interesting moment for me. It was very cordial, but it was really uncomfortable for some people in the audience. But I actually think it's good to be uncomfortable, and those moments can generate things that are important. I almost wish there was more of that.

(for women and transgender people) and racism (toward queer people of color) were significant factors that impact both the forms of violence that LGBTQ people encountered, as well as their perceptions of that violence. Although Meyer does not offer "easy answers" for how a researcher should approach such work, in a recent blog post, he discussed developing the art of reading people as an interviewer "reading what people want to talk about and what they most certainly do not want to talk about."[21] These skills move far beyond a typical "Code of Ethics" aiming to protect research participants and they are equally, if not even more, important for feminist ethnographers aiming to conduct research on sensitive or controversial topics or populations.

(How) Should You "Give Back" to Research Participants?

Many feminist ethnographers want to avoid overburdening participants who often see little direct benefit from ethnographic research. Some may see part of "giving back" as offering participants opportunities to contribute to, or collaborate, in research, such as reviewing interview transcripts. Participants might ask: "Why should I bother reading a transcript and discussing it with you when you'll just include what you want anyway?" Feminist ethnographers need to grapple with this question. What would you be willing to change in your writing based on a participants' comments? Are you willing to note where interpretations differ? How will including participants' perspectives benefit them?

Rarely will one find a completely equal research/participant encounter, as we discussed in chapter 3, despite the best intentions of the feminist ethnographer. In fact, researchers most often hold the pen (or wield the keyboard) and make critical choices—alongside publishers and editors—about what to include and not include in the ethnography. "Giving back" is not only about remuneration; it is also about having respect for the input of participants in your research. There are complicated logistics that often come with that goal. For instance, do participants have the time, finances, and technological ability to be in dialogue (literally or electronically) with you? Do they even care? We do think it is worth mentioning that sometimes our research matters more to us than it does to the people with whom we work.

The issue of what the researcher gives back in return for research participants' willingness to participate in our studies is one that does not have a clear cut answer and is challenging on many fronts. One may question whether it is appropriate, or even desirable, to "give back" in all instances of feminist ethnographic research. This poses complex questions for feminist ethnographers who research conservative movements, like those discussed above. Even if a researcher does determine that they wish to "give back" to participants, challenges remain in figuring out a culturally appropriate way to do so that is respectful of participants' time, expertise, and engagement in the project. On the one hand, typical research compensation, such as offering cash to entice people to participate in an experiment, is different from and may not acknowledge the extent to which many participants may become deeply involved in feminist ethnographic research. Participant-observation may span months, or even years, and some participants may contribute to multiple formal and informal interviews, or be involved in data analysis to varying degrees. Thus, the ways that a researcher might "give back" to individual participants are varied.

While one might offer financial payment, if available, many ethnographers find themselves contributing in other ways, such as buying a meal, assisting with living expenses, offering rides, or babysitting a participant's children might be meaningful gestures for those who offer time and expertise to one's research. Other times, an ethnographer may feel compelled to "give back" in the form of support for the organization they work with by grant writing, developing a website, or other volunteer work that fits their skill sets. Dána-Ain, for example, donated all the royalties from her book sales to the shelter where she conducted the research. Elizabeth Chin donated the royalties from her book *Purchasing Power: Black Kids, America and Consumer Culture* to a scholarship fund in New Haven, the site of her research.[22]

Many feminist ethnographers also hope to "give back" to the people, organizations, and communities with which they work by publishing their research beyond academic audiences with the hope of raising visibility of the issue or group. Contributing to public policy reports or evaluation, or writing op-eds or blogs for nonacademic publications can accomplish this. The challenges we face during fieldwork and the writing process often become the foundation upon which we make decisions about how to present and utilize our data toward a variety of ends. In fact, writing about the ethical concerns and challenges that arise in our research is crucial to feminist ethnographic writing, as we will discuss in the following chapter. Although there is no single "right" answer about how (or even whether) a researcher should "give back," it is a question that should be considered by all feminist ethnographers.

Often feminist ethnographers engage in research that is connected to broad-based social change, which they also see as a way of giving back to communities or organizations with which they work. Many would argue that ethnography, particularly feminist ethnography, has proven extremely useful in studying and moving forward the goals of social change movements. Ethnographic methods, such as oral history, are useful for capturing the development of a movement. The work of feminist ethnographers has been influential within movements, such as Occupy movements internationally, reproductive justice struggles, the battered women's movement, Black Lives Matter, prison reform efforts, domestic worker rights, and welfare rights movements, among others. In chapter 7, we offer detailed examples of how feminist ethnography has worked toward social change.

How Can We Assess the (Potential) Impacts of Feminist Ethnography?

We don't always know what the outcome of our research will be. In fact, we really never do. But feminist ethnographers need to think through the possibilities for impact prior to, and as we conduct research. Some research can emerge from wishing we had contributed (more) to social change in the other aspects of our lives, in an effort to lead to change in the future. This is the case for Kiersten Downs, a graduate student at the University of South Florida in Applied Anthropology, and veteran of the U.S. Air Force. Her dissertation research addresses women veterans' experiences after they leave the service following the prolonged influence of

SPOTLIGHTS

Kiersten Downs on "Feminist Curiosity" and Stamina

***Kiersten Downs** is a doctoral candidate in the Department of Applied Anthropology at the University of South Florida (USF) and a veteran of the United States Air Force (2001–2009). She holds a BA in political science from Binghamton University, a MS in conflict analysis and resolution from Nova Southeastern University, and a graduate certificate in women and gender studies from USF. Her doctoral dissertation research addresses women veterans and reentry to civilian life after military service. Downs keeps a research blog with reflections and updates on her research at: https://womenveteransresearch15.wordpress.com.*

This photo was taken by Devin Mitchell, founder of the Veteran Vision Project. For me, this photo provides a glimpse of my personal experiences and military transition. It tells a story about the motivation behind my work as an applied anthropologist and an activist scholar. It has taken me years of reflection and an intense devotion to higher education to even begin to understand my own experiences as a woman veteran within the complex web of American militarism. There is a part of me that wishes I would have done more to stand up against sexism and gender discrimination while I was still in the military. It has been really difficult to come to the realization that I was part of the problem by keeping quiet about what I was experiencing or observing taking place. But what I also now realize is that my own silence and the silence of others is a byproduct of the gendered institution that we were or still are a part of.

Developing a "feminist curiosity"* takes stamina and according to [international relations scholar] Cynthia Enloe it is not a quiet intellectual pastime. Publicly advocating for gender equity has always been an uphill battle. I realized very quickly that any woman serving in the military or any woman veteran who deliberately analyzes, critiques, and challenges power systems in this arena tends to become an instant target for those in opposition to advancing social justice. It is obvious especially in light of discussions focused on recent current events such as the two women that passed the Army's ranger training along with highly politicized negotiations on expected regulation changes allowing women to serve in all combat roles, that women in today's military continue to provoke mixed responses. Even more interesting to me is the level of condescension coming from some of the men and even other women who were or are part of the military with regards to gender integration. I will elaborate on this latter notion as part of my research analysis.

Like so many other feminist scholars, I am a member of the population that I am researching. There is no way for me to get around the fact that I hold personal biases that likely influence my research. However, this closeness also serves as the motivating force which continues to drive me forward, when even at times the emotional stress of the work has led me to question my efforts in the field. Additionally, I have come to accept that this closeness will always draw criticism from those within academia who feel that we (feminist scholars) have strayed too far from what they understand to be an objective truth. My time in the service has probably aided in the development of my thick skin when it comes to dealing with those colleagues or contentious onlookers who do not hide an exaggerated eye roll the moment the word "feminism" is uttered in relation to social science research or in my case, any work having to do with the military institution. I think it is fair to say that many of us doing this kind of work have experienced damaging and misogynistic rhetoric to a certain degree. I will be up front in saying that at times the continued negativity has gotten to me. Although a burden, it has not stopped me from moving forward with my work.

*Cynthia H. Enloe, *Globalization and Militarism: Feminists Make the Link*, 2007.
Photo: Devin Mitchell, Veteran Vision Project

military masculinity. She foccuses on the challenges that she has faced implementing a feminist mixed-methods study, including an anonymous online survey, semistructured interviews, and participant-observation to explore American women veteran's experiences reentering civilian life. In Downs's case, her aim is to break down the silences around sexism and gender discrimination in the military through her research.

SPOTLIGHTS

Sandra Morgen on Movement Building

Sandra Morgen *received her PhD in 1982 from the University of North Carolina, Chapel Hill. She is professor of anthropology at the University of Oregon, Eugene. Morgen began her career in academia as a doctoral student doing feminist ethnographic work studying the women's health movement in the United States. But it was a challenge because "there wasn't anything called feminist anthropology at that time." She is the author and editor of eight books, including* Women and the Politics of Empowerment *(1988), edited with anthropologist Ann Bookman,* Into our own Hands: The Women's Health Movement in the United States, 1969–1990 *(2002), and as discussed earlier in this chapter,* Taxes are a Woman's Issue *(2006) coauthored with Mimi Abramovitz. Below, Morgen discusses the role that feminist activist ethnography can have in social movements. After having spent a decade conducting research on the impact of welfare reform (the Personal Responsibility and Work Opportunity Reconciliation Act of 1996), she reflects on the success of that research in addressing the policies that made receiving assistance more difficult.*

Our research was part of a national feminist effort to question the mainstream narrative of the success of welfare "reform." We found that most former recipients of welfare continued to experience significant economic hardship and insecurity and struggled to balance low-wage, often inflexible paid employment with their and their children's needs, especially among families of color. Unfortunately, policy decisions were not being made on the basis of research, but on ideologies steeped in racist, sexist and class-based assumptions.

In the advocacy work I was doing on welfare I kept hearing women on welfare compared negatively to this "hard working taxpayer." I realized how little we knew about tax politics or how taxes related to what are traditionally considered "women's issues." So I decided to study tax policy and politics. I coauthored a book with Mimi Abramovitz about women and national tax policy called *Taxes are a Woman's Issue* and then began research on tax politics as expressed in ballot initiative campaigns in Oregon. I have done some advocacy within the research and policy communities to look at gender, race and class as dimensions of tax politics. But also within the feminist community to see the importance of working on tax fairness for women, recognizing that tax fairness means very different things for women in different classes.

I think this kind of work expands what counts as feminist scholarship, a project women of color have been engaged in since the earliest days of feminism. I didn't study taxes because I had an intrinsic interest in tax policy. I did it because my advocacy experience around welfare came smack up against the question of taxes. Is this movement building? I hope it helps point to where progressive, feminist activism needs to be. Even when our scholarship isn't immediately connected to movement building, when it questions and changes paradigms, when it contributes to a feminist critical race, class-conscious way of looking at the world, it is part of the long process of movement-building. I have come to believe that that work should count as important politically. Because we don't know what will build or aid the movements of the future.

Photo: © Robert Hill Long

In some cases, such as Sandra Morgen's discussion on the previous page, feminist ethnography can also contribute to social movement building. For instance, the passage of the 1996 Welfare Reform Bill by U.S. president Bill Clinton led many scholars to examine the impact of the changes in welfare policy. As discussed earlier in this chapter, Morgen is one feminist scholar who spent a decade conducting research on the impact of welfare reform, particularly on women and mothers. That experience led her to shift her research and advocacy agenda far from her previous expertise, to studying tax policy and politics from a feminist perspective.

While at times feminist ethnographers' work is to contribute to the documentation of movement building, at others, a feminist ethnographer may seek to evaluate or critique a social movement. For instance, while Christa's research is supportive of efforts to enhance access to homebirth and legalize midwives, she is critical of the use of "consumer rights" language among middle-class, white organizers, since this strategy can be divisive within the movement. During and following her fieldwork, this often meant having difficult—though also essential and constructive—conversations with activists, many of whom saw little reason to question consumer-based strategies that had proven useful in conversations with legislators. In some cases, these discussions contributed to the inclusion of advocacy strategies, such as highlighting the importance of midwives to improve access to prenatal care among low-income, rural populations. Yet scholarly critique—no matter how constructively intended—is always part of broader legacies of the marginalization of particular voices. The homebirth mothers and families Christa studied frequently bore the brunt of campaigns by powerful medical officials against midwives. In this charged context, her efforts to raise the volume of low-income women's voices within the movement were often met with skepticism. Christa wanted to encourage midwifery advocates to question "sisters in struggle" narratives because they overlooked racialized and socioeconomic disparities in care. For their part, many advocates worried that any questioning of organizing strategies would damage rather than strengthen the movement.[23]

As many researchers learn, once our research moves "off the shelf" (to borrow a phrase from Waterston and Vesperi's *Anthropology Off the Shelf: Anthropologists on Writing*[24]) and into popular consciousness, we relinquish control over how it is interpreted—and ultimately utilized—by both proponents and opponents of our aims. Thus, as well as thinking about how to "give back," we must also be conscious of how our research can be used by others, both in support of, or even against, our aims.

Thinking Through . . .

Ethical Dilemmas

Select one of the issues or figures listed below. Conduct research on the topic. Then write an essay summarizing the ethical issues that you see in relationship to how the research was conducted and what you think a feminist ethnographic approach would have done differently.

- Henrietta Lacks
- Tuskegee Syphilis Experiment
- Stanford Prison Experiments
- Rigoberta Menchu
- Alice Goffman's "On the Run: Fugitive Life in an American City"

Conclusion

It is not always possible for an ethnographer to control the outcomes of their research, but it is essential for feminist ethnographers to consider what possibilities exist and what strategies they can use to anticipate what might emerge, both positive and negative. We also believe that looking back on this process is a worthwhile and fruitful endeavor for feminist ethnographers because it encourages not only personal reflection but also reflexivity within a field devoted to considering and reconsidering challenges as they continue to emerge.

Suggested Resources

Boellstorff, Tom, Bonnie Nardi, Celia Pearce, and T. L. Taylor, eds. (2012) *Ethnography and Virtual Worlds: A Handbook of Method.*

Behar, Ruth (1996) *The Vulnerable Observer: Anthropology that Breaks your Heart.*

Lewin, Ellen, and William L. Leap, eds. (1996) *Out in the Field: Reflections of Lesbian and Gay Anthropologists.*

Longman, Chia, and Tamsin Bradley (2015) *Interrogating Harmful Cultural Practices: Gender, Culture and Coercion.*

The Feminist Ethnographer's Dilemma (September 24, 2011) a panel discussion featuring Orit Avishai, Lynne Gerber, and moderator Margot Weiss at the Barnard Center for Research on Women, http://bcrw.barnard.edu/videos/the-feminist-ethnographers-dilemma/.

For a listing and analyses of Codes of Ethics among Anthropological Associations throughout the world, see World Council of Anthropological Associations:[25] http://www.wcaanet.org/downloads/EthicsTF_emergent%20themes.pdf

Ethics Statements from U.S.-based organizations that relate to ethnography include:

- American Anthropological Association Code of Ethics (1970 [2012]) http://ethics.aaanet.org/category/statement/
- American Sociological Association Code of Ethics (2008) http://www.asanet.org/images/asa/docs/pdf/CodeofEthics.pdf
- Association of American Geographers Statement of Professional Ethics (1998 [2009]) http://www.aag.org/cs/about_aag/governance/statement_of_professional_ethics
- American Psychological Association Ethical Principles and Code of Conduct (1992 [2010]) http://www.apa.org/ethics/code/index.aspx
- American Political Science Association Guide to Professional Ethics (1989 [2012]) http://www.apsanet.org/portals/54/Files/Publications/APSAEthicsGuide2012.pdf

Notes

1 Elizabeth Chin, "The Neoliberal Institutional Review Board, or Why Just Fixing the Rules Won't Help Feminist (Activist) Ethnographers," in *Feminist Activist Ethnography,* eds. Christa Craven and Dána-Ain Davis, 2013.

2 Ibid., 210.

3 For more discussion for her research, see Andrea Queeley. "*Somos Negros Finos*: Anglophone Caribbean Cultural Citizenship in Revolutionary Cuba," in *Global Circuits of Blackness: Interrogating the African Diaspora*, edited by Jean Muteba Rahier, Percy C. Hintzen, and Felipe Smith, 2010.

4 Annette Lareau, "Common Problems in Field Work: A Personal Essay," Appendix to *Home Advantage,* 1989.

5 Diane Bell, Pat Caplan, and Wazir Jahan Karim, *Gendered Fields: Women, Men and Ethnography*, 2013.

6 Diane L. Wolf, ed., *Feminist Dilemmas in Fieldwork*, 1996.

7 Laura Nader, "Up the Anthropologist: Perspectives Gained from Studying Up," in *Reinventing Anthropology*, ed. Dell Hymes, 1972.

8 Ibid., 289.

[9] Karen Ho, *Liquidated,* 2009.
[10] Cynthia Enloe, *Seriously!,* 2013.
[11] Melissa Fisher, *Wall Street Women,* 2012.
[12] Sandra Morgen and Mimi Abramovitz *Taxes are a Women's Issue: Reframing the Debate,* 2006.
[13] Martha K. Huggins and Marie-Louise Glebbeek, eds., *Women Fielding Danger,* 2009.
[14] Ellen Gruenbaum, *The Female Circumcision Controversy,* 2000.
[15] Ibid., 57–58.
[16] Faye D. Ginsburg, *Contested Lives,* 1998.
[17] Faye D. Ginsburg, "Procreation Stories: Reproduction, Nurturance, and Procreation in Life Narratives of Abortion Activists," *American Ethnologist,* 1987.
[18] Tine Davids, "Trying to be a Vulnerable Observer: Matters of Agency, Solidarity and Hospitality in Feminist Ethnography," *Women's Studies International Forum,* 2014.
[19] Kathleen Blee, *Women of the Klan,* 2008 (orig. 1991).
[20] Doug Meyer, *Violence against Queer People,* 2015.
[21] Doug Meyer, "Researching Violence and Asking People to Describe Traumatic Experiences," Accessed September 30, 2015. https://gendersociety.wordpress.com/2015/01/30/researching-violence/.
[22] Elizabeth Chin, *Purchasing Power: Black Kids, America and Consumer Culture,* 2001.
[23] Christa Craven, "Reproductive Rights in a Consumer Rights Era: Toward the Value of 'Constructive' Critique," in *Feminist Activist Ethnography,* eds. Christa Craven and Dána-Ain Davis, 2013.
[24] Alisse Waterston and Maria Vesperi, *Anthropology Off the Shelf: Anthropologists on Writing,* 2009.
[25] These include existing Codes of Ethics by the American Anthropological Association, Anthropological Association of Ireland, Anthropological Association of the Philippines (Ugnayang Pang-Aghamtao, UGAT), Anthropology Southern Africa, Associação Brasileira de Antropologia, Association of Social Anthropologists of Aotearoa/New Zealand, Association of Social Anthropologists (UK), Australian Anthropological Society, and Taiwan Society for Anthropology and Ethnology, as well as others under development in China, France, Hong Kong, India, Portugal, and Romania.

CHAPTER 6

Producing Feminist Ethnography

There are many ways to create, produce, and distribute feminist ethnography. This chapter will explore feminist ethnographic writing, film, performance, and other creative approaches by asking the following questions:

- How does one write feminist ethnography?
- What creative possibilities exist for writing and circulating feminist ethnography?
- How can we make feminist ethnography publicly accessible?
- How do feminist ethnographers engage in creative and artistic projects?

***Spotlights** in this chapter:*

- Aimee Meredith Cox on Writing, Establishing Relationships, and Failure
- Asale Angel-Ajani on Writing (Without Swagger)
- Harjant Gill on Film as a Powerful Feminist Medium

***Essentials** in this chapter:*

- Kirin Narayan, *Alive in the Writing*
- The Sangtin Writers Collective and Richa Nagar, *Playing with Fire*
- Judy DeLoache and Alma Gottlieb, *A World of Babies*
- Gina Athena Ulysse, "My Jelly Platform Shoes" from *Downtown Ladies*

*You will also be **Thinking Through . . .***

- Review & Critique
- Experimental Design
- Developing Creative Ethnography

The most common form of producing and distributing feminist ethnography is through written accounts, which is where we begin this chapter. Traditionally, this takes the form of ethnographic monographs, a book-length manuscript dedicated to the ethnographic study of a single culture. The word "ethnography" is derived from the Greek word "ethnos" (people, ethnic group, and "graphein" to write, or be represented). Creative approaches to producing ethnography also have a storied history that we aim to uncover. Although not feminist in content, one may take a cue in creative production of scholarly work from W. E. B. Du Bois's pageantry genre, which is an instructive dramatic narrative and related to our discussion of representation. In the *The Star of Ethiopia*, Du Bois had thousands of artists dramatize a spectacle on the fiftieth anniversary of the Emancipation Proclamation. There were only four productions in 1913, 1915, 1916, and 1925, in which the history of Blacks is performed in five parts.

Other examples of creative uses of scholarly material can be found in the work of ethnographers like Zora Neale Hurston who wrote ethnographic fiction in the 1940s. In the 1980s ethnographers pointedly interrogated the tradition of ethnographic monographs (intended for academic audiences), and scholarly articles written for academic journals. Feminist ethnographers were a lively part of these discussions and productions. As creative experimentation in ethnographic writing came center stage in the 1990s, feminist ethnographers began to publish more frequently in a variety of genres including fiction, memoir, poetry, and collaborative blogs. Feminist ethnographers also engage in performance art, dance, and other creative methods to showcase their ethnographic work, several of which we will highlight in this chapter.

This chapter offers examples of many forms of ethnographic production—aimed at inspiring you to think innovatively about your own work. We hope that the following discussion encourages you to think about ethnography in new and different ways, and to consider the potential of different approaches for generating research products. We advocate becoming adept (or at least trying your hand) at as many styles of writing and production of ethnographic work as possible. This allows for creativity and can also serve as an important dialogue with your professors about how to best express your work, possibly in multiple forms.

Writing and producing feminist ethnography is an important task, one that can ultimately influence who will come in contact with our work. As mentioned previously, Ruth Behar and Deborah Gordon's groundbreaking edited collection Women Writing Culture in 1995 demonstrated women's robust creative contributions to ethnographic writing. Ethnographers have used various writing styles from fiction to life history, and from critique to memoir. Scholars such as Elsie Clews Parsons, Ella Deloria, and Barbara Meyerhoff, were largely erased from the canon, but their work demonstrated the breadth of what women had produced in written form since the 1800s. Feminist scholars including Louise Lamphere, Dorinne Kondo, Paulla Ebron, and Geyla Frank, resuscitated the silenced innovations of those identified above. That said, innovative and creative approaches—and, we would underscore, engaging and accessible writing—can and should be a part of all (feminist) ethnographic work and we should be open to integrating creative and critical writing. We hope the examples offered here will serve as inspiration and encourage creative thinking about even more novel approaches to circulating feminist ethnography within and beyond the classroom.

How Does One Write Feminist Ethnography?

Writing is not always easy, no matter the genre. Feminist ethnography can be especially difficult because of the expectation to be politically, strategically, ethically, and reflexively engaged. We think that the more freedom and flexibility you give yourself to write badly (at least for your first draft . . . not the one you'll hand in to your professor), the more enjoyable a process it can be. A fantastic short essay on this subject is Anne Lamott's "Shitty First Drafts"—a must read if you ever struggle with writer's block![1] In it, she reminds writers:

> Almost all good writing begins with terrible first efforts. You need to start somewhere. Start by getting something—anything—down on paper. A friend of mine says that the first draft is the down draft—you just get it down. The

second draft is the up draft—you fix it up. You try to say what you have to say more accurately. And the third draft is the dental draft, where you check every tooth, to see if it's loose or cramped or decayed, or even, God help us, healthy.[2]

A classic take on experimentation with different styles of writing is anthropologist Margery Wolf's book *A Thrice Told Tale: Feminism, Postmodernism and Ethnographic Responsibility*.[3] In this book, Wolf, who also wrote the classic ethnography *The House of Lim: A Study of a Chinese Farm Family* in 1968,[4] offers the reader three texts that emerged from her ethnographic fieldwork in Taiwan during the early 1960s. They all center on the story of a young mother, Mrs. Tan, who begins to behave in a strange way that villagers attribute to a variety of possible causes: she is becoming a shaman possessed by a god, she is mentally unstable and in need of hospitalization, or she may be being manipulated by her lazy husband to gain community sympathy and financial support. Wolf notes that although this is a story that has undoubtedly been told numerous times by others who witnessed it, hers are the only written accounts of the events. She is wary of giving them unearned legitimacy, and reminds us to be attentive to the power of writing—inscribing and publishing any story gives it a frozen quality. Wolf is also aware of how her own writing is in some senses polyvocal, incorporating multiple voices: villagers she interviewed, her Chinese research assistant, and her husband who was also conducting fieldwork in the same location.

Wolf begins *A Thrice Told Tale* with a piece of fiction she wrote shortly after the incident in 1960, but never published. Although fictional, and experimental in form, Wolf notes that when she wrote it, she did not think of it as a feminist account. In fact, she highlights the challenges of returning to earlier work as a more experienced, and now, in 1992 decidedly feminist ethnographer. She follows the fictional account with "raw" fieldnotes that she, her field assistant Wu Chieh, and her then-husband Arthur Wolf wrote as the events unfolded. Importantly, she notes, her husband came away with a very different interpretation of the events, despite writing many of the fieldnotes they all agreed upon regarding their accuracy. For Wolf, this makes a useful point, that part of ethnographic responsibility is to present events in a way that allows for multiple interpretations—even by different ethnographers conducting research at the same time.

Finally, Wolf concludes *A Thrice Told Tale* with her academic article from *American Ethnologist* in 1990, analyzing the events from her current perspective as a feminist ethnographer returning to an incident that occurred 30 years prior. A central point that Wolf makes is that ethnographic experience is—and should be—messy. We learn a great deal from challenging and sometimes unpleasant experiences. Her writing evokes this lesson as she demonstrates different styles of experimental/creative writing, polyvocality, reflexivity, and the differences between fiction and ethnography.

Most ethnographers do not have the occasion—or perhaps the inclination—to offer multiple, potentially competing versions of their work. Indeed, it is rare that we get to see an ethnographer's "raw" data or fieldnotes, except in the cases where formal interviews may be archived. In any piece of ethnographic writing, there are many details that are not present, many events that go unanalyzed, and many perspectives that are not emphasized. When most ethnographers begin to write, they sit down with pages and pages of fieldnotes, transcriptions, archives, and the like. It would be impossible to incorporate all the forms of data. The task of the ethnographer as writer is to sift through that material and find stories, events, moments, and ideas that conjure up central aspects of their work. As the example of Margery and Arthur Wolf's different interpretations of the same events above reveals, even two ethnographers working on the same project will have not only different points of view about the events but even within those events different issues may interest them. This is where the importance of a feminist ethnographer's sensibility becomes important and can help sort through their data and begin the process of writing an ethnographic account.

An indispensable book on the process of ethnographic writing, authored by feminist anthropologist Kirin Narayan, is *Alive in the Writing: Crafting Ethnography in the Company of Chekhov*. Narayan introduces students to (as well as invigorates seasoned writers to reconsider) the ethnographic process of writing through reflecting on her own experiences authoring two ethnographies, a novel, and a memoir. Additionally, she shares how she was inspired by Anton Chekov, the Russian physician who wrote short stories and plays during the late 1800s, often based on his travels. Narayan weaves together additional examples from ethnographers and other "ethnographically inclined" nonfiction writers, interspersed with practical advice and targeted writing exercises. Notably, she highlights the significant overlap in style and form among ethnographic writing, creative nonfiction, memoir, biography, nature writing, travel writing, literary journalism, and cultural criticism. Indeed, there is much to be learned from reading, and experimenting, widely.

Taking up Narayan's attention to the power of well-chosen words, we argue that writing is not only a practical or even creative endeavor but also a political one. Indeed, an important political reason for writing feminist ethnography with care is so that people take your feminist concerns seriously. Toward this end, we take inspiration from a broad range of feminist writers—ethnographers, creative writers, journalists, et cetera—who write deliberately and purposefully. For Narayan, writing purposefully means making decisions like limiting freewriting in response to her prompts to under two pages. This strategy both enables and entices others to give you useful feedback, which is less likely if you offer them a long, rambling discussion. Good, concise writing also encourages people to listen to your argument.

Key to this endeavor of writing well—is paying attention to spelling, grammar, and avoiding common writing mishaps. For instance, there are important feminist implications to consider when using passive voice, the sentence construction "(noun) (verb phrase) by (noun)" where the subject is acted on, rather than acting. Although some academic disciplines commonly use passive sentence construction (the natural sciences and psychology, for instance, as in "interviews were conducted"), ethnographers tend to favor "active voice" ("students conducted interviews") because it reveals who is doing the action. Feminist writers have long critiqued passive sentence construction regarding violence, such as "a woman was raped" or "a transwoman of color was murdered," because this grammatical construction can lead a reader to ignore, or a writer to obscure, the fact that someone performed the action.

As with all advice (whether with feminist intent or not), a writer needs to consider the appropriate use of the passive voice. For instance, passive voice does not always hide meaning and can serve useful rhetorical functions. It can allow you to choose what or whom to put in the grammatical subject position. For instance, writing "Student activists were honored at the University" puts the focus on the students, rather than a sentence in active voice that focuses on who honored them, such as "University administrators honored student activists." Like any other grammatical structure or literary convention, if overused or adopted *in order to* hide meaning or harmful actions, it becomes problematic.

In some cases, passive voice may be used effectively when we do not know the agent of the action. For instance, when a writer does not know the identity of an alleged perpetrator, "a woman was raped" may be preferable to "someone raped a woman," because the latter construction privileges a vague perpetrator ("someone")

 **ESSENTIALS**

Excerpt from *Alive in the Writing* by Kirin Narayan

***Kirin Narayan** has written extensively about the craft of ethnographic writing and her long-term fieldwork on oral traditions in South Asia. She earned her PhD in anthropology from the University of California at Berkeley and now teaches at the University of Wisconsin-Madison. She is the author of seven books ranging from an ethnography,* Storytellers, Saints, and Scoundrels: Folk Narrative in Hindu Religious Teaching *(1989), to*

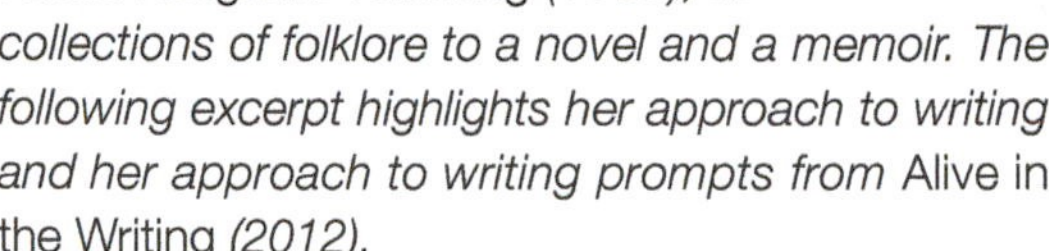

collections of folklore to a novel and a memoir. The following excerpt highlights her approach to writing and her approach to writing prompts from Alive in the Writing *(2012).*

Writing offers the chance to cultivate an attentiveness to life itself, and to enhance perceptions with the precision of words. Writing also potentially communicates images and insights to unseen circles of readers. . . . We all continually improve our ability to describe with vivid accuracy, to lay out ideas with clarity, to make every word count. Writing composed with craft touches readers on several levels—intellectual, emotional, and aesthetic—and the impact lingers longer than words dashed off. Whether in books, essays or articles, grant applications, reviews, letters of application, blogs, or editorials, well-chosen words gather the power to change others' minds and possibly the conditions of our own lives. At its best, strong writing can direct attention to suffering and injustice, deepen compassion and outrage, elaborate imaginative alternatives, and mobilize energies for action. . . .

The boldface prompts throughout the text are meant to initiate freewriting—uninterrupted writing that grows from whatever that seed suggests to you, and that you might later edit and refine. The exercises at the ends of the chapters, though, call for more polished pieces intended for others' eyes. For these exercises, I suggest just two double-spaced pages—not a line more—and here are my reasons. First, learning to write with brevity is a gift to overburdened readers, and especially if you're working as part of a group, a short piece is more likely to receive considered comments. Second, I believe that forcing oneself to be concise renews respect for language itself, for the weight of every word. (xi–xii)

[Throughout Narayan's text, simple prompts, such as "**Start with 'I am most curious about . . .' and write forward. (2 minutes)**" (21) build into more substantive exercises, such as:]

Begin narrating an event that dramatizes the central idea or issue you want to write about. Drawing on all of your senses, use vivid details to describe the people and the place as you follow what happened. For now, don't explicitly say what concept you're trying to illuminate; only show life in process. 2 pages. (22)

Source: Kirin Narayan. *Alive in the Writing: Crafting Ethnography in the Company of Chekhov*. Chicago: University of Chicago Press, 2012, xi–xii, 21–22.
Photo: Shiela Reaves

over "the woman." Additionally, in the statement "a man was raped," the passive voice may actually draw attention to a problematic reality that many people believe that men cannot be victims of rape. In this case, passive voice can rhetorically be used towards the feminist goal of educating readers. Consequently, we emphasize that all feminist writers, including ethnographers who are writing for academic or popular audiences, must make informed and strategic use of grammar to effectively convey the feminist issues we research and care about.

We also choose—with what we write about and how we write about it—to engage with particular issues and not others, highlight particular points of view, and center our accounts on matters that we find meaningful. For feminist ethnographers, it is particularly important to draw inspiration from both our intellectual genealogy and the feminist sensibility that comes from critical and meaningful engagement with fieldwork.

One way some ethnographers ensure that their work is meaningful to those who are part of the research is to engage in collaborative writing. Hence, an ethnographer can create an account that moves beyond polyvocality in the sense that multiple perspectives are incorporated, but toward an even greater engagement with the people and communities under study by integrating their voices into a final product. Collaborative work and authorship, although not inherently feminist, has been an important part of the history of feminist ethnography. Collaboration can be achieved in many ways—from coauthoring academic or popular pieces with a single participant to participatory action research that involves community members in drafting a policy brief. Collaborative writing can also help build feminist solidarity.

The collaborative writing endeavor we highlight here is the book *Playing with Fire: Feminist Thought and Activism Through Seven Lives in India*, written in by the Sangtin Writers, a collective of women employed by a large **NGO (Non-Governmental Organization)** in Uttar Pradesh, India, as activists in their communities. One of those writers is feminist scholar Richa Nagar who, although she is clearly the impetus for bringing the text to academic audiences (by publishing the English version through a university press), joined the collective as a participant and cofacilitator, synthesizer, and editor of the collaborative writing that emerged in the journals of the activists between December 2002 and March 2004.

In all ethnographic writing, it is essential to be aware of intentionality and potential weaknesses. Enlisting the help of others—be they participants in our research, mentors, or peers—can often help us to see and reconsider our work in the context of different theoretical perspectives, ethical dilemmas, and authorial choices. A second example of collaboration is the Latina Feminist Group's *Telling to Live: Latina Feminist Testimonios*,[5] in which poets, oral historians, literary scholars, ethnographers, and psychologists reclaimed the notion of *testimonio*, or life story, to document their experiences as Puerto Rican, Chicana, Native American, Mexican, Cuban, Dominican, Sephardic, mixed-heritage, and Central American women within academia.

This textbook is also an example of collaborative writing, one that does not easily reveal the individual input of both Dána-Ain and Christa. Our process involved each being responsible for writing particular chapters, then each of us reviewing the other's chapter, in turn. After writing this chapter, we reviewed, edited, changed, and debated content via phone, text, and email over 35 times! With each modification, we conferred with each other about how the material should be presented, and what should be included, edited, or omitted. In thinking about the arithmetic of this collaboration, ordinarily one might say that our division of labor was such that this book was written 50% by Dána-Ain and 50% by Christa. In fact, we feel it was written 100% by both of us, because of the collaborative writing process.

Collaborative feminist ethnographic work can also take the form of publishing together about related projects. For instance, Swedish media studies scholars Jenny Sundén and Malin Sveningsson produced what they call a "twin ethnography" in *Gender and Sexuality in Online Game Cultures: Passionate Play*. They write:

> This book . . . develops two parallel stories. The two trajectories of the book are relatively independent, and can be read separately. Then again, there are multiple conversational points of both convergence and divergence between the two storylines, some of which will be made explicit in the collaboratively written

ESSENTIALS

Excerpt from *Playing with Fire* by the Sangtin Writers Collective and Richa Nagar

Richa Nagar's *intellectual, pedagogical, and creative labor has focused on writing lives and struggles across the borders of languages, genres, disciplines, and geographical locations. She is professor in the College of Liberal Arts at the University of Minnesota. Her most recent book,* Muddying the Waters: Coauthoring Feminisms Across Scholarship and Activism *(2014), builds on years of lessons in collaborative building of dreams and worlds, chiefly with Sangtin Writers with whom she coauthored* Playing with Fire: Feminist Thought and Activism through Seven Lives in India *(2006). She has worked with Sangtin Kisaan Mazdoor Sangathan, a movement of farmers and laborers which evolved from the writing of Sangtins, and she has cobuilt a multisited community theater project that brings together amateurs and professional actors to reflect on social issues through literary texts and their own stories (see* http://jananatyachintan.blogspot.com/*). She is also the author or coauthor of five books, The following excerpt, about the process of collaborative writing, is taken from her Introduction to* Playing with Fire *discussing the formation of the sangtins, which translates as close friends or companions. The section is entitled, "Blended, but Fractured 'We'":*

The nine authors of Sangtin Yatra/*Playing with Fire*. Mishrikh, 2004.

The chorus of nine voices in *Playing with Fire* does not remain constant throughout the book. As one of us speaks, the second or third suddenly blends in to give an entirely new and unique flavor to our music. Our notes blend, disperse in ones or twos or sevens, and regroup. . . .

The use of a blended "we" is a deliberate strategy on the collective's part, as is our decision to share quotes from the diaries in a minimal way. Rather than encouraging our readers to follow the trajectories of the lives of seven women, we braid the stories to highlight our analysis of specific moments in those lives. At the same time, our narrative evolves in the same dialogic manner that our journey did, and in the process, it seeks to open up spaces where the primary intended readers of the original book [the original version of the book, *Sangtin Yatra*, published in Hindi]—other NGO workers and members of the authors' own communities—can insert their own narratives and reflections into the dialogue. We want to interrupt the popular practice of representation in the media, NGO reports, and academic analyses, in which the writing voice of the one who is analyzing or reporting as the "expert" is separated from the voice of the persons who are recounting their lives and opinions. One way we have chosen to eliminate this separation is by ensuring that our nine voices emerge as a chorus, even if the diaries of only seven of us are the focus of our discussions.

At no time is this unity meant to achieve resolution on issues of casteism, communalism, and hierarchy within the collective, however. From the outset, the desire that this journey be about "opening sealed boxes tucked away in our hearts" (chapter 1) translated into an assumption that issues of power hierarchies could be raised fearlessly only if there were no expectations of resolution. In other words, the blended "we" hinged on the trust and honesty with which each author could articulate her disagreements and tensions. Bitterness, anger, suspicion, and conflict within the collective produced as many tears in the journey as were produced by the pains and sorrows inflicted by "others." . . . Yet, as an alliance of transnational actors, we want the readers to be aware that the analysis and stances shared in the book are not merely a collection of individual stories but a result of a collective journey.

Source: Sangtin Writers Collective and Richa Nagar. *Playing with Fire: Feminist Thought and Activism through Seven Lives in India.* Minneapolis: University of Minnesota Press, 2006, xxxiv–xxxv.
Photo: David Faust

> closing chapter. In this sense, the chapters can also be read in tandem, guided by our cross-references between chapters as a going back and forth between the "straight" and the "bent," which provides a different reading experience. The first section of the book consists of the ethnography performed by Sveningsson on "straight" game cultures, and opens with the chapter "Go with Your Passion!" . . . . The second section of the book consists of Sundén's ethnographic work on queer cultures of play.[6]

One final example of collaborative feminist ethnographic research that we wish to highlight is the interdisciplinary and comparative work of (In)FERCIT, a research project in Greece on assisted reproduction technologies (ART). Funded by the European Social Fund and the General Secretariat of Research and Technology in Greece, it drew together anthropologists and legal scholars to investigate ART, including feminist anthropologists from Greece, such as Venetia Kantsa and Aspa Chalkidou, and U.S. anthropologist Heather Paxson.[7] The research took place over a three-year research period (September 2012 to September 2015) and focused on generating detailed, multisited ethnographic accounts of ART practices, politics, and technologies in Greece, and relating them to legal issues regarding (in)fertility and reproduction. In subsequent years, (In)FERCIT will provide a comparative perspective comparing the Greek project with similar research conducted in other European and non-European countries: Spain, Italy, Bulgaria, Turkey, Cyprus, and Lebanon.

Even when feminist ethnographers are not writing with a coauthor or working together on their research projects, they often utilize communities of other scholars, as well as participants in their fieldwork to engage in discussions of failure, or perceived failure, in their ethnographic work. These discussions may be situated to position themselves in their work, or as lessons for future researchers.

Yet no ethnographic writing is ever produced in isolation. We draw influences from those whose works inspire us, those whose works make us angry, as well as our contemporary communities that provide support, validation, and allow us to commiserate. Even as we have written this textbook—sometimes struggling when writing came slowly, erratically, or not at all—we have turned our attention to our acknowledgments that appear at the beginning of the book. Recalling and appreciating the influences on your writing, as well as who you want to emulate and write for, can be one of the best motivators when writing gets tough.

What Creative Possibilities Exist for Writing and Circulating Feminist Ethnography?

Much creativity goes into *any* expression of writing, including the evocative stories and theoretical innovations that are part of any well-written ethnographic monograph. In this section, we take up approaches to writing that differ from the classic ethnography in both style and form. For some writers, this may include poetry, creative art, photography, or other original elements in their ethnographic accounts. For others, it means reimagining how to engage with ethnographic data to create short stories, novels, plays, or even imagined childcare guides. Some experiment with parallel writing, and still others draw lessons from the reflexive turn in ethnography—the enhanced attentiveness to our position as feminist ethnographers and our effects on fieldwork—to produce intimate ethnographic accounts through memoir and autoethnography. In this section, we concentrate on creative written forms, and in the next we take up other innovative approaches to circulating ethnography beyond the printed page. The final subsection addresses the possibilities for making ethnography accessible to audiences beyond academia.

SPOTLIGHTS

Aimee Meredith Cox on Writing, Establishing Relationships, and Failure

***Aimee Meredith Cox** received her PhD in anthropology from the University of Michigan. She teaches performance and African and African American studies at Fordham University. She is the author of* Shapeshifters: Black Girls and the Choreography of Citizenship *(2015) and is on the editorial board of* "The Feminist Wire." *Aimee is also a choreographer and dancer. She trained with the Dance Theatre of Harlem, toured extensively as a professional dancer with the Alvin Ailey Repertory Ensemble/Ailey II, and is the founder of The BlackLight Project, a youth-led arts activist organization that operates in Detroit, Michigan, Newark, New Jersey, and Brooklyn, New York. The following are her reflections on writing up her project* Shapeshifters:

AC: I do think how you establish those relationships is a core piece of how you do feminist ethnography. With sincerity and transparency. But I think something that is less talked about in feminist ethnography beyond the methods is how you write it. Do you know what I mean? And I think what I've tried to do, and I don't think this is necessarily a part of how people define feminist ethnography, is to write with lyricism, to not be afraid to cross genres. Because if we're talking about women and the category of "women," however we define that, and we're talking about people who aren't centered for whatever reasons that have to do with gender performance, I think we have to think about the different ways people have to narrate themselves and talk about themselves that aren't always in the social science frame. . . . . The further you are from a normative center, the messier your ways of finding language and finding a style to talk about yourself are, and I want to find a way to talk about that as much as I could, and I wrote those stories.

To do that, I talked with the young women I worked with about what the book should be about. The chapter headings, as well as the chapters themselves really came from what the young women identified as things they wanted to talk about. I was in this site for, almost ten years in various capacities. I could write this book over fifty times and still have a different story. Even using some of the same examples. It was really about what story should be told now, and the young women helped me figure it out. . . .

MC: I'm always so surprised and gratified when ethnographers include stories of failure. Your position within the text has a lot to do with your roles as ethnographer and director. How did you balance those two things?

AC: A lot of why I include myself is because in certain ways I think the way that we do, the language that we do have to talk about Black girls is through the politics of respectability. If we do talk about them it's about their bodies, what they should or shouldn't do, what's appropriate. I felt that what my role in the shelter really highlighted was the politics of respectability.

I was responsible for bringing money into the shelter. It was not a joke. I had the power to hire and fire folks, I could discharge young women, or let them in or not. I think what I did was create cognitive dissonance. As the shelter director, I'm going to act in the best interest of these young women, and as an ethnographer I'm going to write about what all that means. It was very schizophrenic. I think I did more work to not allow the ethnographic work to impact the shelter work than I did vice versa. I really used ethnography as a way to talk about the actions in the shelter rather than the other way around. I was never like, "Oooh a good feminist wouldn't do this." I did what I thought was right based on who I am and how I act in the world, and I had to analyze myself based on that. . . . It's balancing that real desire to want to transform things, and the practical day to day of what happened in the shelter. . . .

The hard part of writing it up was, what part of the stories can be told and the stories are not always going to show the shelter, or the girls, or myself in the best light? And you can't show everything. You can't give a disclaimer for every story. That was hard, letting the stories have a life in the book.

*This interview was conducted by Matthew Chrisler as part of his final project for Dána-Ain's course in *Feminist Ethnographies* at the Graduate Center, CUNY.

SPOTLIGHTS

Asale Angel-Ajani on Writing (Without Swagger)

***Asale Angel-Ajani** received her PhD in anthropology from Stanford University and teaches creative writing at Hong Kong Baptist University. She has conducted research in West Africa, Europe, and South America witnessing the impact of drug trafficking and civil war on the lives of women. She is the author of* Strange Trade: The Story of Two Women Who Risked Everything in the International Drug Trade *(2010). She has also worked with a variety of human rights organizations, including the United Nations Human Rights Commission and Amnesty International. In the following excerpt, Angel-Ajani addresses how the personal experience of having a parent who was involved in drug trafficking impacted the ways she approached writing her book.*

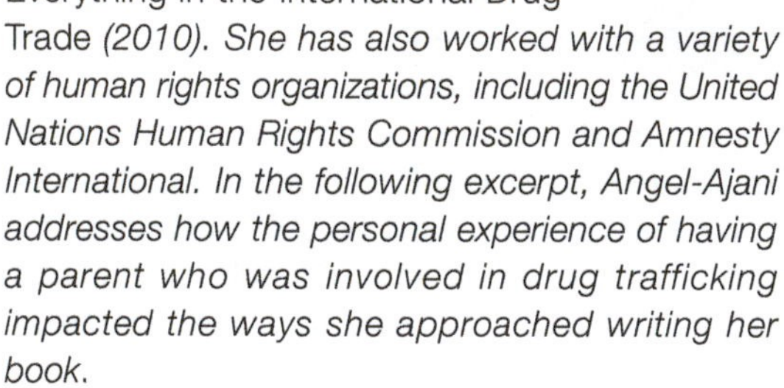

I first came to anthropology through my love of Zora Neale Hurston, mainly her ethnographies—*Mules and Men* and *Tell My Horse*. What I admired most was her ability to strike the balance between studying a particular culture and writing (with humor and without ego) about her place as the anthropologist observing it. She was the first feminist anthropologist that I read. What I learned from her and other feminist ethnographers was to value the stories that were undervalued and less likely to fit in a neat theoretical framework but also to constantly be questioning my personal stakes in the practice of writing and representation.

My book, *Strange Trade*, takes a more narrative approach that is perhaps more emotionally rooted than other books written by anthropologists. Even though there has always been a space for this kind of writing within the discipline, we have moved away from the value of storytelling for language that often obscures and only validates the insular world of the discipline. When we move away from more narrative approaches we lose the possibilities to craft meaningful, transformative, powerful, informed ethnographies that cause us not to look away but to be there, present as readers as actors in the world and that lock on to our memories in the ways that only good stories do.

That said, there are many ways to write about drug trafficking and there are some really good books, important books that treat the subject differently than I do. Journalists like Misha Glenny, Moises Naim and Eric Schlosser have written very succinctly about organized crime and underground economies, including (but not exclusively) drug smuggling, covering the facts and figures and painting rich portraits. But what I found when I was teaching these books was that though the students loved them—I think in part because of the male swagger and exotic locations—they had a hard time remembering that stories of large drug busts or arms deals are peopled by individuals who all have complex reasons that drive their actions. As an anthropologist and a writer, I am always interested in how we choose to tell a particular story. I took a more intimate approach with my own work.

One thing we rarely discuss is an ethnographer's personal impulses to conduct the type of research that they do. Though it wasn't really on my mind while I was conducting fieldwork, my family, my father in particular, with his own history of drug smuggling, was easy and almost natural for me to write about, even though I knew I wanted to try to write a finely rendered account of the lives of Mary and Pauline as they shared them with me. What was difficult was writing about myself as the narrator of this story with emotional candor, which always means sharing vulnerabilities that never make anyone look like a hero. I wanted to be honest about the moral conflicts I faced, the feelings of inadequacy and the loneliness that I felt because I was living a kind of double life in Rome: one of the student and researcher and the other as a sidekick and confidant to a drug lord. At the time, I was not confident with either role. I guess you could say that I had no swagger.

What makes my work a feminist ethnography is the intention behind the writing and publishing of it. I wrote about my research with a much more narrative/literary style because the women who I worked with, who educated me and whose stories allowed me to go on and get a PhD and jobs I felt, should be able to recognize themselves in the pieces that I publish.

Fiction

Examples from early ethnographers—such as Zora Neale Hurston's powerful fiction in the 1920s and 1930s (read an excerpt in chapter 2)—show that ethnographers have long experimented with creative styles of writing about their research. Hurston's work was largely ignored in the academy when it was published, and despite later acclaim—most famously when writer Alice Walker placed a marker at Hurston's grave identifying her as "A Genius of the South" in 1973—Hurston's work remains most commonly assigned in literary courses, not in courses on ethnography. Although her work is recognized as experimental fiction, it also employs familiar ethnographic tropes. She draws on the rigor of ethnographic methods to legitimize her interpretations, as well as the theoretical insights of her mentors, such as Franz Boas, Ruth Benedict, and Margaret Mead. Hurston is also reflective about how her own position as an African American woman who grew up in Eatonville, Florida, one of the first all-Black towns incorporated in the U.S., impacted her fieldwork and writing. She inspired subsequent writers of anthropological fiction to consider the power and politics of ethnographic representation, not only in the ethnographic monograph but also in fictional accounts that may use artistic license to depart from actual events or people.

The same is true of Ella Cara Deloria's novel *Waterlily*,[8] which was originally written in the 1940s, but published posthumously in 1988—coinciding with the increased disciplinary interest in experimental ethnographic writing in the 1980s. Deloria, an anthropologist of European American and Dakota ancestry, who studied with Boas and Benedict, engaged in twenty years of fieldwork studying the history and contemporary practices in Sioux culture before writing her novel that describes Dakota life before the U.S. expansion into Sioux territory. Although the novel was shortened by half, following Benedict's suggestion to focus more centrally upon the plot, it has been heralded as far more compelling than an ethnographic report, but written with equal authority.[9]

In some cases, such as Laura Bohannon's *Return to Laughter: An Anthropological Novel*,[10] ethnographically inspired fiction has been published in lieu of an ethnographic monograph in an attempt to protect participants in ethnographic research. In fact, when the book was first published in 1964, it was credited to Elenore Smith Bowen, Bohannon's pseudonym. *Return to Laughter* chronicles the great difficulty, and at times cruelty, that ensued as an unnamed group in West Africa faced a devastating smallpox epidemic. Since the book is also autobiographical and reflective upon Bohannon's failings as a novice anthropologist, some critics have suggested that her decision to publish under a pseudonym was to protect her professional reputation. Yet, concerns for protecting the anonymity of participants in her research, during a harrowing time for the Tiv in southeastern Nigeria, remain significant.

Another example of what one might call semifictional accounts is the "imagined childcare guides" produced in psychologist Judy DeLoache and anthropologist Alma Gottlieb's *A World of Babies*. Relying on the work of ethnographers in seven different societies, *A World of Babies* provides an engaging format to consider cultural beliefs about infancy and child-rearing. Each chapter imitates the style of Benjamin Spock's *The Common Sense Book of Baby and Child Care*, originally published in 1946, and remains in print after nine subsequent editions. Each chapter of *A World of Babies* is authored by an ethnographer writing as if they are imparting knowledge to new parents as a childcare expert in the given culture, such as a grandmother, midwife, or diviner. *A World of Babies* has become a mainstay in many academic courses on reproduction, and has reached more popular audiences as a frequent gift to new parents.[11]

ESSENTIALS

Excerpt from *A World of Babies* by Judy DeLoache and Alma Gottlieb

Judy DeLoache *earned her PhD in psychology at the University of Illinois and is professor emerita of psychology at University of Virginia. Her specialty is early cognitive development and she has published numerous books and articles on the topic.* ***Alma Gottlieb*** *earned her PhD in anthropology from the University of Virginia, and now teaches anthropology and gender and women's studies at the University of Illinois, Urbana-Champaign. Among other topics, her research addresses infancy and childcare among the Beng in West Africa. In this excerpt, the coauthors describe the breadth and impetus for their creative writing project, A World of Babies.*

Photo of the authors in summer 2015, at Marbach Castle in Germany, where they were completing the new edition of *A World of Babies* (due out in 2016).

People living in different parts of the world and at different historical times hold diverse beliefs about the nature and nurturing of infants. This book celebrates that diversity. Each of its seven chapters is written as though it were an advice manual for new parents in a particular society. The seven societies we highlight include the Puritans of seventeenth-century Massachusetts and six contemporary societies: the Beng of Ivory Coast (West Africa), the Balinese of Indonesia, Muslim villagers in Turkey, the Warlpiri (an Australian Aborigine group), the Fulani of West and Central Africa, and the Ifaluk people of Micronesia. Although these seven by no means represent the range of societies worldwide, they are located on four different continents and differ substantially from one another in many ways. For example, three major world religions—the Judeo-Christian tradition, Islam, and Hinduism—as well as a variety of local religious traditions are represented. The residents of our societies earn their living in a variety of ways, from hunting and gathering to herding, fishing, and farming, to working in the tourist trade. Most importantly for our purposes, these seven societies represent a wide spectrum of beliefs and practices with respect to infants and they all differ radically from industrialized Western societies.

Furthermore, childcare practices differ even within these societies, since subgroups exist within every one. Moreover, all of the contemporary societies we include in this book have undergone significant social change in the course of this century, and, existing at the intersection of many local and international forces, they continue to undergo such change. In the United States today, for example, many Protestants share some child-rearing beliefs and practices with the Puritans while they adamantly reject many more. Within other societies too, many of the "old ways" are no longer followed—a fact no doubt approved by some of their members but deplored by others.

The world of babies is really many different worlds . . .

Source: Judy S. DeLoache and Alma Gottlieb, eds. *A World of Babies: Imagined Childcare Guides for Seven Societies.* Cambridge, New York: Cambridge University Press, 2000, 2–4.

Parallel Writing

Although some (semi-)fictional texts, like *A World of Babies*, are preceded by academic analysis, other authors have engaged in parallel writing, juxtaposing two (or more) distinct texts, often on the same page. Political theorist Annemarie Mol's *The Body Multiple: Ontology in Medical Practice*,[12] interrogates the numerous meanings of atherosclerosis, a disease described as the thickening of the arteries. On the upper half of each page, she documents her participant-observation in medical consultations and procedures, and her interviews with doctors and patients at a Dutch university hospital. On the lower half, she writes in parallel text (made distinct by a different font, and presented as two columns) to reflect on related literature spanning philosophy, feminist theory, science and technology studies, anthropology, and sociology. Ultimately, the texts are in dialogue with each other, aimed at probing the multiplicity and situatedness of Western understandings of disease.

Another compelling example is educator Patti Lather and psychologist Chris Smithies' *Troubling the Angels: Women Living with HIV/AIDS*.[13] The book weaves the authors' experiences conducting participant-observation and interviews with 25 HIV+ women in Ohio, as well as the ways in which the authors became—and remain—emotionally tied to them. Interspersed among transcriptions of interviews is a horizontally split text featuring the authors' reflections on their research—the former in larger font at the top of the page, and the authors' reflections in smaller font underneath. The authors also include what they call "[angel]inter-texts" to serve as "breathers" between the women's experiences and emotions, a deliberate and calculated imposition of scientific interpretation, including "fact boxes" offering statistical and medical context. Finally, the text includes the women's writing in the form of poems, letters, speeches, and e-mails. The combined result is a purposefully discomforting text that delves deeply into the lives of the participants. By denying a straightforward, linear story, *Troubling the Angels* is destabilizing for the reader. In their epilogue, Lather and Smithies even note that participants found an earlier self-published version of the text disconcerting.

Parallel writing can have numerous effects—from successfully bringing varied voices or perspectives together, to pairing different styles of writing, to being quite jarring for the reader (as Lather and Smithies' participants complained). Whatever the ultimate result, which can also be different for different audiences, this style forces us to consider the intent and purposes of what and how we write.

Autoethnography and Ethnographic Memoir

The final creative form of ethnographic writing highlighted in this section involves deep reflection on the ethnographer's role in the process of fieldwork and writing. The term **autoethnography** emerged as a blend of autobiographical and ethnographic writing, and incorporates the perspective and experience of other interlocutors (such as participants in research, but also oftentimes family or colleagues). Although the terms autobiography and memoir are frequently used interchangeably in popular speech, memoir refers to an author's reflection on a particular period of their life. Ethnographic memoirs typically focus on an ethnographer's time conducting fieldwork.

A classic in the autoethnographic tradition in feminist ethnography is anthropologist Ruth Behar's widely read *Translated Woman: Crossing the Border with Esperanza's Story*. She traces her journey as a Cuban American feminist anthropologist with Esperanza Hernández, a Mexican street peddler with whom she became *comadres* during her fieldwork in Mexico. Reflecting on her approach to telling Esperanza's story and her own, Behar writes: "By using both a novelistic style and a dialogical style in this book, I've tried to keep Esperanza's voice at the center of the text, while also showing my efforts to hear and understand her, efforts that led me, ultimately, to my own voice."[14] In her Preface to the Tenth Anniversary edition of *Translated Woman*, Behar notes that weaving her own biography with Esperanza's story, especially the intimate details of her own life that she reveals in the final chapter, received "mixed" responses. Indeed, critics of autoethnography often disparage it as "navel-gazing," merely a chance to write about oneself rather than one's ethnographic work. Feminist ethnographers have taken up this challenge in a variety of ways, including the value of reflecting on one's own position to give context and nuance to ethnographic work is a key feature in this genre.

Anthropologist Irma McClaurin emphasizes that autoethnography is a particular reflexive form that is "simultaneously autobiographical and communal, as the Self encounters the Collective."[15] For an ethnographer who is a "native" in the community they are studying their "work resonates with a reflexivity grounded in a social reality of which [they are] both a product and a producer."[16] McClaurin argues that autoethnography holds particular importance for anthropologists of color, whose work is cited less often, yet whose stories are often appropriated. We should be mindful of the transformative possibilities for particular types of scholarship, as well as historical and disciplinary trends that have extended **ethnographic authority** to some authors and not others.

Another striking example of autoethnography is anthropologist Gina Athena Ulysse's *Downtown Ladies: Informal Commercial Importers, a Haitian Anthropologist and Self-making in Jamaica,* where she writes in what she calls a "third world subaltern female" voice to confront popular archetypes of Black women in the Caribbean.

ESSENTIALS

Excerpt from *Downtown Ladies,* "My Jelly Platform Shoes" by Gina Athena Ulysse

Gina Athena Ulysse *trained as an anthropologist at the University of Michigan, and is an accomplished performance artist, poet, and multimedia artist. She is an associate professor at Wesleyan College and the author of* Downtown Ladies: Informal Commercial Importers, a Haitian Anthropologist and Self-Making in Jamaica *(2007). In this book, Ulysse exposes the personal and professional challenges that reflexivity and autoethnography pose for the young, Black, female ethnographer. Yet, she also eloquently demonstrates throughout the book how things that an ethnographer may initially perceive as trivial—in this excerpt a seemingly mundane fashion choice—can expose the nuanced understanding of intersecting racialized histories, forms of cultural capital, and local norms of consumption. The following is an autoethnographic excerpt from* Downtown Ladies *from a section called "My Jelly Platform Shoes."*

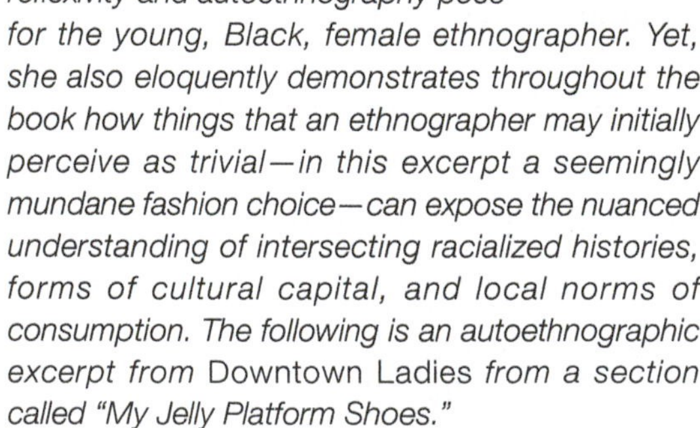

In October 1995, I went to conduct field research in Kingston. One of my prized possessions was a pair of platform jellies. I had worn them the entire summer in Ann Arbor as I had waited to go into "the field." The shoes were in. Throughout the U of M campus, students and even professors wore these jellies or some variation of them. In Jamaica, I wore them everywhere, because they were comfortable, especially during the rainy season. I wore them until the buckle broke. That day, a dark-skinned Jamaican friend, Miss Q. (who is first generation middle class), was visiting. She seemed relieved and expressed happiness that I would finally stop wearing my jellies. "Well, thank God! You won't have to wear those ghastly shoes ever again. They're going in the bin." Surprised, actually shocked, I asked her why. "Oh Gina! Get serious . . . These shoes are so common," she exclaimed. . . .

These moments did not occur in a vacuum but rather within cultural borders with specific definitions of consumption and presentation that affected all interactions. Before I begin an examination of this moment, let me note that historically, in Jamaica, shoes have been a marker of distinction, which at times separated a field hand from a house slave. The cleanliness of one's feet and the type and

(continued)

style of shoes that encase them are visible signs of position. Feet covered in dust differentiate someone who walks to and from a bus from one who rides in a car. Whether feet are sheathed in plastic, synthetic, or leather shoes, these coverings have various capital signs that both mark and reinforce difference. Contemporary anthropological research on shoes is limited. The role of shoes in making gender has been explored more in cultural and literary studies, which have raised a plethora of questions concerning such things as desire, identity, feminism, and globalization. Thicker description* of my platform shoes necessitates a broader field of examination that can ultimately provide knowledge that crosses various disciplines. This is particularly relevant to Caribbean anthropology, where issues of gender and feminism, until recently, were disparate and thus hardly focused on this intersection. Yet, this theoretical crossroads is central to understanding color-, gender-, and class-based inequalities, as these do no rest solely on material differences, but are fully entrenched in the symbolic.

[After further discussing the reception of her jellies, in the context of other fieldwork experiences and interdisciplinary scholarship on race and class, Ulysse concludes:] "Indeed, for dark-skinned, lower-class individuals, money buys character and, in the process, lightens one's color only when it is accompanied with other cultural capital that are determinants of class identities such as education, taste, and presentation."

Source: Gina A. Ulysse, *Downtown Ladies: Informal Commercial Importers, a Haitian Anthropologist, and Self-Making in Jamaica. Women in Culture and Society.* Chicago: University of Chicago Press, 2007, 232.

* Here Ulysse draws on anthropologist Clifford Geertz who describes the term "thick description" as the object of ethnography. Not only should an ethnographer describe human behavior but also offer readers the cultural context to better understand the meaning of such a behavior. Geertz uses the example of a blink or wink of an eye to clarify: is it merely a twitch, someone rapidly contracting an eyelid, or is the person "practicing a burlesque of a friend faking a wink to deceive an innocent into thinking a conspiracy is in motion"? Clifford Geertz, "Thick Description: Toward an Interpretive Theory of Culture,"1973, 7.

A final instructive example of autoethnography is communications scholar Carolyn Ellis's methodological textbook, *The Ethnographic I: A Methodological Novel about Autoethnography,* in which she writes about a fictional graduate course to teach the craft of autoethnographic writing. She favors the terms memoir and autoethnography over what some have called a "confessional," reminiscent of Bronislaw Malinowski's controversial diary,[17] published posthumously, recounting his fieldwork experiences in early twentieth-century New Guinea and the Trobriand Islands in ways that critics have called narcissistic and ethnocentric. Departing from Malinowski's scientific, ostensibly objective presentation of the Trobrianders in his famous 1922 ethnographic monograph, *Argonauts of the Western Pacific,*[18] among other academic publications, when his diaries were published in 1989, his personal writing revealed **ethnocentrism** and insensitivity about his research subjects.

In contrast to autoethnography, which is usually written for an academic audience, ethnographic memoir, which chronicles personal ethnographic experience, is a genre typically intended for a broader readership. An ethnographic memoir that has drawn both praise and criticism is Karla Poewe's *Reflections of a Woman Anthropologist: No Hiding Place,* which she wrote under the pseudonym Manda Cesara.[19] It was one of the first memoirs of ethnography to offer an "extremely revealing account" of an author's experience, which some reviewers have described as "painful," "uncomfortable," and even "tortuous to read."[20] "Cesara" details her early life experiences growing up in Germany, including strained relationships with her Canadian and German family. These experiences serve as background for excerpts from her diary and letters during her fieldwork in Zambia (which she refers to as Lenda in the anonymized account) and extensive conversations about existential philosophy. Her deeply personal reflections include descriptions of her attenuated relationship with her husband and love affairs with a local magistrate and other African men who also served as her informants. "Cesara" positions herself as a feminist in the account, arguing for what she describes as a new feminism, one where "men and women, but especially women . . . realize that another man, even another human being, cannot become their whole existence."[21]

Following the publication of *Reflection of a Woman Anthropologist*, queer feminist anthropologist Esther Newton (see Essential in chapter 2), whose work is cited heavily by "Cesara," wrote her an Open Letter in 1984, which was later published in Newton's *Margaret Mead Made Me Gay*.[22] Newton praised "Cesara's," aka Poewe's "spirit of self-examination and revelation" that she espoused and "courageously practiced." However, Newton fervently contested the use of her work in "a homophobic diatribe worthy of the Moral Majority in the conclusion, citing my work in support of . . . abuse."[23] "Cesara"/Poewe had written, for instance:

> I tolerated homosexuality before I went to the field. While I tolerate it now, I agree with Newton's observation that gays "will always be traitors in the battle of the sexes" (1979:xii). I admired the ongoing "battle of the sexes" in Lenda. By contrast, I deplore the cultural principles which nourish American homosexuality, such as: (1) domination in sex; (2) obsession with youth; (3) obsession with extreme forms of masculinity and femininity; (4) commercialization of physical beauty; (5) egotism; (6) excessive status consciousness; (7) a flippant emotional freedom; (8) manipulation of sex-roles; (9) tendency to produce ersatz cowboys, imitation Hell's Angels, phony oppositions between make-believe men and make-believe woman, and so on. American homosexuality is inauthentic.[24]

Newton's response speaks to what she felt was the blatant misuse of her work: "I put my career on the line to write [*Mother Camp: Female Impersonators in America*, the first ethnography to substantively address a gay and transgender community] (without a pseudonym, I might add). To see you misuse my book to denounce the group I was attempting to dignify . . . is a bitter, bitter irony. As a final insult, you omit my book from your bibliography; readers won't be able to check for themselves."[25] It is important to interrogate texts in light of feminist sensibilities writ large. This is an instructive example: Poewe/"Cesara" represents a scholar who pushed boundaries within the field—in terms of self-revelation and personal reflection—yet also utilizes the anonymity of a pseudonym to make discriminatory claims, and mischaracterize another feminist ethnographer's work.

Thinking Through . . .

Review & Critique

Along with your classmates, choose a variety of different examples of feminist ethnographic work produced in different styles (ethnographic monograph, memoir, autoethnography, a blog, a performance art piece). Analyze the impact or relevance of the styles. Look, for instance, at online responses in blogs, book reviews of academic work, audience questions in response to performance art, etc.

How Can We Make Feminist Ethnography Publicly Accessible?

Many of the creative examples in the previous section aim to make ethnographic work accessible to audiences beyond academia, but that is not—nor should it always be—the intent of all creative work. In fact, creative approaches to collaborative writing or autoethnography (often published by academic presses) can deeply enrich the field of (feminist) ethnography, but may not necessarily reach audiences outside of academia. In this section, we address efforts that explicitly engage with nonacademic audiences. Social scientists have become increasingly "public" in recent years, aiming to extend their work to audiences beyond their scholarly peers. Many ethnographers have become active contributors of op-eds for newspapers, YouTube videos (one of our favorites is "The Anthropology Song: A Little Bit Anthropologist" by Dai Cooper, when she was a Masters Student in Anthropology at the University of Toronto), as well as blogs devoted to ethnography. "Savage Minds: Notes and Queries in Anthropology" is a popular group blog specifically about "doing anthropology in public," which has featured posts by feminist ethnographers, such as Elizabeth Chin, Dána-Ain, Deepa Reddy, and Gina Ulysse. "The Feminist Wire" is another blog operated by an editorial collective of scholars, activists, and writers that provides a sociopolitical and cultural critique of antifeminist, racist, and imperialist politics. It regularly publishes work by feminist ethnographers, such as Dána-Ain and Christa's 2013 op-ed "Equity at the Peril of Normativity: A Feminist Anthropological Take on Race, Marriage and Justice,"[26] and work by feminist ethnographers such as Monica Casper, Aimee Meredith Cox, and Michelle Téllez.

In this vein, feminist ethnographers have made wide use of social media and blogs in recent years to bring their analyses to broader audiences. For instance, many have been featured prominently on *The Huffington Post* and the *King's Review* in the United Kingdom, writing about race and feminism, same-sex marriage, "cyberbullying," and revitalization efforts in Haiti following the 2010 earthquake. To appeal to nonacademic audiences, ethnographers must think about both the accessibility of their language, as well as the placement of research to reach desired audiences. What sorts of journals, magazines, online sites, digital, and nondigital formats should we favor for circulating our work? This answer will vary based on the ethnographer's goals. It is worthwhile for feminist ethnographers committed to analyzing inequalities to ask themselves questions like: What about my study would be interesting, relevant, or meaningful to those beyond academia? Earlier we discussed being attentive to the desires of those we study, and as we prepare to make our work more public, what would engage readers who may not know very much about the subject or geographical location? While not every ethnographic study lends itself to broad audiences, we would argue that for feminist ethnographers, part of contributing to social justice is considering how our work might cross these boundaries.

Another format for making ethnography more publically accessible is film. Since the 1980s, ethnographers have moved beyond presenting visual images as merely supplementary to ethnographic insights, using visual images as an alternative. These attempts have broken from a conventionally discursive or didactic mode of knowledge production. Filmmaker and women's studies scholar Trinh T. Minh-Ha has produced numerous films that have brought into question notions of memory, sensation, and perception in the ethnographic encounter. She is widely known for her award-winning film *Reassemblage* (1982), in which she aims "not to speak about/just speak nearby," the lives of rural women in Senegal. In her important 1989

SPOTLIGHTS

Harjant Gill on Film as a Powerful Feminist Medium

Harjant Gill *received his PhD from American University and teaches anthropology at Towson University, Maryland. His research examines the intersections of masculinity, modernity, transnational migration, and popular culture in India. Gill is also an award-winning filmmaker and has made several ethnographic films, including* Roots of Love *(2011) which looks at the changing significance of hair and turban among Sikh men in India and* Mardistan (Macholand), *discussed on the next page. He is currently filming his forthcoming film,* Sent Away Boys *focusing on how provincial communities are transformed by the exodus of young men giving up farming to seek a better future abroad, funded by Wenner-Gren Foundation and Woodrow Wilson Career Enhancement Fellowship. He has served on the board of directors of Society for Visual Anthropology (SVA) and codirected the SVA Film & Media Festival (2012–2014). His website is* www.TilotamaProductions.com.

My films [use] queer, feminist and transnational studies' theoretical frameworks to explore how masculinities are defined and reinforced within traditionally patriarchal societies like Punjab. While these films are not autoethnographic, they are equally informed by personal interests and experiences having grown up as a man with a Punjabi Sikh family in North India. Having been introduced to feminist and queer studies during my undergraduate training in Anthropology at San Francisco State University, the two have [also] profoundly shaped my own approach to ethnographic film, in terms of how I think about the content, the form, the style, and treatment of my films. In making *Milind Soman Made Me Gay*, I drew directly on the works of feminist and queer ethnographers and filmmakers like Trinh T. Minh-Ha, Cherríe Moraga, Gloria E. Anzaldúa, Marlon Riggs, Pratibha Parmar, Richard Fund, Safina Uberoi. The title *Milind Soman Made Me Gay* is a direct reference to Esther Newton's seminal text, *Margaret Mead Made Me Gay*, which was my introduction to queer anthropology. Unlike the conventional approaches to ethnographic film and documentary which seems to perennially concern itself with boundary policing (trying to determine what is and what is not a ethnographic film?), I found feminist and queer approaches very liberating, permitting me to disregard conventions by placing individual narratives before the form, permitting me to experiment with different conceptual styles and approaches, and thereby defining my own perimeters for ethnographic/documentary film. Similarly, treatment of my more recent films on Indian masculinities including *Roots of Love* and *Mardistan* has been influenced more so by feminist and queer approaches to ethnography in thinking about the experiences of men in India, and in critiquing the role the State and the legal system plays in keeping patriarchal privilege intact. Feminist studies, particularly the scholarship of bell hooks, has also taught me the importance of treating my participants (the subjects of my documentaries) with love and compassion, stressing the importance of depicting them as individuals with agency rather than mere victims of their circumstances.

While I produce work both in filmic and textual forms, I find film to be a much more accessible form of disseminating my research and scholarship, and engaging with audiences both within and outside of the academy. As an anthropologist deeply invested in the idea of doing public anthropology, I find film as an effective tool for dialogue, engagement, and advocacy. I also find that film can offer a kind of an immediate sensorial experience of a given topic or community, through the use of image and sound, which make up the medium, in ways that text alone cannot accomplish. Audiences (including my students) are able to visualize and experience what a young Sikh boy experiences the first time a turban is tied around his head, or what a young Sikh man experiences when he has his first haircut. The affective quality and experience of film as a medium is incredibly powerful for audiences being introduced to narratives or communities they have not encountered before. More so than text, film as a medium allows our

(*continued*)

participants/our interlocutors to speak and share their experiences in their own voice, which is incredibly important within a discipline with a history marred with issues and concerns around representation. Film can and has been used as a powerful collaborative tool for anthropologists to work with the community members, empowering them to share their own stories in their own voice rather than speaking on their behalf.

While film is a powerful medium, I also recognize its limitations—in not being able to provide the kinds of contextual and analytic insights text or a monograph can offer. I don't think film and text should be mutually exclusive. In fact, in my personal experience the two mediums are most effective when they complement each other. I have written extensively about my film work, and I've used film as windows of insight into my larger, more expansive project on Punjabi masculinities, which I am in the process of developing into a monograph. Currently I am most excited about the possibility of using new media technologies to incorporate my films into my writing in the form of interactive and dynamic e-books, areas with tremendous opportunities for experimentation and growth.

---

book, *Woman, Native, Other: Writing Postcoloniality and Feminism*,[27] she positions her work as (un/non)ethnography, in contrast to more conventional ethnographic documentary films.

Anthropologist Harjant Gill also produces elegant documentary films, which interrogate topics related to gender, sexuality, and religion in India and among Indians in the diaspora. His academic writing examines notions of belonging and citizenship among gay South Asian men. His most recent film, "Mardistan (Macholand)" explores a range of Indian masculinities.

> Mardistan (Macholand) is an exploration of Indian manhood articulated through the voices of four men from different generations and backgrounds. A middle-aged writer trying to make sense of the physical and sexual abuse he witnessed studying in an elite military academy, a Sikh father of twin daughters resisting the pressure to produce a son, a young 20-year-old college student looking for a girlfriend with whom he can lose his virginity, and a working-class gay activist coming out to his wife after twenty years of marriage. Together, their stories make up different dimensions of what it means to be a man in India today. Mardistan (Macholand) starts a conversation on critical issues including patriarchy, son preference, sexual violence and homophobia in a nation increasingly defined by social inequalities.[28]

Gill's work has been screened at academic institutions and conferences—which we had the pleasure of viewing at the 2015 American Anthropological Association conference—as well as public film festivals, and it has been shown on BBC World News, PBS, and Doordarshan (Indian National TV). The film's wide distribution has reached audiences far beyond academia.

How Do Feminist Ethnographers Engage in Creative and Artistic Projects?

As evidenced above, the creative processes of conducting fieldwork and crafting ethnography can also lend themselves to producing creative formats for circulation. In this section, we focus on feminist ethnographers who have distributed their work through performance, dance, song, plays, and film. In the late 1980s, for instance, Faye V. Harrison wrote and performed "Three Women, One Struggle," a one-woman show organized around the voices of three Black women from Washington,

DC, Jamaica, and South Africa. Performed in Louisville, Kentucky, on International Women's Day, Harrison writes that "anthro-performances . . . even when published are much more than what can be read from a printed page. Although performances can be recorded through video or film, and hence, viewed by bigger audiences, the dynamics of the wider social event(s) of which a performance is a part may be hard to capture."[29]

More recently, Gina Athena Ulysse's TEDx Talk "Untapped Fierceness/My Giant Leaps," is a beautiful example of her use of song, dance, performance, and personal revelation—and well worth watching. She opens the talk by singing and follows with a performance of her poetry about containment. "You either do that [contain yourself] or you disappear," she says. And then asks rhetorically, "Why do they think that so many Black women in anthropology keep turning to the arts?" The piece she performed is one she wrote after defending her dissertation as a first-generation student. Her "giant leaps" through academia as a Haitian American woman are told through monologue, poetry, and song. She concludes by explaining that her own "untapped potential" is in the merging of her childhood goals of being a rock star and her academic journey to theorize oppression and serve as a change agent in her birth country, Haiti. Through performance, she dramatizes her ethnographic work, and her scholarly work informs her performance. As she says "Little bits of theory started to spill into my songs. And then I started to reference everybody . . . to such a point that when you hear me [sing], you need a bibliography." Her CD *I am Storm: Songs and Poems for Haiti* has received critical acclaim and her one-woman performance piece "Because God is too Busy: Haiti, Me and The World" is a dramatic monologue that weaves spoken word poetry and Vodou chants into a fierce critique of the post-earthquake dehumanization of Haitians in the global media.

Another example is Argentine political theorist and anthropologist Marta Elena Savigliano, who pairs textual analysis with multiart presentation in *Angora Matta: Actos Fatales De Traduccion Norte-Sur/Fatal Acts of North-South Translation*, a bilingual, interdisciplinary text that incorporates what Savigliano calls "writerly experimentation [that] challenges the conventions of fiction and scholarly writing."[30] *Angora Matta* was originally conceived as a libretto for a thriller opera of tangos, developed with composer Ramon Pelinski, choreographer Susan Rose, and animation director Miguel Angel Nanni. The main portion of the text features the original Spanish on the left-hand column and translation/*traducción* of English "subtitles" on the right, interspersed with photos, scene description, and other performative elements. Savigliano builds upon her training in dance, political science, and anthropology to challenge the racialized, exoticized, and eroticized representations of "other" in "traditional" dance forms fetishizing and isolating the communities that perform them from the global flow of international politics. In addition, she coproduced an experimental presentation of this work in 2002, involving 30 U.S. and Argentine artists in the Teatro Presidente Alvear of Buenos Aires. Savilgiano draws upon feminist scholarship to critique the representational politics of ethnography, but she offers novel alternatives.

For the sake of comparison, it is instructive to look at Savigliano's work in relation to anthropologist Julie Taylor's *Paper Tangos,* which also takes up the art and politics of tango in Argentina in the context of military dictatorships and violence.[31] Taylor is a classically trained ballet dancer born in the United States, who chronicles her life crossing borders between the United States and Latin America. A notable element of the book is the experimental design, which includes photographs on the lower corner of every right-hand page so that when a reader thumbs through it a flip-book sequence of a tango appears. Taylor describes this as an effort to convey

Thinking Through . . .

Experimental Design

Read Marta Elena Savigliano's *Angora Matta* and Julie Taylor's *Paper Tangos*. Write a brief comparison of the ways that each author characterizes the experimental design of her work. What differences do you see in an explicitly feminist approach versus one that does not identify as such?

body knowledge by introducing movement onto each page of her written words. Yet, unlike Savigliano, Taylor does not explicitly position her account as emerging from feminist theory or ethnographic practice.

Lastly, Dána-Ain and Aimee Meredith Cox created an experimental performance designed to engage and enliven discussion at the American Anthropological Association (AAA) conference in 2009. The piece was developed as part of a performative session organized by Elizabeth Chin, and was eventually included in written form in *Katherine Dunham: Recovering an Anthropological Legacy, Choreographing Ethnographic Futures*.[32] The AAA session celebrated the work of Katherine Dunham (1909–2006), a dancer, choreographer, social activist, and anthropologist who was a pioneer in ethnochoreography, African American modern dance, and an expert on religion and culture in Haiti. Dána-Ain and Cox, who took Dunham Technique classes with Joan Peters who had trained at the Katherine Dunham School of Theatre Dance,[33] crafted "The Script," never giving it a formal name:

> *The Script* was meant to do heavy lifting; as an intellectual statement or expression of postmodernism, as a performance, as a tribute to Miss Dunham, and as an example of the participatory anthropology that both Aimee and I do. After examining some of Dunham's techniques and dancing we chose to highlight three elements of Dunham's dance technique and put those movements in the service of interpretive experimentation; Breathing, Contraction and Fall and Recovery. Interpretive experimentation meant that others were invited to participate in embodying the techniques/movements. These would include a third person who would perform with Aimee and myself, and the audience. First, I would read the "meaning" of the technique using the auditory as the first point of entry for comprehension of the technique. Then, Aimee would perform the technique to create a visual understanding. Karen Williams, who at that time was a graduate student, interpreted each movement, as she saw fit. Finally following our performance, the audience was asked to perform and interpret the movements. The structure itself was punctuated by postmodernism, in that there were layers of interaction and layers of meaning, all valid—in essence all self-centralized (not self-centered). The self, in this sense, meant that you begin with your own point of reference to understand something, but then it becomes part of a space—literally, figuratively or performatively, that is embraced by, supported by—indeed influenced by, others. The variability of the meaning begins with the person, but then expands in definition . . .[34]

Even years later, audience members who were present at that panel have approached Dána-Ain commenting that they remain inspired by witnessing "an alternative way of thinking about and doing anthropology."

Conclusion

As this chapter demonstrates, there are many ways to produce interesting, engaging, and impactful feminist ethnography. One thing gained from ethnographic performance and creative nontraditional forms of ethnography is the ability to reach various audiences. We also gain the chance to be emotive as scholars—feeling, not just theorizing in isolation, our way through crises, challenging situations, the traumas we may witness, or the joys we may encounter. These creative mechanisms are a useful way to share the stories of participants and to translate theory. Through creative production we open up the possibility of moving our viewers, listeners, and readers to think, act, and respond critically. It is certainly a productive alternative to generating data in more positivist terms. Creativity then may be viewed as an interpretive domain, which expands critical **pedagogy**, the philosophy of teaching and learning, as well as scholarship.

Thinking Through . . .

Developing Creative Ethnography

If you have been working on an ethnographic project this term, take this opportunity to write, create, or perform about it in a way that is new to you. Presumably, you have turned in a paper about the project aimed at your professor (an academic audience). What would it look like to write a fictional account about an event you observed? Or create a dance performance inspired by your fieldwork? Think about your options and choose one aimed at distributing your ethnographic knowledge in a different way. Write a brief reflection on the differences you observe in the two styles.

Suggested Resources

Ruth Behar, and Deborah A. Gordon (1996) *Women Writing Culture.*

Toni Morrison (2007) *Playing in the Dark.*

Kirin Narayan (2012) *Alive in the Writing: Crafting Ethnography in the Company of Chekhov.*

Gina Athena Ulysse (2013, May 4) "Untapped Fierceness/My Giant Leaps." TEDxUofM Talk, https://www.youtube.com/watch?v=xHhngXU8Zw4.

Go to museums, dance performances, and other performative events.

Read well-written work—fiction, poetry, ethnography, whatever inspires you.

Notes

1 Anne Lamott, "Shitty First Drafts," in *Bird by Bird,* 1995.
2 Ibid., 25–26.
3 Margery Wolf, *A Thrice Told Tale: Feminism, Postmodernism and Ethnographic Responsibility,* 1992.
4 Margery Wolf, *The House of Lim: A Study of a Chinese Farm Family,* 1968.
5 The Latina Feminist Group, *Telling to Live: Latina Feminist Testimonios,* 2001.
6 Jenny Sundén, and Malin Sveningsson, *Gender and Sexuality in Online Game Cultures,* 2012, 17, 19.

[7] See also, Venetia Kantsa, and Aspasia Chalkidou, "Doing Family 'In the Space Between the Laws': Notes on Lesbian Motherhood in Greece," *lambda nordica*, eds. Ulrika Dahl and Jenny Gunnarsonn Payne, 2014, and Heather Paxson, *Making Modern Mothers*, 2004.

[8] Ella Cara Deloria, *Waterlily*, 1988.

[9] Susan Gardner, "Introduction" to *Waterlily*, 2009, xxxiii.

[10] Elenore Smith Bowen (Laura Bohannon), *Return to Laughter: An Anthropological Novel*, 1964.

[11] A fully revised second edition will be coming out in 2016 featuring imagined childcare guides for eight new societies. Both editions demonstrate, without a doubt, the myriad "right" ways to raise a child, as well as an inventive and accessible approach to ethnographic writing.

[12] Annemarie Mol, *The Body Multiple: Ontology in Medical Practice*, 2003.

[13] Patricia Lather and Chris Smithies, *Troubling the Angels*, 1997.

[14] Ruth Behar, *Translated Woman*, 2003, 13–14.

[15] Irma McClaurin, *Black Feminist Anthropology*, 2001, 69.

[16] Ibid., 67.

[17] Carolyn Ellis, *The Ethnographic I*, 2004; Bronislaw Malinowski, *A Diary in the Strictest Sense of the Term*, 1989.

[18] Bronislaw Malinowski, *Argonauts of the Western Pacific*, 1922.

[19] Manda Cesara, *Reflections of a Woman Anthropologist*, 1982. Poewe's pseudonym is acknowledged on her website.

[20] John L. Wengle, *Ethnographers in the Field*, 1988; Martha Ward, "Reflections of a Woman Anthropologist: No Hiding Place. Manda Cesara (Book Review)," *American Anthropologist*, 1985; Carolyn Sargent, "Manda Cesara, 'Reflections of a Woman Anthropologist. No Hiding Place' (Book Review)," *Canadian Journal of African Studies/Revue Canadienne Des Études Africaines*, 1983.

[21] Manda Cesara, *Reflections of a Woman Anthropologist*, 1982, 188.

[22] Esther Newton, *Margaret Mead Made Me Gay*, 2000.

[23] Ibid., 227.

[24] Manda Cesara, *Reflections of a Woman Anthropologist*, 1982, 211.

[25] Esther Newton, *Margaret Mead Made Me Gay*, 2000, 227.

[26] Dána-Ain Davis, and Christa Craven, "Equity at the Peril of Normativity: A Feminist Anthropological Take on Race, Marriage and Justice," *The Feminist Wire*, 2013. http://thefeministwire.com/2013/06/equity-at-the-peril-of-normativity-a-feminist-anthropological-take-on-race-marriage-justice/.

[27] Trinh T. Minh-Ha, *Woman, Native, Other*, 2009.

[28] Harjant Gill, "MARDISTAN (MACHOLAND) Reflections on Indian Manhood 28 Mins. In Punjabi & English W/subtitles Directed by Harjant Gill Produced by PSBT (Public Service Broadcasting Turst),"2014. http://www.tilotamaproductions.com/Tilotama_Productions/MARDISTAN_%28MANLAND%29.html.

[29] Faye V. Harrison, *Outsider Within*, 2008, 291.

[30] Marta Savigliano, *Angora Matta*, 2003, xi.

[31] Julie M. Taylor, *Paper Tangos*, 1998.

[32] Elizabeth Chin, ed., *Katherine Dunham*, 2014.

[33] Cox also trained with the prestigious Alvin Ailey American Dance Theater and was a member of Ailey II.

[34] Dána-Ain Davis, "Katherine Dunham Made Me. . .," in *Katherine Dunham*, ed. Elizabeth Chin, 2014, 118.

CHAPTER 7

Feminist Activist Ethnography

In order to identify and evaluate the role activism can play in feminist ethnography, this chapter will guide you through the following questions:

- What does it mean to be a feminist activist ethnographer?
- What should feminist activist ethnography seek to accomplish?
- Is feminist ethnography inherently activist?
- What forms can feminist activist ethnography take?
- How can feminist activist ethnographers reflect upon our practice?

***Spotlights** in this chapter:*

- Leith Mullings on Making Feminist Ethnography Meaningful
- Marianne Maeckelbergh on Being a Feminist Activist Scholar
- Tom Boellstorff on New Technologies and Activism
- Michelle Téllez on Activism Through Storytelling in Visual Media
- Jennifer Bickham Mendez on the Relevance of Activist-Scholarship

***Essentials** in this chapter:*

- Susan Brin Hyatt, "'Water is Life—Meters Out!'"
- Fed Up Honeys on Stereotypes of Young Urban Womyn of Color
- *Poto Mitan: Haitian Women, Pillars of the Global Economy*, a Documentary
- Dorothy Hodgson, *Comparative Perspectives on the Indigenous Rights Movement in Africa and the Americas*

*You will also be **Thinking Through . . .***

- Engaging in Public Scholarship
- Working with Activists

In 2003, then American Anthropological Association president Louise Lamphere argued that an engaged anthropology was vital, given the host of critical issues that anthropologists were researching.[1] Similarly, in his Presidential Address to the American Sociological Association (ASA) in 2004, Michael Burawoy spoke about the critical turn toward public scholarship within sociology:

> As mirror and conscience of society, sociology must define, promote and inform public debate about deepening class and racial inequalities, new gender regimes, environmental degradation, market fundamentalism, state and non-state

> violence. I believe that the world needs public sociology—a sociology that transcends the academy—more than ever. Our potential publics are multiple, ranging from media audiences to policy makers, from silenced minorities to social movements. They are local, global, and national. As public sociology stimulates debate in all these contexts, it inspires and revitalizes our discipline. In return, theory and research give legitimacy, direction, and substance to public sociology.[2]

Over the past decade many disciplines have increased their commitment to more public and engaged scholarship. In fact, a decade after these conversations began at ASA and AAA conferences, AAA president Leith Mullings noted in her 2013 address to members, that calls for engaged, public, and activist scholarship have ignited the discipline of anthropology and making such interventions have not only become accepted, but often expected.

This chapter examines the role of activism within feminist ethnography, and a variety of ways that feminist ethnographers engage in activist work. Many would argue that being a feminist activist ethnographer is practicing a form of scholarship committed to human liberation. It requires that you have commitments beyond the academy—that you are committed to a struggle.

SPOTLIGHTS

Leith Mullings on Making Feminist Ethnography Meaningful

***Leith Mullings** is distinguished professor of anthropology at the Graduate Center of the City University of New York. Mullings graduated from the University of Chicago and served as president of the American Anthropological Association. She links her scholarship to—and has organized or been involved in—activist organizations for racial, economic, and social justice. She is the author of influential articles, such as "Households Headed by Women," and the book* On Our Own Terms *(1996). More information about her work can be found at www.leithmullings.com. In her interview for this book, Mullings describes her work as socialist feminist ethnography to signal an emphasis on the analysis of inequality, the ways in which it is produced and reproduced, and how it can be addressed. She explained that at this point in time, feminist anthropology is generally accepted in the academy, particularly the stream that emphasizes cultural critique. One challenge Mullings noted is in making one's scholarship meaningful.*

It is one thing to do analytic, scholarly work that your colleagues read. It's quite another thing to do work that can affect people's lives for the better. That is a challenge that I would hope feminist ethnography would address. As scholars, we have to think about how that can be done from the very outset of our work. But not all scholars are necessarily concerned about that. . .

The challenge of making your work meaningful to the problems of ordinary people is first to make it accessible with respect to language and availability and second to the extent that you can, to work in the context of and with social movements that can use your work to help bring about change. In an era where social movements are not as intense as they were in the 60s and 70s this may be more difficult. Collaborative research helps to address that. If you work with communities, not only does it make your research better, but you are more likely to produce work that is relevant, that can help people and can be used to empower subaltern populations.

*This interview was conducted by Talisa Feliciano as part of her final project for Dána-Ain's course in *Feminist Ethnographies* at the Graduate Center CUNY.

To explore the subject of activist ethnography, as it intersects with feminist ethnography, there are several things that should be considered. First, ethnographers collect data that can be used to illuminate social problems and can often have an impact on policy or serve as a mechanism to activate community groups. Second, feminist social inquiry owes a debt to politically engaged action, particularly the civil rights and feminist movements of the 1960s and 1970s. Feminist ethnography is unquestionably indebted to the visions, risks, and sacrifices that have enabled gender-conscious struggles for the rights of full citizenship and for human rights and dignity into the twenty-first century.[3] Third, social critique by feminist scholars has played an important role in contemporary understandings of social justice.

Feminist ethnographic research and activism have contributed to the development of the activist-scholar model. For instance, in a recent discussion of the perils and possibilities for feminist scholar-activists and activist-scholars, sociologist Manisha Desai reflects on her experiences with activist ethnography in the early 1980s, when she came to the U.S. for graduate school following her training in social work in India:

> I assumed the identity of a scholar-activist from the beginning of my graduate school career. This identity was facilitated by changes in the U.S. academy at the time, in particular the institutionalization of feminist scholarship, which highlighted the intrinsic relationships between the intellectual and activist projects of feminism. It was understood that feminist scholars would have an activist commitment, which often was the focus of their research, and that this commitment would be reflected in their analysis and writing.[4]

Feminism is a prescriptive project, with a social justice vision that attempts to explain, in analytical terms, power differentials of a number of processes including colonialism, capitalism, militarism, ableism, homophobia, among others. We recognize that the term "scholar-activist" is the term most commonly used by activist researchers, and that some, like Desai, utilize both terms to describe their work. However, we choose the term "activist-scholar" strategically, to underscore how feminist activism and principles so often guide the research of those we discuss in this chapter.

Critics of activist scholarship have claimed that researchers may lose objectivity if they work with a particular group or community for extended periods of time and view themselves as part of that groups' goals—in other words, we run the risk of "going native." In our view, it is often the passion for issues—be it reproductive justice, LGBTQI+ rights, antiracist initiatives, access to public safety nets, or prison reform—that leads many of those who become feminist ethnographers to pursue an academic career in the first place. In turn, formal training in feminist ethnography, epistemology, and theory provides the tools to engage critically with inequity and contribute to social justice.

What Does It Mean to Be a Feminist Activist Ethnographer?

Given that feminist politics both respond to and draw from a social justice perspective, an element of that sensibility is to think about the ethnographer's role in how information is gathered, for whom or in whose interest the research being done. Ida Susser, an anthropologist whose research is on HIV/AIDS, among other topics, argues that it is almost impossible to engage in ethnography and not intervene or advocate when you do research with people who have preventable illnesses or face challenges that can be addressed, such as homelessness. In these instances, she posits, it is an integral part of the research.[5] The political contexts in which research and activism occur vary over time. For instance in the neoliberal moment, market- and consumption-based strategies are advanced as the solution for addressing social problems and feminist activist research helps to demystify and highlight other ways of knowing. Commitments beyond the academy play an important part in being an activist-scholar. Yet, only making one's work available to various publics does not constitute engaging in activism; it requires a particular intent on the part of the feminist ethnographer.

Many researchers, come to feminist ethnography with pre-existing involvements in activist struggles, such as human rights advocacy, racial and economic justice, disability rights, anti-domestic violence, and/or LGBTQI+ equity. A history of engagement in activist efforts undoubtedly shapes, and may become part of the ways we approach our research. For some, this may guide them toward particular research projects. For others, these commitments may influence the way they approach a topic that may have no direct relation to their previous work.

Being an activist-scholar has a long history in disciplines like anthropology and sociology, some dating that relationship to early-twentieth-century figures, such as Ruth Benedict, Katherine Dunham, and Margaret Mead. What did it mean to be a public ethnographer advocating what would now be characterized as feminist goals in the 1920s? In many ways, it was a personal decision to be a **public intellectual.** Using Mead as our example, she had a public persona and wrote for popular journals, using the knowledge she had gathered through ethnographic fieldwork. She entered into public conversation about contemporary societal concerns. Mead wrote a column in the 1960s for *Redbook*, a popular magazine targeted at young married women, and engaged in public dialogue about subjects from adolescence to women's sexuality to environmentalism on radio and television. She was a public scholar in that she engaged in public debates. For example, Mead gave Congressional testimony toward the legalization of marijuana. And at the time of her death, she was working on the Congressional passage of childhood nutrition legislation. Her notoriety, indicated by the political and media responses to her efforts, is a strong indication of her role as a public intellectual. In 1969, the then-governor of Florida Claude Kirk referred to Mead as a "dirty old lady," and various cartoons during the 1960s and 1970s mocked Mead's position on the legalization of marijuana and presented her being searched by customs at the U.S.-Mexico border, presumably for drugs.[6]

How does Mead's public engagement and activism differ from more contemporary feminist ethnographers' activist roles? One might say that being a public intellectual today centers around a commitment to ensuring that one's scholarship is accessible to the general public in the form of films, writing for popular newspapers or blogs, or participating on talk shows or in events that are live-streamed for public consumption. In that regard, being a public ethnographer during Margaret Mead's time is not so different from the contemporary moment—apart from the technologies that are used to do it.

The contributions feminist ethnographers have made to activism and activist scholarship are evident by engaging in critical analysis of social situations aimed at changing social structures. For instance, consider the legions of feminist ethnographers whose work has contributed boldly to reproductive health struggles. In illuminating and challenging the intentions of some conservatives to undermine women's reproductive rights, research by feminist scholars has informed those debates. Exploring the politics of reproduction and reproductive access within the context of shifting economic strategies, Emily Martin's *The Woman in the Body: A Cultural Analysis of Reproduction* was one of the first to illuminate how medical language exploited industrial metaphors to describe and pathologize women's bodies.[7] Other scholars confronted the logic of positioning fetuses as more important than women, such as Monica J. Casper's *The Making of the Unborn Patient: A Social Anatomy of Fetal Surgery*.[8] Still others examined the implications of new reproductive technologies, such as sociologist Barbara Katz Rothman in her text on how prenatal testing changed the landscape for women's experience of pregnancy, *The Tentative Pregnancy: How Amniocentesis Changes the Experience of Motherhood*, and anthropologist Sarah Franklin's scholarship on the cultural dimensions of assisted reproduction and the debates surrounding them, documented in *Embodied Progress: A Cultural Account of Assisted Conception* and *Biological Relatives: IVF, Stem Cells and the Future of Kinship*.[9] Interventions may also be found in the work of scholars who use a critical race perspective both within activist efforts and scholarship on reproduction. For instance, legal scholar Dorothy Roberts's *Killing The Black Body: Race, Reproduction, and the Meaning of Liberty* argues that one can never understand reproduction without considering race.[10] Anthropologist Khiara Bridges explores how processes of racialization are evident in prenatal care in *Reproducing Race: An Ethnography of Pregnancy as a Site of Racialization.*[11] Social critique can be valuable for activist scholars, because it works to transform our thinking in ways that can influence organizing strategies and approaches, as well as open up new avenues of inquiry and intervention for other scholars to pursue.

Other scholars are involved in activist work more directly, engaging with and in movements for social change. One example that builds on the social critique of reproductive politics highlighted above is the Advocacy Committee established by the Council on Anthropology and Reproduction (CAR), a special interest group of the Society for Medical Anthropology. CAR has been active for the past decade, working with groups like National Advocates for Pregnant Women and contributing to policy brief drafts used to influence policy. For instance, CAR published

Thinking Through . . .

Engaging in Public Scholarship

One way to engage in public scholarship is to edit a public resource like Wikipedia. This is particularly important for feminists because Wikipedia's articles on women, people of color, LGBTQI+ figures, and feminist/queer organizations are often incomplete, "stubs," of low quality, or simply non-existent. Wikipedia is the 7th "most read" website on the Internet (falling behind only search engines, YouTube, and social media sites).

Look up WikiProjects on Feminism, Gender Studies, LGBT Studies, or WikiProjects relevant to countering systematic bias. From those pages, you can choose a "stub" (an incomplete article), conduct your own research, and add your content. See also, Wikipedia links to "How to" Guides (and a video tutorial), as well as suggestions for writing about women, transgender, non-binary, and intersex people linked to the WikiProjects mentioned above. Write a brief reflection about the experience (why did you chose a particular topic? what state was it in prior to your intervention? why did you make the changes that you did? what interactions, if any, did you have with Wikipedia administrators and/or other users?).

a statement vehemently opposing legislation that creates barriers to safe abortion care, encouraging readers to contact lawmakers opposing such legislation and work with organizations like Planned Parenthood that provide reproductive healthcare to low-income women and are being targeted by these laws.[12]

What Should Feminist Activist Ethnography Seek to Accomplish?

Feminist ethnographers contribute to many types of activism, including those that lean toward conservatism (see discussion of Poewe/"Cesara's" ethnographic memoir in chapter 6). This textbook is primarily oriented toward engagement or activism that is politically *progressive*, indeed concerned with both feminism and social justice. By social justice we mean understanding how power works, and seeking to ensure equitable treatment.

In the twenty-first century, being an activist-scholar often means developing formal relationships with organizations or community-based programs in which research priorities are determined by the organizations for their benefit. Whether engaged, activist or public, any one of these terms (often used interchangeably by scholars) mean that feminist ethnographers consciously put themselves in public dialogue about issues of injustice. That public may be a general listening public, a government-related public, or a community-based public, such as an activist organization. The point is that the feminist ethnographer who seeks to be public, engaged, or activist aims to accomplish research that is meaningful for those who participate in it.

In "'Water Is Life, Meters Out!' Women's Grassroots Activism and the Privatization of Public Amenities,"[13] anthropologist Susan Brin Hyatt discusses her ethnographic project on the privatization of water in a deindustrialized town in the United Kingdom. Essentially, Hyatt attempts to see the way that women, through the lens of activism, understood their structural disadvantage. One of the things that Hyatt found in researching and documenting activist work was that people could envision the possibility of making common cause with other groups whom they previously had seen as the root of the problem.

Women organized campaigns against companies that were selling water, which they thought should be provided by the state. Privatizing water increased the likelihood that poor and working class families would be unable to pay their bills at some point. In order to have a "seat" at the table to air their concerns, the women bought shares in the water company so they could attend the annual shareholders meeting. Hyatt also bought one share and she too attended. This offers a glimpse of into the role that a feminist activist ethnographer can play in both conducting research and contributing to the issue under study.

A second example illustrating feminist activist ethnography is evident in Bianca Williams' work. Williams embodies being an academic and an activist. She is a coleader of Black Lives Matter 5280, the Denver chapter of the national Black Lives Matter (BLM) organization. Williams's research includes focusing on the emotional well-being of Black women as it contributes to the group's five Community Commitments, including striving for justice; affirming Black women leadership; inclusivity; serving Black communities; and cultivating Black love. Her activism informs her scholarship such that in the past year and a half, as Black women across the globe have risen as founders, organizers, and leaders in the BLM movement, Williams is undertaking a research project that documents and analyzes how they participate in radical self- and communal care. As part of their initiative, BLM encourages organizers and leaders to prioritize self-care in the struggle for racial

ESSENTIALS

Excerpt from "Water Is Life—Meter's Out!" by Susan Brin Hyatt

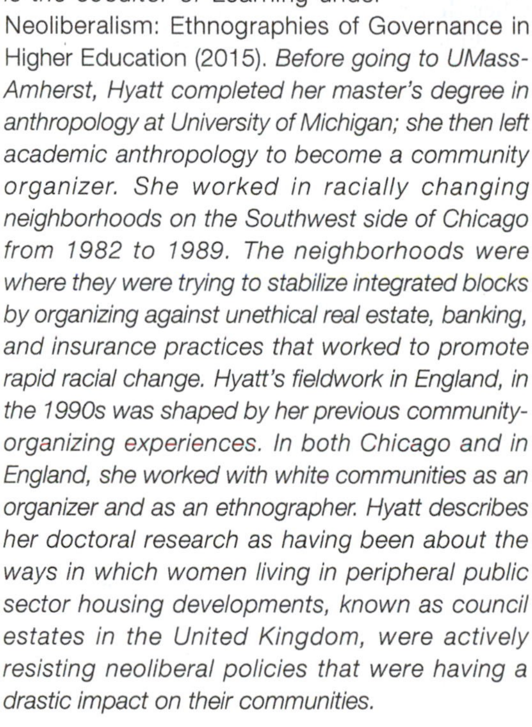

Susan Brin Hyatt *is an associate professor of anthropology at Indiana University-Purdue University at Indiana, where she is the founding director of the MA program in applied anthropology. She considers herself to be a feminist ethnographer because she looks at gender as one of many ways in which people become arrayed along a continuum of inequality and privilege. She received her PhD from University Massachusetts at Amherst. She is the coeditor of* Learning under Neoliberalism: Ethnographies of Governance in Higher Education (2015). *Before going to UMass-Amherst, Hyatt completed her master's degree in anthropology at University of Michigan; she then left academic anthropology to become a community organizer. She worked in racially changing neighborhoods on the Southwest side of Chicago from 1982 to 1989. The neighborhoods were where they were trying to stabilize integrated blocks by organizing against unethical real estate, banking, and insurance practices that worked to promote rapid racial change. Hyatt's fieldwork in England, in the 1990s was shaped by her previous community-organizing experiences. In both Chicago and in England, she worked with white communities as an organizer and as an ethnographer. Hyatt describes her doctoral research as having been about the ways in which women living in peripheral public sector housing developments, known as council estates in the United Kingdom, were actively resisting neoliberal policies that were having a drastic impact on their communities.*

One of the most active campaigns I observed and participated in was a campaign organized and participated in primarily by low-income women against the effects of water privatization. . . .

The annual meeting was scheduled for a day in late September 1994. We decided that we would have a little demonstration outside of the building where the meeting was to be held before it began. I suggested that we collect some bottled waters (which I bought in the supermarket) and set up a little "stand" where we would display the bottled waters alongside other bottles labeled, "Water from the Meters of Lower Grange." Everyone agreed to this plan and we spent an afternoon making placards with the message, "Water for Sale! Is Social Justice Also for Sale?" and fliers that read: First there was the craze for Perrier, then it was other bottled waters like Highland Spring or Buxton. Will the next fashion for expensive, overpriced water be Water from the Meters of Lower Grange? SHOULD WATER FEEL MORE LIKE A LUXURY THAN A NECESSITY?

We arrived at the shareholders' meeting early the next morning in festive spirits. Needless to say, the majority of shareholders were not sympathetic to the cause, but the media and various and sundry other groups who were also there to protest came by the table we had set up and chatted with us.

Source: Susan Brin Hyatt. "'Water is Life—Meters Out!' Women's Grassroots Activism And the Privatization of Public Amenities." Occasional Papers on Globalization. University of South Florida. Vol. 1(7), (2004), 8.

justice, going as far as to have a "Healing Justice" committee dedicated to creating strategies "to assist communities who are rising up and fighting back against anti-Black state and state-sanctioned violence to care for themselves, move through grief, heal from trauma, and attend to their emotional and physical safety in protest spaces."[14]

In contrast, it is not always feasible for scholars (feminist or otherwise) to identify themselves during fieldwork as activists or engage in direct activism. Sometimes this is the case due to geopolitical constraints, which may be a barrier for assuming the role of activist or advocate. Geopolitics is a complex and complicated issue that can be unpredictable in the ways it motivates and/or encumbers an ethnographer. Nonetheless, feminist activist researchers often find alternative ways to engage in change. For example, serving in an intermediary capacity allow one to take part in a dialogue or conversation, while at the same time maintaining a kind of distance from the issue under discussion, in ways that may prove to be more useful to a long-term project.

Is Feminist Ethnography Inherently Activist?

As Indigenous rights activist and education scholar Linda Tuhiwai Smith has written, "There is no easy or natural relationship between activism and research. Although some activists are also researchers, and have to undertake their own research, and researchers may also be activists, the roles are very different."[15] However, we believe it is accurate to say that most feminist ethnographers have shaped their work in relation to broader political concerns, despite the fact that professional ethnographers are sometimes treated with skepticism from the academy when they engage in activism. When you consider yourself a feminist activist ethnographer, it is a priority to have feminist principles as a researcher that merge both research and activism. In so doing, there is a shift in the responsibility that a feminist ethnographer has to those they study.

Performance studies scholar D. Soyini Madison has written on the use of what she terms critical ethnography, which we view as similar to activist ethnography:

> Critical ethnography . . . begins with an ethical responsibility to address processes of unfairness or injustice within a particular lived domain. By "ethical responsibility" I mean a compelling sense of duty and commitment based on moral principles of human freedom and well-being and hence a compassion for the suffering of living beings. The conditions for existence within a particular context are not as they could be for specific subjects; as a result, the researcher feels a moral obligation to make a contribution toward changing those conditions toward greater freedom and equity. The critical ethnographer also takes us beneath surface appearances, disrupts the status quo, and unsettles both neutrality and taken-for-granted assumptions by bringing to light underlying and obscure operations of power and control. Therefore, the critical ethnographer resists domestication and moves from "what is" to "what could be."[16]

One thing is certain: proponents of feminist activist ethnography are opposed to the idea that any research can be "objective" or neutral. In fact, they highlight that discussing inequities is, in effect, a political position itself. Feminist activist ethnographers are conscious of—and must be reflective about—their desire for their research to be politically relevant.

One of the mid-twentieth century's most vocal activist feminist scholars in the discipline of anthropology was Eleanor "Happy" Leacock who believed that feminist anthropology was part of a broader radical critique of the origins of inequality in which detailed attention needed to be paid to historical processes. Her scholarship covered many subjects, such as Indigenous issues, poverty, education, and racism in schools, and one of the most important contributions to feminist scholarship was Leacock's introduction to the reissue of Friedrich Engels's *Origins of the Family, Private Property and the State*,[17] which locates the origins of women's oppression in economic systems. Although she struggled to find academic employment during the 1950s because of her political work—for example, as an activist with the group Harlem Fight Back—Leacock modeled what is means to be a feminist and activist. Leacock was a founder of the New York Women's Anthropology Caucus, which among other things, challenged sexism in the academy. Her research among the Montagnais-Naskapi in the northern Labrador region of Canada shed light on how industrial capitalism impacted Indigenous people's lives, essentially destroying egalitarian relationships. It was Leacock's political commitments to equality that often drove her research. During the McCarthy era, many Americans were accused of being Communists or Communist sympathizers and Leacock was careful about calling herself an "activist."

The simplest answer to the question in this section is that not every feminist ethnographic project is activist in intent, and not every ethnographic project on feminist activism produces feminist ethnography. One would be hard pressed to pose ethnography as intrinsically activist. Yet we believe that learning about activist possibilities enhances all work that aims to be attentive to issues of power, privilege, and inequality.

What Forms Can Feminist Activist Ethnography Take?

Many feminist activist ethnographers engaged in social issues are viewed as experts. In fact, feminist ethnographers' expertise may be used in many ways: from teaching to public education, from publishing to collaboration, and from conducting research to working on campaigns. They use their skills and **cultural capital** to raise awareness, inform policy, engage with media, and serve as expert witnesses in human rights and legal cases.

In many instances, feminist scholars have sought to develop projects that bridged the gaps between the researcher and the researched, between subjectivity and objectivity, between theory and practice. Here we might reconsider the import of expertise. Ethnographic knowledge can serve as a form of witnessing and exploring the processes through which activist practice can emerge. In the field of theology, we see the use of ethnography as a form of witnessing. According to Christian theologians Christian Scharen and Aana Marie Vigen in *Ethnography as Christian Theology and Ethics*, when scholars divest themselves from being an expert, they can become "witnesses to truth on a more profound level."[18] Likewise, women's studies scholar Deborah Gordon in the article "Border Work: Feminist Ethnography and the Dissemination of Literacy,"[19] discusses witnessing and the role it plays in reinventing stories of suffering that can be used in support of social justice. Accordingly, witnessing can be a fundamentally important component of feminist activist ethnography.

While there are many forms that feminist activist ethnography can take, the scales of that activism—that is, how much a researcher interacts with organizers, the intention of their ethnographic work, et cetera—differ across projects. Zethu Matebeni is an interdisciplinary feminist scholar and activist whose research is linked to queer issues, sexuality, gender, race, HIV and AIDS, film, cinema, and photography. Along with three other scholars—psychologist Vasu Reddy, clinical psychiatry research scientist Theo Sandfort, and LGBTI program coordinator for the Open Society Initiative for Southern Africa Ian Southey-Swartz—Matebeni wrote about a community study based on in-depth interviews with 24 self-identifying African lesbians living with HIV in South Africa, Zimbabwe, and Namibia. The study focused on the women's personal experiences and circumstances, making the point that women's experiences shed light on and challenges popular notions of lesbian risk. Matebeni also curates exhibits and book projects, including "Jo'burg TRACKS: Sexuality in the City," and the book project *Reclaiming Afrikan: Queer Perspectives on Sexual and Gender Identities*.[20]

Feminist activist ethnographers often document and analyze local or community-based movements. Consider, for example, Michelle Marzullo's analysis of a local instantiation of same-sex marriage. In her article, "Seeking Marriage Material: Rethinking the U.S. Marriage Debates Under Neoliberalism,"[21] Marzullo examines the circumstances and outcome of Mayor Jason Wests's decision to perform same-sex marriages in the Hudson Valley city of New Paltz, New York, in 2004. Wests's decision was prompted by his interest in his city doing its part to contribute to the larger goal of legalizing same-sex marriage. Marzullo's focus on this particular local effort may be viewed in contrast to a researcher who might document and analyze same-sex marriage conceptually in terms of family making or national efforts to legalize same-sex marriage.

Another feminist scholar who has engaged in activism on a variety of local, as well as international issues, is anthropologist Marianne Maeckelbergh. She began engaging in activism by attending animal rights protests in New York City, and quickly became involved in organizing protests around issues ranging from human rights to prisoner support to environmental activism. Maeckelbergh was involved in campaigns to stay the execution of Mumia Abu-Jamal, to divest from Burma, to prevent the Mitsubishi Corporation from cutting old growth forests, and to stop the forced relocation of the Dineh people from their homelands to a nuclear waste dump site.

As is the case with most feminist activist ethnographers, it is exposing hierarchies and power structures of the state that Maeckelbergh finds most useful to her work. She reveals that although she still doesn't understand how all the practices

SPOTLIGHTS

Marianne Maeckelbergh on Being a Feminist Activist Scholar

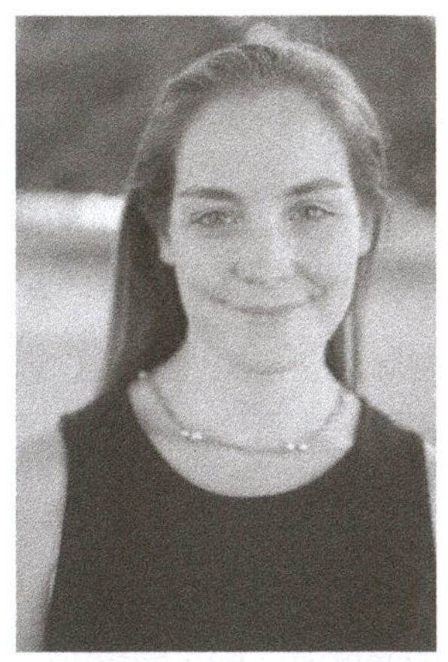

Marianne Maeckelbergh *is an associate professor in cultural anthropology and development sociology at Leiden University, Netherlands, and she received her PhD from the University of Sussex. She has been actively involved in grassroots movements since the mid-1990s. Here is what she says about her activism.*

A turning point for me was the 1999 anti-WTO protests in Seattle, where so many of these divergent issues came together. The escalation of those protests into a full-scale conflict zone left a strong and lasting impression on me. On the one hand, thousands of people taking over the streets and the world seemingly opening up in front of us with endless possibilities in a truly empowering and inspiring way, while on the other hand, the police using pepper spray, tear gas, batons and rubber bullets indiscriminately on tens of thousands of protestors, and on random residents of Seattle. For me, it was a moment that laid bare the global power dynamics of the world we live in. Since then I've attended many of the anti-summit protests around the world as well as the European Social Forum in 2003 and 2004 and the World Social Forum in 2004, usually arriving early to help organize. Since 2011, I've been working on the film project www.globaluprisings.org and have been trying to create connections and exchange of information between the many movements, uprisings, revolts and revolutions that have emerged around the world.

It was my involvement in these movements that led me to want to better understand how power operates. It was also these movements that made me want to understand how people can and do organize to change the way power operates.

of power operate, she says, "My experiences as an activist (for example, being confronted by angry and completely irrational police using violence against me and fellow activists) and my experiences as a scholar (experiencing the forms of authority academia implies, as well as the skepticism towards this form of authority from those without it) continuously contribute to the long learning process. There is much left to analyze."

Participatory Action Research

Engaging in collaborative research can profoundly affect how the research is shaped. Participatory action research (PAR) is one form of such collaboration. PAR, as described briefly in chapter 4, involved methods that are developed for a research project *with* the people being studied. Anthropologist Luke Eric Lassiter discusses feminist approaches to collaborative research in *The Chicago Guide to Collaborative Ethnography*, such as cowriting the outcome of the research with the participants.[22] Ideally, this process will benefit both the researcher and the subjects of inquiry, enabling participants to serve as partners in the production of knowledge. Participants are valued and consulted in almost all steps in the research process.

An early example of collaborative research was the four-year literacy project that was directed by urban affairs and public policy scholar Rosa Torruellas, along with oral historians Ana Jurabe and Rina Benmayor. Between 1985 and 1989, the Center for Puerto Rican Studies at Hunter College in New York City initiated and ran a Spanish-language adult literacy program in East Harlem.[23] The researchers created the project to study educational patterns in a community with high dropout rates and promoted women's empowerment through Spanish-language literacy. The most profound outcome of collaborative and public scholarship is that it shifts the role of more passive research informants to consultants or participants who may take on a number of roles such as cointerpreters, coresearchers, or collaborators.

A more contemporary example of collaborative research is environmental psychologist Caitlin Cahill's community-based PAR project with young people investigating the everyday experiences of global urban restructuring. The project "Makes Me Mad: Stereotypes of Young Urban Womyn of Color," involved Cahill and six young women researchers living on the Lower East Side of Manhattan.[24] Together they investigated the relationship between the gentrification of their community, public (mis)representations, and their self-understanding. Because the project was developed for and by young urban womyn of color, it reflects their concerns.

Dána-Ain worked on a PAR project with students from Queens College with the Office of Community Studies (OCS) and the Griot Circle, an organization founded to meet the needs of elder LGBT people of color. Wanting to address the problem of Access-a-Ride, a paratransit service for people with limited mobility, operated by New York's Mass Transit Authority (MTA), Griot sought a research partner to help understand the problems its members had with Access-a-Ride. Due to time and budgetary constraints, they agreed to use survey methodology. They wanted the OCS student researchers and Dána-Ain to conduct the research, analyze the data, and develop an agenda to advocate for better services. Members of Griot and the executive director collaborated in developing the first draft of the survey. Then Dána-Ain, working with three masters-level students, refined the survey after consultation with OCS staff. A second draft went back to Griot Circle for members to review. In return, they received a third draft, which OCS staff finalized. At the moment that Dána-Ain thought they had finished with the back and forth, the executive director sent an email stating that since the survey would not only be aimed at Griot members but members of other elder-focused programs, they too wanted some input in the survey instrument. Although this project is not inherently feminist, the analysis of the data will include attention to gender and gender variance in relationship to accessing these services. The back and forth that Dána-Ain experienced with Griot is not unusual in the PAR process. In order to maintain the integrity of a participatory research project grounded in feminist principles, a researcher must be willing to accept the full participation of community members in the process. This can be daunting and quite a bit of time is necessary to ensure that all parties experience full investment and ownership in the project.

 **ESSENTIALS**

Excerpt from the Fed Up Honeys on Stereotypes of Young Urban Womyn of Color

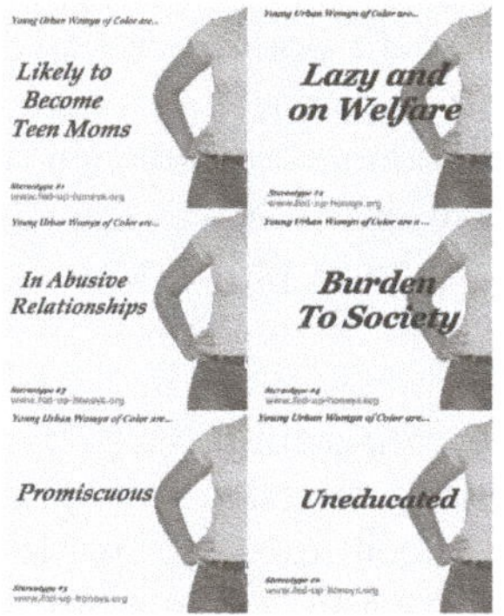

The Fed Up Honeys formed a collaborative community-based participatory action research (PAR) project to address the concerns of women of color living in the Lower East Side in New York City. One of the researchers is feminist ethnographer Caitlin Cahill, an environmental psychologist from New York City, who specializes in PAR research. Committed to interdisciplinary, engaged scholarship, Cahill has received a Taconic Fellowship from the Pratt Center for Community Development and a special recognition from the American Civil Liberties Union (ACLU) for her work with young people on educational rights. Together, Indra Rios-Moore, Erica Arenas, Jennifer Contreras, Na Jiang, Tiffany Threatts, Shamara Allen, and Caitlin Cahill published a research report "Makes Me Mad: Stereotypes of Young Urban Womyn of Color" and launched the website www.fed-up-honeys.org. Cahill has also published extensively on collaborative PAR research. The following excerpt from one coauthored publication by Cahill, Rios-Moore, and Threatts discusses the genesis of their collaborative research and activist outcomes of the Fed Up Honey's work.

Our study considered the relationship between the lack of resources in our community, the Lower East Side neighborhood of New York City, and mischaracterizations of young women. When we first began our project, we did not know what we were going to research. The area of investigation was open as the study was broadly defined as "the everyday lives of young women in the city." We collectively determined the focus of the project after working together for several weeks, and after doing preliminary research on our neighborhood and our own everyday experiences. . . . The project is for and by young urban women of color and is reflective of our own concerns and the issues that personally affected us. We represent a diverse collection of personalities and backgrounds; the fact that we all felt so passionately about this topic is a testament to its likely importance to all young women affected by stereotypes that are pervasive in popular culture and the self-image issues that stem from them. . . .

As is evident in the title for our project "Makes Me Mad," we wanted to express our anger in order to engage others, depending on who they are, to either feel their own pain or experience the pain and guilt of acknowledging racism. With our "stereotype stickers" we wanted to "prick the 'psychic amnesia' that has infected America" (Torre and Fine 2006). Each sticker features a stereotype about young urban women of color including: "Likely to become teen moms," "In abusive relationships," "Promiscuous," "Uneducated," "Lazy and on Welfare," and "Burden to society." In the sticker campaign we hoped to upset and motivate "to go against the grain, to prove everyone wrong" and "to realize what it is we have against us." We created the stickers especially for other young women of color, but we posted them all over our neighborhood as we hoped to provoke the public in general into rethinking these stereotypes and how they related

(continued)

to the gentrification of our community. We also used the stereotype stickers to "advertise" our website.

Our website www.fed-up-honeys.org, "created by young womyn of color for young womyn of color," is a kind of one-stop-shop experience where visitors can find out about the "Makes Me Mad" research project. On our website you can download our study and learn more about our research. We have a page devoted to the Lower East Side that includes links to community organizations and businesses that connect to young people's interests. We have a page of resources especially for young women (links to other websites with information about health, sexuality, financial resources). We also have a "rant" page because venting was key to our own process so we wanted to create a virtual space for self-expression, where people can post their frustration. Another page includes poetry of relevance to other young people of color and features a beautiful poem about taking cold showers in the projects. . . .

Through the fed-up-honeys website and our sticker campaign, we want to stress the importance of self-directed and community-supported action for change. Using the vehicles of action research, research products such as our stickers, and the website, we want to help in the process of motivating and taking part in a revitalization of active community participation. We believe that by simply living your truth and encouraging others to do the same, you can participate in your community's growth. In the process of being true to yourself and the network of people that make up your community, you can help to knock down the myths that hold down our communities.

Source: Caitlin Cahill, Indra Rios-Moore, and Tiffany Threatts. "Different Eyes/Open Eyes." *Revolutionizing Education*, 2008, 94, 117–119.

Social Media and Film

Social media, according to some, has changed activism because it facilitates an almost lightening-speed circulation of information. It generates an urgency in ways that are almost unprecedented. For example, in 2014, a full-fledged campaign "Bring Back Our Girls" took off on social media, in response to the kidnapping of 276 school girls in Nigeria. The ensuing campaign received widespread coverage on Facebook, Twitter, and other social media.

In an article in the *New Yorker Magazine* in 2010, however, columnist Malcolm Gladwell wrote an editorial critical of such "new" forms of activism, in which he describes the 1960 scene in Greensboro, North Carolina, where "Negro" students staged a sit-in at Woolworth's protesting the fact that Blacks were not served.[25] They risked their lives and limbs during the protest and Gladwell distinguishes between this form of activism versus cyberactivism, whereby one can push a button to sign a petition or post their outrage over a particular injustice on Facebook or Twitter. Gladwell holds that these forms of digital protest are weak.

But social media has clearly changed activism and there are possibilities for cyber-engagement that can draw activist-scholars into struggles beyond clicking a button, or buying a coffee to support a particular cause. The possibilities are ones that we hope will engage a new generation of feminist ethnographers. In our interview with anthropologist Tom Boellstorff, who has conducted extensive ethnographic research in virtual communities, he offers a more optimistic perspective than Gladwell, which we appreciate (see Spotlight on the next page).

A powerful use of visual media as a form of feminist activist ethnography is the use of film. In 2010, an earthquake hit Haiti and the viewing public witnessed the devastation, largely via social media. The popular media portrayed Haiti as a miserable country with little ability to deal with the catastrophe. The groundbreaking 2009 film *Poto Mitan: Haitain Women, Pillars of the Global Economy* has served as an important counter-narrative. With anthropologist Mark Schuller as codirector and coproducer, anthropologist Gina Athena Ulysse and international education

SPOTLIGHTS

Tom Boellstorff on New Technologies and Activism

***Tom Boellstorff** received his PhD in anthropology at Stanford University and teaches anthropology at the University of California, Irvine. His publications include* The Gay Archipelago: Sexuality and Nation in Indonesia *(2005) and* Coming of Age in Second Life: An Anthropologist Explores the Virtually Human *(2008, with a new second edition in 2015). He has served as editor-in-chief of* American Anthropologist, *the flagship journal of the American Anthropological Association and has been engaged in HIV/AIDS and LGBT activism in the United States, Indonesia, Malaysia, and Russia, with groups such as the International Gay and Lesbian Human Rights Commission. In our interview, Boellstorff addressed the virtual possibilities for activism and feminist ethnography.*

Thinking about the multiple meanings of activism as they are changed by technology is really important. I do agree that there's a critique of this kind of "Click a link activism" where people are like "Oh I'm so activist, I clicked on this link that audoubon.org had." But at the same time, if a million people pick up one piece of trash. . . . I don't want to throw out the baby with the bathwater and just say that's meaningless. I think these new emerging technologies do give us ways to do half-hearted activism, busy activism, multi-tasking activism, that could be meaningful and actually part of the equation for making social change. Not that it's better or necessarily more effective, but I get worried about [calling it] inauthentic or bad. That, to me, is a little too hasty and prevents us from thinking about what might be some cool things that are happening in this space that we could be using for activist work and that could play a role in building coalitions and informing people and doing other kinds of stuff. For newer generations, as these technologies continue to transform the world in so many ways, thinking about technology and activism is something that I'm interested in. And what really interests me are things that we can do that make these new intersections of technology and activism not a way to be self-satisfied and not do the real thing, but a way of doing the real thing. Because technology nowadays *is* part of the real thing.

scholar Claudine Michel as associate producers, and filmmaker Renée Bergan, the documentary sought to make Haitian women's voices more accessible to U.S. audiences. *Poto Mitan* is based on Schuller's ethnographic work and features the perspectives of five women and how they have survived neoliberal globalization by using their collective activism to make change:

> *Poto Mitan's* unique quality rests upon the women's acute understanding of the power of film. Citing the Haitian proverb, "hearing and seeing are two different things," the women implored Dr. Schuller to share their stories with people in the U.S., people who have the power to make change.[26]

Schuller returned to Haiti as a member of one of the first teams to respond following the devastating 7.0 earthquake in 2010 through a grassroots medical mission in his neighborhood. His objective in producing this film was to raise Haiti's profile and standards for media about Haiti, increase awareness of revitalization efforts within Haiti, identify funds to support that work, and to promote people's voices to demand change.

Importantly, as Schuller has emphasized in his scholarly presentations, he realizes that his role is to document and observe social and political conditions, but not

Thinking Through . . .

Working with Activists

Identify an organization online, based anywhere in the world, that addresses an activist issue (an antiviolence campaign, LGBTQ right, disability rights, anti-racism, et cetera). Write a brief summary, explaining their mission and organizational goals, and reflect on how a feminist activist ethnographer could collaborate with organizers to assist their work, virtually or in person.

necessarily spearhead public activism. Distinguishing himself from local activists allowed him to connect with people in power with whom he might not otherwise have been able to access. Schuller's ability to bring issues pertaining to Haiti to the forefront of people's attention is not necessarily embedded in activism but rather with him serving as an interlocutor.

The power of social justice film, documentaries, and social media is that they have the ability to make you think, make you mad, or make you act. Visual media also has the power to motivate people, because when it documents or narrates inequality, abuse and devastation, they are often produced out of passion and anger. Indeed, the intent is to stimulate discussion among the viewers. Consider, for instance, two popular films, *An Inconvenient Truth* and *Born into Brothels*, both of which had wide releases and deeply influenced the public's perception about global warming and the children of prostitutes living in Calcutta, India, respectively. Media, whatever the form, can help shape and circulate ideas about subjects that may not be well understood. We expect to be told real things about life and situations and to have our awareness raised. That is why some feminist activist ethnographers may decide to make films, or use social media to stimulate the public's interest in issues of inequity or discrimination, and sometimes to rally the public to respond.

A final example of a feminist ethnographic film that has been used widely by worker's rights activists, as well as in the academy, is Michelle Téllez's "Workers on the Rise." Téllez collaborated with an Phoenix-based editor Justine García and members of the Arizona Worker Rights Center, which tracks labor rights violations, challenges abusive employers, promotes worker-friendly legislation, and develops worker leadership and community in Phoenix. The film was originally sold in hard

ESSENTIALS

Poto Mitan: Haitian Women, Pillars of the Global Economy, a Documentary

The documentary can be viewed at http://www.potomitan.net.

Poto Mitan: Haitian Women, Pillars of the Global Economy is a film by Tèt Ansam Productions, with narration by Edwidge Danticat, released in 2009.

Photo: Renée Bergan

Edele Joseph, Port-au-Prince, 2007.

SPOTLIGHTS

Michelle Téllez on Activism Through Storytelling in Visual Media

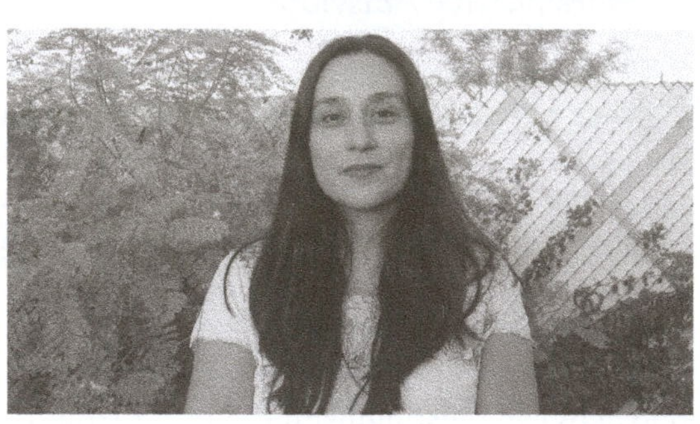

Michelle Téllez *is an interdisciplinary scholar trained in sociology, Chicana/o studies, community studies, and education.* She received her PhD in *education, with an emphasis in critical community studies from Claremont Graduate University and is a faculty member in sociology and ethnic studies at Northern Arizona University. Her work seeks to uncover stories of identity, transnational community formation, gendered migration, resistance, and Chicana mothering. In addition to publications on her scholarship, she writes for online outlets such as "The Feminist Wire" and uses visual media to engage a variety of audiences. Her most recent video* "Workers on the Rise" *(2012) documents labor struggles in Maricopa county, Arizona. Téllez is also a founding member of the Arizona Ethnic Studies Network, the Entre Nosotr@s collective and sits on the editorial review board for Chicana/Latina Studies: The Journal of Mujeres Activas en Letras y Cambio Social.*

There is a quote I live by: "No hay que luchar para destruir hay que luchar para crear; We mustn't struggle to destroy, we must struggle to create." Feminist praxis requires reflexivity and a desire to produce research that can transform—transform our minds, our ideologies, our perceptions of truth—and without an intersectional lens that centers the voices that are often ignored in positivist research paradigms then we are not pursuing that transformation. When I learned about ethnography, it gave me the tools to tell the stories that I so deeply wanted to tell . . . . I came across visual media through the women's multimedia center of Claremont, California and it opened brand new possibilities of storytelling to me. I've played with different methods behind the camera and mostly I've found that coediting and filming, that is, collaborating on a project, shapes what stories are told, what voices are centered and the final product becomes a radical way of shifting how documentaries are made and by whom.

Gender is something that is ignored oftentimes when we're trying to tell stories, right? So what lens is being used to tell a story? I'm a feminist, I'm a feminist ethnographer and so this kind of goes with me everywhere I go. It's almost like second nature, so I'm always thinking about what story hasn't been told, what visual hasn't been shared, what experience is often ignored. That is what feminism is about, right? It's not just about what is found in the theoretical field, it's about transformation. For me, it's bringing to life [the stories]. Writing is one way of getting out the stories that must be heard. But when you actually get to see the experience, the visual experience, it tells something different, especially for those that are unfamiliar with the topic. This is true for migration, this is true for activism, this is true for community members trying to revive and share their cultural center. Visuals create relationality and viewers can find their mutual humanity in that. That is an essential part of feminist ethnography, right? That's storytelling. You're trying to transform, and I think that storytelling through visual media is absolutely important because it's accessible.

copy to fundraise for the nonprofit organization it is centered around and is now available for free viewing on Vimeo.[27]

Serving as an Interlocutor

Like Mark Schuller, some feminist ethnographers do not assume the identity of being an activist—at least not in ones field sites. Rather they prefer to serve as interlocutors, whereby they can offer social critique and simultaneously disentangle the webs of power in which people live. This is the case for anthropologist Dorothy Hodgson, who does ethnography in Tanzania, where she positions herself as an interlocutor. In her documentation of the continuing land grabs of Maasai land, her position as researcher/interlocutor (rather than being directly identified as an activist) enabled her Maasai participants to use her documentation work in a court cases toward their own political project.

While value is often derived from scholars' data collection used toward social movements or social justice, it is possible that participants may be placed at risk for being associated with a scholar who identifies as an activist, making the very term problematic since sometimes activists are viewed as agitators. Engaging in activist research must account for the ways in which researchers often have resources upon which they can call if their participation instigates or involves some form of danger or harm. It is important to be sensitive to the fact that research participants associated with scholars who identify as activists can experience danger but may not have the same access to resources. This is particularly significant since it is the

 ESSENTIALS

Excerpt from the Introduction to *Comparative Perspectives on the Indigenous Rights Movement in Africa and the Americas* by Dorothy Hodgson

Dorothy Hodgson *earned her PhD in anthropology at the University of Michigan and is professor of anthropology and graduate program director at Rutgers University. She has published numerous books on gender and social inequality among Maasai, including her most recent,* Being Maasai, Becoming Indigenous: Postcolonial Politics in a Neoliberal World *(2011).*

[Feminist ethnographers have] a range of overlapping positions, from advocacy and collaboration, to dialogue and discussion, to scholarly detachment. Some anthropologists like David Maybury-Lewis have been relentless advocates for indigenous rights, working through nonprofit organizations such as Cultural Survival, IWGIA, and Survival International to facilitate and finance indigenous networking and advocacy. Others, like Les Field, argue for a position that combines scholarship and collaboration. Field describes himself as

> an academic who works within the metropolitan academy as a theorist critical of conventional and particularly colonial-derived categories and also collaborates with an indigenous community and its intellectuals in their various projects, attempting to negotiate and reconcile these very different kinds of work. [Field 1999:195]

Some anthropologists, like myself, might characterize our position as "interlocutors" rather than "collaborators," that is, as scholars who share our ideas and work with indigenous groups in ongoing, constructive, and, perhaps, even occasionally contentious dialogues and debates in an effort to inform and shape their policies and practices, without directly aligning ourselves with one group or faction of the movement (cf. Jackson 1999). As I have written elsewhere, drawing on Gupta and Ferguson (1997:30), I see our "political task not as 'sharing' knowledge with those who lack it but as forging links between different knowledges that are possible from different locations and tracing lines of possible alliance and common purpose between them" (Hodgson 1999:214). As such, our "interlocutors" may be many and varied, including not just indigenous activists but the constituencies, institutions, organizations, and people with which we, and they, engage and interact.

Source: Dorothy L. Hodgson. "Introduction: Comparative Perspectives on the Indigenous Rights Movement in Africa and the Americas." *American Anthropologist* 104(4):1037–1049. 2002, 1044–1045.

researcher's responsibility to not only do no harm, but if one is an activist-scholar, we have a responsibility to attempt to do good.

How Can Feminist Activist Ethnographers Reflect Upon Our Practice?

When we look back on the practice of feminist activist ethnography, we must not obscure its conflictual history. Many scholars view activism as an important goal of feminist and progressive research. However, others critique the idea of being politically engaged when one is an intellectual. Anthropologists Setha Low and Sally Engle Merry's article, "Engaged Anthropology: Diversity and Dilemmas,"[28] lays out some of the issues that have been raised. One point is that anthropologists from the U.S. in particular have been engaged since the discipline's beginning. We saw evidence of this in the work of Margaret Mead, a public academic. Low and Engle chronicle the inclusion of scholars in projects supported by the Works Progress Administration during the 1930s and 1940s, the largest project to promote the development of public infrastructure, such as roads and buildings, in the United States. In some instances, this engagement was not representative of the kind of progressive politics we have highlighted in this text. A different form of engagement arose after World War II when scholars based in the U.S. were asked to provide their knowledge and expertise to projects financed by the military, creating ethical controversy about the appropriate role of the ethnographer as both a researcher and a citizen.

Low and Engle identify three difficulties scholars may face when being activists. The first is whether one should be involved in the research or serve as a non-biased observer. On the one hand, the argument is that the dynamics of the research changes when you become involved. On the other hand, what about the ethics of not responding when an intervention is necessary? The second dilemma concerns criticizing those who have power over the people or situation you are researching, particularly if you are conducting research in someplace other than your home country. The final concern is the longstanding debate over providing anthropological insights to governments, militaries, and development agencies. One challenge is the possibility that those entities could appropriate an ethnographer's data, and potentially use it to harm research participants or their communities.

Further, anthropologist Charles R. Hale notes that activist scholarship may be called into question when it is posed in terms that are too celebratory or sanguine, as opposed to being in relation to confrontation and contradiction.[29] Some would argue that there are consequences for pointing out contentious social issues and then being directly in the line of fire when people disagree with the researcher's perspective. In addition to the dilemmas laid out by Low and Engles, and Hale—and there are certainly others—we would add the possibility that the researchers' agenda may differ from those of the participants. For example, Dána-Ain points out in *Battered Black Women and Welfare Reform: Between a Rock and a Hard Place*,[30] that one major goal of her research was to reshape welfare policy and the negative perspectives many policymakers held about working class and poor women on welfare. However, women's priorities were much more individually oriented because they needed housing and employment and implored Dána-Ain to assist them in securing those resources, which she tried to do, as an advocate. Dána-Ain came to see more clearly after reflecting back on her research, that her advocacy had very limited outcomes.

Morgensen (see Spotlight in chapter 1) points out that neither activism nor advocacy guarantees justice, empowerment, or resources: "If anti-oppressive commitments are crucial to feminist activist ethnography, all who wish to pursue such work must take care not to imagine that their activist sites provide a counter or a solution to the power relations in their research."[31] What feminist activist ethnography does, however, is reveal the various ways in which power can be negotiated in the research context and that critical reflection may generate, as Morgensen notes, potentially productive tactics. A potent example of this is anthropologist and visual artist Beth Uzwiak's research on an international women's human rights agency in New York City.[32] Her research reveals a dramatic disconnection between the NGO's feminist mission and the façade it creates to maintain legitimacy with transnational human rights structures. Uzwiak calls into question the inequitable internal labor practices of feminist NGOs, which often go unnoticed—even by worker/activists themselves—in the context of the laudable broader goals of feminist organizations to achieve social justice for women around the world. Ultimately, the NGO creates an environment where workers are ideologically committed to women's human rights but, because of this commitment, do not openly refute their own mistreatment within the agency. Uzwiak questions: how much (or *how*) should we, as feminist activist ethnographers, reveal in our critical work, especially when such revelations can potentially complicate unwavering support of feminist organizations? We side with Uzwiak in this debate. Ultimately, we believe that it is incumbent upon feminist activist ethnographers to remain reflective and critical both about our own work, as well as the work of organizations with feminist goals.

To this end, in her article, "Globalizing Scholar Activism,"[33] sociologist Jennifer Bickham Mendez points out that discussions about activist research have not always included the contribution of feminism. Yet, feminists have shown that lived realities or oppositional narratives can be packaged in order to carry meaning and leverage within decision and policymaking circles. Other audiences may include the general public. Writing can be an important way to support activism, and the craft of writing for a nonacademic audience is key to many feminist ethnographic

SPOTLIGHTS

Jennifer Bickham Mendez on the Relevance of Activist-Scholarship

Jennifer Bickham Mendez *trained in sociology at University of California, Davis, and now teaches at the College of William and Mary in Virginia. She has written extensively on the possibilities for activism in feminist scholarship. Her book* From the Revolution to the Maquiladoras: Gender, Labor and Globalization in Nicaragua *(2005) received the 2008 Annual Book Award from the Political Economy of the World System Section of the American Sociological Association as well as an honorable mention from the Global Division of the Society for the Study of Social Problems. Here she speaks about conducting activist, politically engaged research and the importance of cultivating understandings of the needs and challenges of local communities as part of a political project.*

For me, feminist ethnography is politically engaged ethnography. It's politically engaged research. That is not the case for all feminist ethnographers . . . but it seemed like in the late nineties suddenly [ethnographers] re-discovered politically engaged research, it suddenly became okay to do because we were coming out of that postmodern haze: research had to mean something. But I think feminism had articulated some of the core ideas of scholar-activism for a long time—the attention to accountability, that you can never escape power dynamics, that power is all around us.

(continued)

I think feminist activist ethnography begins with understanding the way that [a group you are studying] assigns meanings to the world. Once you do, then you can also begin to understand what the particular needs of this community are, and how you might be able to use your research in service of those needs, but in ways that are participative and inherently political. I'm not talking about traditional "needs assessment" which can be incredibly patronizing—or matronizing. What I'm referring to is academic theorizing used to inform political strategy. It's the connection of on-the-ground practice with theory that, to me, opens a space of strategy. Bringing those two worlds together and assessing how knowledge generated by the academy could be of strategic use to the community requires that one understand the power of knowledge and where it can be inserted.

Beyond doing no harm, you have to establish relationships that are not just based on taking and using people's stories. Of course, the ethnographic relationship is imperfect, but I think that most researchers don't even think about this stuff. Every way of studying the world has its weaknesses. But I would rather that my weaknesses be through the trying and striving to understand the needs of those I study with feminist principles in mind and guided by those principles. It takes time. It's not just something you can dabble in.

And we must remember the feminist adage that the personal is also political. We can't separate immediate, everyday needs and strategizing to meet them, from a vision of social change. For instance, if there is something that can be done that solves an immediate problem and we can do that, then that, to me, is part of our responsibility as feminist ethnographers. It's not the same thing as charity, like going and building houses in Honduras like many of our wonderful students do. But they come back and have no real sense of what they just did in the broader political sense, except for they built somebody's house. And that's great, that's wonderful, and I don't want to belittle that. But what I'm talking about is something different. I'm not just talking about meeting needs, like giving somebody a ride, as merely an act of charity, I'm talking about giving somebody a ride because in that moment, they needed a prescription medication, and as a researcher I need to be accountable to that. And also seeing the importance of that mundane act within a broader social change agenda. Politically engaged research involves expanding our conversations and understanding of research ethics. It isn't okay to adopt the position of a detached observer to avoid thorny ethical issues. As a feminist, politically engaged researcher when you confront concrete sorts of needs that are on the table, you shouldn't turn your gaze away from them. They are real. And you should engage those physical and immediate needs—my baby has a fever that won't subside, or I've had severe dental pain and need a ride to the clinic. Under particular circumstances providing ride to the dental clinic might be a necessary step in your research. And you have to confront what that means for how you interact with a community of people. For me, confronting repeated access issues within the Latino community as I conducted ethnographic research here in Williamsburg, Virginia led me to sit on the board of our community safety net clinic. One of the biggest questions for me as I begin a project (or my students begin a project) is: what does it mean to you to be an engaged researcher in the community?

---

projects. Translating our work using accessible, jargon-free language and participating in public forums beyond academic ones are important ingredients of acting as a "public intellectual."

Whatever forms of engagement feminist ethnographers commit to, it is worthwhile to remember that there is the potential for burnout and self-care is important to remaining involved in the long term. As Tom Boellstorff reminds us, it is essential to draw boundaries and maintain healthy limits in our activist work and why sometimes we just "gotta watch Game of Thrones":

> To me, the activist spirit is . . . that activism is sort of like breathing, it's what you're doing regardless. If you choose not to engage and catch up on Game of Thrones, that is [not always seen as germane to activism itself]. But if you

> *don't* watch some Games of Thrones and you're only out there doing activism, you'll go crazy and you'll burn out, and so sometimes you gotta watch Games of Thrones . . . There are those of us who are privileged to be able to opt out or have some kind of relatively safe space in their homes or our work place where we aren't confronting it 24/7 and that gives us the ability to breathe and make those decisions about how much breathing do we do. You know, at least what I've seen, the activists who make the biggest difference, they take Saturdays off sometimes.

Conclusion

We have discussed activism and its connection to feminist ethnography and want to conclude by considering how activism has changed during the time that feminist ethnography has emerged as a field. Consider, for instance, how aspects of activism have transformed as social change has become increasingly linked to consumption. The (RED) Campaign, for instance, founded by U2 singer Bono and Bobby Shriver in 2006 involved business and individual consumers in the fight against AIDS, by shopping. In order to create sustained flows of capital to fight AIDS, through the sales of products like Starbucks and Gap, they advocated a consumer-based approach to social change. These consumerist shifts have not necessarily changed what feminist ethnographers feel committed to in developing activist scholarship, but they are problematic for reducing activism to a financial enagagement that is more available to some than to others. Indeed, consumer-based activism has not diluted the need for research, nor our willingness to participate in social movements. It is knowing of people's burdens that motivates many feminist ethnographers to do what we do, and engage with activist movements and organizations.

Suggested Resources

Caitlin Cahill (2004) "Defying Gravity? Raising Consciousness through Collective Research." *Children's Geographies.*

Julia Sudbury and Margo Okazawa-Rey (2009) *Activist Scholarship: Antiracism, Feminist and Social Change.*

Lynne Phillips and Sally Cole (2013) *Contesting Publics: Feminism, Activism, Ethnography.*

Jeffrey S. Juris, and Alex Khasnabish, eds. (2013) *Insurgent Encounters: Transnational, Activism, Ethnography, and the Political.*

Jennifer R. Wies and Hillary J. Haldane, eds. (2015) *Applying Anthropology to Gender-Based Violence: Global Responses, Local Practices.*

Mary K. Anglin (2006) "Whose Health? Whose Justice? Examining Quality of Care and Breast Cancer Activism through the Intersections of Gender, Race, Ethnicity, and Class." In Health at the Intersections of Gender, Race, and Class.

New Day Films https://www.newday.com/films.

Notes

[1] Louise Lamphere, "The Perils and Prospects for an Engaged Anthropology: A View from the United States," *Social Anthropology*, 2003.

[2] Michael Burawoy, "2004 American Sociological Association Presidential Address: For Public Sociology," *American Sociological Review*, 2005.

[3] Faye V. Harrison, "Navigating Feminist Activist Ethnography," in *Feminist Activist Ethnography*, eds. Christa Craven and Dána-Ain Davis, 2013.

[4] Manisha Desai, "The Possibilities and Perils for Scholar-Activists and Activist-Scholars," in *Insurgent Encounters,* edited by Jeffrey S. Juris and Alex Khasnabish, 2013, 90.

[5] Ida Susser, "The Anthropologist as Social Critic: Working Towards a More Engaged Anthropology." *Current Anthropology*, 2010.
[6] Library of Congress, "Margaret Mead As a Cultural Commentator," 2001.
[7] Emily Martin, *The Woman in the Body: A Cultural Analysis of Reproduction*, 2001.
[8] Monica J. Casper, *The Making of the Unborn Patient: A Social Anatomy of Fetal Surgery*, 1998.
[9] Barbara Katz Rothman, *The Tentative Pregnancy: How Amniocentesis Changes the Experience of Motherhood*, 1993; Sarah Franklin, *Embodied Progress: A Cultural Account of Assisted* Conception, 2002 and Biological *Relatives: IVF, Stem Cells and the Future of Kinship*, 2013.
[10] Dorothy Roberts, *Killing The Black Body: Race, Reproduction, and the Meaning of Liberty*, 1998.
[11] Khiara Bridges, *Reproducing Race: An Ethnography of Pregnancy as a Site of Racialization*, 2011.
[12] Council on Anthropology and Reproduction Advocacy Committee, "CAR Opposes Legislation that Creates Barriers to Safe Abortion Care," *Medical Anthropology Quarterly*, 2015.
[13] Susan Brin Hyatt, "'Water is Life—Meters Out!' Women's Grassroots Activism And the Privatization of Public Amenities," 2004.
[14] "Black Lives Matter," accessed October 4, 2015, http://blacklivesmatter.com/.
[15] Linda Tuhiwai Smith, *Decolonizing Methodologies*, 2012, 217.
[16] Soyini D. Madison, *Critical Ethnography*, 2005, 5.
[17] Eleanor B. Leacock, "Introduction to The Origin of the Family, Private Property, and the State, by Frederick Engels," 1972.
[18] Christian Scharen and Aana Marie Vigen, *Ethnography as Christian Theology and Ethics*, 2011, 22.
[19] Deborah A. Gordon, "Border Work: Feminist Ethnography and the Dissemination Literacy," in *Women Writing Culture*, eds. Ruth Behar and Deborah A. Gordon, 1995, 383.
[20] Zethu Matabeni, ed. *Reclaiming Afrikan*, 2014.
[21] Michelle Marzullo, "Seeking 'Marriage Material': Rethinking the U.S. Marriage Debatees Under Neoliberalism," in *Feminist Activist Ethnography*, eds. Christa Craven and Dána-Ain Davis, 2013.
[22] Luke Eric Lassiter, *The Chicago Guide to Collaborative Ethnography*, 2005.
[23] Rina Benmayor, Rosa M. Torruellas, and Ana L. Juarbe. Responses to Poverty among Puerto Rican Women, 1992.
[24] Indra Rios-Moore, et al., *Makes Me Mad: Stereotypes of Young Urban Womyn of Color*, 2004.
[25] Malcolm Gladwell, "Small Change, Why the Revolution Will Not Be Tweeted," *New Yorker*, 2010.
[26] "Poto Mitan: Haitian Women Pillars of the Global Economy," accessed October 4, 2015. http://potomitan.net/.
[27] Michelle Téllez, "Workers on the Rise," 2012, https://vimeo.com/85164509.
[28] Setha M. Low and Sally Engle Merry, "Engaged Anthropology: Diversity and Dilemmas," *Current Anthropology*, 2010.
[29] Charles R. Hale, *Theory, Politics and Methods of Activist Scholarship*, 2008.
[30] Dána-Ain Davis, *Battered Black Women and Welfare Reform*, 2006.
[31] Scott L. Morgensen, "Reflection: Fearlessly Engaging Complicity," in *Feminist Activist Ethnography*, eds. Christa Craven and Dána-Ain Davis, 2013, 72.
[32] Beth Uzwiak, "Fracturing Feminism: Activist Research and Ethics in a Women's Human Rights NGO," in *Feminist Activist Ethnography*, eds. Christa Craven and Dána-Ain Davis, 2013.
[33] Jennifer Bickham Mendez, "Globalizing Scholar Activism: Opportunities and Dilemmas Through a Feminist Lens," in *Engaging Contradictions*, 2008.

CHAPTER 8

Thinking Through the Future of Feminist Ethnography

Conversations with Feminist Ethnographers

> At this point in our history, we need feminist activists and ethnographers more than we ever did. Darwinist individualism is not going away. It's here to stay. And the pressure on social scientists in terms of objectivity is also stronger than it's ever been. The power of taking a stand—in public—continues. Those of us who do that, we continue to face state institutional oppression, including co-opted versions of diversity, and co-opted versions of inclusivity and inclusion. These pose challenges to holding onto the value of collective activists and scholarship in various performative outlets. . . . Renewed commitment to engaging in embodied, critical, reflexive, and intersectional work remains critical to preserving feminist activist principles of anti-oppressive and ethical research.
>
> —Nancy A. Naples, feminist sociologist, National Women's Studies Association Conference, San Juan, Puerto Rico, 2014

In the Introduction to this textbook, we discussed the multiple ways of thinking through feminist ethnography—as project, process, product, and outcomes that can be linked to the aims of social justice. A central part of this engagement has been constructing a history of the field. Clearly, we have placed quite a bit of emphasis on the past, which is suggestive of our thinking about its importance. In our opinion, charting the past also helps to understand the present, as well as future possibilities. We invoke the past, as it relates to feminist ethnography by thinking through histories. Knowing the histories of feminist ethnography, from the early contributions of female ethnographers to the diverse and critical strands that have emerged in recent years, facilitates achieving some degree of intellectual integrity.

Our process of working on this book—interviewing over thirty feminist scholars and activists, rereading texts, identifying new feminist ethnographic works, and transcribing two sessions we co-organized on Feminist Activist Ethnography in 2014—has yielded so much more than uncovering this rich history. It has encouraged us to explore the aspirations that feminists across disciplines have for feminist ethnography.[1] In this conclusion, we look back to look forward, by engaging in a conversation of sorts with the many inspirational activists and scholars we interviewed for this project and with whom we served on conference panels. We share their reflections on the past and visions for the field to reveal the textured possibilities for thinking through feminist ethnography long into the future.

Reflecting on the influences of feminist ethnography in the development of queer studies, Tom Boellstorff praises feminism for paying attention to and drawing from a rich past. He advises that we listen to our elders and know our history:

> [I] mean that in a diachronic, as well as the synchronic sense. I mean listening to elders historically, as well as listening to a group of people at a field site. That listening goes through time as well. That's a really important principle and it's not only because it is a way to learn about ideas and what's been done before, but it's also about a way to build coalitions and communities.

What you can learn from examining histories is not only about the scope of the research and ethnography that came before, but also how it has changed. Louise Lamphere, in response to a student's question about the history of feminist anthropology and activism at the 2014 American Anthropological Association panel replied that the practice of feminist ethnography has become more widely accepted, contributing to feminist activist aims over time.

> In the 70s . . . first of all, a lot of us hadn't done any work on women. We got involved in the [feminist] movement and we thought, "Shoot, we've got to be teaching about women. Let's see what anthropology has got to say." We dug around in the books that we had been reading. Out of that came work like *Woman, Culture, and Society*. Then, a bunch of us decided, "Okay, we'll do some fieldwork on women," and sure enough we went to do fieldwork on nuns in Nepal, and I started doing work on women in factories, and so on. We also had students that wanted to do stuff, so there's this whole cadre of people that started doing fieldwork in the mid- to late 70s, early 80s. . . .When women started going out doing fieldwork on women, we were just using the regular old theories that anthropology had to offer and the regular old methodologies. It wasn't until the 80s when we began to think about it in a feminist light and ask, "What are the power relationships between ourselves and our subjects and what's our own 'positionally' (i.e., social position) and that of the people we were studying?" So, although much has changed, a commitment to reflecting on feminist ethnographic scholarship to suggest pathways for social change continues in the field.

One the most common themes that emerged from almost all of the interviews was that feminist ethnography is much more than a practice, more than theory, more than principles and producing texts, performances, and engaging in social media. Feminist ethnography is praxis—an actively engaging process that is embodied, taught, learned, and relearned. And, more than that, most feminist ethnographers with whom we spoke think that feminist ethnography has great value because of its potential to move us toward a just and equitable world.

Feminist ethnography—as a process, practice, and product—motivates us to think politically about our work. Talisa Feliciano, a PhD student, indicates that feminist ethnographers, especially students, have the opportunity to destabilize trends toward monolithic definitions of feminist politics.

> Feminism often becomes equated with middle-class Western white women's struggles. While I do not want to downplay those particular concerns, it is important that we remember that feminism encompasses more than a singular way of being a woman. I think this tendency in mainstream feminism certainly bleeds into feminist ethnography. Are we overproducing certain types of knowledge? More importantly does the knowledge we produce help? How does it

> hurt? These questions are in my mind, and the minds of my peers, as we slowly become another generation of feminist ethnographers.

Interdisciplinary scholar Michelle Téllez sees feminist ethnography as a place of possibility:

> The advice I want to give my students is to ask themselves: why are they doing what they're doing? This is it. We have this one life to live. Are we going to add the tallies to whatever checklist we are supposed to be following, or do we want to be committed to a life of balance, harmony, and justice? I think feminism is often misunderstood, but it's really a place where we can critique. It's not just about women, it's about gender, and it's about transformation, it's about transnational politics, it's about experiences, and abilities. . . For me, it's a place of possibility.

Feminist ethnography is an approach that opens up possibilities for understanding the world in new ways and ushering in social change. Leith Mullings explains:

> [Feminist ethnography is] the ability to step out of the traditional canon to understand and engage in analyses that can lead you to a different place, a different conclusion, a different way of seeing the world, and perhaps a different way of participating in changing the world. I do not believe that all feminist ethnography necessarily leads us to this place. It is about a philosophical worldview and political commitments. There are many different ways of doing feminist ethnography and many different types of commitment. Feminist ethnography that focuses on the conditions of women and takes a collaborative methodological approach is exciting, but for me what is much more exciting is a feminist ethnography that seeks to understand the foundations of inequality and to change them.

Students engage in this same approach. Ashley Chavez-White, for instance, graduated from the College of Wooster in 2015 with a double major in anthropology and women's, gender, and sexuality studies and plans to apply to master's programs in the field of midwifery. Reflecting on writing her undergraduate thesis, *Once upon the Fifteenth Year: An Exploration of Identity Formation Within the Cultural Practice of Quinceañeras in Contemporary Nicaragua*, she says:

> Feminist ethnography is such a growing library. New research, like my first feminist ethnographic project on quinceañeras, forces students to keep asking questions, to keep looking deeper. What feminist ethnography did for me was to push me to ask lots of questions about power and gender. By finding new ways of using a feminist lens during ethnographic research, any research actually, I hope that new feminist ethnographic research by undergraduate and graduate students is helping shape the ways that more established scholars approach their research as well.

Activating Activism

The pulse of change, a phrase used by Faye V. Harrison in her book *Outsider Within: Reworking Anthropology in the Global Age,*[2] aptly characterizes how feminist ethnography can intersect with activism. Many of the people we interviewed realize the force activism carries, even when it comes in different forms. Some have made choices about how to best position themselves so that they can do activist work—whether that be movement building, teaching, political lobbying, et cetera. Activist and public health scholar Lynn Roberts makes a strong case for finding the right space to do the work you want to do as she reflected on her own life and career:

> I gave birth to a child at two months shy of my eighteenth birthday—that officially made me a teen mom. I did not have a feminist nor ethnographic lens in that encounter, but I did figure out pretty quickly that I felt that the researcher in that instance, who was a graduate student at Howard University, was clueless about my . . . situated knowledge. And it would eventually inspire me to want to become a researcher myself and to strive to do it better, somehow. I think I've been on that quest ever since. It also made me want to work in an applied field. I am in an institution where we are constantly looking in public health to have large impact on population health. Although I don't really identify with the discipline since I'm not specifically trained in public health, I began teaching in the sub-field of community health because I had been involved in public health work for many years in New York City around HIV/AIDS and violence prevention, and around programs for women and youth. I was invited to apply for a position in an action research center and later applied for a faculty position left vacant by a highly esteemed colleague. I sometimes like to say my entry to the academy was through a "back door". . . So, I want to say this—particularly to younger scholars—that if what you want to do most in life is to make a difference, then you have to decide where you want to be situated to do that. . . . where can you be the most satisfied personally, professionally, and also have the most impact?

However, the possibilities for linking scholarship to activism were not always available to academics, as Louise Lamphere recalls.

> I don't think the kind of activism that [some of the younger] people on the panel are talking about was as possible in the 70s and 80s. . . . And when you get up to the 2000s, first of all—there are a lot of social movements that people have been studying that focus on different issues like climate, sustainability, food insecurity, LGBT marriage issues. And folks are studying those movements and are working in activist movements themselves, so the line between "I do my activism on Sundays or Saturdays and in the evenings and I do my teaching over here" has collapsed. I think [a lot of activism] has been going on among feminist anthropologists and other anthropologists for a long time. But there are other, more collaborative things [now] and the actual work on policy and/or on working for political change because you're part of a movement that's doing demonstrations or whatever, that's the new piece. . . . It doesn't mean we weren't doing some activist stuff, but we didn't engage, it wasn't possible at that point to do it in our writing and in our research in quite the same direct way that it's possible now.

Envisioning the Possibilities of Feminist Ethnography

When we asked people about what advice they had for the next generation of feminist ethnographers, some talked about the possibilities that have opened up for refining our methods and discussing them more robustly and strategically with our students and in our work. Aimee Meredith Cox points out that this is a necessary aspect of feminist ethnographic production:

> I think we need new methods. Maybe it's just how we talk about it. We need to refine the way we talk about it. What does participant-observation mean? I would challenge the next generation to refine the way we talk about methods, and to create new methods. And I'm sure some of you are already doing that with technology and social media. I think we need to enliven the way we think about methods and practice, and how we talk about our methods. I don't think we're doing justice, ethnographies are not doing justice to the way they

> capture data. It's easy to say, "I did interviews, I took notes, I was there, and I was watching." I think especially in that realm of participant-observation, we need a way to talk about ethnography that is [not only] rooted in anthropology because everyone is doing ethnography, including historians and journalists. I think it's imperative to the discipline that we are more specific about what we mean by participant-observation and the theory behind it. . . . The challenge is a way to talk about the methods and enact them. . . . How do we do something different?

Anthropologist Michelle Marzullo's response offered useful insights into the possibilities for combining qualitative and quantitative methods.

> What we do as anthropologists is not just telling stories. We're brokers of knowledge. We're able to break into these problems to make them real and we have privilege into data that our informants do not. In that way, we can become sort of this vessel for them. To make it much more concrete for you, what I'm talking about is thinking very strategically about your research design. [For example,] I do not like statistics, I'm not a statistician but I do use quantitative work. I do surveys and I use reports, government reports, that have numbers in them. This is because politicians only hear two things: they hear statistics and they hear budget numbers. If you don't have those two things, then what you're talking about might be nice, and they might notice if perhaps their kid has been involved in this or was impacted by it, but otherwise they won't notice. It's really thinking very strategically about the impact you want to have and how you might take and ferry the affect, the emotions, stories of people that you're working with joined with a picture painted with statistics. . . . You can help structure the story or help voice the things that [participants in your research] just don't have access to or they just don't have time for. A community leader once said to me, "Oh my God, I love this subject, I'm just so busy, I don't know how to get this information." That's our job! Right? Is to get this information out, it's not to put ourselves forward, it's to put our communities forward.

The possibilities envisioned by feminist ethnographers often centered around its production. Some people wanted to see more results of ethnographic research publicized beyond academic circles. While feminist scholars and activists have been doing this for many years, it is something that sociologist Jennifer Bickham Mendez says students are particularly adept at.

> I think that students today already have gained exposure to the idea of writing to multiple audiences, more so than you and I did because of the Internet, and because of all the fantastic examples of blogs and other platforms and forums for writing for, and reaching multiple audiences.

Mendez notes that she learns how to do this, often side by side with her students. Cox urges all of us to consider the possibilities of performative writing and for finding ways to engage with narratives and characters in more literary format:

> We have to think of new ways of writing. How are we presenting what we're finding? Is there another way to do it beyond "These were my methods, this is what I found"? I just read this book, and in the introduction she tells me everything she found. I don't want to read the book now! I want something to be revealed in the stories. I think there's a reason why we call them narratives, why we get so invested in novels and characters. They change and they grow, and things are revealed to us along the way. I wonder if it's possible to do that with ethnography. Is there a way to travel with the characters, to be more present in real time with the interlocutors?

Feminist ethnographers produce ethnography in many ways—both on the page and off, through performance, film, and other creative projects—and there are still many opportunities for innovative work. Supporting this perspective, when the National Women's Studies Association panelists were asked how junior scholars could approach feminist ethnography and activism without the protection of tenure, Nancy A. Naples responded:

> I encourage my students to think about their writing as a creative project. . . . The academic literature is not going to take you to the analysis. What do you really wanna say? Right? It's often a distraction. . . . And so what I train them to do is what I call "translation work" . . . I help them start with the literature, but segueway in creative ways to really legitimately demonstrate why that literature doesn't get us where we want to go. It is their insights from conducting fieldwork that do. I think you can do that as a graduate or undergraduate student. I think you can do that as a junior faculty member. I think it's about translation. So, I encourage you to not see theoretical inquiry and creative work as a mutually exclusive thing.

In this way, the choices we make about how we conduct research, who we cite, and how we produce and circulate our work must also extend to our commitments to foster the work of feminist ethnography both within and outside academia. As we point out throughout the book, ultimately the onus remains on each of us—scholars and students of feminist ethnography—to assure that we actively seek out and hold up the innovative work by women, scholars of color, authors outside of the Global North, and groups that have been frequently overlooked in previous scholarship. In this way, we are each in a position to enhance not only our own scholarship, but to create a future for feminist ethnography that continues to push against boundaries and invigorate the field.

Notes

[1] At the 2014 annual meeting of the National Women's Studies Association we organized a roundtable, "Interdisciplinary Perspectives on Feminist Ethnography & Activism," with sociologist Nancy A. Naples, community and public health scholar Lynn Roberts, social psychologist and dance studies scholar Rosemarie Roberts, and anthropologist Alisse Waterston. The second roundtable we organized was "Producing Feminist Activist Anthropology," with anthropologists Elizabeth Chin, Jennifer Goett, Louise Lamphere, and Michelle Marzullo at the 2014 annual meetings of the American Anthropological Association.

[2] Faye V. Harrison, *Outsider Within,* 2008.

Glossary

abolitionist movement A movement to end slavery; in the United States, the movement sought to end the African and Indian slave trade and free enslaved Africans.

adjudication board Organizational bodies that assess the merits of a claim (i.e., against ethical standards) and assess a legal punishment.

Afrofuturism Afrofuturism is philosophy that imagines alternative visions of the future and aesthetically synthesizes astral jazz, African American sci-fi, hip-hop, historical fiction, fantasy, Afrocentricity, magic realism, and technology. It is a critique of the dilemmas that people of color experience and offers a reexamination of possibilities.

agency The capacity for an individual to act.

androcentric A focus on men, often concerning research focused primarily on men.

autoethnography A form of writing that uses self-reflection and the researcher's experience in relation to broad cultural meanings.

binary Having two parts in contrast to each other, for example, black/white or public/private.

canon A body of work influential in shaping a topic or discipline.

Chican@/Latin@ Gender-neutral alternative to Chicano or Chicana, Latino or Latina; scholars also use Chicana/o and Latina/o, and more recently Chicanx and Latinx.

code A process of looking at data and identifying or labeling themes.

confidentiality A primary responsibility a researcher has to keep a person's information private.

consanguinity Relation by blood.

cultural capital The nonfinancial assets, such as family status or political influence, one has to promote mobility and access to resources.

cultural relativism The notion that a culture must only be judged within its own cultural context.

cyberfeminism A term used to describe feminists involved in the use of new media technology.

donor agency An entity that provides financial resources for projects.

economic liberalism An economic perspective centered on the belief that individuals should make the greatest number of economic decisions.

emic The perspective of a person within a community.

empirical Verifiable research, based on observation or experience.

epistemology The nature and scope of knowledge.

essentialize/essentialism To reduce to an essence; to attribute a "natural" set of characteristics to a specific group, such as, "women are emotional."

ethnocentrism The belief that one's own culture is the appropriate standard against which to measure all others.

ethnographic authority The notion that an ethnographer holds authority by virtue of having "been there" in the field.

etic The analytical perspective of a researcher.

etiology The cause of a condition.

eugenics Controversial beliefs, laws, practices with the goal of improving genetic quality of human populations.

feminist standpoint theory An argument that when women recognize and confront the systems that keep them oppressed, they can understand that oppression from the perspective of who they are.

genocide The intentional killing of a group, usually an ethnic, racial, or religious group.

geopolitics Issues relating to nation, geography and economics, such as diplomacy, security, financial markets, and sometimes civil disruption.

heteronormativity A perspective that heterosexuality is the "normal" sexual orientation.

hierarchize To arrange in a ranked order.

hybridity A cross between two things.

intellectual genealogy Refers to the authors one has read and who have influenced their thinking.

interdisciplinary Crossing academic or disciplinary boundaries.

intersectionality A term coined by legal scholar Kimberlé Crenshaw to describe an analysis of intersecting identities—such race, class, gender, sexuality, ability, and nation—in relation to systems of oppression.

informed consent The permission granted to the researcher by the research participant to conduct research.

interlocutor A person who participates in a dialogue.

IRB (Institutional Review Board) A committee designated to review and approve research projects involving human subjects.

longitudinal Something that occurs over a long period of time, often used to describe a long-term research project and/or one where a researcher returns to the field after a period of time to obtain additional data.

means of production The nonhuman items needed to produce things, such as machines, buildings, and tools.

mestizo (masculine, or mestiza, feminine) A term used to describe a person who is of combined descent.

mixed-methods Utilizing qualitative and quantitative methods, or using different methodological strategies in concert to collect data.

moral relativism A philosophical argument that all standards of right and wrong are products of time and culture; thus, we should tolerate all cultural behaviors, even when we disagree about the morality of them.

NAFTA (North Atlantic Free Trade Agreement) The 1994 agreement between Canada, the United States, and Mexico, that created a trilateral rules-based trade block.

neoliberalism An economic approach that shifts away from government spending to privatization.

NGO (Non-Governmental Organization) An organization that is typically set up by citizens as a nonprofit and is not run by any government agency.

participatory action research (PAR) A research approach involving participation and action by members of a community or group under study.

participant-observation A method or process in which the researcher participates in activities with and observes a group.

patriarchy A societal form where men hold power and women are largely excluded from it.

pedagogy A method of teaching.

periodize To divide into portions of time.

polyvocality Use of multiple voices as a way to narrate.

positionality Describes how one is situated in relation to others.

positivist Knowledge based on observable facts.

postmodernism A late-twentieth-century movement away from modernism. In the social sciences is resulted in skepticism about cultural interpretation. It is often associated with new forms of writing.

post-structuralism A mid- to late twentieth-century intellectual movement that developed in Europe away from structuralism. As a strategy, it interrogates linguistic and other structures to demonstrate how knowledge is produced by understanding objects—such as texts.

praxis The application of knowledge and skills.

public intellectual A person whose scholarship and ideas go beyond the academy and circulate in nonacademic spheres.

reflexive/reflexivity To be self-referential, looking back on one's actions.

reproductive justice The complete physical, mental, spiritual, political, social, and economic well-being of women and girls based on the full achievement and protection of women's human rights.

reproductive labor Refers to the work that is done in the domestic sphere, which sustains the household and society.

taxonomy Classification of things.

temperance movement A nineteenth-century social movement against consuming alcohol.

Title VII Part of the Civil Rights Act of 1964, prohibiting discrimination against employees based on sex, race, color, national origin, and religion.

transcripts Typed copies of a recorded interview.

Bibliography

Abramovitz, Mimi, and Sandra Morgen, eds. *Taxes Are a Woman's Issue: Reframing the Debate*. New York: Feminist Press, 2006.

Abu-Lughod, Lila. "Can There Be A Feminist Ethnography?" *Women & Performance: A Journal of Feminist Theory* 5, no. 1 (1990): 7–27.

———. *Veiled Sentiments: Honor and Poetry in a Bedouin Society*. Updated ed. with a new preface. Berkeley: University of California Press, 1999 (orig. 1986).

———. *Do Muslim Women Need Saving?* Cambridge, MA: Harvard University Press, 2013.

Aenerud, Rebecca. "Thinking Again: This Bridge Called My Back and the Challenge to Whiteness." In *This Bridge We Call Home: Radical Visions for Transformation*, edited by Gloria Anzaldúa and AnaLouise Keating, 2002.

Agathangelou, Anna M., and Lily H. M. Ling. "An Unten (ur) Able Position: The Politics of Teaching for Women of Color in the US." *International Feminist Journal of Politics* 4, no. 3 (2002): 368–98.

Ahmed, Sara. *The Cultural Politics of Emotion*. New York: Routledge, 2004.

———. *Queer Phenomenology: Orientations, Objects, Others*. Durham: Duke University Press, 2006.

———. *The Promise of Happiness*. Durham: Duke University Press, 2010.

Alexander, M. Jacqui, and Chandra Talpade Mohanty. *Feminist Genealogies, Colonial Legacies, Democratic Futures*. New York: Routledge, 1997.

Allen, Jafari. *¡Venceremos?: The Erotics of Black Self-making in Cuba*. Durham, NC: Duke University Press, 2011.

American Anthropological Association. "Code of Ethics of the American Anthropological Association." *AAA Ethics Blog: A Forum Sponsored by the AAA Committee on Ethics*, 2012. http://ethics.aaanet.org/category/statement/.

American Sociological Association. "American Sociological Association Code of Ethics." The American Sociological Association, 2008. http://www.asanet.org/images/asa/docs/pdf/CodeofEthics.pdf.

Andaya, Elise. *Conceiving Cuba: Reproduction, Women, and the State in the Post-Soviet Era*. New Brunswick, NJ: Rutgers University Press, 2014.

Angel-Ajani, Asale. *Strange Trade: The Story of Two Women Who Risked Everything in the International Drug Trade*. Berkeley, CA: Seal Press, 2010.

Anglin. "Whose Health? Whose Justice? Examining Quality of Care and Breast Cancer Activism through the Intersections of Gender, Race, Ethnicity, and Class." In *Health at the Intersections of Gender, Race, and Class*, edited by Amy Schulz and Leith Mullings, 313–41. New York: Jossey-Bass/Pfeiffer, 2006.

Anzaldúa, Gloria. *Borderlands/La Frontera: The New Mestiza*. San Francisco: Aunt Lute, 1987.

———. "Toward a New Consciousness." In *The Post-Colonial Studies Reader*, edited by Bill Ashcroft, Gareth Griffiths, and Helen Tiffin, 208–10. New York: Taylor & Francis, 2006.

Aretxaga, Begoña. *Shattering Silence: Women, Nationalism, and Political Subjectivity in Northern Ireland*. Princeton: Princeton University Press, 1997.

Asch, Adrienne, and Michelle Fine. "Shared Dreams: A Left Perspective on Disability Rights and Reproductive Rights." *Radical America* 18, no. 4 (1984): 51–58.

Association for Queer Anthropology. "Awards." *Association for Queer Anthropology*, n.d. http://queeranthro.org/awards/.

Atay, Ahmet. *Globalization's Impact on Cultural Identity Formation: Queer Diasporic Males in Cyberspace*. Lanham, MD: Lexington Books, 2015.

Babb, Florence. *Between Field and Cooking Pot: The Political Economy of Marketwomen in Peru*. Austin: University of Texas Press, 1989.

———. *After Revolution: Mapping Gender and Cultural Politics in Neoliberal Nicaragua*. Austin: University of Texas Press, 2001.

———. *The Tourism Encounter: Fashioning Latin American Nations and Histories*. Stanford: Stanford University Press, 2011.

Baca Zinn, Maxine, and Bonnie Thornton Dill, eds. *Women of Color in U.S. Society*. Philadelphia: Temple University Press, 1993.

Baker, Lee D. *From Savage to Negro: Anthropology and the Construction of Race, 1896–1954*. Berkeley: University of California Press, 1998.

———. *Anthropology and the Racial Politics of Culture*. Durham: Duke University Press, 2010.

Baker, Lee, ed. *Life in America: Identity and Everyday Experience*. Malden, MA: Wiley-Blackwell, 2003.

Bailey, Marlon M. *Butch Queens Up in Pumps: Gender, Performance, and Ballroom Culture in Detroit*. Ann Arbor: University of Michigan Press, 2013.

Bates, Daisy. *My Natives and I*. Edited by Peter J Bridge. Carlisle, Western Australia: Hesperian Press, 2004.

Battle-Baptiste, Whitney. *Black Feminist Archaeology*. Walnut Creek, CA: Left Coast Press, 2011.

Baumgardner, Jennifer, and Amy Richards. *Manifesta: Young Women, Feminism and the Future*. New York: Farrar, Straus and Giroux, 2000.

Behar, Ruth. *The Vulnerable Observer: Anthropology That Breaks Your Heart*. Boston: Beacon Press, 1996.

———. *Translated Woman: Crossing the Border with Esperanza's Story*. 2nd ed. Boston: Beacon Press, 2003.

Behar, Ruth, and Deborah A. Gordon. *Women Writing Culture*. Berkeley: University of California Press, 1996.

Bell, Diane, Pat Caplan, and Wazir Jahan Karim. *Gendered Fields: Women, Men and Ethnography*. New York: Routledge, 2013.

Benmayor, Rina, Rosa M. Torruellas, and Ana L. Juarbe. *Responses to Poverty among Puerto Rican Women: Identity, Community, and Cultural Citizenship. Centro de Estudios Puertorriqueños*, Hunter College of the City University of New York, 1992.

"Black Lives Matter." Accessed October 4, 2015. http://blacklivesmatter.com/.

Blackwood, Evelyn. *The Many Faces of Homosexuality: Anthropological Approaches To Homosexuality*. New York: Routledge, 1986.

———. "Tombois in West Sumatra: Constructing Masculinity and Erotic Desire." *Cultural Anthropology* 13, no. 4 (1998): 491–521.

———. *Falling Into the Lesbi World: Desire and Difference in Indonesia*. Honolulu: University of Hawaii Press, 2010.

Blackwood, Evelyn, and Saskia Wieringa, eds. *Same-Sex Relations and Female Desires: Transgender Practices Across Cultures*. New York: Columbia University Press, 1999.

Blee, Kathleen. *Women of the Klan: Racism and Gender in the 1920s*. Berkeley: University of California Press, 2008 (orig. 1991).

Boddy, Janice Patricia. *Civilizing Women: British Crusades in Colonial Sudan*. Princeton: Princeton University Press, 2007.

Boellstorff, Tom. *The Gay Archipelago: Sexuality and Nation in Indonesia*. Princeton: Princeton University Press, 2005.

———. "Queer Studies in the House of Anthropology." *Annual Review of Anthropology* 36 (2007): 17–35.

———. *Coming of Age in Second Life: An Anthropologist Explores the Virtually Human*. Princeton: Princeton University Press, 2008.

———. *Coming of Age in Second Life: An Anthropologist Explores the Virtually Human*. Princeton: Princeton University Press, 2015 (orig. 2008).

Boellstorff, Tom, Bonnie Nardi, Celia Pearce, and T. L. Taylor, eds. *Ethnography and Virtual Worlds: A Handbook of Method*. Princeton: Princeton University Press, 2012.

Bolles, A. Lynn. *Sister Jamaica: A Study of Women Work and Households in Kingston*. Lanham, MD: University Press Of America, 1996.

———. *We Paid our Dues: Women Trade Union Leaders of the Caribbean*. Washington, DC: Howard University Press, 1996.

———. "Telling the Story Straight: Black Feminist Intellectual Thought in Anthropology." *Transforming Anthropology* 21, no. 1 (2013): 57–71.

Bookman, Ann and Sandra Morgen, eds. *Women and the Politics of Empowerment*. Philadelphia: Temple University Press, 1988.

Bourque, Susan, and Kay Warren. *Women of the Andes: Patriarchy and Social Change in Two Peruvian Towns*. Ann Arbor: University of Michigan Press, 1981.

Bowen, Elenore Smith. *Return to Laughter: An Anthropological Novel*. New York: Anchor, 1964.

Bridges, Khiara M. *Reproducing Race: An Ethnography of Pregnancy as a Site of Racialization*. Berkeley: University of California Press, 2011.

Bridgman, Rae, Sally Cole, and Heather Howard-Bobiwash, eds. *Feminist Fields: Ethnographic Insights*. Ontario: Broadview Press, 1999.

Brodkin Sacks, Karen. *Caring by the Hour: Women, Work, and Organizing at Duke Medical Center*. Champaign: University of Illinois Press, 1988.

Browne, Kath, and Catherine J. Nash, eds. *Queer Methods and Methodologies: Intersecting*

Queer Theories and Social Science Research. Farnham, Surrey, England; Burlington, VT: Ashgate, 2010.

Brown University, Pembroke Center for Teaching and Research on Women. "Exhibit - The Lamphere Case: The Sex Discrimination Lawsuit That Changed Brown," 2015. http://www.brown.edu/research/pembroke-center/archives/christine-dunlap-farnham-archives/louise-lamphere-v-brown-university/exhibit-lamphere-case-.

Burawoy, Michael. "2004 American Sociological Association Presidential Address." In *American Sociological Review* 70 (2005): 4–28.

Cahill, Caitlin. "Defying Gravity? Raising Consciousness through Collective Research." *Children's Geographies* 2, no. 2 (2004): 273–86.

Cahill, Caitlin, Indra Rios-Moore, and Tiffany Threatts. "Different Eyes/Open Eyes." *Revolutionizing Education* (2008): 89–124.

Caldwell, Kia Lilly, Kathleen Coll, Tracy Fisher, Renya K. Ramirez, and Lok Siu, eds. *Gendered Citizenships: Transnational Perspectives on Knowledge Production, Political Activism, and Culture*. New York: Palgrave Macmillan, 2009.

Casper, Monica J. *The Making of the Unborn Patient: A Social Anatomy of Fetal Surgery*. New Brunswick, NJ: Rutgers University Press, 1998.

Cesara, Manda. *Reflections of a Woman Anthropologist: No Hiding Place*. Studies in Anthropology. London, New York: Academic Press, 1982.

Chari, Sharad, and Henrike Donner. "Ethnographies of Activism." Special Double Issue, *Cultural Dynamics* 22(2)–23(1) (2010).

Cheater, Christine. "Kaberry, Phyllis Mary (1910–1977)." In *Australian Dictionary of Biography*. Canberra: National Centre of Biography, Australian National University. Accessed October 4, 2015. http://adb.anu.edu.au/biography/kaberry-phyllis-mary-10654.

Chin, Elizabeth. *Purchasing Power: Black Kids, America and Consumer Culture*. Minneapolis: University of Minnesota Press, 2001.

———. "The Neoliberal Institutional Review Board, or Why Just Fixing the Rules Won't Help Feminist (Activist) Ethnographers." In *Feminist Activist Ethnography: Counterpoints to Neoliberalism in North America*, edited by Christa Craven and Dána-Ain Davis, 201–16. Lanham, MD: Lexington Books, 2013.

———. *My Life with Things: The Consumer Diaries*. Durham: Duke University Press, 2016.

Chin, Elizabeth, ed. *Katherine Dunham: Recovering an Anthropological Legacy, Choreographing Ethnographic Futures*. Advanced Seminar Series. Santa Fe: School for Advanced Research Press, 2014.

Chodorow, Nancy. Family Structure and Feminine Personality. In *Woman, Culture, and Society*, edited by Michelle Rosaldo and Louise Lamphere, 43–66. Stanford: Stanford University Press, 1974.

City University of New York Graduate Center, PhD Program in Anthropology. "The Impact of Welfare Reform on Two Communities in New York City." *W. K. Kellogg Foundation*. Accessed January 15, 2016. http://www.wkkf.org/resource-directory/resource/2003/01/the-impact-of-welfare-reform-on-two-communities-in-new-york-city.

Clair, Robin Paric. "The Changing Story of Ethnography." In *Expressions of Ethnography: Novel Approaches to Qualitative Methods*, edited by Robin Paric Clair, 3–28. Albany: State University of New York Press, 1992.

Cohen, Cathy J. *Democracy Remixed: Black Youth and the Future of American Politics*. Oxford; New York: Oxford University Press, 2010.

———. "Black Youth Project." *Black Youth Project*. Accessed October 4, 2015. http://www.blackyouthproject.com/.

Cole, Sally Cooper, Rae Bridgman, and Heather Howard-Bobiwash. *Feminist Fields: Ethnographic Insights*. Ontario: Broadview Press, 1999.

Combahee River Collective. *The Combahee River Collective Statement: Black Feminist Organizing in the Seventies and Eighties*. New York: Kitchen Table, Women of Color Press, 1986.

Council on Anthropology and Reproduction. "The Council on Anthropology and Reproduction (CAR) Opposes Legislation That Creates Barriers to Safe Abortion Care." *Medical Anthropology Quarterly* (2015).

Cox, Aimee Meredith. *Shapeshifters: Black Girls and the Choreography of Citizenship*. Durham: Duke University Press, 2015.

Craven, Christa. *Pushing for Midwives: Homebirth Mothers and the Reproductive Rights Movement*. Philadelphia: Temple University Press, 2010.

———. "Reproductive Rights in a Consumer Rights Era: Toward the Value of 'Constructive' Critique." In *Feminist Activist Ethnography: Counterpoints to Neoliberalism in North America*, edited by Christa Craven and Dána-Ain Davis, 100–16. Lanham, MD: Lexington Books, 2013.

Craven, Christa, and Dána-Ain Davis, eds. *Feminist Activist Ethnography: Counterpoints to*

Neoliberalism in North America. Lanham, MD: Lexington Books, 2013.

Crenshaw, Kimberlé. "Mapping the Margins: Intersectionality, Identity Politics and Violence Against Women of Color." *Stanford Law Review* 43, no. 6 (1991): 1241–99.

Dahl, Ulrika. "Femme on Femme: Reflections on Collaborative Methods and Queer Femmeinist Ethnography." In *Queer Methods and Methodologies*, edited by Kath Browne and Catherine J. Nash, 143–66. Farnham, Surrey, England; Burlington, VT: Ashgate, 2010.

Dahl, Ulrika, and Jenny Payne Gunnarson, eds. "Special Issue: Kinship & Reproduction." *Lambda Nordica*, no. 3/4 (2014). http://www.lambdanordica.se/en/2015/06/03/nytt-nummer-3-42014-kinship-reproduction/.

Dahl, Ulrika, and Del LaGrace Volcano. *Femmes of Power: Exploding Queer Femininities*. London: Serpent's Tail, 2009.

Dave, Naisargi. *Queer Activism in India: A Story in the Anthropology of Ethics*. Durham: Duke University Press, 2012.

Davids, Tine. "Trying to Be a Vulnerable Observer: Matters of Agency, Solidarity and Hospitality in Feminist Ethnography." *Women's Studies International Forum* 43, no. March–April (2014): 50–58.

Davis, Angela Y. *Women, Race, & Class*. New York: Vintage, 2011.

Davis, Dána-Ain. *Battered Black Women and Welfare Reform: Between a Rock and a Hard Place*. Albany: State University of New York Press, 2006.

———. "Border Crossings: Intimacy and Feminist Activist Ethnography in the Age of Neoliberalism." In *Feminist Activist Ethnography: Counterpoints to Neoliberalism in North America*, edited by Christa Craven and Dána-Ain Davis, 29–38. Lanham, MD: Lexington Books, 2013.

———. "Katherine Dunham Made Me . . ." In *Katherine Dunham: Recovering an Anthropological Legacy, Choreographing Ethnographic Futures*, edited by Elizabeth Chin, 101–26. Advanced Seminar Series. Santa Fe: School for Advanced Research Press, 2014.

Davis, Dána-Ain, Ana Aparicio, Audrey Jacobs, Akemi Kochiyama, Leith Mullings, Andrea Queeley, and Beverly Thompson. "Working It Off: Welfare Reform, Workfare and Work Experience Programs in New York City." *Souls: A Critical Journal of Black Politics, Culture and Society* 5, no. 2 (2003): 22–41.

Davis, Dána-Ain, and Christa Craven. "Equity at the Peril of Normativity: A Feminist Anthropological Take on Race, Marriage and Justice." *The Feminist Wire*, 2013. http://thefeministwire.com/2013/06/equity-at-the-peril-of-normativity-a-feminist-anthropological-take-on-race-marriage-justice/.

———. "Revisiting Feminist Ethnography: Methods and Activism at the Intersection of Neoliberal Policy." *Feminist Formations* 23, no. 2 (2011): 190–208.

Davis, Dána-Ain, and Shaka McGlotten, eds. *Black Genders and Sexualities*. New York: Palgrave Macmillan, 2012.

Deacon, Desley. *Elsie Clews Parsons: Inventing Modern Life*. Women in Culture and Society Series. Chicago, IL: University of Chicago Press, 1997.

DeLoache, Judy S., and Alma Gottlieb, eds. *A World of Babies: Imagined Childcare Guides for Seven Societies*. Cambridge; New York: Cambridge University Press, 2000.

Deloria, Ella Cara. *Waterlily*. Lincoln: University of Nebraska Books, 1988.

Deomampo, Daisy. "Transnational Surrogacy in India: Interrogating Power and Women's Agency." *Frontiers: A Journal of Women Studies* 34, no. 3 (2013): 167–88.

Desai, Manisha. "The Possibilities and Perils for Scholar-Activists and Activist-Scholars: Reflections on the Feminist Dialogues." In *Insurgent Encounters: Transnational Activism, Ethnography, and the Political*, edited by Jeffrey S. Juris and Alex Khasnabish, 89–107. Durham: Duke University Press, 2013.

di Leonardo, Micaela, ed. *Gender at the Crossroads of Knowledge*. Berkeley: University of California Press, 1991.

———. "Introduction: Gender, Culture and Political Economy: Feminist Anthropology in Historical Perspective." In *Gender at the Crossroads of Knowledge*, edited by Micaela di Leonardo, 1–49. Berkeley: University of California Press, 1991.

di Leonardo, Micaela, and Roger Lancaster. "Gender, Sexuality, Political Economy." *New Politics* 6, no. 1 (1996).

Dill, Bonnie Thornton, and Ruth Enid Zambrana, eds. *Emerging Intersections: Race, Class, and Gender in Theory, Policy, and Practice*. New Brunswick, NJ: Rutgers University Press, 2009.

Dominguez, Virginia, Matthew Guttman, and Catherine Lutz. "Problem of Gender and Citations Raised Again in New Research Study." *Anthropology News*, 2014: 19.

Downs, Kiersten. "Women Veterans and Re-Entry: A Research Study." Accessed October 5, 2015. https://womenveteransresearch15.wordpress.com/.

Ellis, Carolyn. *The Ethnographic I: A Methodological Novel aboutAautoethnography*. Lanham, MD: Rowman Altamira, 2004.

Engebretsen, Elisabeth L. *Queer Women in Urban China: An Ethnography*. New York: Routledge, 2015.

Engebretsen, Elisabeth L., William F. Schroeder, and Hongwei Bao, eds. *Queer/Tonzhi China: New Perspectives on Research, Activism, and Media*. Copenhagen, Denmark: Nordic Institute of Asian Studies Press, 2015.

Engels, Frederich. *The Conditions of the Working Class in England*. Leipzig, Germany: Otto Wigand, 1845.

———. *Origin of the Family, Private Property and the State*, Hottingen-Zürich, Germany: Verlag der Schweizerischen, Volkbuchhandlung, 1884.

Enloe, Cynthia. *Seriously! Investigating Crashes and Crises as If Women Mattered*. Berkeley and Los Angeles: University of California Press, 2013.

Enloe, Cynthia H. *Globalization and Militarism: Feminists Make the Link*. Lanham, MD: Rowman & Littlefield, 2007.

Erikson, Susan L. "Global Ethnography: Problems of Theory and Method." In *Reproduction, Globalization, and the State: New Theoretical and Ethnographic Perspectives*, edited by Carole Browner and Carolyn Sargent, 23–37. Durham: Duke University Press, 2011.

Erzen, Tanya. *Straight to Jesus: Sexual and Christian Conversions in the Ex-Gay Movement*. Berkeley: University of California Press, 2006.

———. *Fanpire: The Twilight Saga and the Women Who Love It*. Boston: Beacon Press, 2012.

Espiritu, Yen Le. *Asian American Panethnicity: Bridging Institutions and Identities*. Philadelphia: Temple University Press, 1993.

Families of Choice in Poland, Institute of Psychology, Polish Academy of Sciences. "Conference: Queer Kinship and Relationships," June 2015. https://www.ncfr.org/events/calendar/queer-kinship-and-relationships-2015-conference.

Feministing. "Katherine Cross Archive." Accessed October 4, 2015. http://feministing.com/author/katherinecross/.

feministkilljoys. "Making Feminist Points." *Feministkilljoys*, September 11, 2013. http://feministkilljoys.com/2013/09/11/making-feminist-points/.

Fernandez-Kelley, Maria Patricia. *For We Are Sold, I and My People: Women and Industry in Mexico's Frontier*. Albany: State University of New York Press, 1984.

Fernea, Elizabeth Warncock. *Guests of the Sheik: An Ethnography of an Iraqi Village*. New York: Doubleday Anchor, 1969.

Field, Les W. "Complicities and Collaborations: Anthropologists and the 'Unacknowledged Tribes' of California." *Current Anthropology* 40, no. 2 (1999): 193–210.

Fine, Michelle, Maria Elena Torre, Iris Boudin, Judith Clark, Donna Hylton, Migdalia Martinez, "Missy" Melissa Rviera, Rosemarie Roberts, Pamela Smart, and Debora Upegui. *Changing Minds: The Impact of College In a Maximum-Security Prison*. A Collaborative Research Project by the Graduate Center of the City University of New York and the Women in Prison at the Bedford Hills Correctional Facility, 2001.

Fisher, Melissa. *Wall Street Women*. Durham: Duke University Press, 2012.

Fisher, Tracy. *What's Left of Blackness: Feminisms, Transracial Solidarities, and the Politics of Belonging in Britain*. Comparative Feminist Studies. New York: Palgrave Macmillan, 2012.

Fletcher, Alice Cunningham, and Francis A. LaFlesche. *The Omaha Tribe*, Vol 2. Bison Book Edition reproduced form the 27th Annual Report of the Bureau of American Ethnology to the Secretary of the Smithsonian Institution, 1905–1906. Washington: Government Printing Office, 1911.

Franklin, Sarah. *Embodied Progress: A Cultural Account of Assisted Conception*. New York: Routledge, 2002.

———. *Biological Relatives: IVF, Stem Cells, and the Future of Kinship*. Durham: Duke University Press, 2013.

Frederickson, Mary E., and Delores M. Walters, eds. *Gendered Resistance: Women, Slavery, and the Legacy of Margaret Garner*. New Black Studies. Urbana: University of Illinois Press, 2013.

Freeman, Carla. *High Tech and High Heels in the Global Economy: Women, Work, and Pink-Collar Identities in the Caribbean*. Durham: Duke University Press, 2000.

Freidan, Betty. *The Feminine Mystique*. New York: W. W. Norton, 1963.

Freire, Paulo. *Pedagogy of the Oppressed*. 30th anniversary ed. New York: Continuum, 2000.

Gardner, Susan. "Introduction." In *Waterlily*, xxxiii. University of Nebraska, 2009.

Geertz, Clifford. "Thick Description; Toward an lnterpretive Theory of Culture." In *The Interpretation of Cultures*, 3–30. New York: Basic Books, 1973.

Gill, Harjant, dir. Milind Soman Made Me Gay. 27 Mins. In Punjabi & English w/ subtitles, Produced by Tilotama Productions, 2007. http://www.tilotamaproductions.com/Tilotama_Productions/MILIND_SOMAN_MADE_ME_GAY.html.

———. "Roots of Love" 26 mins, In Punjabi & English w/subtitles. Produced by PSBT (Public Service Broadcasting Trust), 2011. http://www.tilotamaproductions.com/Tilotama_Productions/ROOTS_OF_LOVE.html.

———. Mardistan (Macholand) Reflections on Indian Manhood. 28 Mins. In Punjabi & English w/ subtitles, Produced by PSBT (Public Service Broadcasting Trust), Tilotama Productions, 2014. http://www.tilotamaproductions.com/Tilotama_Productions/MARDISTAN_%28MANLAND%29.html.

Ginsburg, Faye. "Procreation Stories: Reproduction, Nurturance, and Procreation in Life Narratives of Abortion Activists." *American Ethnologist* 14, no. 4 (1987): 623–36.

———. *Contested Lives: The Abortion Debate in an American Community*. Berkeley: University of California Press, 1998.

Gladwell, Malcolm. "Small Change, Why the Revolution Will Not Be Tweeted." *New Yorker*, October 4, 2010.

Gordon, Deborah A. "Border Work: Feminist Ethnography and the Dissemination of Literacy." In *Women Writing Culture*, edited by Ruth Behar and Deborah A. Gordon, 373–89. Berkeley, University of California Press, 1995.

Gottlieb, Alma, and Philip Graham. *Parallel Worlds: An Anthropologist and a Writer Encounter Africa*. Chicago: University of Chicago Press, 1994.

———. *Braided Worlds*. Chicago: University of Chicago Press, 2012.

Gray, Mary L. *Out in the Country: Youth, Media, and Queer Visibility in Rural America*. New York: New York University Press, 2009.

———. "Why LGBT Communities and Our Allies Should Care about Net Neutrality." *The Huffington Post*, 2014. http://www.huffingtonpost.com/mary-l-gray-phd/why-lgbt-communities-and-_b_6147802.html.

———. "Stop Blaming Dharun Ravi: Why We Need To Share Responsibility For The Loss Of Tyler Clementi." *The Huffington Post*, 2012. Accessed October 5, 2015. http://www.huffingtonpost.com/mary-l-gray-phd/tyler-clementi_b_1317688.html.

Gupta, Akhil, and James Ferguson. "Discipline and Practice: 'The Field' as Site, Method, and Location in Anthropology." *Anthropological Locations: Boundaries and Grounds of a Field Science* 100 (1997): 1–47.

Gutmann, Matthew C. *The Meanings of Macho: Being a Man in Mexico City*. Men and Masculinity 3. Berkeley: University of California Press, 1996.

Hale, Charles R. *Engaging Contradictions: Theory, Politics, and Methods of Activist Scholarship*. Berkeley: University of California Press, 2008.

Harding, Sandra G. *Feminism and Methodology: Social Science Issues*. Bloomington: Indiana University Press, 1987.

Harrison, Faye V. "'Three Women, One Struggle': Anthropology, Performance, and Pedagogy." *Transforming Anthropology* 1, no. 1 (1990): 1–9.

———. "Feminist Methodology as a Tool for Ethnographic Inquiry on Globalization." In *The Gender of Globalization: Women Navigating Cultural and Economic Marginalities*, edited by Nandini Gunewardena and Ann Kingsolver, 23–31. Santa Fe, NM: School for Advanced Research Press, 2007.

———. *Outsider Within: Reworking Anthropology in the Global Age*. Chicago: University of Illinois Press, 2008.

———. "Navigating Feminist Activist Ethnography." In *Feminist Activist Ethnography: Counterpoints to Neoliberalism in North America*, edited by Dána-Ain Davis and Christa Craven, ix–xv. Lanham, MD: Lexington, 2013.

Harrison, Faye V., ed. *Decolonizing Anthropology: Moving Further Toward an Anthropology for Liberation*. Washington, DC: Association of Black Anthropologists, American Anthropological Association, 1991.

Herdt, Gilbert. *Guardians of the Flutes: Idioms of Masculinity: A Study of Ritualized Homosexual Behavior*. New York: McGraw-Hill Book Co, 1981.

Hernández, Graciela. "Multiple Mediations in Zora Neale Hurston's Mules and Men." *Critique of Anthropology* 13, no. 4 (1993): 351–62.

Hesse-Biber, Sharlene Nagy. *Feminist Research Practice: A Primer*. 2nd ed. Thousand Oaks, CA: SAGE Publications, 2014.

Hill Collins, Patricia. *Black Feminist Thought: Knowledge, Consciousness, and the Politics of Empowerment*. 2nd ed. Routledge Classics. New York: Routledge, 2009.

Ho, Karen. *Liquidated: An Ethnography of Wall Street*. Durham: Duke University Press, 2009.

Hodgson, Dorothy L. "Critical Interventions: Dilemmas of Accountability in Contemporary Ethnographic Research." *Identities* 6, no. 2–3 (1999): 201–24.

———. "Introduction: Comparative Perspectives on the Indigenous Rights Movement in Africa and the Americas." *American Anthropologist* 104(4):1037–1049. 2002, 1044–1045.

———. *Being Maasai, Becoming Indigenous: Postcolonial Politics in a Neoliberal World*.

South Bend, IN: Indiana University Press, 2011.

hooks, bell. *Feminist Theory: From Margin to Center*. Cambridge, MA: South End Press, 2000.

Huggins, Martha K., and Marie-Louise Glebbeek, eds. *Women Fielding Danger: Negotiating Ethnographic Identities in Field Research*. Lanham, MD: Rowman & Littlefield Publishers, 2009.

Hunter, Nan D. "Contextualizing the Sexuality Debates: A Chronology 1966–2005." In *Sex Wars: Sexual Dissent and Political Culture*, edited by Lisa Duggan and Nan D. Hunter, 10th Anniversary Edition, 15–28. New York: Taylor & Francis, 2006.

Hurston, Zora Neale. *Mules and Men*. Urbana and Chicago: University of Chicago Press, 1978 (orig. 1935).

———. *Their Eyes Were Watching God*. New York: Harper Perennial Modern Classics, 2013 (orig. 1937).

———. *Tell my Horse: Voodoo and Life in Haiti and Jamaica*. New York: Harper Collins, 1990 (orig 1938).

Hurtado, Aida. *The Color of Privilege: Three Blasphemies on Race and Feminism*. Ann Arbor: University of Michigan Press, 1997.

Hyatt, Susan Brin. "Water Is Life—Meters Out! Women's Grassroots Activism And the Privatization of Public Amenities." *Globalization Research Center. Occasional Papers on Globalization* University of South Florida, no. Vol 1 (7) (June 2004).

Hyatt, Susan Brin, Boone W. Shear, and Susan Wright, eds. *Learning under Neoliberalism: Ethnographies of Governance in Higher Education*. New York: Berghahn Books, 2015.

Inhorn, Marcia C. *Quest for Conception: Gender, Infertility and Egyptian Medical Traditions*. Philadelphia: University of Pennsylvania Press, 1994.

———. *The New Arab Man: Emergent Masculinities, Technologies, and Islam in the Middle East*. Princeton: Princeton University Press, 2012.

Jackson, Antoinette T. "Daisy M. Bates: Ethnographic Work among the Australian Aborigines." Unpublished paper, 1998.

Jackson, Jean. "The Politics of Ethnographic Practice in the Colombian Vaupés." *Identities Global Studies in Culture and Power* 6, no. 2–3 (1999): 281–317.

Juris, Jeffrey S., and Alex Khasnabish, eds. *Insurgent Encounters: Transnational Activism, Ethnography, and the Political*. Durham: Duke University Press, 2013.

Kaberry, Phyllis Mary. *Aboriginal Woman: Sacred and Profane*. London; New York: Routledge, 2004.

Kanaaneh, Rhoda Ann. *Birthing the Nation: Strategies of Palestinian Women in Israel*. Berkeley: University of California Press, 2002.

Kantsa, Venetia, and Aspasia Chalkidou. "Doing Family 'In the Space Between the Laws': Notes on Lesbian Motherhood in Greece." *Lambda Nordica*, edited by Ulrika Dahl and Jenny Gunnarson Payne. no. 3/4 (2014): 86–108.

Kingston, Maxine Hong. *The Woman Warrior: Memoirs of a Girlhood among Ghosts*. Vintage, 2010 (orig. 1976).

Lamott, Anne. "Shitty First Drafts." In *Bird by Bird: Some Instructions on Writing and Life*, 20–27. New York: Anchor Books, 1995.

Lamphere, Louise. "The Perils and Prospects for an Engaged Anthropology. A View from the United States," *Social Anthropology* 11, no. 2 (2003): 153–68.

———. "Feminist Anthropology Engages Social Movements: Theory, Ethnography and Activism." In *Mapping Feminist Anthropology in the Twenty-First Century*, edited by Ellen Lewin and Leni M. Silverstein. New Brunswick, NJ: Rutgers University Press, forthcoming.

Lamphere, Louise, Eva Price, Carole Cadman, and Valerie Darwin. *Weaving Women's Lives: Three Generations in a Navajo Family*. Albuquerque: University of New Mexico Press, 2007.

Lamphere, Louise, Helena Ragoné, and Patricia Zavella, eds. *Situated Lives: Gender and Culture in Everyday Life*. New York: Routledge, 1997.

Lamphere, Louise, Rayna Rapp, and Gayle Rubin. "Anthropologists Are Talking About Feminist Anthropology." *Ethnos* 72, no. 3 (2007): 408–26.

Lamphere, Louise, Patricia Zavella, and Felipe Gonzales. *Sunbelt Working Mothers: Reconciling Family and Factory*. Ithaca, NY: Cornell University Press, 1993.

Landes, Ruth *City of Women*. New York: Macmillan, 1947.

Lareau, Annette. *Home Advantage: Social Class and Parental Intervention in Elementary Education*. Lanham, MD: Rowman & Littlefield Publishers, 1989.

———. "Common Problems in Fieldwork." In *Journeys Through Ethnography: Realistic Accounts of Fieldwork*, edited by Annette Lareau and Jeffrey Shultz, 195–236. Boulder: Westview Press, 1996.

———. "Reflections on Longitudinal Ethnography and the Families' Reactions to Unequal Childhoods." In *Unequal Childhoods: Class,*

Race, and Family Life, 2nd ed., 312–32. Berkeley: University of California Press, 2011.

———. *Unequal Childhoods: Class, Race, and Family Life*. 2nd ed. Berkeley: University of California Press, 2011.

Lassiter, Luke Eric. *The Chicago Guide to Collaborative Ethnography*. Chicago: University of Chicago Press, 2005.

Lather, Patricia, and Chris Smithies. *Troubling the Angels: Women Living with HIV/AIDS*. Boulder, CO: Westview Press, 1997.

The Latina Feminist Group. Telling to Live: Latina Feminist Testimonios. Durham: Duke University Press, 2001.

Lather, Patti. "Postbook: Working the Ruins of Feminist Ethnography." *Signs: Journal of Women and Society* 27, no. 1 (2001): 199–227.

Leacock, Eleanor B. "Introduction to *The Origin of the Family, Private Property, and the State*, by Frederick Engels," 7–67. New York: International, 1972.

Leacock, Eleanor. "Theory and Ethics in Applied Urban Anthropology." In *Cities of the United States*, edited by Leith Mullings, 317–36. New York: Columbia University Press, 1987.

Leacock, Eleanor, and Richard Lee. *Politics and History of Band Societies*. Politics and History of Band Societies. New York: Cambridge University Press, 1982.

Lewin, Ellen, *Lesbian Mothers: Accounts of Gender in American Culture*. Ithaca, NY: Cornell University Press, 1993.

———. *Recognizing Ourselves*. New York: Columbia University Press, 1999.

———. *Gay Fatherhood: Narratives of Family and Citizenship in America*. Chicago: University of Chicago Press, 2009.

Lewin, Ellen, ed. *Inventing Lesbian Cultures*. Boston: Beacon Press, 1996.

———. *Feminist Anthropology: A Reader*. Malden, MA: Wiley-Blackwell, 2006.

Lewin, Ellen, and William L. Leap, eds. *Out in Public: Reinventing Lesbian/Gay Anthropology in a Globalizing World*. Chichester, UK; Malden, MA: Wiley-Blackwell, 2009.

———. *Out in the Field: Reflections of Lesbian and Gay Anthropologists*. Urbana: University of Illinois Press, 1996.

———. *Out in Theory: The Emergence of Lesbian and Gay Anthropology*. Urbana: University of Illinois Press, 2002.

Library of Congress. "Margaret Mead As a Cultural Commentator - Margaret Mead: Human Nature and the Power of Culture | Exhibitions - Library of Congress." Web page, November 30, 2001. http://www.loc.gov/exhibits/mead/oneworld-comment.html.

Longman, Chia, and Tamsin Bradley. *Interrogating Harmful Cultural Practices: Gender, Culture and Coercion*. Farnham, Surrey, England; Burlington, VT: Ashgate, 2015.

López, Iris. *Matters of Choice: Puerto Rican Women's Struggle for Reproductive Freedom*. New Brunswick, NJ: Rutgers University Press, 2008.

———. "Negotiating Different Worlds: An Integral Ethnography of Reproductive Freedom and Social Justice." In *Feminist Activist Ethnography: Counterpoints to Neoliberalism in North America*, edited by Christa Craven and Dána-Ain Davis, 145–80. Lanham, MD: Lexington Books, 2013.

Lorber, Judith. *Gender Inequality: Feminist Theories and Politics*. New York: Oxford University Press, 2010.

Love, Barbara J., ed. *Feminists Who Changed America, 1963–1975*. Urbana: University of Illinois, 2006.

Low, Setha M, and Sally Engle Merry. "Engaged Anthropology: Diversity and Dilemmas." *Current Anthropology* 51, no. S2 (2010): S203–S226.

Lurie, Nancy O. "Women in Early American Anthropology." In *Pioneers of American Anthropology: The Uses of Biography*, edited by June Helm, 29–82. Seattle: University of Washington Press, 1966.

Lutz, Catherine, and Jane Lou Collins. *Reading National Geographic*. Chicago: University of Chicago Press, 1993.

Madison, Soyini D. *Critical Ethnography: Methods, Ethics, Performance*. Los Angeles: Sage, 2005.

Maguire, Patricia. *Doing Participatory Research: A Feminist Approach*. Amherst, MA: Center for International Education, School of Education, University of Massachusetts, 1987.

Malinowski, Bronislaw. *Argonauts of the Western Pacific: An Account of Native Enterprise and Adventure in the Archipelagoes of Melanesian New Guinea*. London: George Routledge & Sons, Ltd., 1922.

———. *A Diary in the Strictest Sense of the Term*. Vol. 235. Stanford University Press, 1989.

Manalansan IV, Martin F. *Global Divas: Filipino Gay Men in the Diaspora*. Durham: Duke University Press, 2003.

Marcus, Eric. "Stonewall Revisited." In *Independent Gay Forum*, Vol. 30 (1999).

Marcus, George E. *Ethnography through Thick and Thin*. Princeton: Princeton University Press, 1998.

Martin, Emily. *The Woman in the Body: A Cultural Analysis of Reproduction*. Boston: Beacon Press, 2001.

Marzullo, Michelle. "Seeking 'Marriage Material': Rethinking the U.S. Marriage Debatees Under Neoliberalism." In *Feminist Activist Ethnography: Counterpoints to Neoliberalism*, edited by Dána-Ain Davis and Christa Craven, 77–100. Lanham, MD: Lexington Books, 2013.

Matabeni, Zethu, ed. *Reclaiming Afrikan: Queer Perspectives on Sexual and Gender Indentities*. Cape Town, South Africa: Modjaji Books, 2014.

Matebeni, Zethu, Vasu Reddy, Theo Sandfort, and Ian Southey-Swartz. "'I Thought We Are Safe': Southern African Lesbians' Experiences of Living with HIV." *Culture, Health & Sexuality* 15, no. 1 (2013): 34–47.

Matto de Turner, Clorinda *Aves Sin Nido*. Lima: Imprenta del Universo de Carlos Prince, 1889.

Maynard, Mary. *Researching Women's Lives from a Feminist Perspective*. New York: Routledge, 2013.

McClaurin, Irma. *Black Feminist Anthropology: Theory, Politics, Praxis, and Poetics*. New Brunswick, NJ: Rutgers University Press, 2001.

McGlotten, Shaka and Dána-Ain Davis, eds. *Black Genders and Sexualities*. Critical Black Studies. New York: Palgrave Macmillan, 2012.

Medicine, Beatrice. "Native American (Indian) Women: A Call for Research." *Anthropology and Education* 19, no. 2 (1988): 86–92.

Mendez, Jennifer Bickham. *From the Revolution to the Maquiladoras: Gender, Labor and Globalization in Nicaragua*. Durham: Duke University Press, 2005.

———. "Globalizing Scholar Activism: Opportunities and Dilemmas Through a Feminist Lens." In *Engaging Contradictions: Theory, Politics, and Methods of Activist Scholarship*, edited by Charles R. Hale, 136–63. Berkeley: University of California Press, 2008.

Meyer, Doug. *Violence against Queer People: Race, Class, Gender, and the Persistence of Anti-LGBT Discrimination*. New Brunswick, NJ: Rutgers University Press, 2015.

———. "Researching Violence and Asking People to Describe Traumatic Experiences." Accessed September 30, 2015. https://gendersociety.wordpress.com/2015/01/30/researching-violence/.

Minh-Ha, Trinh T. *Woman, Native, Other: Writing Postcoloniality and Feminism*. Bloomington: Indiana University Press, 2009.

Mohanty, Chandra Talpade. "Cartographies of Struggle: Third World Women and the Politics of Feminism." In *Third World Women and the Politics of Feminism*, edited by Chandra Talpade Mohanty, Ann Russo, and Lourdes Torres, 1–47. Bloomington: Indiana University Press, 1991.

———. "Under Western Eyes." In *Third World Women and the Politics of Feminism*. Bloomington: Indiana University Press, 1991.

———. *Feminism Without Borders: Decolonizing Theory, Practicing Solidarity*. Durham: Duke University Press, 2003.

Mohanty, Chandra Talpade. "'Under Western Eyes' Revisited: Feminist Solidarity through Anticapitalist Struggles." *Signs: Journal of Women and Society* 28, no. 2 (2003): 499–535.

Mohanty, Chandra Talpade, Ann Russo, and Lourdes Torres, eds. *Third World Women and the Politics of Feminism*. Bloomington: Indiana University Press, 1991.

Mol, Annemarie. *The Body Multiple: Ontology in Medical Practice*. Durham: Duke University Press, 2003.

Monáe, Janelle. The Electric Lady. © 2013 by Bad Boy, Atlantic, Wondaland Arts Society. Digital Recording.

Moore, Henrietta L. *Feminism and Anthropology*. Feminist Perspectives. Cambridge, UK: Polity Press in association with B. Blackwell, Oxford, UK, 1988.

Moore, Mignon R. *Invisible Families: Gay Identities, Relationships, and Motherhood among Black Women*. Berkeley: University of California Press, 2011.

Moraga, Cherríe, and Gloria Anzaldúa. *This Bridge Called My Back: Writings of Radical Women of Color*. New York: Kitchen Table, Women of Color Press, 1983.

Morgan, Robin. *Sisterhood Is Global: The International Women's Movement Anthology*. New York: The Feminist Press at City University of New York, 1996.

Morgen, Sandra. *Into our Own Hands: The Women's Health Movement in the United States, 1969–1990*. New Brunswick, NJ: Rutgers University Press, 2002.

Morgen, Sandra, ed. *Gender and Anthropology: Critical Reviews for Research and Teaching*. Washington, DC: American Anthropological Association, 1989.

Morgensen, Scott L. *Spaces Between Us: Queer Settler Colonialism and Indigenous Decolonization*. Minneapolis: University of Minnesota Press, 2011.

———. "Reflection: Fearlessly Engaging Complicity." In *Feminist Activist Ethnography: Counterpoints to Neoliberalism in North America*, edited by Christa Craven and Dána-Ain Davis, 69–74. Lanham, MD: Lexington Books, 2013.

Morrison, Toni. *The Bluest Eye*. New York: Random House, 1999 (orig. 1970).

———. *Song of Solomon*. New York: Random House, 2014 (orig. 1977).

———. *Playing in the Dark*. New York: Vintage, 2007.

Mullings, Leith. "Households Headed by Women: The Politics of Race, Class and Gender." In *Conceiving the New World Order: The Global Politics of Reproduction*, edited by Faye D. Ginsburg and Rayna Rapp, 122–39. Oakland: University of California Press, 1995.

———. *On Our Own Terms: Race, Class, and Gender in the Lives of African-American Women*. New York: Routledge, 1997.

———. "African American Women Making Themselves: Notes on the Role of Black Feminist Research." *Souls: A Critical Journal of Black Politics, Culture and Society* 2, no. 4 (2000): 18–29.

Mullings, Leith, and Amy J. Schulz. "Intersectionality and Health: An Introduction." In *Gender, Race, Class, and Health: Intersectional Approaches*, edited by Amy J. Schulz and Leith Mullings, 3–19. San Francisco: Jossey Bass, 2006.

Mullings, Leith, and Alaka Wali. *Stress and Resilience: The Social Context of Reproduction in Central Harlem*. New York: Kluwer Academic/Plenum Publishers, 2001.

Muñoz, Lorena. "Brown, Queer and Gendered: Queering the Latina/o 'Street-Scapes' in Los Angeles." In *Queer Methods and Methodologies*, edited by Kath Browne and Catherine J. Nash, 1:55–67. Farnham, Surrey, England; Burlington, VT: Ashgate, 2010.

Mwaria, Cheryl. "Biomedical Ethics, Gender, and Ethnicity: Implications for Black Feminist Anthropology." In *Black Feminist Anthropology: Theory, Politics, Praxis, and Poetics*, edited by Irma McClaurin, 187–210. New Brunswick, NJ: Rutgers University Press, 2001.

———. Questioning the Role of Race and Culture Versus Racism and Poverty in Medical Decision-Making." In *Health at the Intersections of Gender, Race, and Class*, edited by Amy Schulz and Leith Mullings, 289–312. New York: Jossey-Bass/Pfeiffer, 2006.

Naaeke, Anthony, Anastacia Kurylo, David Linton, Michael Grabowski, and Marie L Radford. "Insider and Outsider Perspective in Ethnographic Research." 9. *Proceedings of the New York State Communication Association*, 2011. http://docs.rwu.edu/cgi/viewcontent.cgi?article=1017&context=nyscaproceedings.

Nader, Laura. "Up the Anthropologist: Perspectives Gained from Studying Up." In *Reinventing Anthropology*, 284–311. New York: Vintage Books, 1972.

Nagar, Richa. *Muddying the Waters: Coauthoring Feminisms across Scholarship and Activism*. Chicago: University of Illinois Press, 2014.

Naples, Nancy A. *Grassroots Warriors: Activist Mothering, Community Work, and the War on Poverty*. New York: Routledge, 1998.

———. *Feminism and Method: Ethnography, Discourse Analysis, and Activist Research*. New York: Routledge, 2003.

Naples, Nancy A., and Karen Bojar, eds. *Teaching Feminist Activism: Strategies from the Field*. New York: Routledge, 2002.

Naples, Nancy A., and Manisha Desai, eds. *Women's Activism and Globalization: Linking Local Struggles to Global Politics*. New York: Routledge, 2002.

Naples, Nancy A. and Jennifer Bickham Mendez, eds. *Border Politics: Social Movements, Collective Identities, and Globalization*. New York: New York University Press, 2014.

Narayan, Kirin. *Storytellers, Saints, and Scoundrels: Folk Narrative in Hindu Religious Teaching*. Philadelphia: University of Pennsylvania Press, 1989.

———. "How Native Is a 'Native' Anthropologist?" *American Anthropologist* 95, no. 3 (1993): 671–86.

———. *Alive in the Writing: Crafting Ethnography in the Company of Chekhov*. Chicago: University of Chicago Press, 2012.

Nash, June. *We Eat The Mines and the Mines Eat Us: Dependency and Exploitation in Bolivian Tin Mines*. New York: Columbia University Press, 1979.

Navarro, Tami, Bianca Williams, and Attiya Ahmad. "Sitting at the Kitchen Table: Fieldnotes from Women of Color in Anthropology." *Cultural Anthropology* 28, no. 3 (2013): 443–63.

Nelson, Jennifer. *Women of Color and the Reproductive Rights Movement*. New York: New York University Press, 2003.

Newton, Esther. *Mother Camp: Female Impersonators in America*. Englewood Cliffs, NJ: Prentice-Hall, 1972.

———. *Cherry Grove, Fire Island: Sixty Years in America's First Gay and Lesbian Town*. Durham: Duke University Press, 1993.

———. *Margaret Mead Made Me Gay: Personal Essays, Public Ideas*. Durham: Duke University Press, 2000.

———. "Too Queer for College: Notes on Homophpbia 1987." In *Margaret Mead Made Me Gay: Personal Essays, Public Ideas*, 219–24. Durham: Duke University Press, 2000.

Oakley, Ann. "Gender, methodology and people's ways of knowing: Some problems with feminism and the paradigm debate in social science." *Sociology* 32, no. 4 (1998): 707–31.

Ong, Aihwa. *Spirits of Resistance and Capitalist Discipline: Factory Women in Malaysia.* Albany: State University of New York Press, 1987.

Parezo, Nancy J. "Matilda Coxe Stevenson: Pioneer Ethnologist." In *Hidden Scholars: Women Anthropologists and the Native American Southwest*, edited by Nancy J Parezo, 38–62 Albuquerque: University of New Mexico Press, 1999.

Parsons, Elsie Worthington Clews. *The Journal of a Feminist.* Bristol, United Kingdom: Thoemmes Continuum, 1994.

Pascoe, C. J. *Dude, You're a Fag: Masculinity and Sexuality in High School.* 2nd ed., With a New Preface edition. Berkeley: University of California Press, 2011.

Paxson, Heather. *Making Modern Mothers: Ethics and Family Planning in Urban Greece.* Berkeley: University of California Press, 2004.

Pérez, Gina M. *The Near Northwest Side Story: Migration, Displacement, and Puerto Rican Families.* Berkeley: University of California Press, 2004.

———. "Methodological Gifts in Latina/o Studies and Feminist Anthropology." *Anthropology News* 48, no. 7 (October 1, 2007): 6–7.

Personal Narratives Group. *Interpreting Women's Lives: Feminist Theory and Personal Narratives.* Bloomington: Indiana University Press, 1989.

Phillips, Lynne, and Sally Cole. *Contesting Publics: Feminism, Activism, Ethnography.* London: Pluto Press, 2013.

Pinho, Osmundo. "Ethnographies of the Brau: Body, Masculinity and Race in the Reafricanization in Salvador." *Estudos Feministas* 13, no. 1 (2006): 127–45.

Powdermaker, Hortense *After Freedom: A Cultural Study In the Deep South.* New York: Viking, 1939.

"Poto Mitan: Haitian Women Pillars of the Global Economy." Webpage, accessed October 4, 2015. http://potomitan.net/.

Queeley, Andrea. "*Somos Negros Finos*: Anglophone Caribbean Cultural Citizenship in Revolutionary Cuba." In *Global Circuits of Blackness: Interrogating the African Diaspora*, edited by Jean Muteba Rahier, Percy C. Hintzen, and Felipe Smith, 201–22. Champaign: University of Illinois Press, 2010.

Radcliffe-Brown, A. R. "The Social Organization of Australian Tribes." *Oceania* 1, no. 1 (1930): 206–46.

Ransby, Barbara. *Eslanda: The Large and Unconventional Life of Mrs. Paul Robeson.* New Haven and London: Yale University Press, 2013.

Rapp, Rayna. *Testing Women, Testing the Fetus: The Social Impact of Amniocentesis in America.* New York: Routledge, 1999.

Raymond, Janice G. *The Transsexal Empire: The Making of the She-Male.* Boston: Beacon Press, 1979.

Reinharz, Shulamit. *Feminist Methods in Social Research.* New York: Oxford University Press, 1992.

Reiter (now Rapp), Rayna. *Toward an Anthropology of Women.* New York: Monthly Review Press, 1975.

Rios-Moore, Indra, Erica Arenas, Jennifer Contreras, Na Jiang, Tiffany Threatts, Shamara Allen, and Caitlin Cahill. "Makes Me Mad: Stereotypes of Young Urban Womyn of Color." New York: Center for Human Environments, The Graduate Center, City University of New York, 2004.

Roberts, Dorothy. *Killing the Black Body: Race, Reproduction, and the Meaning of Liberty.* New York: Vintage, 1998.

Rodriguez, Cheryl. "Black Feminist Anthropology for the 21st Century." *Anthropology News* 48, no. 7 (2007): 7.

Rodriguez, Cheryl R., and Dzodzi Tsikata, and Akosua Adomako Ampofo, eds. *Transatlantic Feminisms: Women and Gender Studies in Africa and the Diaspora.* Lanham, MD: Lexington Books, 2015.

Rooke, Alison. "Queer in the Field: On Emotions, Temporality and Performativity in Ethnography." In *Queer Methods and Methodologies*, edited by Kath Browne and Catherine J. Nash, 1:25–41. Farnham, Surrey, England; Burlington, VT: Ashgate, 2010.

Rosaldo, Michelle, and Louise Lamphere, eds. *Woman, Culture, and Society.* Stanford: Stanford University Press, 1974.

Rothman, Barbara Katz. *The Tentative Pregnancy: How Amniocentesis Changes the Experience of Motherhood.* New York: W. W. Norton & Company, 1993.

Rubin, Gayle. "The Traffic in Women: Notes on the 'Political Economy' of Sex." In *Toward an Anthropology of Women*, edited by Rayna Reiter, 157–209. New York: Monthly Review Press, 1975.

———. "Thinking Sex: Notes for a Radical Theory of the Politics of Sexuality, in Pleasure and

Danger: *Exploring Female Sexuality,* edited by Carole Vance, 143–78. New York: Routledge, 1984.

Sandoval, Chela. *Methodology of the Oppressed.* Theory out of Bounds, v. 18. Minneapolis: University of Minnesota Press, 2000.

Sanford, Victoria, and Asale Angel-Ajani, eds. *Engaged Observer: Anthropology, Advocacy, and Activism.* New Brunswick, NJ: Rutgers University Press, 2006.

Sangtin Writers Collective, and Richa Nagar. *Playing with Fire: Feminist Thought and Activism through Seven Lives in India.* Minneapolis: University of Minnesota Press, 2006.

Sargent, Carolyn. "Manda Cesara, 'Reflections of a Woman Anthropologist. No Hiding Place' (Book Review)." *Canadian Journal of African Studies/Revue Canadienne Des* Études Africaines 17, no. 3 (1983): 564.

Savigliano, Marta. *Angora Matta: Actos Fatales De Traduccion Norte-Sur/Fatal Acts of North-South Translation.* Lebanon, NH: University Press of New England, 2003.

Scharen, Christian, and Aana Marie Vigen. *Ethnography as Christian Theology and Ethics.* London: Continuum International Publishing Group, 2011.

Schrock, Richelle D. "The Methodological Imperatives of Feminist Ethnography." *Journal of Feminist Scholarship* 5, no. 1 (2013): 48–60.

Schuller, Mark, and Renée Bergan, dirs. Poto Mitan: Haitian Women Pillars of the Global Economy. Produced by Tèt Ansanm Productions, 2009. http://www.potomitan.net/.

Shabazz, Rashad. *Spatializing Blackness: Architectures of Confinement and Black Masculinity in Chicago.* Chicago: University of Illinois Press, 2015.

Shostak, Marjorie. *Nisa: The Life and Words of a !Kung Woman.* Ann Arbor: University of Michigan Press, 1981.

———. *Return to Nisa.* Cambridge, MA: Harvard University Press, 2000.

Silliman, Jael Miriam, Marlene Gerber Fried, Loretta Ross, and Elena Gutiérrez. *Undivided Rights: Women of Color Organize for Reproductive Justice.* Cambridge, MA: South End Press, 2004.

Skeggs, Beverly. "Feminist Ethnography." In *Handbook of Ethnography*, edited by Paul Atkinson, Amanda Coffey, Sara Delamont, John Lofland, and Lyn Lofland. London: Sage Publications, 2001.

Smith, Barbara. *The Truth That Never Hurts: Writings on Race, Gender, and Freedom.* New Brunswick, NJ: Rutgers University Press, 1998.

Smith, Dorothy E. *Writing the Social: Critique, Theory, and Investigations.* Ontario: University of Toronto Press, 1999.

———. *Institutional Ethnography: A Sociology for People.* The Gender Lens Series. Walnut Creek: AltaMira Press, 2005.

Smith, Linda Tuhiwai. *Decolonizing Methodologies: Research and Indigenous Peoples.* 2nd ed. London: Zed Books, 2012 (orig. 1999).

Smiths, Mary. *Baba of Karo, a Woman of the Muslim Hausa.* New Haven: Yale University Press, 1954.

South African History Online. "Charlotte (née Manye) Maxeke." Text, February 17, 2011. http://www.sahistory.org.za/people/charlotte-n%C3%A9e-manye-maxeke.

Spector, Janet. *What This Awl Means: Feminist Archaeology at a Wahpeton Dakota Village.* St. Paul: Minnesota Historical Society Press, 1993.

Speed, Shannon. *Rights in Rebellion: Indigenous Struggle and Human Rights in Chiapas.* Stanford: Stanford University Press, 2008.

Speed, Shannon, R. Aída Hernández Castillo, and Lynn M. Stephen, eds. *Dissident Women: Gender and Cultural Politics in Chiapas.* Austin, TX: University of Texas Press, 2006.

Sprague, Joey. *Feminist Methodologies for Critical Researchers: Bridging Difference.* Walnut Creek, CA: Alta Mira, 2005.

Stacey, Judith. "Can There Be A Feminist Ethnography?" *Women's Studies International Forum* 11, no. 1 (1988): 21–27.

———. *Brave New Families: Stories of Domestic Upheaval in Late-Twentieth-Century America.* Berkeley: University of California Press, 1990.

———. *Unhitched: Love, Marriage, and Family Values from West Hollywood to Western China.* New York: New York University Press, 2011.

Steinmetz, Katy. "Which Word Should Be Banned in 2015?" *Time Magazine*, November 12, 2014. http://time.com/3576870/worst-words-poll-2014/.

Sterk, Claire E. *Tricking and Tripping: Prostitution in the Era of AIDS.* Putnam, New York: Social Change Press, 2000.

Strathern, Marilyn. "An Awkward Relationship: The Case of Feminism and Anthropology." *Signs: Journal of Women and Society* 12, no. 2 (1987): 276–92.

Sudbury, Julia, and Margo Okazawa-Rey, eds. *Activist Scholarship: Antiracism, Feminism, and Social Change.* Boulder: Paradigm Publishers, 2009.

Su, Karen. "Translating Mother Tongues: Amy Tan and Maxine Hong Kingston on Ethnographic

Authority." *Feminist Fields: Ethnographic Insights*, edited by Rae Bridgman, Sally Cole, and Heather Howard-Bobiwash, 33–53. Ontario: Broadview Press, 1999.

Sundén, Jenny, and Malin Sveningsson. *Gender and Sexuality in Online Game Cultures: Passionate Play*. Routledge Advances in Feminist Studies and Intersectionality 8. New York: Routledge, 2012.

Susser, Ida. "The Anthropologist as Social Critic: Working Towards a More Engaged Anthropology." *Current Anthropology* 51, no. 2 (2010): S227–33.

Swarr, Amanda Lock. *Sex in Transition: Remaking Gender & Race in South Africa*. Albany: State University of New York Press, 2012.

Taylor, Julie M. *Paper Tangos*. Public Planet Books. Durham: Duke University Press, 1998.

Te Awekotuku, Ngahuia, and Manatu Maori. *He Tikanga Whakaaro: Research Ethics in the Maori Community*. Wellington, New Zealand: Manatu Maori, 1991.

Téllez, Michelle. "Doing Research at the Borderlands: Notes from a Chicana Feminist Ethnographer." *Chicana/Latina Studies* 4, no. 2 (2005): 46–70.

Téllez, Michelle, dir. Workers on the Rise, 2012. https://vimeo.com/85164509.

"The Feminist Ethnographer's Dilemma." Accessed October 5, 2015. http://bcrw.barnard.edu/videos/the-feminist-ethnographers-dilemma/.

Torre, Maria E., and Michelle Fine. "Participatory Action Research (PAR) by Youth." Youth Activism: An International Encyclopedia 2 (2006): 456–462.

Tristan, Flora. Promenades dans Londre. Paris: H.-L. Delloye; Londres: W. Jeffs, Libraire, 1840.

Tsing, Anna Lowenhaupt. *In the Realm of the Diamond Queen: Marginality in an Out-of-the-Way Place*. Princeton: Princeton University Press, 1993.

Ulysse, Gina Athena. *Downtown Ladies: Informal Commercial Importers, a Haitian Anthropologist, and Self-Making in Jamaica*. Women in Culture and Society. Chicago: University of Chicago Press, 2007.

———. I Am Storm: Songs and Poems for Haiti, © 2010. Compact disc.

———. "Faye V. Harrison and Why Anthropology Still Matters." The Huffington Post, December 20, 2013, http://www.huffingtonpost.com/gina-athena-ulysse/anthropology-still-matters-faye-v-harrison_b_4259423.html.

———. *Untapped Fierceness/My Giant Leaps*. TEDxUofM, 2013. https://www.youtube.com/watch?v=xHhngXU8Zw4.

Underhill, Ruth Murray. *Papago Woman: An Intimate Portrait of American Indian Culture*. Case Studies. Prospect Heights, IL: Waveland Press, 1985 (orig. 1936).

Uzwiak, Beth. "Fracturing Feminism: Activist Research and Ethics in a Women's Human Rights NGO." In *Feminist Activist Ethnography: Counterpoints to Neoliberalism in North America*, edited by Christa Craven and Dána-Ain Davis, 119–136. Lanham, MD: Lexington Books, 2013.

Valentine, David. *Imagining Transgender: An Ethnography of a Category*. Durham: Duke University Press, 2007.

Venugopal, Arun. "Museums as White Spaces," 2015. http://www.wnyc.org/story/museums-white-spaces/?utm_source=sharedUrl&utm_medium=metatag&utm_campaign=sharedUrl.

Visweswaran, Kamala. *Fictions of Feminist Ethnography*. Minneapolis: University of Minnesota Press, 1994.

———. "Histories of Feminist Ethnography." *Annual Review of Anthropology* 26 (1997): 591–621.

Viteri, María Amelia. *Desbordes: Translating Racial, Ethnic, Sexual, and Gender Identities Across the Americas*. Albany: State University of New York Press, 2014.

Walker, Alice. *Meridian*. Open Road Media, 2011 (orig. 1976).

———. *The Color Purple*. New York: Harcourt Brace Jovanovich, 1982.

Walker, Rebecca "Becoming the Third Wave." Ms. Magazine, 11, no. 2 (1992): 39–41.

Walters, Delores. "Cast Among Outcastes: Interpreting Sexual Orientation, Racial, and Gender Identity in the Yemen Arab Republic." In *Out in the Field: Reflections of Lesbian and Gay Anthropologists*, edited by Ellen Lewin and William L. Leap, eds. 58–69. Urbana and Chicago, IL: University of Illinois Press. 1996.

Wane, Njoki, Jennifer Jagire, and Zahra Murad, eds. *Ruptures: Anti-Colonial & Anti-Racist Feminist Theorizing*. Rotterdam, Holland: Sense Publishers, 2013.

Wang, Carolyn, and Mary Ann Burris. "Photovoice: Concept, Methodology, and Use for Participatory Needs Assessment." *Health, Education & Behavior* 24, no. 3 (1997): 369–87.

Ward, Martha. "Reflections of a Woman Anthropologist: No Hiding Place. Manda Cesara (Book Review)." *American Anthropologist* 87, no. 2 (1985): 476–78.

Waterston, Alisse. *My Father's Wars: Migration, Memory, and the Violence of a Century*. New York: Routledge, 2013.

Waterson, Alisse, and Vesperi, eds. *Anthropology Off the Shelf: Anthropologists on Writing.* New York: Blackwell, 2009.

Weiner, Annette. *The Trobrianders of Papua New Guinea.* Ann Arbor: University of Michigan Press, 1988.

Weiss, Margot. *Techniques of Pleasure: BDSM and the Circuits of Sexuality.* Durham: Duke University Press, 2011.

Wekker, Gloria. *The Politics of Passion: Women's Sexual Culture in the Afro-Surinamese Diaspora.* New York: Columbia University Press, 2006.

Wengle, John L. *Ethnographers in the Field: The Psychology of Research.* Tuscaloosa: University of Alabama Press, 1988.

Weston, Kath. *Families We Choose: Lesbians, Gays, Kinship.* New York: Columbia University Press, 1991.

Wies, Jennifer R., and Hillary J. Haldane, eds. *Applying Anthropology to Gender-Based Violence: Global Responses, Local Practices.* Lanham, MD: Lexington Books, 2015.

Wilchins, Riki. *Read My Lips: Sexual Subversion and the End of Gender.* Ithaca, NY: Firebrand Books, 1997.

Williams, Erica Lorraine. *Sex Tourism in Bahia: Ambiguous Entanglements.* Chicago: University of Illinois Press, 2013.

Wolf, Deborah Goleman. *Lesbian Community.* Berkeley: University of California Press, 1979.

Wolf, Diane L. *Beyond Anne Frank: Hidden Children and Postwar Families in Holland.* Berkeley: University of California Press, 2007.

Wolf, Diane L., ed. *Feminist Dilemmas in Fieldwork.* Boulder: Westview, 1996.

Wolf, Margery. *The House of Lim: A Study of a Chinese Family.* Princeton: Pearson, 1968.

———. *A Thrice-Told Tale: Feminism, Postmodernism, and Ethnographic Responsibility.* Stanford, CA: Stanford University Press, 1992.

Wollstonecraft, Mary. *A Vindication of the Rights of Woman.* London: Joseph Johnson, 1792.

Yale University Lesbian, Gay, Bisexual, and Transgender Studies. "Conference: Queering Anthropology." *Yale University Lesbian, Gay, Bisexual, and Transgender Studies,* February 2015. http://lgbts.yale.edu/event/conference-queering-anthropology.

Zavella, Patricia. *Women's Work and Chicano Families: Cannery Workers of the Santa Clara Valley.* Ithaca: Cornell University Press, 1987.

———. "Feminist Insider Dilemmas: Constructing Ethnic Identity with Chicana Informants." In *Feminist Dilemmas in Fieldwork,* edited by Diane L. Wolf, 138–59. Boulder: Westview, 1996.

Zinn, Maxine Baca, and Bonnie Thornton Dill, eds. *Women of Color in U.S. Society.* Women in the Political Economy. Philadelphia: Temple University Press, 1994.

Index

Page references for illustrations are italicized.

About the Authors

Dána-Ain Davis's training covers a range of fields: an undergraduate degree in film and a certificate in Black Studies, a master's in public health, and a PhD in anthropology. She has taught across a range of departments and programs including Global Black Studies, women's studies, and media, society, and the arts. She currently teaches in anthropology at the Graduate Center, City University of New York (CUNY) and is associate chair of the master's program in urban studies at Queens College, CUNY. Her work centers on examining the manifestations and articulations of neoliberalism in a range of contexts: race, reproduction, violence against women, and welfare reform policy. She is the author of *Battered Black Women and Welfare Reform: Between a Rock and a Hard Place* (2006). Other intellectual interests include feminist activism, reproductive justice, and community organizing. Dána-Ain's current research involves examining the racial politics of prematurity and neonatal intensive care units. She also coedited *Black Genders and Sexualities* with Shaka McGlotten (2012), coedited *Feminist Activist Ethnography: Counterpoints to Neoliberalism in North America* with Christa Craven (2013), served as coeditor with Aimee Meredith Cox of *Transforming Anthropology*, the journal of the Association of Black Anthropologists (ABA), and served as president of ABA.

Christa Craven holds a joint appointment in anthropology and women's, gender, and sexuality studies (WGSS) at the College of Wooster, a small liberal arts college in Ohio. She is currently chair of the WGSS program. Her research interests include women's health and reproductive justice, lesbian/gay/bi/trans/queer reproduction, midwifery activism, feminist ethnography & activist scholarship, and feminist pedagogy. She is the author of *Pushing for Midwives: Homebirth Mothers and the Reproductive Rights Movement* (2010) and coeditor of *Feminist Activist Ethnography: Counterpoints to Neoliberalism in North America* with Dána-Ain Davis (2013). Craven's current research project is on reproductive loss (miscarriage, infertility, and adoption loss) in lesbian, gay, bisexual, transgender, and queer (LGBTQ) communities. She is working on a book based on that research aimed at LGBTQ parents and health and adoption professionals. She is the former cochair of the Society of Lesbian and Gay Anthropologists (now the Association for Queer Anthropology) and currently serves as the of the Program Administration and Development Co-Chair for the National Women's Studies Association.

Lightning Source UK Ltd.
Milton Keynes UK
UKHW02f0638160918
328882UK00010B/107/P